INVESTIGATING VARIATION

OXFORD STUDIES IN SOCIOLINGUISTICS

General Editors:

Nikolas Coupland
Adam Jaworski
Cardiff University

Recently Published in the Series:

Talking about Treatment: Recommendations for Breast Cancer Adjuvant Treatment
Felicia D. Roberts

Language in Time: The Rhythm and Tempo of Spoken Interaction
Peter Auer, Elizabeth Kuhlen, Frank Müller

Whales, Candlelight, and Stuff Like That: General Extenders in English Discourse
Maryann Overstreet

A Place to Stand: Politics and Persuasion in a Working-Class Bar
Julie Lindquist

Sociolinguistic Variation: Critical Reflections
Edited by Carmen Fought

Prescribing under Pressure: Parent-Physician Conversations and Antibiotics
Tanya Stivers

Discourse and Practice: New Tools for Critical Discourse Analysis
Theo van Leeuwen

Beyond Yellow English: Toward a Linguistic Anthropology of Asian Pacific America
Edited by Angela Reyes and Adrienne Lo

Stance: Sociolinguistic Perspectives
Edited by Alexandra Jaffe

Investigating Variation: The Effects of Social Organization and Social Setting
Nancy C. Dorian

Investigating Variation

The Effects of Social Organization and Social Setting

Nancy C. Dorian

UNIVERSITY PRESS

2010

OXFORD
UNIVERSITY PRESS

Oxford University Press, Inc., publishes works that further
Oxford University's objective of excellence
in research, scholarship, and education.

Oxford   New York
Auckland   Cape Town   Dar es Salaam   Hong Kong   Karachi
Kuala Lumpur   Madrid   Melbourne   Mexico City   Nairobi
New Delhi   Shanghai   Taipei   Toronto

With offices in
Argentina   Austria   Brazil   Chile   Czech Republic   France   Greece
Guatemala   Hungary   Italy   Japan   Poland   Portugal   Singapore
South Korea   Switzerland   Thailand   Turkey   Ukraine   Vietnam

Published by Oxford University Press, Inc.
198 Madison Avenue, New York, New York 10016

www.oup.com

Oxford is a registered trademark of Oxford University Press

Library of Congress Cataloging-in-Publication Data
Dorian, Nancy C.
Investigating variation: the effects of social organization and
social setting / Nancy C. Dorian.
    p. cm.—(Oxford studies in sociolinguistics)
Includes bibliographical references.
ISBN 978-0-19-538593-9; 978-0-19-538592-2 (pbk.)
1. Scottish Gaelic language—Dialects—Scotland—Sutherland.
2. Scottish Gaelic language—Variation.   3. Scottish Gaelic language—
Social aspects.   4. Fishers—Scotland—Sutherland—Language.   I. Title.
PB1598.S96D62 2009
491.6'37—dc22   2008046388

9 8 7 6 5 4 3 2 1
Printed in the United States of America
on acid-free paper

For the Gaelic speakers of Embo, welcoming and generous beyond telling to the linguist who turned up in their midst in 1963, and most especially to my faithful telephone partners and visitors of 1993 and after, without whom it would have been impossible to bring this study to completion: Babbie, Jessie Wulina, Kenna, Bella Bheag, Jessie, Jenny, Wilma, and Isabel.

Acknowledgments

More than forty years after I first began to investigate the Gaelic spoken by the East Sutherland fisherfolk and their descendants, I consider it now, fully as much as I did then, an incomparable privilege to have been deeply engaged with the people who spoke this variety of Gaelic and their family circles. The four books to which that engagement has given rise are strong testimony to the almost inexhaustible interest of working with the people in question, but their unfailing generosity deserves its own testimony. "Highland hospitality" is legendary, and in these communities it went far beyond the usual sphere to emerge also in the kindness shown in making an inquisitive linguist's work as personally rewarding as it was professionally fruitful. Humanly and professionally, the years of my association with the people of the former East Sutherland fishing communities have been rich to a degree that words do not easily express. All of these kind people have my lasting gratitude, but in truth the debt is one that can never be repaid.

There is a sense in which every East Sutherlander with whom I ever had a conversation about local conditions or events or practices contributed to the present book. The most immediate contributions, however, are those of the individuals at every level of Gaelic proficiency who provided the linguistic material discussed in this study and displayed (in the case of the active speakers) in its tables. I enter them here according to village of origin.

Of Brora: Mrs. Bella Coul; Miss Jean Dempster; Mrs. Catherine McDonough; Mrs. Dorothy MacRae MacKay; Mrs. Jessie MacLennan; Mr. Donald MacLeod; Mrs. Sarah MacRae and Mr. John MacRae; Miss Bella MacRae; Mr. William MacRae; Miss Bella Jean Sutherland.

Of Golspie: Mr. Hugh MacDonald; Mrs. Margaret MacKay; Miss Jean MacRae; Mrs. Betty Sutherland and Mr. Sinclair Sutherland; Mrs. Elizabeth Sutherland and Mr. Alexander Sutherland.

Of Embo: Mr. Dan Banks; Mr. James Cumming; Mrs. Nana Cumming; Mr. Donald Hugh Cumming; Mrs. Sophia Davey; Mrs. Isabel Ross Finch; Mrs. Christina Fraser and Mr. John Fraser; Mrs. Jessie MacKay Fraser and Mr. Thomas Fraser; Mr. Thomas Fraser; Mrs. Jessie MacKay Frew; Mrs. Bella Grant; Mrs. Isobel Sutherland Hadden; Mrs. Nana MacPhail Johnston; Mr. Alexander MacKay; Mr. Andrew MacKay; Mrs. Bella MacKay; Mrs. Betsy MacKay and Mr. Harold MacKay; Mr. David MacKay; Mr. Donald MacKay; Mr. James MacKay; Mrs. Jenny Cumming MacKay; Mrs. Lena MacKay and Mr. Kenneth MacKay; Mr. Lindsay MacKay; Mr. Thomas MacKay "Brown"; Mr. Thomas MacKay; Mrs. Jessie Fraser Ratell; Mrs. Bella Ross Roach; Mr. Alex Ross; Mrs. Barbara Ross; Mrs. Bella Ross; Mr. Donald Ross; Miss Jessie Ross; Mrs. Jessie Ann Ross and Mr. Donald Ross; Miss Margaret Ross; Mr. Paul Ross; Mr. Peter Ross; Miss Wilma Ross; Mr. Donald Sutherland; Mrs. Margaret Taylor, Mrs. Georgie Watt; Mrs. Isabel Joan Fraser Wilton.

During the preparation of this book, a number of colleagues answered questions or in some cases read bits or chapters of early manuscript drafts. In that connection I would like to thank Colleen Cotter, Bill Jancewicz, Ruth King, Paul Lewis, Ronald Macaulay, Robin Sabino, Suzanne Romaine, and Sally Thomason. Colleen Cotter, Ronald Macaulay, and Suzanne Romaine in particular sent critiques or questions in response to an early draft of the first three chapters that were invaluable in helping me present the idiosyncratic, socially neutral linguistic variation of East Sutherland fisherfolk Gaelic in a way that would be as intelligible as possible to readers with no personal experience of such variation phenomena. Two reviewers for Oxford University Press likewise supplied useful critiques at a much later stage in the enterprise. Suzanne Romaine and Robin Sabino kindly sent me copies of articles I would otherwise not have known about that proved relevant to parts of my presentation. The availability of Summer Institute of Linguistics (SIL) phonetic fonts to the general public was a boon for which I am very grateful (and for being steered to them by Robin Sabino and her graduate student Norman Hubbard), as I am also for the kindness of SIL's Mark Anderson in locating an early user's manual for the fonts I adopted. Series editors Nikolas Coupland and Adam Jaworski made the suggestion that resulted in the main title for this book.

Finally a word of appreciation for East Sutherland fisherfolk Gaelic itself. Peripherally aberrant it may be, but to anyone who comes to it without preconceived ideas of what Scottish Gaelic should sound like, it is a lovely dialect, graced by its long, Scandinavian-sounding vowels; people passing my office and hearing it on recordings occasionally asked if it were a variety of Swedish. Those of us who speak only this variety of Gaelic easily recognize the folk wisdom of the proverb: 'S geal leis an fhitheach an isean fhein, "White to the raven is its own chick."

Contents

Phonetic/Phonological Values of Symbols Appearing
in the Text, xxi

1 The Variation Puzzle, 3
1 Linguistic Variation without Social Weighting 3
2 High Levels of Socially Neutral Linguistic Variation
   in Three Socioeconomically Undifferentiated
   Minority-Language Enclaves 5
3 Exposure to Standard-Language or Mainstream Norms
   and Deviations from Those Norms in English
   and in Gaelic 6
   3.1 English and Its Dialect Forms. 7
   3.2 Vernacular Gaelic and Formal Gaelic 8
   3.3 Local Speech Features in the East Sutherland
       Fisherfolk Context 10
4 Initial Encounters with Variability 11
   4.1 Encountering the Language .12
   4.2 Encountering Intra-Community Variation. 12
   4.3 Age-Related Variation 13
       4.3.1 Establishing an Age-and-Proficiency
            Continuum. 15
5 Inter-Speaker and Intra-Speaker Variation
   in the Gaelic-Speaking Communities. 16

5.1 Examples of Inter- and Intra-Speaker Differences
     in the Use of Two Variables 17
5.2 The Evidence of Dialect Geography 18
5.3 The Possible Effect of Gender 19
5.4 The Possible Effect of Style 19
5.5 The Possible Effect of Kinship or of Household
     Membership 20
5.6 The Prevalence of Idiosyncratic, Socially Neutral
     Variation 20
6 Coming to Grips with the Variation Puzzle 21
   6.1 The Inadequacy of Obsolescence as an
        Explanation for Idiosyncratic Variation 22
7 Researcher Responses to Seemingly Idiosyncratic
   Variation among Speakers 23
   7.1 Residual Prescriptivism 23
   7.2 Data Control via Source Selection 25
   7.3 Search for an Assumed Uniformity 26
   7.4 Concentration on the Group Rather
        than the Individual 28
   7.5 Expectation of Linguistic Focusing within Small,
        Tight-Knit, Highly Interactive Communities 29
   7.6 Expectation of Linguistic Accommodation
        to Other Speakers 30
   7.7 Expectation of Linkage between Variation
        and Social Differentiation 31
   7.8 Researcher Responses: Summary 32
8 Variation within and across Village Boundaries 32
   8.1 Local Responses to Variation:
        Inter-Village Variation 33
   8.2 Local Responses to Variation:
        Intra-Village Variation 34
   8.3 Fisherfolk Populations United
        and Divided by Gaelic 36
9 Plan of the Remainder
   of the Book 38

2 **The East Sutherland Fishing Communities, 39**
   1 Introduction: Fishing as a Subsistence Mode 39
   2 Creation of the East Sutherland Fishing Communities:
      The "Improvement" Era 40
      2.1 The Highland Clearances
           in the East Sutherland Context 41
   3 Fishing as a Way of Life in East Sutherland 43
      3.1 The Local Fishery: Line Fishing 43
      3.2 The National Fishery: Herring Fishing 45

4 The East Sutherland Fisherfolk as a Socially
   and Linguistically Distinctive Population 47
   4.1 Separateness and Poverty. 47
   4.2 Separateness and Language 48
        4.2.1 Settlement History and Dialect
               Distinctiveness 49
        4.2.2 Geographically Based Differences
               in the Gaelic of the Fishing Communities 51
        4.2.3 The Church as a Potentially Unifying
               Institution 51
   4.3 Separateness and Endogamy 52
        4.3.1 Maintenance of Kin Ties 53
        4.3.2 Naming Practices and the Maintenance
               of Kin Ties 53
        4.3.3 Maintaining Less Familiar Degrees
               of Kinship. 54
        4.3.4 Focus on Kinship 55
5 The Fishing Communities as Face-to-Face
   Communities. 55
   5.1 Geographic and Demographic Characteristics. 56
   5.2 Egalitarianism as a Fishing Community Norm 59
   5.3 Gender-Distinctive Work Roles 61
   5.4 Multiplex Roles 61
   5.5 Community Membership. 62

3 **Dimensions of Linguistic Variation in a
   Socioeconomically Homogeneous Population, 64**
   1 Introduction: The Residual Fisherfolk Populations
      in the 1960s and After. 64
   2 Varieties of Variation in East Sutherland Gaelic 65
   3 Geographically Based Variation in Fisherfolk Gaelic 67
      3.1 An Example of Geographically Based Variation 67
      3.2 Establishing the Existence of Geographically
           Based Variation 69
   4 Age-Related Variation in Fisherfolk Gaelic. 69
      4.1 An Example of Age-Related Variation. 70
      4.2 Establishing the Existence of Age-Related
           Variation 73
   5 Style-Related Variation in Fisherfolk Gaelic. 73
      5.1 An Example of Style-Related Variation 74
      5.2 Establishing the Existence of Style-Related
           Variation 75
   6 Personally Patterned Variation in Fisherfolk Gaelic 76
      6.1 An Example of Personal-Pattern Variation. 76

6.2 Cases of Age-Related Variation
and Personal-Pattern Variation Compared 78
6.2.1 Contrasting Cases Involving Analogical
Regularization 79
6.2.2 A Single Variable Demonstrating Both
Age-Related and Personal-Pattern Variation . . . 82
6.3 Age-Related and Personally Patterned Variation
Compared: Summary. 82
6.4 The Idiosyncratic Variant-Use Patterns
of a Key Embo Sibling Pair. 83
6.4.1 Variables for Which the Siblings Favored
Different Variants 84
6.5 Establishing the Existence of Personally
Patterned Variation 86
7 The Challenges of Investigating Personally Patterned
Variation in the Fisherfolk Communities 87
7.1 Assembling a More Adequate Database. 87
7.2 Establishing Lack of Social Weighting in Connection
with Individual Variant Selections 88
7.2.1 Evidence from Apparent Unawareness of
Alternative Forms 90
7.2.2 Evidence from Dyadic Conversational Material:
Repetitions Using Different Variants 91
7.2.3 Evidence from Intra-Speaker
Variant Alternation 93
7.2.4 Evidence from Traditional Material 94
7.2.5 Evidence from Responses to One Pair
of Socially Weighted Variants 95
7.2.6 Evidence from Reaction to Gratuitous
English Loanwords 96
7.3 Summary: Absence of Social Evaluation in
Personally Patterned Variation 98

4 A General Introduction to Speakers and Variables, 100
1 Introduction 100
2 The Database. 101
2.1 Elicited Material 101
2.2 Freely Spoken Material 102
3 Focus on Embo Gaelic 103
4 Sources 104
4.1 Village of Origin 104
4.2 Age 105
4.3 Sex 105
4.4 Proficiency: Descriptive Proficiency-Level
Labels 106

4.5 Proficiency: Evaluative Proficiency-Level
Labels 106
5 Speakers 109
5.1 Factors in Gaelic-Language Social
Interaction Patterns 111
6 Variables: Introduction 112
6.1 Selection of Variables for Presentation 113
6.2 Particular Variable Features Selected
for Discussion 114
6.3 Choices in the Identification of Variant Forms 115
6.4 Representation of the Variables 117
6.4.1 Adopting English Glosses 117
6.4.2 Avoiding a Main-Variant Nomination 118
6.5 Inclusion of Repetitions and Broken-Off
Variants in Token Counts 120
7 Selection and Presentation of Variables: Summary 122

5 A Close Look at Some Embo Variables and Their Use, 123

Part I: The Variables

1 Introduction 123
2 Order of Presentation and Percentage of Use 125
3 Features of Variant Use 126
3.1 The Significance of Personal-Pattern Ubiquity:
Brora and Golspie Parallels 127
3.2 Absolute Numbers versus Percentage of Use 127
3.3 Elicited versus Freely Spoken Variants and Other
Possible Stylistically Cued Patterns of
Variant Use 128
4 Multivariant Variables: Five-Variant Variables 128
4.1 The Variable Adverbial ('in') 128
4.1.1 Use of Multiple Variants 130
4.1.2 Patterns of Variant Preference by
Age and Sex 131
4.2 The Variable Conjunctional ('when') 131
4.2.1 Use of Multiple Variants 133
4.2.2 Patterns of Variant Preference by
Age and Sex 134
4.3 The Variable ('along with') 134
4.3.1 Use of Multiple Variants 136
4.3.2 Patterns of Variant Preference by
Age and Sex 137
5 Gender and Multiple- or Single-Variant Use
for the Five-Variant Variables 137

6 Alignment of Individual Variant Preferences:
Three Five-Variant Variables 139
6.1 Variant-Preference Distributions 140
6.2 Variant-Preference Clusterings 141
6.3 Clusterings by Sex of Speaker 142
6.4 Invariance 142
6.5 The London-Embo Speaker Group 142
6.6 Patterns of Atypical Variant Preference 143
7 Multivariant Variables: Four- and Three-Variant
Variables.................................. 143
7.1 The Variable ('would go') 143
    7.1.1 A Case of Linguistic Variation Together with
           Linguistic Change...................... 144
    7.1.2 The Role of Acoustic Salience............. 146
    7.1.3 Use of Multiple Variants 146
    7.1.4 Patterns of Variant Preference by
           Age and Sex......................... 147
7.2 The Variable ('family') 148
    7.2.1 Use of Multiple Variants 149
    7.2.2 Patterns of Variant Preference by
           Age and Sex......................... 150
7.3 The Variable ('from, off, of') 150
    7.3.1 Use of Multiple Variants 152
    7.3.2 Patterns of Variant Preference by
           Age and Sex......................... 153
7.4 The Variable (preterite particle) before Front
    Vowel 153
    7.4.1 Use of Multiple Variants 155
    7.4.2 Patterns of Variant Preference by
           Age and Sex......................... 156
7.5 The Variable ('potato') 156
    7.5.1 Use of Multiple Variants 157
    7.5.2 Patterns of Variant Preference by
           Age and Sex......................... 158
8 Alignment of Individual Variant Preferences:
Eight Multivariant Variables...................... 158
9 Two-Variant variables 162
9.1 The Variable ('wasn't/weren't') 162
    9.1.1 Use of More than One Variant 163
    9.1.2 Patterns of Variant Preference by
           Age and Sex......................... 164
    9.1.3 The Analogical Factor................... 164
9.2 The Variable ('came')........................ 165
    9.2.1 Use of More than One Variant 166
    9.2.2 Patterns of Variant Preference by Age and Sex 167

9.3 The Variable ('tomorrow'). 167
  9.3.1 Use of More than One Variant 168
  9.3.2 Patterns of Variant Preference by
         Age and Sex. 169
  9.3.3 Variables with Structurally Parallel
         Variants in /-ax/ and /-iç/ 169
9.4 The Variable ('saw') 170
  9.4.1 Use of More than One Variant 172
  9.4.2 Patterns of Variant Preference by
         Age and Sex 172
9.5 The Variable Demonstrative ('that') 174
  9.5.1 Use of More than One Variant 175
  9.5.2 Patterns of Variant Preference by
         Age and Sex 175
9.6 The Variable Affirming ('is/are') 176
  9.6.1 Use of More than One Variant 177
  9.6.2 Patterns of Variant Preference by
         Age and Sex 178
9.7 The Variable ('needing') 179
  9.7.1 Use of More than One Variant 180
  9.7.2 Patterns of Variant Preference by
         Age and Sex 180
9.8 The Variable ('this') 180
  9.8.1 Use of More than One Variant 181
  9.8.2 Patterns of Variant Preference by
         Age and Sex. 182
9.9 The Variable ('out'). 182
  9.9.1 Use of More than One Variant 183
  9.9.2 Patterns of Variant Preference by
         Age and Sex 183
9.10 The Variable ('near'). 184
  9.10.1 Use of More than One Variant 184
  9.10.2 Patterns of Variant Preference by
          Age and Sex. 185

Part II: Variant Use by Speech Functions,
          Variability by Speaker and Variable, and
          Speakers' Levels of Variant-Preference
          Agreement and Disagreement

10 The Effect of Elicitation on Variant Use 186
  10.1 Variables with Analogically Formed Variants 186
  10.2 Variables with Both Disyllabic
        and Monosyllabic Variants 187
  10.3 Other Variables 188

11 Other Potentially Style-Related Patterns of
    Variant Use 189
    11.1 Variant-Use Patterns in Traditional Material 189
    11.2 Variant-Use Patterns in Stories with Sharp
          Differences in Tone and Affect 190
    11.3 Variant-Use Patterns in Extended Discourse 191
          11.3.1 The "Gift Tape" 191
          11.3.2 The "Ceilidh Tapes" 192
    11.4 Variant-Use Patterns with Different
          Interlocutors 194
    11.5 Conclusion 195
12 Variability as a Property of Variables and of Speakers . . 196
    12.1 Individual Speakers' Levels of Variation 197
    12.2 Variables Compared by the Number of
          Individuals Using More than One Variant 199
13 Speakers Compared by the Typicality or Aberrance
    of Their Variant Preferences 200
14 Speakers' Levels of Agreement and Disagreement
    with Fellow Speakers 201
    14.1 Relatively High Levels of Agreement on Variant
          Preference 202
          14.1.1 High Agreement Levels by Sex
                  and Proficiency Level 202
          14.1.2 High Agreement Levels between Spouses 203
          14.1.3 High Agreement Levels within the
                  London-Embo Group 205
          14.1.4 High Agreement Levels outside the
                  London-Embo Group 205
    14.2 Relatively Low Levels of Agreement on Variant
          Preference 205
          14.2.1 Low Agreement Levels by Sex
                  and Proficiency Level 207
    14.3 Unpredictable Outcomes in Levels of Agreement
          on Variant Preferences 207

6 Kin Groups, Peer Groups, and Variation, 209
    1 Introduction 209
    2 The Influence of Family and Peer Group 210
    3 The Centrality of Kin Groups in Embo's Social Structure 212
    4 Working with the Members of Key Sibling Sets 213
    5 Variant Selections by Percentage of Use among
       Family-Group Members: Introduction 217
       5.1 Group 1 218
       5.2 Group 2 221
       5.3 Group 3 224

5.4 Group 4 226
 5.4.1 Full-Family Comparison in the
        Lexical-Retention Study 232
 5.4.2 Across-the-Family Variant-Preference
        Differences. 233
6 Variant-Preference Patterns among Members of
   a Self-Identified Peer Group. 234
7 Summary. 236

7 Speech Norms, Accommodation, and Speaking Well in Gaelic Embo, 237

1 Introduction 237
2 Social Responses to Linguistic Divergence 238
 2.1 Social Responses to Divergent Variant Choices 238
 2.2 Social Responses to Divergent Language Choice . . .240
 2.3 Social Responses to Geographically
      Divergent Forms 241
 2.4 Language and Identity 243
3 Absence of Community-Internal Accommodation to
   Personal-Pattern Variation 244
 3.1 Accommodation and Non-accommodation to the
      Usage of Gaelic-Speaking Outsiders: Conversational
      Interactions with Speakers of Other Dialects 245
 3.2 Accommodation and Non-accommodation to
      the Usage of a Non-local Speaker of the Local
      Fisherfolk Gaelic. 246
 3.3 Non-accommodation in Variant Selection within
      Multispeaker Interactions 247
4 Accommodation and the Effect of Translation Tasks 248
 4.1 Elicitation Responses to an Outsider Speaking
      the Local Gaelic 249
 4.2 Elicitation Responses to a Speaker of Non-local
      Gaelic. 251
5 The Exception to the Rule: A Variable with Negatively
   Weighted Variants 253
 5.1 Older Speakers' Practices and Attitudes
      with Regard to Gerund Formation 253
 5.2 Younger Speakers' Attitudes and Practices
      with Regard to Gerund Formation 254
 5.3 Individual Differences in Sensitivity to Analogical
      Gerund Formation. 255
 5.4 Gerund Formation with Verbs Borrowed
      from English 256
 5.5 Responses to Variation in Gerund Formation
      Compared with Responses to Variation in Other
      Linguistic Forms 257

6 Low Awareness of Within-the-Community Variation
Revisited. 259
7 Speaking Well in a Community with an Unwritten
Vernacular 260
7.1 The Menomini Indians and the Embo Fisherfolk as
Bilingual/Multilingual Communities in Transition . .261
7.2 Components of Being a "Good" Speaker in a
Community without Mother-Tongue Literacy. 262
7.3 The Committed Speaker as a "Good" Speaker 263
7.4 "Good" Menomini Speakers Compared with
"Good" Fisherfolk Gaelic Speakers 265
7.5 Speaking Well Reconsidered. 266
8 Assessing Speaker Skills. 266
8.1 Disparate Skills at the Low End of the Proficiency
Continuum 268
8.2 Assessing Speaker Skills: Conclusion. 270

**8 Socially Neutral Linguistic Variation: Where, Why,
What For, and How?, 271**
1 Introduction: Discounting Variation. 271
2 Inter-Speaker Variation among Close Kin
and Agemates 273
3 Factors in the Persistence of Socially
Neutral Variation. 274
3.1 Absence of Linguistic Codification and
Home-Language Literacy in Small, Isolated
Minority-Group Communities 274
3.2 Socioeconomic Homogeneity, Together with
Weakness of Other Potential Social and Linguistic
Correlations. 275
3.3 Population Mixture and Language Contact 277
3.3.1 The Process of Dialect Leveling 277
3.3.2 Population Mixture with Limited
or Absent Leveling 278
4 Absence of Social Weighting of Variants
in Inter-Speaker and Intra-Speaker Variation 281
5 Socially Neutral Individual Variation
and Obsolescence. 282
6 Contributory Factors in Socially Neutral Individual
Variation: Summary. 285
7 Ideological Factors Bearing on Socially Neutral
Individual Variation and Its Recognition 287
7.1 Recognizing Alternative Ideologies 287
7.2 Recognizing One's Own Ideology. 288
7.2.1 The "Homogeneity Assumption" 289

8 The "What For?" Issue in Socially Neutral
   Individual Variation 290
   8.1 Variability, Variant Selection, and Personal Voice . . 292
9 How Is Personally Patterned Variation Transmitted? 295

9 Conclusion, 297

1 Introduction 297
2 Contrary to Expectations: Personally Patterned Variation
   in Embo Gaelic 298
   2.1 Rampant Inter-Speaker and Intra-Speaker
        Variation in a Small, Densely Interactive,
        and Socially Homogeneous Community 298
   2.2 Ongoing Maintenance of High Variation Levels 299
   2.3 Non-participation of Personal-Pattern Variables
        in Marking Group Membership 299
   2.4 The Social Neutrality of Variants 300
   2.5 Low Awareness of Acoustically Salient Variation . . . 300
3 Remaining Questions 301
   3.1 Are Largely Uniform Descriptive
        Accounts Justified? 301
   3.2 Is the Linguistic System of the Community More
        Regular than That of the Individual? 302
   3.3 What of "Structured Heterogeneity" and
        Implications for Language Change? 304
   3.4 Is There a Place for the Individual
        in Linguistic Analysis? 305
4 Methodological Implications of Embo Personal-Pattern
   Variation 307
   4.1 Beginning with the Variants or Beginning
        with the Group That Uses Them. 308
   4.2 Implications for Dialect Geography 308
   4.3 Selection of Sources and Inclusion
        or Exclusion of Data 310
5 Social Structure and Linguistic Variation 311

Notes, 315

References, 327

Index, 335

Phonetic/Phonological Values of Symbols Appearing in the Text

The vowels /i/, /e/, /ɛ/, /u/, /o/, /ɔ/ have their standard phonetic values; the same vowel symbols with /:/ are the equivalents with phonemic length. All are "pure" vowels without on- or off-glides.

The vowels printed as /a/ and /a:/ represent phonetic [ɑ] and [ɑ:]. The vowel printed as /ə/ represents [ə], [ɣ], or a backed [ɪ], and the vowel printed as /ə:/ represents high, back, unrounded [ɯ:]. All vowels have phonemically nasal counterparts.

Diphthongs are essentially combinations of the above, but [i] and [u] can act as off-glides that contrast with two-vowel sequences occupying a full two morae, such as [pi.əu] 'food' versus [pi.ɑ.u] 'feed'.

The consonants printed as /č/ and /ǰ/ represent the affricates [tš] and [dǯ]. The consonant /r/ represents an abbreviated (one- or two-tap) trill initially, single-flap medially, and an abbreviated (and occasionally voiceless) trill finally. The consonant printed as /ł/ represents a velarized lateral. Except in compounding, only the consonant /n/ can appear with phonemic length.

The labial, dental, and velar stops and the affricate appear aspirated, unaspirated, or voiced, but the three possibilities appear contrastively only in word-initial position, where the voiced series occurs morphophonemically in response to a triggering element that is often absent from the surface structure. The contrast between the aspirated and unaspirated series of voiceless stops and affricate is neutralized in medial position (see the diminutive of /kʰatʰ/ below, in which the originally aspirated final stop loses its aspiration when the suffix is added). Word-finally only the voiceless aspirated and voiced stops and affricate appear.

Initial contrasts

/kʰatʰ/ 'cat'	[kʰɑtʰ]
/katʰ/ 'swelling' (gerund)	[kɑtʰ]
/(ə) gatʰ/ 'the cat'	[(ə) gɑtʰ]

Final contrasts

/kʰatʰ/ 'cat'	[kʰɑtʰ]
/ad/ 'hat'	[ɑd]

Medial contrasts

/kʰatan/ 'kitten' = 'cat' + masculine diminutive suffix /-an/ [kʰɑtɑn]
/adag/ 'small hat' = 'hat' + feminine diminutive suffix /-ag/ [ɑdɑg]

The first syllable of disyllabic or polysyllabic words is normally stressed, for example, /ˈmɔriçɛn/ 'fisherfolk'. The exceptions, apart from a very few English loanwords of longstanding and many recent English loanwords, are adjectives or verbs with prefixes that are still at least somewhat productive, for example, the adjectival prefix /mi-/ 'un-, non-', the verbal prefix /a-/ 're-'.

INVESTIGATING VARIATION

The Variation Puzzle

1 LINGUISTIC VARIATION WITHOUT SOCIAL WEIGHTING

Two equally interesting questions are at the heart of this book: how an extraordinary degree of idiosyncratic linguistic variation can coexist with an extraordinarily homogeneous speaker population, and how linguists might overlook the possibility of their coexistence.

One answer to these questions is that speech communities take a variety of forms, and that while one type of social and economic organization has been growing more dominant around the world (socioeconomically stratified societies with increasingly urbanized populations), other types have been decreasing and have grown unfamiliar to linguists who are the products of the dominant variety. Another aspect of this same picture is that socioeconomically stratified societies are to be found in both urban and rural settings (in precontact Hawaii as well as postcontact Hawaii, for example), while societies without social and economic stratification are only to be found in rural and usually rather isolated settings; the latter are less accessible as well as less common in recent times. When William Labov allows for just one exception to the universality of the uniformitarian principle ("knowledge of processes that operated in the past can be inferred by observing ongoing processes in the present"; Labov 1994:21, citing Christy 1983:ix), he couches that exception in terms of differences in social organization across time. He warns that the uniformitarian principle is secure where the physiological basis of language is concerned but is "more problematic where social differences are concerned," so that "we must...be wary of extrapolating backward in time to neolithic, pre-urban societies with an entirely different social organization" (Labov 1994:23). This is a useful caution, but it needs to be extended to include the possibility of *contemporary* societies with an entirely different social organization: those without socioeconomic stratification, for example, like the originally single-occupation communities to be introduced here, or those with only a family-level social organization, like the Matsigenka Indians of south-eastern Peru (Johnson 2003).

Variationist sociolinguistics, focusing chiefly on variation in phonology, has produced results that are especially impressive for their replicability in a wide variety of locations, most of them urban but some rural. But the fact that two conditions fundamental to the variationist approach are not universally present in contemporary societies raises the possibility of other, less well-recognized forms of variation. One of the conditions in question is socioeconomic stratification, and the other is a set of linguistic variants that can be construed as standard variants. The two interact, since in the absence of social and economic stratification, there is less likely to be one social group whose usage comes to be especially positively evaluated and so becomes established as standard in the sense of being normative for the community. The centrality of standard usage for variationist sociolinguistics is made clear by Chambers in his textbook devoted to Labovian urban dialectology: "certain variants...take on social significance depending upon their phonetic distance from the standard variant, or...their phonetic differentness from the standard variant" (Chambers 1995:25). If no variant is established as standard, however, then even when there is quite an array of coexistent variants, absence of social hierarchy among the community of speakers allows for the possibility that the variants will take on no social significance relative to one another— that is, will remain socially neutral.

The possibility of acoustically salient but socially unweighted variation can be difficult for speakers of long-standardized languages to credit fully, since most of us are accustomed to making social distinctions on the basis not just of easily detectable grammatical alternates but also of small and subtle differences in pronunciation. Responding as strongly as we do to such phenomena, we are inclined to doubt that speakers of other languages might be either oblivious of blatant variation or indifferent to it if they should become aware of it. The evidence proves to be very strong, however, that where a community population is socioeconomically undifferentiated to a remarkable degree and few (if any) community-external norms are brought to bear on local usage, pervasive individual variation, in the phonemic realization of morphemes in the chief case to be discussed here, not only can flourish but can do so without linguistic variants developing social values. This flies in the face of widely accepted generalizations such as the following:

> Perhaps the only real sociolinguistic universal introduced so far in this chapter is
> social differentiation. The claim underlying this universal is that there are always

differences in speech communities and that those differences correlate with the existence of social groups within a community. (Southerland and Anshen 1989:332)

It is a commonplace of linguistics...that variation in speech (aside from age and gender...) is a function of (a) region, (b) social group, and (c) situation. (Honey 1997:92)

Small and profoundly homogeneous minority-language communities whose socio-economic structure is undifferentiated and whose vernacular escapes the pressures of community-external language norms are not without social groups, of course, since a family of some sort constitutes an unavoidable minimum and the extended kin group its usual extension. But there need not, in such communities, be a corre-lation between social groups and variable linguistic features. Where small population size, high interaction density, and egalitarian social structure prevail, linguistic accommodation may be minimal or absent. I propose to discuss here one set of communities characterized by a great deal of linguistic variation largely uncorrelated with community-internal social groups apart (in some cases) from broad age groupings and examine in as much depth as possible the idiosyncratic but socially neutral linguistic variation that prevails in one of these communities. Subsequently I introduce communities in very different parts of the world that appear on the basis of linguists' accounts to show similarities to this one in social structure and to offer linguistic variation of a similar sort. The social structure in question is fundamental to the existence of a pronounced degree of socially neutral linguistic variation, and the rarity of this sort of social structure in our times (though not perhaps in earlier times) helps account for contemporary lack of attention to the possibility that social homogeneity and linguistic heterogeneity will coexist.

2 HIGH LEVELS OF SOCIALLY NEUTRAL LINGUISTIC VARIATION IN THREE SOCIOECONOMICALLY UNDIFFERENTIATED MINORITY-LANGUAGE ENCLAVES

The language at the heart of this study is East Sutherland fisherfolk Gaelic, a rubric that can serve as a cover term for a cluster of dialects that came into being in the early years of the nineteenth century as the result of a harsh local history that will be detailed chapter 2. This dialect cluster served as the vernacular of a substantial population of fisherfolk in several villages along the east coast of Sutherland, in the far northeast Highlands of Scotland, until the end of World War I. Thereafter they were spoken by a dwindling population of former fisherfolk and their descendants in the three villages of Brora, Golspie, and Embo along that same coast.

Bilingual community members who still spoke Gaelic fluently in the early 1960s, when I first met them, had acquired their distinctive local form of Gaelic at a time when all who spoke that form of Scottish Gaelic belonged to what amounted in each of the three villages to a single, socioeconomically undifferentiated ethnic group. Members of that group had been virtually occupationally uniform (all fisherfolk), economically situated at a single level (all poor), residentially segregated (all housed in a few crowded streets at the seafront), nearly all minimally educated to the same standard (schooled only in English and only to the legal school-leaving age of fourteen), and kept almost entirely endogamous by severe stigmatization (deep-seated bias against the impoverished fisherfolk). For most ethnic group members who acquired fluency by being born into a fisherfolk household, Gaelic remained the routine language of intra-group communication.

Despite the striking socioeconomic uniformity of the fisherfolk populations during the childhood and young adult years of fluent 1960s speakers, and despite those speakers' regular use of Gaelic in the home and within contemporary kin networks, even the oldest fluent community members spoke a Gaelic that abounded in idiosyncratic linguistic variation. In addition, there was a good deal of variation representing linguistic change in progress, especially among somewhat younger but still fully fluent speakers in the isolated village where Gaelic persisted best. Although linguistic variation of both types was prevalent, very few variants carried any social weighting. Apart from a pair of disfavored and much mentioned variants in gerund formation, there appeared to be no generally stigmatized variants. Patterns of self-correction or patterns of variant avoidance sometimes suggested that an individual speaker had an idea that one variant of a particular variable was preferable to another, without any evidence emerging that the notion was shared by other speakers. Occasional patterns of linguistic conditioning appeared, but they also tended to be idiosyncratic: one speaker might show a tendency to use a particular variant in negated sentences, for example, without other speakers showing the same tendency. By and large, individual variation was socially neutral.

3 EXPOSURE TO STANDARD-LANGUAGE OR MAINSTREAM NORMS AND DEVIATIONS FROM THOSE NORMS IN ENGLISH AND IN GAELIC

As it turns out, the Gaelic-speaking fisherfolk communities that are the focus of interest here are not unique in exhibiting simultaneously an absence of social stratification and the presence of abundant, socially unweighted linguistic variation in their ancestral minority-group language; a community profile significantly associated with just such a combination is introduced in chapter 8. In a good many such cases, lack of any dialectal relationship between the local speech form and the standard language of the region or the country is an important co-occurrent social setting feature. The very process of standardization tends to eliminate the possibility of social neutrality where variants are concerned, so that regional or social dialects of a language that has a standardized form are inevitably placed in a negative light by the mere existence of the standard. Minority-community speech varieties escape the weight of that particular comparison if they are not dialects of a superordinate standardized language, and, provided socioeconomic differentiation is absent, any variation they display is more likely to escape social weighting than is variation in the dialects of standardized languages.

3.1 English and Its Dialect Forms

The forms of English to which twentieth-century fisherfolk bilinguals were exposed included a slightly Scottish-tinged variety of Received Pronunciation (RP), the most prestigious variety of British English, and the local variety of Highland English, a vernacular with strong regional phonological features as well as some regional syntactic features. In their working lives, many men and women from the fishing communities also had considerable exposure to Scots, a Lowland Scottish form of English, and their own English showed considerable Scots influence. The east coast Scottish herring fishery was dominated by Scots speakers from Banffshire, Morayshire, and Aberdeenshire, and East Sutherland fishermen regularly hired themselves out in ones and twos as seasonal hands on large herring fishing boats owned and otherwise manned by Scots speakers. Women who contracted to work as herring packers and gutters in coastal curing stations also had a good deal of exposure to Scots, since women from the same three shires were well represented in that workforce. In addition, there had been some very early contact with Scots at the time of the East Sutherland fishing communities' establishment, because the estate to which two of the villages belonged brought in a few experienced fisher families from Scots-speaking areas to serve as models and instructors to the inland evictees now destined to become fishermen (Loch 1820:135–36; see chapter 2). These Scots speakers may well have been the first mother-tongue speakers of any variety of English with whom the Gaelic-speaking evictees had extended direct contact; quite possibly any English acquired by the newly created East Sutherland fisherfolk showed Scots influence from the start.

In the East Sutherland setting, Scots dialect forms such as *no'* for *not, canna* for *cannot, oot* for *out*, and the like were and are every bit as strongly stigmatized as they are elsewhere in Scotland. The East Sutherland fisherfolk were well aware of the negative social weighting of these non-standard usages in their English. English, after all, has long been both the medium of schooling and a school subject, and Scots dialect variants of English are well-established targets of prescriptive teaching in Scottish schools, in East Sutherland as much as elsewhere. Schoolteachers emphasized "correct English", and Scots vernacular forms were clearly not a part of that variety. There was considerable consciousness among the bilingual fisherfolk that Scots-influenced forms were to be avoided in their English when they were aiming at their best linguistic behavior, though such forms appeared to be deeply engrained speech habits among older speakers in particular and were not entirely absent in the English speech of even some of the youngest bilinguals.

Fisherfolk English also showed some degree of influence from Gaelic syntax, and Gaelic turns of phrase were likewise to be heard. In addition there was a good deal of influence from Gaelic phonology. One rather striking feature of fisherfolk English, for example, was lack of any phonemic contrast between /ɪ/ and /ə/, just as in the local Gaelic, so that what would ordinarily be the minimal pair *limp* and *lump* fell together, with a vowel much closer to that of the latter word in standard forms of English than to that of the former. Gaelic-influenced features of fisherfolk English carried negative social weighting, just as Scots-influenced features did, since both sorts of influence conflicted with the norms fostered in schooling.

3.2 Vernacular Gaelic and Formal Gaelic

Whereas Highland English was both a public-sphere language and a private-sphere language in East Sutherland, fisherfolk Gaelic was essentially a private-sphere language, an intimate language rarely used outside the domestic and neighborhood spheres. Local Gaelic speakers had considerable passive exposure to two different non-local sorts of public-sphere Gaelic, however, both encountered in religious life. One was the Gaelic of the Bible, a variety distant in terms both of time and of place: the Bible was translated into Gaelic in the second half of the seventeenth century in Argyllshire, a west coast location far to the south. Bible Gaelic was familiar through frequent exposure to Scripture readings and from regular congregational singing of the metrical version of the psalms, lined out during worship services by a solo singer, the precentor, whom the congregation then followed in a repetition (with melodic variation) of each successive line. Bible Gaelic represented a pinnacle of prestige among forms of Gaelic, but it was wholly unsuitable as a model for actual speech behavior. The lexicon and the grammar were both archaic, representing norms that no contemporary speaker could realistically adopt, least of all a speaker of an unusual peripheral dialect cluster like that of the East Sutherland fisherfolk.

Church services routinely presented fisherfolk congregations with a second non-local variety of Gaelic as well, namely an educated form of whatever dialect the parish minister had as his mother tongue. Since no minister in living memory had ever been of local origin, the dialect in question was always that of some other area, usually a west coast or Hebridean island variety. Parishioners could expect to hear the prosody and the phonetic stamp of a dialect very different from their own; grammatically, too, the differences were large. East Sutherland Gaelic diverges conspicuously from more mainstream Gaelic dialects in certain high-frequency aspects of grammar, and the complete absence of a number of grammatical forms required for the production of grammatically conservative constructions makes it impossible for a fisherfolk speaker to model his or her own local speech after that of a mainstream dialect speaker without ceasing to speak the local Gaelic altogether. Local speakers reported that they became used to the accent and phraseology of whichever minister was in the pulpit, provided he stayed long enough in the parish and was speaking about more or less predictable religious subjects (Dorian 1981:90–91). But educated speakers of western dialects were not much more realistic as speech models than the Bible, and familiarity with such forms of Gaelic was a matter of passive knowledge. Most important, there was neither uniformity among such more conservative varieties of Gaelic as fisherfolk speakers were exposed to (they included a modest amount of broadcast Gaelic, in addition to the varieties heard in church), nor reinforcement of any of them in the form of regular educational support.

From exposure to these rather elevated forms of Gaelic, local East Sutherland speakers were more likely to become aware that their own form of Gaelic was aberrant ("wrong") than to acquire a sense that some particular other form of Gaelic and its features were "right". That is, passive exposure to more favored varieties of Gaelic did not produce the kind of hierarchy of acceptability among competing linguistic forms that typically appears in literate populations once standardization and school instruction are established. Some individuals were aware of certain written-Gaelic models through their own literacy efforts, through training as potential precentors (a church-based training given to many young boys), from familiarity with the Gaelic Bible and the metrical psalms, and from very minimal and ineffective instruction in book Gaelic offered at the Embo primary school at one period or another (only to boys, during the chief such period); a few were inclined to introduce the occasional written-language lexical item into their own Gaelic. Others who had acquired impressions of more mainstream usage from interactions with west-coast and Hebridean Gaelic speakers also introduced non-local words or expressions from time to time. Especially among older speakers who had had the longest and most intensive church-related experience, occasional lexical shifting might suggest that they knew that just one out of a set of local variants coincided with mainstream dialect forms or with written forms while the others did not. But lexical shifts of this kind were characteristic of particular individuals and were not generalized across whole age groups or across full social networks.

All of the alternative forms of Gaelic to which fisherfolk speakers were exposed—Bible Gaelic, the Gaelic of preaching, broadcast Gaelic, the book Gaelic taught intermittently and unproductively at the Embo primary school, and the western dialects of Gaelic that could be heard at the fishing stations—were regarded by fisherfolk speakers as "better" than their own Gaelic. One or two Gaelic heartland dialects that predominated at the herring curing stations were familiar in a purely passive sense to east coast speakers who had spent time there, particularly what East Sutherlanders called "Stornoway Gaelic", that is, any dialect spoken in Lewis, the most populous of the Outer Hebridean islands and a major curing station site. Many East Sutherlanders found Lewis Gaelic all but unintelligible, but Lewis Gaelic was nonetheless accorded higher standing than their own Gaelic, if only because it represented a region where Gaelic was still widely spoken and deeply rooted, as it no longer was in their own part of the country.

Although Gaelic has not gone unstandardized—codified Gaelic exists, represented in grammar books and promoted in recent decades in Gaelic medium education—East Sutherland fisherfolk speakers had no effective access to this sort of Gaelic. There were no serious efforts under way on the local scene to introduce and promote any "proper" form of Gaelic during the childhood or young-adult periods of even the youngest fisherfolk speakers, nor were there any efforts being made to preserve or promote the local Gaelic. "Good Gaelic" and "the right Gaelic" loomed large as concepts in local speakers' minds, and certainly biblical and church Gaelic constituted a prestigious frame of reference for Gaelic. But people were hard pressed to identify "the right Gaelic" with any specific form of spoken Gaelic, and they had no expectation of speaking such a Gaelic themselves. Because of the importance of Gaelic in religious life, the relationship between Gaelic and English was not strictly diglossic: in the religious sphere Gaelic rivaled English as the High language. Apart from this one sphere, however, English represented the language of power, while among bilinguals fisherfolk Gaelic served as the language of intimacy and solidarity.

3.3 Local Speech Features in the East Sutherland Fisherfolk Context

Features of a local speech variety take on social meaning by reason of their oppositional value: certain features may index membership in certain groups as opposed to others or be emblematic of particular identities as opposed to others. The isolation and enclavement of the Gaelic speakers in each of the East Sutherland fishing villages, together with the homogeneity of each enclaved population, largely precluded such developments, except across the three villages themselves. Both written Gaelic and mainstream Gaelic varieties were too weakly present in East Sutherland to operate as realistic counterpoints to the local Gaelic. No officially codified form of Gaelic was introduced and promoted there; consequently no opposition developed between a set of local linguistic features emblematic of a strictly local identity as opposed to other features representing a regionally neutral overarching identity. No persistent local dialect features became emblematic among East Sutherland Gaelic speakers, that is, in the way that they are reported to have done among young locals in Oiartzun, in the Spanish Basque Country, where a standardized, supra-regional Batua has been introduced and vigorously promoted by schools and government (Haddican 2007). Without any contrasting class and neighborhood speech differences, furthermore, social networks in the East Sutherland fishing villages did not exhibit distinctive use of particular local features to index network membership in the fashion reported for the Belfast English of Northern Ireland (Milroy 2002). Instead, local features served to index the identity of one entire homogeneous set of villagers as opposed to another—to mark Embo community membership as opposed to Brora or Golspie community membership, that is.

It is not impossible, even in communities where language shift is well under way, for social subgroups to develop and express distinct identities via linguistic features. In a dwindling Dyirbal-speaking community in Australia, two adolescent peer groups were found to use their distinctive forms of Young Dyirbal mostly horizontally, within the peer group, "adjust[ing] their speech to a recognizable set of linguistic norms, thus using language variety functionally to express group loyalty and identity" (Schmidt 1985:131). Nothing of this sort emerged in the one East Sutherland fishing village with a relatively substantial number of young, imperfect speakers; Embo semi-speakers used their Gaelic almost entirely vertically, with relatives older than they, rather than horizontally with agemates.

4 INITIAL ENCOUNTERS WITH VARIABILITY

Our failure as linguists to reckon with the specific combination of socioeconomic uniformity and a high degree of unweighted idiosyncratic linguistic variation (most notably in small communities speaking unwritten minority languages), and to allow for that combination when formulating linguistic principles, has more to do with what we presuppose than with what is available for observation. Much as we might wish to, we do not come to the research enterprise conceptually unencumbered. Some of the conditions that shape our ordinary daily environment are so broadly and deeply pervasive that it is difficult to be aware of them, much less disencumber ourselves of the expectations they create. There is our training to reckon with as well, the procedures and methodologies that are transmitted to us in the course of our studies and during our early apprenticeship in the profession. At least initially, each professional works within the descriptive and interpretive traditions of his or her time. The combination of a daily environment that shapes some of our assumptions, on the one hand, and of methodological traditions that shape our investigative procedures, on the other hand, can block for longer or shorter periods our perception of certain phenomena or, if they do register with us, our inclination to engage with them.

I make these statements with some self-consciousness, since this book deals with a variation phenomenon that came to my attention fairly early in my field research; yet it was only several decades later that I began to engage with it in a serious way. That is, I knew the phenomenon was there, and in fact I reported on it quite conscientiously. But for a long while I neither tried to explain the phenomenon in question nor considered the broader implications it might have for linguistic work in general. With the present study I hope to make partial amends for my lapses in this regard, but regrettably I delayed too long in taking up the task. The fuller account and more thoroughgoing explanations that might have been available if I had grappled with the same questions earlier are unobtainable now for the saddest of reasons: many of the speakers who could have supplied key data had died before I turned specifically to these questions. Still, despite a late start I can now add significantly to the evidence that was available from early materials, and the directions in which the evidence points are interesting and provocative enough to call for exposition and discussion. They raise questions that are useful to consider, even if the answers remain partial.

The exposition here contains a thread of chronological narrative, since the research focus at issue took shape gradually over some considerable time and in the wake of a number of differently targeted investigations, each of which contributed something to subsequent inquiries and understandings. Recapitulating the winding path I took will be the most effective way of indicating why the path wound so much and why it eventuates where it does.

4.1 Encountering the Language

In the autumn of 1963 I went to coastal eastern Sutherland in the Scottish Highlands to investigate the Gaelic spoken by East Sutherland fisherfolk and their descendants in the villages of Brora, Golspie, and Embo (taken from north to south along the central part of that coast). The research was the fieldwork stage of my dissertation, but the location was selected by the Gaelic division of the Linguistic Survey of Scotland, to whose ongoing work I had linked my study. My Survey assignment (a phonological description) required that I deal with the Gaelic-speaking populations of all three coastal villages, and to my consternation each fisherfolk population proved to speak a slightly different variety of eastern Sutherland-shire Gaelic. All had some striking regional features in common, but each had certain local features as well. There were village-by-village differences in morphophonology and in the phonological realization of various words, the Brora and Golspie versions usually but not always coinciding as opposed to the Embo version. In a few cases, lexical items in use in two villages differed altogether from the equivalent in the third, and in very rare cases each village used a slightly different word. Nominal gender occasionally varied by village, furthermore, and quite a number of morphosyntactic structures likewise.

These local differences were meat and drink to a dialect-geography undertaking like the Linguistic Survey of Scotland, and because such differences were legion (upward of 250 words have a distinctive phonological realization in at least one of the three villages; Dorian 1978:151–58), I devoted a great deal of time to establishing differences by village, not just during my first year of fieldwork but on subsequent field trips as well, as I moved on to differences in morphosyntax. Both by temperament and by training I was committed to faithful representation of whatever data emerged in the course of my work, and the fact that I was working in three linguistically distinguishable subcommunities meant that I needed to work with several sources in each population, to be sure that any geographically distinctive forms were represented accurately. From the first year of fieldwork onward, therefore, I gathered material from multiple sources.

4.2 Encountering Intra-Community Variation

The dialect-geography orientation of my original work in East Sutherland made a concentration on differences inevitable in a study that covered three villages. Beyond the differentiation associated with the three separate villages, however, I very soon found that even within the same village, fully fluent individual speakers might produce different versions of a considerable number of items.

In my initial year's fieldwork, I used the elicitation techniques that had been emphasized in a field methods course I had taken. The fluid, kin-rich social environment in many fisherfolk households meant that a number of household members and some additional kinfolk were often present when I was eliciting forms. Many East Sutherland Gaelic speakers took easily to elicitation. In fact, it was an exercise that proved to be simplicity itself for people who routinely passed along any supposedly direct-quotation remarks in whatever language they regularly used with their interlocutor, regardless of which language the original remarks had been in (Dorian 1997a). In a number of households some individuals were particularly eager to supply translations, and it was not always the elderly speaker I was most hoping to hear from who gave the Gaelic forms I requested. It seemed to me that the courteous thing to do was to take down whatever was offered, no matter who was speaking; I did that, waiting if necessary for some later chance to get the same forms from the elderly speaker in whose usage I was especially interested.

I also spent a fair bit of general social time in several of the households where I was working, and because I had the use of a car (a small van lent me by the Survey) at a time when most local people did not, I undertook some transport duty, too, taking people to visit relatives in hospital, on shopping trips to the nearest larger towns (more than two hours away by the routes then available), or to social events (sheepdog trials, musical evenings).[1] Everyone knew that I was interested in their Gaelic and was trying to learn it, and among my friends there was a benevolent tolerance of my tendency to take notes not just during formal work sessions but even during conversations at which I was at first more nearly a listener-learner than an active participant. As a result, both elicitation sessions and social occasions offered opportunities to make direct comparisons between individual speakers' renditions of various structures.

4.3 Age-Related Variation

The linguistic differences that struck me most, in my early interactions with various households and with the social networks of their principal members, were those in Embo village that appeared to be associated with differences in age. I thought I was hearing distinctions made by older Embo speakers that were not always made by younger fellow villagers and constructions used by older speakers that were not used, or were used in some modified form, by younger speakers. In the 1960s the fisherfolk were a social and linguistic aberration in the East Sutherland setting overall, still using Gaelic as their home language in a region where other segments of the local population had mostly stopped speaking Gaelic, some of them a full half-century earlier. It was clear, however, that even among the fisherfolk Gaelic was passing out of use. By the mid-1960s, even in the most Gaelic-speaking of the communities, no children were acquiring the language. Since fishing for a living had virtually ceased by the middle of the twentieth century and the fisherfolk were no longer economically and socially set apart from everyone else by their occupation and its distinctive lifeways (or by the social stigma that attached to a poverty-level subsistence mode), it was not surprising that greater integration into the general population of the region was producing a shift in language behavior.

In two of the former fishing communities, Brora and Golspie, speakers of fisherfolk Gaelic by then made up only a very small subgroup within the village population as a whole, 3.6 percent and 4.6 percent respectively, in 1964. All of the regular Gaelic speakers in these two villages were over fifty years of age, but despite not having transmitted Gaelic to their children, nearly all of them used it on a daily basis within their own households and kin networks. Those who were fully fluent demonstrated fairly comparable levels of grammatical control of Gaelic in many (though not all) constructions. What one fully fluent speaker offered in exemplification of a first-person singular verb in the conditional, for example, or of a possessive modifying a noun, was generally quite similar to what the other fully fluent speakers would offer. Change in progress could be detected (loss of grammatical gender in pronoun reference was very clearly under way, for example), but the incidence of change seemed moderate for a speaker population that in opting not to transmit their home language had also opted for language shift. Such conspicuously aberrant grammatical structures as I heard in Brora came in response to translation tasks solely from a particular set of imperfect speakers, younger individuals (relatively speaking) who had either lost the fuller control they had had as very young children or had never acquired Gaelic to full proficiency.[2]

Conditions in Embo were considerably more favorable to Gaelic in at least some respects. Embo had been almost wholly a fishing village, and even in the early 1960s the village was a little better than 38 percent Gaelic-speaking. Because moorland, fields, and pasturage separate the village from nearby farms and from the nearest English-speaking village, Embo's residents were much more isolated from regular contact with English monolinguals than were the fisherfolk of Brora and Golspie, who lived near (or by then even in, in some cases) the English-speaking parts of their villages. Although a transmission failure shift from Gaelic-English bilingualism to English monolingualism was under way in Embo, just as in the other two villages, it was less far advanced in Embo. In addition to the many fluent speakers between ages ninety and forty, a few fluent Gaelic speakers in their thirties could still be found in the Embo of the early 1960s, as well as some still younger individuals comparable to Brora's imperfect younger speakers. But at the same time, Embo's fluent Gaelic speakers were showing a degree of flux in grammatical constructions (and to a lesser extent in phonology) that was much less prevalent among the fluent speakers of Brora or Golspie. Across Embo's considerably broader age range of fully fluent Gaelic speakers, differences could often be heard between what a speaker at the higher age range offered in exemplification of a first-person singular conditional verb, or of a possessive modifying a noun, and what speakers at the lower age range were likely to offer for the same construction (less or no use of a synthetic inflection in the first case, less use of prenominal possessive pronouns in the second). Differences that correlated with age and proficiency were quite prominent in fluently spoken Embo Gaelic, in fact, quite apart from the lesser control of grammar and phonology that the imperfect youngest speakers displayed.

4.3.1 Establishing an Age-and-Proficiency Continuum

Once I had recognized the relevance of age to grammatical, lexical, and phonological differences in Embo Gaelic speech, I established among my sources an age and proficiency continuum that divided the Embo pool of fully fluent speakers into an older fluent speaker (OFS) group, those above sixty as of 1970 (roughly the midpoint of my frequent though intermittent on-site fieldwork over the years 1963 through 1978), and a younger fluent speaker (YFS) group, those sixty and under in 1970. This division was an artificial one in that the community itself made no such distinction. The division point I used, drawn between those over sixty and those sixty or under, can be justified readily enough for the particular speaker sample I happened to work with. The youngest member of my OFS group was widely regarded as a superior speaker with an especially rich store of local knowledge; her seniority in language and lore seemed to be recognized by the speakers grouped here as younger fluent speakers. But any entirely age-based grouping of speakers will include both more and less thoroughgoing exemplars of the features that typify the group in general. Just as individual older fluent speakers were not all equally conservative on every grammatical or lexical feature, individual younger fluent speakers showed different degrees of conservatism versus innovation with regard to particular grammatical features or lexical items in flux. (See chapter 4 for further discussion of these matters, and chapter 8 for a close discussion of the difficulties involved in attempting to evaluate speaker skills for the purpose of creating a speaker typology.)

Fluent Embo speakers themselves seemed not to notice the differences between what those at the higher end of the fluent speaker age range said and what those at the lower end were saying, but they did notice the more conspicuous deviations of a number of imperfect speakers who were younger still than the youngest fully fluent Gaelic speakers. These last were similar in their incomplete control of Gaelic phonology, grammar, and lexicon to the imperfect youngest speakers in Brora. Individuals who, like these, spoke an imperfect Gaelic that in Embo village drew the conscious attention and explicit disapproval of more fully fluent speakers, are recognized here as a separate proficiency group. In giving them a designation of their own, I am in this case acknowledging the Embo community's recognition of them as a distinct speaker group and generalizing that recognition to Brora, where I did not undertake comparable discussions. The Embo fluent speakers used no separate term in speaking of the imperfect speakers, but for analytic purposes I termed them *semi-speakers* (Dorian 1973, 1977). Apart from their noticeably imperfect control of Gaelic phonology, grammar, and lexicon, they differed from fully fluent speakers in one important social respect as well. Whereas all fully fluent speakers had some conversation partners with whom

Gaelic was the unmarked language of verbal interaction, this was not true of semi-speakers. Some semi-speakers spoke Gaelic more often or more eagerly than others, but none had any conversation partners with whom they routinely and regularly spoke Gaelic by preference.[3]

Both in dialect geography and in descriptive linguistics, young speakers have traditionally been considered less desirable sources of information, even when they are as fully fluent as were the Embo younger fluent speakers. Their speech, compared to that of their elders, is deemed more likely to be contaminated by importations (loanwords, features from neighboring areas, slang, influence from a school-taught standard) and less likely to preserve the most conservative features of strictly local speech. Never mind that today's conservative elderly speakers were yesterday's suspect youngsters at some previous point: the current crop of younger speakers is carefully avoided, typically, by the serious dialect geographer or descriptive linguist, at least if elderly speakers are still available. Methodological bias as strongly entrenched over a considerable period as this one has been is bound to have consequences. The findings that result are necessarily skewed toward oldest-speaker conservatism, and the speech variety that is canonized in published atlases and descriptive grammars seldom (if ever) represents the full spectrum to be met with in the community of speakers. Some potential sources and directions of distortion are discussed later in this chapter (see §7).

5 INTER-SPEAKER AND INTRA-SPEAKER VARIATION IN THE GAELIC-SPEAKING COMMUNITIES

Raising questions about the validity of selective traditional field practices was certainly not part of my original objective in undertaking work on East Sutherland Gaelic, nor was challenging established descriptive principles. Like any other fieldworker, I hoped to describe the local Gaelic in its fullest possible form, and in consequence I had the usual strong descriptivist interest in the way the oldest available speakers said things. But since the oldest speakers did not by any means always agree among themselves in East Sutherland, any field researcher who hoped to avoid dealing ceaselessly with speaker-by-speaker variation would have had to try, at least as an initial strategy, to locate a single fully fluent source in each fisherfolk community and then describe that lone individual's speech production. This approach is far from unknown in descriptive work, in fact. Edward Sapir, legendary fieldworker though he was, wrote his grammar of Southern Paiute on the basis of work with a single schoolboy, sent to him at the University of Pennsylvania for the purpose by the Indian School in Carlisle, Pennsylvania (Sapir 1992).

Among the East Sutherland fisherfolk, however, even this drastically selective approach would not have eliminated the need to deal with a considerable degree of variation. Not only did fluent elderly Gaelic speakers not necessarily agree among themselves about grammatical structures, even within the bounds of a single village, but they also showed a good deal of variation on various other items, grammatical or lexical, within their own individual usage. In all of the villages intra-speaker variation was as conspicuous as inter-speaker variation.

5.1 Examples of Inter- and Intra-Speaker Differences in the Use of Two Variables

The rather startling extent of this variation can best be demonstrated by consideration of one or two actual examples. One useful case is the monosyllabic prepositional element meaning 'on her' as it appeared in Golspie usage. Looking at material drawn from the five oldest speakers in that village, all of them fine, high-proficiency speakers falling within a nine-year age range, we find that four different forms of the monosyllabic prepositional element meaning 'on her' (variable ('on her') hereafter)[4] were in use in structurally common and equivalent environments; that is, the difference in variant forms was not prosodically or grammatically motivated. It also attracted no notice and carried no social loading. Two of the five fluent elderly speakers made use of more than one of the forms in comparable environments, so taking just one of the speakers as sole source would not necessarily have eliminated the problem of variation. In Embo village, as a second example, five forms of the compounded preposition 'along with' (variable ('along with') hereafter) were in use. Among them, six older high-proficiency Embo sources within a fifteen-year age range of one another produced freely spoken instances of ('along with') that included all five of the variants; again, since three of the six made use of more than one variant, working with just one Embo speaker could not have been counted on to eliminate the variation.

High-frequency, socially unweighted, idiosyncratic variation of this sort was a feature of fisherfolk Gaelic but not of fisherfolk English; in the latter, competing forms had the sort of social weighting typical of other varieties of English. The differences in form that Gaelic variants of variables such as ('on her') and ('along with') took could not be explained away as the product of Gaelic-English bilingualism. Both variables are conjugating prepositions (prepositions that literally conjugate for number and person), a prominent feature of Gaelic but one without a match in English. The variants exhibited by the two prepositional variables did not constitute the sort of progressive weakening that might arise from gradual disuse in the repertoires of a population experiencing a shift to English; they were instead consonant with the kind of variation to be met with in Gaelic dialect geography (see the next section).

Although these and other variables of the idiosyncratic-variation type were attended to little or not at all by the speakers who produced them, the differences between variants were not small in articulatory terms. The four Golspie forms of 'on her' are /ɛr, ɔir, ɔiç, ɔi/, while the five Embo forms of 'along with' are /kʰɔ̃:ɬa ri, kʰɔr(a) ri, kʰɔ̃n(a) ri, kʰɔ̃rn(a) ri, kʰɔi/ (with the vowels in parentheses subject to syncopation); with the exception of the last variant cited, all of these variant forms are potentially possible in any structural and semantic environment for which the conjugating preposition in question is suitable. The five Embo variants of ('along with') can be seen to form a series of phonologically related forms with various liquids and/or nasals appearing as second consonant, or, in the case of the mono-syllabic variant /kʰɔi/, with the second consonant eliminated altogether. As a group they have a degree of phonological coherence, exhibiting modifications (including elimination) of the second consonant. The most reduced form, it should be noted, is used chiefly by speakers fifty-eight years old or more and is rare among the youngest and least proficient speakers (see table 5.5 in chapter 5); that is, it does not represent an articulatory reduction produced by imperfect acquisition.

It bears repeating, in connection with both sets of variants, that all of the speakers in question were fully fluent and were regular speakers of Gaelic. That is to say, there was no possibility of dismissing their variant forms as aberrations arising from disuse of the language. And while the age range of the six oldest Embo speakers who provided freely spoken instances of ('along with') spanned fifteen years, those fifteen years represented just the uppermost quarter of the fifty-eight-year age spectrum available in Gaelic-speaking Embo.

5.2 The Evidence of Dialect Geography

Gaelic dialect geography provides further evidence that the East Sutherland Gaelic variants appearing in inter-speaker variation, apart from a very few that were ana-logically formed, did not represent a fading of Gaelic proficiency in a bilingual district. The seemingly overabundant variants of the East Sutherland fisherfolk variables were generally to be found in use in the Gaelic of one or more other dialect areas within the northerly part of the Highland mainland. This suggests what patronymic evidence also suggests (see chapter 2, §4.2.1), namely, that dialect mixture took place in the early years of the fishing villages' existence. The Gaelic division of the Linguistic Survey of Scotland happens to have included 'on her' as one of the items in its lengthy questionnaire, for example, and three of the four Golspie variants are recorded for other Highland districts. The variant /ɛr/, which is used exclusively by nearly all Brora and Embo speakers and exclusively or alternatively by four of seven Golspie speakers, seems unusual at first blush in terms of the written language and more mainstream dialects. But the Survey records it for other parts of eastern and central Sutherland and likewise for the fishing villages of Easter Ross, the next county to the south. Forms phonemically parallel to /ɔi/, used alternatively by two of the seven Golspie speakers in my sample and exclusively by one, appear in Assynt, on the western coast of Sutherland, and in Wester Ross, in the next county to the south, and still closer by in southern Caithness, just to the north of the East Sutherland fishing commu-nities. Forms resembling /ɔir/, used alternatively by two Golspie speakers and offered exclusively by one, are rarer, recorded for single speakers in northwestern and northeastern Inverness-shire locations, not far to the south.[5] Only /ɔiç/, the less common of two variants used by a single highly fluent Golspie speaker (the second-oldest in my sample), appears nowhere else among the Survey's question-naire point responses. But since those points were selective rather than compre-hensive, the absence of a form elsewhere on the Survey maps does not guarantee that it was not in use in other locations—or for that matter that it was not in use as an alternative form among sampled speakers. Indeed, the Survey's sole Golspie entry, provided by a single Golspie source in 1958, corresponds to /ɛr/, offering no hint of the actual variety of forms that was in use in Golspie Gaelic.

The Gaelic survey did not include 'along with' among its questionnaire items, but evidence of nearby use of at least two of the Embo variants of 'along with' comes from a collection of Easter Ross fishing village texts collected orally in the 1960s, where the writings *comhla ri* /kʰɔ̃:ɫa ri/ and *cona ri* /kʰɔ̃na ri/ both appear (Watson 2007).

5.3 The Possible Effect of Gender

The ('along with') variant selections of six Embo older fluent speakers indicates that the sex of the speaker can no more account for the differences in variant selection than age and proficiency can, since the elderly males and the elderly females differ among themselves. The three oldest Embo males (aged eighty-two, seventy-five, and seventy, respectively) used three different variants among them. The oldest of them heavily favored /kʰɔ̃n(a) ri/, in elicitation as well as freely spoken), but in addition he made one lone use of /kʰɔra ri/. The second oldest male also provided one instance of /kʰɔra ri/ (his only freely spoken variant, though his dominant variant in elicitation was /kʰɔ̃rna ri/). This minimally shared used of /kʰɔra ri/ constitutes the sole instance of overlap among the three male speakers' variant choices, since the youngest of the three used only /kʰɔi/, both freely spoken and in elicitation. The three oldest Embo women who provided freely spoken instances of ('along with'), aged (?)seventy-four, sixty-seven, and sixty-four, respectively, used just one variant in common, namely, /kʰɔ̃:ɫa ri/. Two instances of /kʰɔ̃:ɫa ri/ are the only variants produced by the oldest of the three, but the other two used several additional variants as well. The sixty-seven-year-old made fully as much use of /kʰɔi/ as of /kʰɔ:ɫa ri/, with /kʰɔ̃na ri/ as a rare variant choice for her. The sixty-four-year-old by contrast strongly favored /kʰɔ̃rna ri/, with /kʰɔ̃na ri/ as her next most common variant choice and /kʰɔra ri/ and /kʰɔ̃:ɫa ri/ as rarely used variants. This complex picture rules out any straightforward gender effect, at least for this variable and these speakers.

5.4 The Possible Effect of Style

Stylistic differences represent another possible explanation for differences in variant choice. Some inherent difficulty existed, where my East Sutherland work was concerned, in ruling out style differentiation as a factor in variant choice, both because stylistic range is confined to a comparatively narrow spectrum in a single-class population using a strictly local, strongly stigmatized, and unwritten vernacular, and because a great deal of the available recorded material was directed to a single unvarying audience of one, namely, a familiar researcher who spoke the self-same dialect. In a few cases, however, an interviewer previously unknown to one of my sources conducted an interview of which I was given a copy, and in these interviews there is occasionally a style shift toward formality in the form of at least one obvious lexical substitution in which a more mainstream Gaelic form is introduced instead of the usual local form. An unfamiliar radio broadcaster conducted a phone interview with the sixty-four-year-old Embo woman already mentioned, for example, during which she took the trouble to substitute non-local *balaich* 'boys' for strictly local *brogaich*. But even though her strongly favored ('along with') variant, /kʰɔ̃rn(a) ri/, was just as distinctly local (and nonstandard) as *brogaich*, she made no effort to substitute a more standard form in the one instance of ('along with') that she produced; instead, she used her preferred local form in the interview just as she did in conversation. Persistence with her own local variant preference is indicated by similar behavior in the cases of four other variables that appeared either once or twice in her radio interview: in each case, she used with the radio broadcaster the same variant forms that she favored in conversation with fellow villagers, with me, and with a fieldworker colleague of mine whom she had come to know and like.

This finding is not actually very surprising, in view of the fact that fisherfolk speakers pay no apparent attention to variant selection differences within their own villages and seem to have trouble even noticing the variation when it is pointed out to them (see §8.2 later). However, given the impact of formal versus casual style on the more familiar socially weighted variables of variationist studies, it is important to introduce the question of style here as well. It will be considered again briefly in chapter 3, §5, and again in connection with a particular set of variables in the second part of chapter 5.

5.5 The Possible Effect of Kinship or of Household Membership

Two of the six older Embo speakers who provided freely spoken instances of ('along with') were close kin: the seventy-year-old male and the sixty-seven-year-old female were a brother and sister who also lived in the same household. They shared the variant /kʰɔi/, but while that was the brother's sole variant in his available materials, either freely spoken or elicited, the sister used two additional variants in her freely spoken materials and a third additional variant in elicitation. Selecting closely related individuals as sources or selecting sources from a single household would therefore also not automatically eliminate the problem of variation for an investigator of East Sutherland fisherfolk Gaelic.

5.6 The Prevalence of Idiosyncratic, Socially Neutral Variation

The unavoidable fact of the matter was that variables with multiple variant forms existed in profusion in these villages, and even elderly speakers of the highest proficiency differed on which variant they used, both from instance to instance in their own speech and from speaker to speaker.[6] This fact is remarkable chiefly when other salient facts about the East Sutherland fisherfolk subcommunities are considered: that they had consisted of only a single socioeconomic class, essentially undifferentiated as to occupation, income, and educational level at the time when the fluent speakers of the 1960s were growing up; that they had furthermore been small, face-to-face communities with a pronounced history of endogamy and a high level of social interaction; and that, while transmission had ceased, regular intra-group use of Gaelic remained the norm among fluent speakers. And yet, despite the presence of a strikingly large amount of inter-speaker and intra-speaker variation, common patterns of variant selection had not developed into membership markers for distinct social subgroups within these socioeconomically undifferentiated enclaves. Consciousness of within-the-village variation remained extremely low, and competing variants remained socially neutral.

Of course I did not initially anticipate the full extent of the variability I was encountering, and in the early years of my East Sutherland work I had other research priorities. I therefore documented variation that seemed unrelated to age and proficiency when I encountered it, but I did not set out to determine its range or its limits and I left possible explanations for it unexplored, in spite of the questions raised by its surprising proportions.

6 COMING TO GRIPS WITH THE VARIATION PUZZLE

Research focuses are always susceptible to serendipitous change, and the event that redirected mine was the appearance in 1983 of a colleague's review of my 1978 descriptive study of East Sutherland Gaelic (Ó Dochartaigh 1983). The colleague in question had also done dialect geography work for the Gaelic Division of the Linguistic Survey of Scotland in the 1960s and was highly knowledgeable about Scottish Gaelic dialects. Experienced dialect geographer that he was, however, he had not worked in a relic area where a nucleated community of fluent speakers still made use of Gaelic in constant daily interactions, as the East Sutherland fisherfolk continued to do, most notably in Embo but within certain kin networks also in Brora and Golspie. In reading my descriptive study, Ó Dochartaigh was struck by the repeated mention of lack of agreement among my sources. In giving the particulars for the conjunction that translates as 'before', for example, I had reported that Brora and Golspie sources used the form /məs/, except for one who used /mər/ instead, and that although all Embo speakers in my sample used /mə(n)/ (the /-n/ appearing before vowel-initial verbs) for 'before', for some of them the conjunction produced a change in the initial consonant of a following verb, while for others it did not (Dorian 1978:137). In the conjugation for the preposition 'on', I had supplied three of the four Golspie forms of 'on her', furthermore (omitting only the infrequent /ɔiç/ form with which I was not yet properly acquainted), and for the compounded preposition 'along with' I had entered all five of the Embo forms. With many instances such as these in mind, Ó Dochartaigh wrote (1983:123): "One major thread running through all of this work is that of the decay and loss of the Gaelic language in this area. For instance, in the chapter on grammar we are constantly being reminded, in Dorian's many comments on alternative forms, of the nature and extent of this language death." Reading this comment was a turning point for me. I saw immediately how he might have arrived at that interpretation: a lot of seemingly fluent speakers disagreed on a lot of grammatical matters, and the dialect was dying. It seemed highly plausible that the one could be explained by the other.

6.1 The Inadequacy of Obsolescence as an Explanation for Idiosyncratic Variation

In spite of its plausibility, the explanation was not workable. The speakers who differed on such matters as the form of the conjunction 'before' and its effect on following consonant-initial verbs were high-proficiency and full-fluency speakers of East Sutherland Gaelic, just like the Golspie speakers who differed on ('on her') and the Embo speakers who differed on ('along with'). Furthermore, many of the variant forms in question were familiar in other mainland dialect areas, as noted in §5.1, some of them quite close by. The /mər/ form of 'before', used by just one of my sample of Brora speakers and by none of the Golspie sample, was nonetheless in frequent use in the fisherfolk Gaelic of nearby Hilton, in Easter Ross, for example, just as both the /kʰɔ̃:ɬa ri/ and /kʰɔ̃na ri/ forms of Embo 'along with' occurred there.

There was a great deal of proficiency-related variation appearing in East Sutherland Gaelic, to be sure, but it turned up in more chronologically ordered fashion than this, the forms of elderly speakers differing quite sharply from those of semi-speakers and in Embo also tending to differ from those of younger fluent speakers. In age- and proficiency-related variation, that is, change was characterized by directionality; typically some innovative development appeared, increasing in frequency as speakers' ages decreased. Whatever explained the fact that five Embo speakers within the older age range (including the oldest who provided instances of the structure) produced an altered initial consonant in consonant-initial verbs that followed /mə(n)/ 'before', while three others (including the second-oldest who provided instances) did not, it could not be a purely age-related matter of proficiency, since all of these individuals were older, high-proficiency speakers.

As noted in §5.1, age and proficiency were also inadequate to explain the different forms used for 'on her' in Golspie and 'along with' in Embo. If such conspicuous individual variation as this could exist, yet could not be accounted for by age and proficiency levels or by such features as social class membership or community-internal social groupings, the most fundamental question that remained was whether the same sort of variation appeared in other speech forms besides East Sutherland fisherfolk Gaelic, and if so, why it was not recognized and discussed in the ever more extensive literature on variation. Were linguists just as unlikely to pay attention to acoustically striking but socially unweighted variation such as the four Golspie forms of ('on her') and the five Embo forms of ('along with') as Golspie and Embo speakers themselves were to notice that they were producing it? An unexpectedly high degree of unexplained variation is not necessarily a welcome feature in a fieldworker's growing database, of course, and as Ó Dochartaigh's ready (though unworkable) explanation for the East Sutherland fisherfolk variation indicates, there are often conventional viewpoints ready to hand that allow the fieldworker to avoid accepting such variation as a regular feature of the speech form under study. The next section discusses some familiar lines of thinking that make it possible for linguists to avoid engaging with the full range of variation they may encounter and notes the aspects of my East Sutherland fieldwork that ultimately prevented me from adopting them.

7 RESEARCHER RESPONSES TO SEEMINGLY IDIOSYNCRATIC VARIATION AMONG SPEAKERS

Linguists may register the fact that their sources show a surprising lack of agreement with one another and yet not grapple adequately with the issue of disagreement, as my own case demonstrates. The experience of one seasoned fieldworker led him to offer the following comment and advice to fellow fieldworkers: "The language practices of any speech community, no matter how small or monolithic (I have worked with language communities with a grand total of 200 speakers!), are never homogeneous. Variation is the rule; don't paper over this" (Foley 2003:86). As Foley's final exhortation suggests, it can be tempting for researchers to ignore an unexpected degree of variation and proceed with a description that gains apparent coherence thereby. A variety of familiar assumptions, expectations, or methodological practices help account for the inclination to follow such a course.

7.1 Residual Prescriptivism

One major factor in the tendency to leave findings of seemingly inexplicable variation out of account lies, I suspect, in the largely unconscious expectations of investigators socialized in literate and linguistically mainstream societies. For a literate mother-tongue speaker of a standardized language, it seems natural—even unavoidable—that "good" speakers of any language will recognize some forms of whatever language they speak as "preferable" to others, and that several such "good" speakers will largely concur on which forms are preferable.[7] The very process of standardization creates a linguistic environment in which one form is viewed as the "correct" form and competing forms are then automatically judged to be less acceptable, even though they may be perfectly equivalent in purely structural terms to the favored form. Milroy and Milroy cite the example of *different to*, *different than*, and *different from*, showing that the grammatical reasonableness of each form can be established by a particular line of argument. But within the prescriptive ideology that a standardized language brings into being, one and only one of the set of items that can follow *different* in the spoken vernacular is recognized as appropriate for the formal uses to which a standard language is frequently put (Milroy and Milroy 1985:14). Once one form is anointed as "correct", the others are inevitably disfavored and their use frowned on.

Most linguists consider that they have put prescriptive notions behind them in the course of their professional training, but James Milroy has marshaled a good deal of evidence showing that language professionals are susceptible to a prescriptivism of their own. He demonstrates, for example, that historians of English have perpetuated "the myth of the Anglo-Norman scribe", so as to be able to discount the rampant variant spellings of Middle English:

> There is no hard evidence for it [i.e., variation-producing Anglo-Norman scribes]— but...it is a very powerful myth which leaves its traces everywhere—in onomastics, ME dialectology, standard histories of language and handbooks of ME, and in important work on early English pronunciation by Jespersen, Wyld, Dobson and others. It is clearly an extension of the argument put forward by Sweet, Marsh and others that some forms (or changes) are legitimate and others illegitimate. The alleged Anglo-Norman spellings are illegitimate and can be ignored. (Milroy 2000:21)

Historical linguists are by no means the only offenders, in Milroy's view. He sees the grammaticality judgments of transformational grammar as part of the same mind-set (Milroy 2000:12; see also Ross 1979 and Johnstone 1996:11 in this connection), and he and L. Milroy note that features of English that appear with some frequency in unplanned spoken discourse, as demonstrated by Ochs (1979), are nowhere mentioned in descriptive grammars of English. Referring to Ochs's research and similar findings by Crystal (1980) and by Miller and Weinert (1998), the Milroys conclude:

> Coherent linguistic descriptions of planned discourse are apparently accepted as norms for the language as a whole by those who, for professional purposes, need such descriptions, while unplanned discourse is characterised as containing "error" or as "unstructured" in relation to the norms of planned discourse. (Milroy and Milroy 1999:120)

In a similar vein, Cheshire reports on syntactic structures that are prevalent in spoken English but ignored in conventional descriptions of English syntax. She attributes what she calls "our failure to understand the nature of spoken syntax" at least partly to the fact that the frameworks of analysis we use "conform to the views of language that we have acquired during our education rather than to the variety of language that we produce during face-to-face interaction" (Cheshire 1999:129).

Other critics have noticed a reluctance on the part of descriptive linguists to give a realistic account of everyday speech when that sort of speech regularly shows features of admixture. Mougeon and Beniak, urging researchers to give quantitatively reliable accounts of the influence of language contact on the speech forms they are studying, concur with a colleague's assessment that linguists are inclined to underreport linguistic transfer:

> In research on minority languages, unfortunately, the tendency has also lately been to...neglect interference. As Flora Klein-Andreu sees it (p.c.)—a viewpoint which we share as well—a stigma is attached to interference: 'It seems to me that the reason for this neglect is a kind of covert purism: the results of transfer are considered undesirable or "bad"; therefore they are ignored or seriously downplayed, as kind of courtesy to the population under study. (Mougeon and Beniak 1991:184)

Interestingly, this may be the case even when the transfer is from a more formal variety of the same language: "Linguists have found it fairly easy to describe [Arabic] vernaculars but have always resorted when doing so to an unconfessed purism, editing out without acknowledgement the prestigious, 'literary'-cum-vernacular forms of the language that are in fact probably its commonest manifestation" (Mitchell 1982:124–25).

Where East Sutherland Gaelic was concerned, most of these forms of purism were minimized for me by the fact that I had only the barest acquaintance with any other form of Scottish Gaelic and was a very long way from genuinely literate in the language. I often asked friends residing in Golspie, native speakers of a west coast dialect, what they said for some phrase or construction I was learning from local fisherfolk speakers, but such comparisons were of purely intellectual interest for me. For a strictly locally oriented field-site language learner, they lacked the social power that standard language forms usually have for classroom learners and native speakers alike.

7.2 Data Control via Source Selection

In the fundamental matter of selecting sources ("speakers", "informants", "consultants", "assistants"; see Newman and Ratliff 2001:2–4 for a good discussion of the range of terminology), linguists make choices that shape the record they leave when they describe a language. One very common choice is to select for the relative linguistic conservatism that advanced age is likely to confer, as both descriptivists and dialect geographers have regularly done. C. M. Voegelin, for example, was "interested in recording the 'best' variety of the language he was studying" and followed the general practice of anthropological linguists when he "neglected" the young people who still spoke Tübatulabal in favor of working with elderly or middle-aged speakers (Voegelin and Voegelin 1977:336).

Another fairly common choice is reliance on a single primary source, as Sapir did in producing his grammar of Southern Paiute. If only one intelligent and cooperative source is consulted, the likelihood that the researcher will have to confront high variability is reduced, though not necessarily eliminated. The last monograph on a particular Scottish Gaelic dialect to appear before my own on East Sutherland Gaelic was Magne Oftedal's excellent full-scale description of Gaelic in Leurbost, a village of (at the time) about 535 people on the Isle of Lewis in the Outer Hebrides (Oftedal 1956). Oftedal worked primarily with a single source—a disabled weaver with ample time to devote to the project. This man, Roddy Martin, supplied "the majority of words, forms, and expressions" in Oftedal's material (1956:16). The reader might suppose that Oftedal's chief source represented a small community's very uniform speech variety if it were not for the fact that Oftedal comments explicitly on differences between the Gaelic spoken by the weaver and his wife ("her dialect differed on some points from Roddy's, both in phonemic distribution and in grammar", 1956:17), differences made truly remarkable by the fact that husband and wife were both Leurbost natives and had spent their childhoods as next-door neighbors. Oftedal also notes that "minor dialectal differences" appear over Leurbost's two-mile length (1956:14). Though the wife was at the sessions with Oftedal and her husband, and sometimes stood in for him in his absence, her variants are not explicitly treated in the text, nor are the "minor dialectal differences" across the dialect. Other contributors are mentioned as supplying connected texts in the form of stories and in one case lexical material, and "occasional informants" constituting "nearly everybody in the central part of Leurbost" are likewise mentioned (1956:17–18), but no individual differences in forms are discussed, and the dominance of the source material from the disabled weaver is maintained throughout the description.

Because the original dialect geography assignment in East Sutherland covered three villages and required identification of the genuinely local in each location, my work necessarily involved several sources from each village from the beginning and therefore confronted me almost immediately with the marked degree of individual variation typical of the Gaelic of these villages.

7.3 Search for an Assumed Uniformity

A fieldworker can also press for a consensus that may or may not actually exist. Paul Friedrich, investigating dialectal variation in Tarascan phonology in Mexico, speaks of conducting interviews "with two speakers or even a small group (to control individual variation)" (Friedrich 1971:170). He worked in twenty-six villages, in interviews usually lasting two hours, focusing on 50 to 130 key words contextualized in one or more Tarascan utterances. The working assumption seems to have been that speakers of a single village dialect would agree on the pronunciation of the words in question, but the mention of "control" for individual variation raises some question about whether this was strictly so. Friedrich's interest lay in village-by-village differentiation, however, and the matter of possible intra-village variation is not discussed.

Among the few remaining Tolowa speakers of northern California, James Collins ran headlong into a view of linguistic variability strongly at odds with his own. Discovering that the Tolowa language materials used in a test for Indian Teacher Education certification at a state-university–affiliated Center for Community Development included some incorrect or incorrectly labeled forms (e.g., a past tense form glossed as present tense), Collins initially declined to supply the expert approval of the test that he was asked for. This created funding problems for the Center and was interpreted as behavior hostile to Tolowa efforts to preserve their language, even though Collins had also offered to help in revising the test materials. In his subsequent work with local speakers of varying proficiency in Tolowa, Collins found that they had no concept of a single "correct" or "real" Tolowa, in terms of an originally stable structural system such as academic scholars conventionally recognized, so that they would only say of forms such as those he had criticized that their own family in a particular Tolowa settlement did not say things that way. Collins comments: "Unlike many Americans who assume that cultural chaos reigns unless there is an official standard language . . . , Tolowa skeptics question the effort to have a *general* linguistic description for the entire speech community" (1998:267; emphasis in original). The Tolowa position in effect challenges the practice of producing structurally uniform overall language descriptions, based on the assumption of a uniformity that would justify a title like the one Oftedal gave his monograph (*The Gaelic of Leurbost*). Their position challenges perhaps even our practice of referring to unwritten and unstandardized languages in the singular (Tarascan, Tolowa, East Sutherland Gaelic), as if languages could always be assumed to exist in a single more or less uniform state, in terms of some underlying consensus if not in surface form.

As Collins notes, this difference in viewpoints speaks to the question of whether language is fundamentally the same for any two active speakers who are members of the same social aggregate. In a few respects there were differences as conspicuous within the Gaelic of Embo itself, even when a good many age-related change processes are discounted, as there were between the Gaelic of Embo and that of Golspie; yet conventional linguistic description would readily recognize the Embo versus Golspie differences and much less readily the differences within Embo Gaelic, except for precisely those age-related differences that can be associated with the decline of Gaelic proficiency. The descriptive tradition that presents a largely uniform account of most newly described languages (especially in the case of a geographically concentrated and socially egalitarian speech community) is deeply entrenched, but the idiosyncratic variation that was so striking a feature of fisherfolk Gaelic in Sutherland clearly called for a different approach. I was not swift to begin searching for a more satisfactory approach, but the linguistic literature ultimately provided indications that Embo (as the only East Sutherland fisherfolk community with enough Gaelic speakers to have offered the abundant data required) represents a distinct social profile and a distinctive social setting, associated with high individual variation in languages in other parts of the world, too, though not previously recognized for that association (see chapter 8, § 6).

7.4   Concentration on the Group Rather than the Individual

A methodological approach that organizes and presents data for socially based groups of speakers but not for individual speakers has long been considered problematic because of the potential for ignoring lack of isomorphism between individual and group (Romaine 1982:20). Returning to this problem in the light of their fieldwork findings and reviewing the variation analysis practices of correlational sociolinguistic work, Wolfram and Beckett identify what they call a "homogeneity assumption": they point out that presenting data for a set of speakers as if that set were a homogenous group implies that individual variation is insignificant in the description of linguistic and social covariance (2000:5–6). If in-group variance nonetheless appears prominently in a group that was delimited in terms of apparently meaningful social boundaries, the corrective in the correlational sociolinguistic tradition is taken to be division of the group into "numerous small groups with subtle, special relationships to the whole" (Chambers 1995:100). Such strikingly atypical speakers as may remain even after subdivision can be treated as exceptional cases (e.g., Nathan B. in Labov 1979).

Just as Ochs, Cheshire, and others found that spoken-language structures were omitted in grammatical treatments of English, and Collins found that his conception of a whole-community structural description of Tolowa was not shared by Tolowa speakers, Wolfram and colleagues found that data analysis based on the group did not work well in their field site. In Hyde County, a very isolated, rural, and biracial region of North Carolina's Outer Banks, the researchers found patterns of "inexplicable" individual variation that led them to conclude that individualized life histories and personal identities were necessary to understanding variation in that locale (Wolfram and Beckett 2000:27; Wolfram and Thomas 2002:182). In the small, isolated Hyde County communities where everyone knew everyone else, they found that considerable individual variation could appear even when individuals had a demographic profile in common. African American speakers from Hyde County exhibited uniformity with respect to some core African American Vernacular English (AAVE) features, but at the same time they showed significant individual variation with respect to others (Wolfram and Thomas 2002:179). Despite the great isolation of the region, no uniform regional version of AAVE had developed, but neither did African American speech in Hyde County converge with the regional dialect of the area's European American population. The social identities recognized in correlational sociolinguistic analysis remained important; but individualized life histories and personal identities had to be taken into consideration to account for those patterns of seemingly inexplicable individual variation. (See chapter 9, §7.2 for further discussion.)

In the socially isolated fisherfolk communities of East Sutherland, similarly, virtually identical demographic profiles often did not result in uniform linguistic usages, even on the part of individuals who interacted constantly in Gaelic. Although in age-related variation some predictable directionality typically

appeared, making variability interpretable in terms of group-based age and proficiency differences, this was not the case with the idiosyncratic variation equally
conspicuous in fisherfolk Gaelic. Ultimately it seemed clear that group-based data
presentation was less well suited to idiosyncratic variation than to age-related
variation.

7.5 Expectation of Linguistic Focusing within Small, Tight-Knit, Highly Interactive Communities

There has often been an expectation of more agreement in speech behavior, or at
least more agreement on the evaluation of speech behavior, within small and
tightly knit communities than in larger, more socially diverse communities, and
simultaneously an expectation of lesser linguistic divergence among speech
community members who relate to one another through multiplex roles, interacting with one another constantly, than among members of large, socially complex
communities in which people have uniplex roles with a great many different people but multiplex roles with relatively few. One form such expectations take is the
designation of some communities as "focused" and others as "diffuse", with different assumptions about the degree of linguistic variability to be met with in each
type of community:

> Among tightly-knit and closely-interactive communities—those which we shall refer
> to as *focussed*—the sharing of [linguistic] rules, and the regularity of rules, can be
> considerable. (Le Page and Tabouret-Keller 1985:5)

> "Focussing" will imply greater regularity in the linguistic code, less variability; "dif-
> fusion" the converse. (Le Page and Tabouret-Keller 1985:116)

Each of the Gaelic-speaking fishing communities of coastal East Sutherland could
certainly be described as tightly knit and closely interactive—that is, as focused
communities in social terms. The expected regularity in linguistic rules did not
appear, however: witness the fully proficient Brora speaker who used /mər/ instead
of /məs/ for 'before', and the division of fully proficient Embo speakers into those
for whom /mə(n)/ 'before' changed the initial consonant of a following verb and
those for whom it did not (§6.1). The communities in question can realistically be
described, it seems, as socially focused but linguistically diffuse, a combination
not anticipated in the literature.

One major aspect of life in very small and socioeconomically undifferentiated communities is overlooked when expectations such as those of Le Page and
Tabouret-Keller are voiced: members of such communities share an extremely
high level of information both about local history and lifeways and about other
community members and their families; under such circumstances, there is a
much reduced incentive for individuals to adjust their speech to that of other

community members. The smaller focus of linguistic accommodation in the fisherfolk villages of East Sutherland will be taken up in chapter 8, §3, but the doubtful general expectation of greater regularity in focused speech communities merits some further discussion precisely with reference to accommodation.

7.6 Expectation of Linguistic Accommodation to Other Speakers

Dialect mixture in the establishment of a new geographical settlement (presumably present in the early years of the East Sutherland fishing communities; see chapter 2, §4.2.1) is widely acknowledged to result in the presence of multiple variants, but researchers influenced by standard language environments have an expectation that the "excessive" variation will diminish over time: "As time passes and focusing begins to take place, particularly as the colony or new town begins to acquire an independent identity, the variants present in the mixture will begin to be subject to reduction. This will take place as a result of accommodation between speakers in face-to-face interactions" (Trudgill 1999:197). Documentary evidence for a progression of just this sort is actually available for English in New Zealand. Trudgill, working with New Zealand broadcasting archives, found "astonishing variability" in both consonant and vowel realizations among close-in-age speakers, all born in the same small town on New Zealand's South Island, who had grown up together and were in many cases also related to one another. Their parents were English speakers, but they hailed from a variety of English-speaking areas: Ireland, Scotland, England, and Australia. Trudgill explained the variability exhibited in the English of the locally born children by the number of different linguistic models the children were exposed to. In the absence of a single peer dialect, the multiplicity of models gave rise, according to Trudgill's hypothesis, to "much greater freedom in the selection of which linguistic model to follow than would normally be the case" (Trudgill 1999:200). Trudgill calls this "the chaos before the order", since New Zealand English ultimately coalesced around more unitary phonological norms. But English of course has a long history of standardization, and no regional form of the language escapes the looming presence of the standard language, or, as in New Zealand, of the local colonial standard.

It is entirely possible that the Gaelic of the three East Sutherland fishing communities showed still more variability in the early years after the communities' founding than it showed in the latter half of the twentieth century. But is certain, at any rate, that it still showed very much more variability 150 years after the founding of the fishing communities than Trudgill found in the English of the first native-born generation of Otago townspeople on New Zealand's South Island, and among people just as similar in age and as closely linked by kinship and social background as the Otago townsfolk, if not more so. To adopt Trudgill's terms, the linguistic "chaos" in the East Sutherland fishing communities never did give way to "order". Contrary to the expectations of literate researchers from standardized language traditions, "accommodation between speakers in face-to-face interaction" does not automatically take place; in its absence, "the reduction of variants that accompanies focusing, in the course of new-dialect formation" (Trudgill 1999:197) may not take place either. Accommodation operates powerfully in East Sutherland, as I discuss in chapter 8, but for practical reasons it does not operate in terms of individual variant choices from among same-village variants. Instead, use of Gaelic with Gaelic-speaking interlocutors and use of strictly local village variants with other fisherfolk Gaelic speakers are the essential elements of fisherfolk linguistic accommodation, as will be shown in that chapter.

7.7 Expectation of Linkage between Variation and Social Differentiation

The expectation of focusing also gives rise to an assumption that even if usage differs within such communities, the differentiation will be stable and will display regular variation patterns with clear-cut social functions:

> Agreement on norms (as consequence of close-knit and stable social patterns) results not in uniformity of usage within a community, but on agreement on a pattern of stable differentiation. In a relatively focused community such as Ballymacarett [a Belfast neighborhood], therefore, we observe much greater regularity in the patterning of the variable elements than we do in less focused communities, and we may further suggest that the variants used in such a focused community develop a clear and consistent pattern in their social functions.... The less focused the community is, the less clear will be the relationship of specific linguistic variants to their various social functions. (Milroy 1992:90)

The expectations expressed in this passage appear to be confirmed by the findings of the Milroys in Belfast, where a working-class population maintains its vernacular norms despite all the pressures brought to bear by the promotion of a standardized language in schools and by the espousal of that same standardized language in such high-status institutions as mass media, religion, and government (Milroy 1987a). And yet in Embo, a highly focused working-class community entirely without the socioeconomic differentiation so prominent in Belfast, most of the many variable elements in a local Gaelic unconstrained by the pressures of standardization escaped any association whatever with social function and social evaluation.

The complex kin ties running through a strongly endogamous population such as Embo's (and those of the fisherfolk subsections of Golspie and Brora) had a powerful effect on social interaction. Most individuals grew up in large families and had available a very large number of blood kin and affines, with many of whom they regularly interacted. Both the natural social interactions of kin groups within the village or subvillage—each a compact, densely populated area—and the occupational interactions necessitated by fishing as a livelihood (boat crews among the men and gutting and packing crews among the women; see chapter 2) encouraged constant face-to-face contact. This was highly effective in keeping the fisherfolk communities Gaelic in speech, but it resulted neither in community-wide consensus within each village on the forms that many words or grammatical constructions should take nor in the assignment of different social weight to each of the variants representing a given variable.

7.8 Researcher Responses: Summary

None of the responses noted here and none of the practices associated with them is inherently unreasonable, much less blameworthy. On the contrary, these have been standard, useful, and successful practices for professional linguists. The eminent names cited in connection with various traditional descriptive practices—including those of Sapir, Oftedal, Voegelin, Friedrich, and Labov—make it clear that the practices in question have enabled gifted linguists to produce invaluable descriptive, analytic, and theoretical work that deserves the high regard in which it is held. My point in reviewing these expectations and practices is only to suggest that while they support the recognition and identification of a great many important linguistic phenomena, they may nonetheless delay the recognition of others. The particular variation phenomenon at issue here is one of these. I have already acknowledged that my own attempt to identify the full extent of this phenomenon and offer an explanation for it was seriously delayed by the effect of some of these assumptions on my own thinking. Only the stubborn refusal of the fisherfolk Gaelic data to conform satisfactorily to established expectations forced me to think otherwise and look elsewhere. The difficulties of dealing realistically and accurately with rampant, socially unweighted, idiosyncratic variation, for linguists who are mother tongue speakers of standardized languages and members of socioeconomically stratified societies, is a theme that is revisited in subsequent chapters, especially chapters 3 and 8.

8 VARIATION WITHIN AND ACROSS VILLAGE BOUNDARIES

The findings of both rural and urban dialectology indicate that speech behavior is frequently deployed in the service of social boundary marking, a function it serves supremely well. Even a small, rural community may present social divisions that are reflected in linguistic differences, as Holmquist found in Spanish Cantabria (1988). But not all small, rural communities present internal social divisions that are reflected in speech differences, and in Embo's single-class, single-ethnicity environment, internal social groupings such as the descent-based collectivities recognized by shared by-names (see chapter 2) do not find any expression in shared linguistic features. A look at the striking difference between fisherfolk Gaelic speakers' responses to variation *between communities* in East Sutherland, as opposed to their responses to variation *within their own community*, highlights this point.

8.1 Local Responses to Variation: Inter-Village Variation

Literate speakers of standardized languages tend to assume that most variation in language will be salient and socially evaluated, and indeed most alternative pro-nunciations and alternative grammatical forms in a standardized language such as English are inescapably subject to social evaluation relative to one another, so that the pronunciation "vahs" is assigned to a superior set of vases, for example, as Labov famously documented for one informant (1972:251, note 42), and *regardless* is considered preferable to the redundant *irregardless*).[8] Despite minimal or non-existent literacy, Brora, Golspie, and Embo bilinguals were actually far from indifferent to linguistic variation in Gaelic—they were deeply preoccupied with one form of it, in fact. The oddity in connection with East Sutherland Gaelic speakers' interest in linguistic variation was the radical imbalance of response that they demonstrated to the two most prevalent kinds of variation: speakers showed an extreme sensitivity to much of the variation in geographical terms (inter-village variation) and an even more extreme obliviousness to strictly local variation in individual terms (intra-village variation). This striking contrast pre-vailed in spite of the fact that the kinds of differences typical of inter-village var-iation were occasionally also typical of intra-village variation. To take a moderately high-frequency example, speakers were generally aware of the difference between the Brora/Golspie pronunciations of the placename *Golspie*, which has a shibilant [kəi:ʃpi], and the Embo pronunciation, which has a sibilant [kəi:spi], but Embo speakers showed no parallel awareness of the intra-village variation that produced either shibilant or sibilant in initial consonant clusters with a lateral as second element ([ʃl'ig ~ sl'ig] 'a shell', [ʃɫɔtʰ ~ sɫɔtʰ] '[a particular kind of] seaweed') within their own village.

East Sutherland Gaelic speakers could and often did discuss cross-village differences at great length. Indeed, differences of this sort constituted a favorite topic of conversation. Brora and Golspie speakers commented with half-amused wonder on what Embo speakers said for a given item, and Embo speakers did the same in reverse where Brora and Golspie speakers were concerned. Most of these explicit comments dealt with the phonological form of lexical items, and most of them represented a short list of well-known stereotypes trotted out frequently for just such discussions. But though they tended to bring up the same set of words repeatedly, speakers from each village were well aware of far more cross-village differences than the ones that were stereotypically mentioned. During elicitation sessions, it was not unusual for speakers to volunteer, just for the curiousness of it all, other-village lexical items well beyond those of the stereotypical list. They

also proved sensitive to far more than just lexical differences, accurately identifying certain particles or syntactic structures as peculiar to the speakers of another
village. They had an unusually large number of occasions to comment on these
things because of my own unavoidable lapses as a "local" Gaelic speaker. I lived
in a Gaelic-speaking household in Golspie during nearly all periods of my fifteen
years of intermittent on-site fieldwork, but my work took me to at least one of the
other villages, and often both, every day. If I began to use a word or a construction
I had only recently acquired, I would quite naturally produce it in the form typical
of the village where I had heard it and newly learned it. In cases where another
village used a slightly different word or construction from the one I was reproduc-
ing, I was likely to be made aware of the inter-village variation by the mild
amusement or mock rebuke of my other-village conversation partner.

8.2 Local Responses to Variation: Intra-Village Variation

When it came to intra-village variation, the situation could hardly have been more
different. I would look up from my note-taking, surprised at hearing a spouse or a
sibling give a version of a word or a construction that differed from the version
given by the immediately preceding speaker, only to find them quite unaware their
versions had differed. Even when I asked them to repeat the items in question in
quick succession, they seemed unable to hear what I heard. An Embo brother and
sister not far apart in age, living next door to one another and regularly in
conversation with each other in Gaelic, gave different versions of the locational
adverb 'out'. The sister, the older by four years, used with almost complete consistency a form that ended with a consonant, /mwĩç/, while the brother completely
consistently used the vowel-final version /mwĩ/. (This distinction is phonemic and
therefore perfectly perceptible for local speakers, see /i/ 'she' versus /iç/ 'eat.')
There were other people in Embo who used each of these variants, but it struck me
as remarkable that these siblings, immediate neighbors and constant conversation
partners, would use two different variants. They were quite unaware that they used
different variants, however, and for some time disbelieved my assurance that they
did, even when they had repeated the word turn by turn, each of them producing
what was to me a blatant difference in syllable structure. The brother eventually
recognized the difference, but acknowledged that it was difficult for him to hear.

By a happy chance I captured on tape a particularly striking instance of the
salience of inter-village variation for two Golspie speakers, husband and wife, as
contrasted with their apparent unawareness of intra-village variation. A great
many sessions with this couple were recorded because they were the central figures in an oral history of the East Sutherland fisherfolk that I was preparing. Most
sessions were in English, but frequent Gaelic terms, phrases, quotations, and
anecdotes quite naturally emerged as they spoke of their childhood days and their
early adulthood in a still wholly Gaelic-speaking fisherfolk community. In this
particular instance, the wife was talking about the imperfect knowledge of English

among older people in those days, and she quoted an elderly Embo woman's com-
ical mixture of Gaelic and English in attempting to answer an English-speaking
customer's question about how cockles should be cooked: " 'Well, you put them
first in a /puːrn mə̃ː vɫɔː/ ['a lukewarm water'] and then they'll /skɛ/ ['spew'] out
all the /kɛruax/ ['sand'].' " In response I teasingly remarked that the Embo woman
surely never said that cockles would spew out "/kɛruax/". As everyone present
was aware, the Embo version of the word *sand* was quite different from the
Golspie version, even stereotypically so—one Golspie woman liked to refer to
Embo as "sandy Embo" precisely because of this well-recognized isogloss. The
wife agreed with my comment, acknowledging with a smile that the old Embo
woman certainly had said /kãnax/, as any Embo Gaelic speaker would have, not
/kɛruax/.

At this point her husband, a thoughtful man more than usually given to
reflecting on his native language, joined in with a comment of his own: "Why is
Golspie and Brora /kɛruax/? I don't know where that came from." Remarkable
here is just how inaccurate this exceptionally reflective man's comment was.
Three of the four Golspie speakers who provided renditions of 'sand' in my materials did *not* in actuality use the form /kɛruax/—and they included himself. Some
time previously he had supplied the word for 'sand' when discussing the term for
quicksand, and as it happened he had used the alternative Golspie variant,
/kɛrəvax/. His wife, by contrast, did seem regularly to use the variant /kɛruax/;
I have four elicited and four freely spoken instances of 'sand' from her, and all
are /kɛruax/. What emerges from the husband's remark, at any rate, is the salience
of geographical variation for him, compared with the failure of intra-village variation to register with him, even when he and his wife were among the people who
might use different variants.[9] The social sameness of one's own fellow villagers
seems to have rendered much or even most same-village linguistic variation undetectable; since it reflected no social group distinctions, it attracted no notice.
Other-village variation, by contrast, signaled a powerful them/us social distinction and attracted very intense notice (see chapter 7, §2.3).

The Golspie couple's responses to Golspie/Golspie variation versus Golspie/
Embo variation are typical rather than atypical. Linguistic variation across villages, brought up with great frequency by local Gaelic speakers, was almost
always accurately rendered. Throughout innumerable discussions of the topic,
I can recall only one or two inaccurate attributions of a geographical variant. A
very understandable one was a Brora woman's attribution of /mwir/ 'sea', a
strictly Golspie form, to Embo. This form was alien to Brora, and since Brora and
Golspie usage generally coincided at least in part, with Embo usage as the nonconforming case, she responded according to the overwhelmingly dominant
pattern in attributing the nonconforming usage to Embo. Intra-village variation,
by contrast, was only rarely mentioned, and then usually in response to some
expression of surprise on my part. The occasional speaker who did note the
existence of other local variants typically understated the variation considerably.
In a discussion of adverbial 'in', for example, the Embo brother mentioned before
accepted as widespread, and readily produced in sample sentences, two variants

of adverbial 'in', /sčɛ/ and /sčax/, for both directional and locational purposes; he claimed that Embo speakers did not use /stɛ/ for adverbial 'in'. The oddity in this instance was not just that he made no mention of the additional variants /sčɛx/ and /stɛx/, but that the variant he explicitly rejected, /stɛ/, was the variant his sister next door overwhelmingly favored in everyday conversational use.

8.3 Fisherfolk Populations United and Divided by Gaelic

In their attentiveness to inter-village variation and their inattentiveness to intra-village variation, fisherfolk Gaelic speakers were responding realistically to geographical, administrative, and social boundaries. Each fishing community was geographically quite separate, and each formed a subcommunity oriented to a distinct English-speaking village, the Brora and Golspie fisherfolk to the otherwise largely monolingual villages of Brora and Golspie, and the Embo fisherfolk to the almost entirely monolingual village of Dornoch. Brora and Golspie people (fisherfolk and non-fisherfolk alike) were profoundly affected by their position as parts of the vast estate belonging to the local aristocratic family, the House of Sutherland. Dunrobin Castle, the imposing seat of this family, stood on the shore between Brora and Golspie, though much closer to the latter than to the former. Embo, by contrast, lay on the far side of Loch Fleet, a sea loch formed by the mouth of the river Shin, and belonged to a different and much smaller estate. In Embo's case, the subcommunity status arose from its position as a satellite village to Dornoch, once the foremost ecclesiastical center of the far northern Highlands and currently the site of a venerable cathedral and the county's court of justice. As Dunrobin Castle represented the hegemony of the non-Gaelic world and the ascendancy of an alien (non-Highland) family in Brora and Golspie, so Dornoch Cathedral represented outside hegemony in Embo, while Dornoch's status as a royal burgh (chartered as such by the English monarchy in 1628) paralleled for Embo the social ascendancy of a non-Gaelic aristocratic family in the other two villages. (The next chapter treats local history and its effects in greater detail.)

During the nineteenth century and the first quarter of the twentieth century, the sharpest social demarcation in the local population was that of occupation: one either fished for a living or one did not, and the fisherfolk were fundamentally and profoundly distinct from all who did not. Over the course of the twentieth century, as other working-class occupational groups became monolingual in English, this binary occupational division became associated with an equally binary linguistic division: the fisherfolk (Gaelic *maraichean* /mɔriçɛn/) grew up with a local variety of Gaelic as the home language, while all others (termed *tuathanaich* /tʰũãniç/ in the local Gaelic, a cover term for all non-fishing occupations) grew up with a local variety of English as the home language (Dorian 1980a). Reflecting these social realities, members of the three fisherfolk communities stated when questioned on the subject that they felt closer to the *maraichean* of the other two villages than they did to the *tuathanaich* of their own village.

Although this fundamental sense of a common fisherfolk identity was strong, a number of features interacted to make each community quite distinct. The road miles between villages made social interaction rather infrequent for families who lacked independent transport, even such minimal transport as the horse and cart that a crofter usually had.[10] The local train line, regularly used in connection with marketing fish, entailed an expense that could seldom be accepted for purely social purposes. Young people from Golspie or Embo on a fine Sunday might make a walk of several miles to the small-boat ferry that crossed Loch Fleet to pay a visit to kin in the other village, but their elders seldom had time or energy for such a trek on the one day of the week that was not fully occupied with obtaining a labor-intensive livelihood. Religious life was vigorous in all of the villages, but each fisherfolk population was situated in a different parish and attended the local church of the relevant denomination. Each village also had its own primary school, so that fisherfolk children had no cross-village contact through schooling. During storms from a particular wind direction, Golspie and Embo fishermen both made use of Loch Fleet as a harbor, but access to the safe reaches of this loch was made so difficult by sand bars and narrow channels that neither set of fishermen used it regularly; its intermediate location therefore produced less cross-village contact than might have been supposed by looking at a map.

Apart from occasional visits to kinfolk already married into one of the other two fisherfolk populations, the most frequent cross-village contacts between fisherfolk seem, by contemporary autobiographical accounts, to have arisen from the travels that the seasonal herring fishing entailed. A great number of three-woman crews consisting of two gutters and a packer traveled from each of the villages to various herring fishing stations during the herring season, and although each crew was normally made up of women from a single village, the various East Sutherland village crews interacted with one another to some extent at the stations. Similarly, East Sutherland fishermen who hired out, often singly, to serve as crew members on the big boats used by Scots-speaking herring fishers of east coast regions well to the south met and mingled in the ports where fish were landed. Some cross-village marriages seem to have arisen from herring season contacts among East Sutherland men and women working in the same sequence of ports around the coasts over the course of the herring migration (as did some marriages "out" to Scots-speaking fisherfolk, too). These cross-village marriages were never common, however, and most of an individual's kin (insofar as they remained in the area at all) would be in his or her own village.

For all their joint identity as *maraichean*, then, the members of each fishing community maintained a distinct local identity as well. Where Gaelic was concerned, the historical factor of estate ownership was central. Fisherfolk natives of the two villages within the Sutherland estate, Brora and Golspie, considered their Gaelic more indistinguishable than it actually was from a linguist's point of view, while both they and the natives of the one village that fell within a separate estate, Embo, considered Embo Gaelic quite different. Embo villagers considered that they and their fellow villagers spoke an undifferentiated local form of Gaelic, while they took speakers from the other two communities to speak a recognizably different form of Gaelic. The differing degrees of attentiveness to inter-village and intra-village variation reflect these points of view.

9 PLAN OF THE REMAINDER OF THE BOOK

In subsequent chapters of this book I first introduce the East Sutherland fisherfolk and their lifeways so as to illuminate the powerful impact of fishing on every facet of people's lives (chapter 2). Only when the intensely interdependent and interactive character of village life and the enforced separateness of fisherfolk existence over more than a century is clear does the striking presence of high-frequency but socially unweighted intra-village and intra-speaker linguistic variation come properly into focus.

Chapter 3 expands on the nature of this sort of idiosyncratic variation and offers evidence for the absence of social weighting in connection with nearly all of it, focusing necessarily on Embo, where Gaelic was still spoken by a considerable number of people at the outset of my work and by some few even at the end of the twentieth century. Chapter 4 introduces the sources for this study, while chapter 5 presents the variants; their incidence; their possible correlations with age, gender, and distinctive discourse functions; and the level of agreement or disagreement between speakers. Chapter 6 examines the effect of the kin network and, to the lesser extent possible, the effect of the age cohort. Community language norms are explored in chapter 7, where language-related behaviors that evoke strong responses are compared with personal-pattern variation, which generally evokes no response at all, and the components of being deemed to speak the local Gaelic well are examined.

The idiosyncratic variation displayed by East Sutherland fisherfolk Gaelic has its own inherent interest, but its larger significance lies in the fact that it makes its appearance under social and sociolinguistic conditions that are not unique to these communities. In chapter 8 I introduce other speech communities that present idiosyncratic variation phenomena akin to those of the East Sutherland fisherfolk communities and identify some of the social setting features that give rise to such phenomena; rare in our own time, the social settings that produce such phenomena were in all likelihood much more widespread in earlier times. The questions of what purpose idiosyncratic variation serves and how it may be acquired are also considered in this chapter.

The final chapter reviews Embo findings that run counter to expectations expressed in the sociolinguistic literature, raises some questions prompted by the Embo findings, and points to still other kinds of social setting and social organization that are likely to harbor equally unforeseen patterns of language use, including, quite possibly, other patterns of linguistic variation.

The East Sutherland Fishing Communities

1 INTRODUCTION: FISHING AS A SUBSISTENCE MODE

How people earn their livelihoods can have a powerful effect on the way they live and interact, and the effect is seldom more evident than among fisherfolk. With no need for a spread of fields around them, and with boat crews to assemble at the constantly changing hours decreed by the tides, fishermen typically live in tight clusters of dwellings along a sea front. Whereas agriculturalists need one another's help chiefly at harvest season, and hunters chiefly for relatively large-scale undertakings, fishermen regularly work together, with crew size determined by the size of the boat and the type of fishing engaged in. Farmers' daily work entails little inherent bodily risk, at least in settled conditions, while the risk run by hunters typically varies according to the size and ferocity of the animal being pursued. The hunter's risk will be great on occasion, when the game is large or has its own formidable weaponry, and in extreme climates such as the Arctic or the desert it can be inherently risky; but with most smaller forms of game and in many climates, risk will be limited. Most fishermen, by contrast, work routinely in an environment that poses a risk to life, and this is especially so in northerly climates. A sudden change in the weather or an equipment failure, both common occurrences, can set a fisherman's life at risk in a matter of seconds.

Living patterns in the fishing communities of coastal East Sutherland were strongly shaped by these general features of fishing as an economic activity and by certain aspects of local history as well. In Brora, Golspie, and Embo, the three villages central to this study, the fisherfolk lived in a few streets close by the sea, mostly in two-family houses with an internal separating wall. The houses stood close together in a very straight line along shorter or longer streets. Density of population in these streets was very high, especially since large numbers of children were not only welcome for their own sake but also economically desirable. Fishing as practiced in this region was extremely labor-intensive as well as risk-laden, and the combined efforts of a large household were needed to secure a livelihood at even the most basic level.

While occupational needs such as ready access to the sea and speed in assembling boat crews account for the seafront residence patterns, they do not by themselves account for the fact that in East Sutherland the fisherfolk lived in what amounted to social segregation: few individuals who were not members of a fishing family lived in the streets where the fisherfolk were clustered (the chief exceptions being craftsmen, such as the occasional cartwright, carpenter, tailor, or mason), and in two of the three communities there was a clear physical separation between the fisherfolk residential areas and the residential areas where others lived. Understanding this segregation and some of its linguistic correlations requires a brief review of the history of the communities as it relates to both residential and social patterns.

2 CREATION OF THE EAST SUTHERLAND FISHING COMMUNITIES: THE "IMPROVEMENT" ERA

Fishing was not a well-developed traditional subsistence activity in this far northern coastal region. Apart from the seasonal taking of salmon in a number of local rivers, there was little fishing activity in these parts up to the end of the eighteenth century. One obvious explanation emerges from a look at the coastline: this stretch of coast offers almost no natural harbors, and the few locations that might seem to offer harborage (chiefly river mouths) are made problematic by navigational hazards, such as sandbars or silting. Fishing was introduced as a major form of livelihood in this part of Sutherland, as in other parts of the county, by design and by compulsion. At the very end of the eighteenth century and the beginning of the nineteenth, an era of what was euphemistically known as "improvement" began in the Scottish Highlands with the introduction of large-scale (and therefore more efficient) farming practices. The traditional ways of wresting a livelihood from the land were not proving adequate for the support of a steadily growing population, but, more important from the point of view of the Highland chiefs who had become the owners of great estates, they provided very little in the way of a cash income. By this date, the Scottish clan system had been effectively destroyed, in the determined extension of Anglo-Saxon governance and custom following the two failed Jacobite risings (1715 and 1745), and such clan chiefs and chieftains as remained in possession of ancestral lands for the most part had left Scotland and taken up residence in or near London, the seat of all real power.

The aristocratic House of Sutherland was in any case not indigenous but was the creation of early Norman power in Scotland. Extensive lands in what we now know as Sutherland were granted in the first half of the twelfth century to a family closely associated with newly established Norman power. On the evidence of his original surname, the land-grant recipient was among the Flemish allies of the Normans, but he took the name De Moravia (Anglicized as Murray), reflecting a still earlier Norman land grant to the same family in Moray. Ennobled in the thirteenth century, the House of Sutherland had as its official seat Dunrobin Castle, just outside Golspie, but the family was never connected linguistically or culturally to the existing Gaelic culture of the region. Always oriented to the south, the earls of Sutherland took wives almost exclusively from outside the Gaelic aristocracy and were frequently absent from the north for extended periods (Dorian 1981:14). Effective roles in the power struggles of the times required that ambitious aristocrats be nearer the geographical centers of power, Edinburgh before the Act of Union in 1707 and London thereafter.

2.1 The Highland Clearances in the East Sutherland Context

At the dawn of the improvement era, the countess of Sutherland and her incomparably wealthy English husband, George Granville Leveson-Gower, marquis of Stafford, were, like most of the other great aristocratic families of the Highlands, based in London. As was the case in other such families, the management of their estates was left to functionaries known as factors. The new economic wisdom of the era called for a general modernizing of the Highland economy and an end to the long-standing practice of leasing small holdings to great numbers of tenants, many of them connected by surname if not blood to the local chiefly family. Highland small-holders mostly operated at a level that was barely above subsistence in favorable years, and in bad years they might easily fall below it; they were always hard-pressed to pay their rents, and defaults occurred with some frequency. A new breed of managers, mostly Lowlanders considered to be up to date in their economic thinking and their management practices, proposed to put an end to such uneconomical arrangements and make Highland estates profitable, as few of them were in terms of the cash income needed to support aristocrats maintaining a London lifestyle. The means employed to effect such improvements was a general clearing away of the numerous tenantry, followed by the establishment of large sheep farms in the previously tenanted areas. In another somewhat euphemistic turn of speech, this period of Highland history is known in English as the Clearance period; in East Sutherland Gaelic, the local language, it is called more bluntly *teamhair an iomruagadh*, 'the time of the persecution' or 'of the dispersion'.

A great many ordinary Highlanders lived in extremely precarious economic circumstances at the time when the fishing communities came into being, but the involuntarily resettled inlanders destined by estate plan for a new life as fishing families were impoverished beyond the usual degree. In the evictions, often effected with conspicuous callousness and even brutality (notoriously so in parts of eastern Sutherland), they suffered the loss of their dwellings, their crops, their livestock, and a good part of whatever modest household goods they had managed to acquire. They found themselves refugees, cast up destitute in an unfamiliar setting and demoralized by being turned out of lands their ancestors had inhabited since time out of memory. The isolation of Highland settlements could be extreme in the eighteenth century, especially in the interior. Up to the beginning of the Clearance period, Highland roads were no better than tracks, and bridges were largely nonexistent. The difficult Highland terrain and the likewise difficult climate made travel exceedingly slow and hazardous, so that it was seldom undertaken without a compelling reason. It is possible that some of the women and children evicted from inland glens at no great distance from the coast had never seen the sea except as a distant shimmer before their abrupt removal to its immediate vicinity. Certainly they knew nothing at all about gaining subsistence from the sea, and their menfolk knew nothing about managing a boat or about saltwater fish and the methods employed to catch them.

A good many Highland estates encouraged the emigration of large numbers of evicted tenantry, but the Sutherland estate took a different tack. Unexpected and highly unusual difficulties in recruiting soldiers to the Sutherland military regiment had arisen in 1799, and a young law agent was employed to tour the estate and look into problems with the tenantry. The program he recommended in due course was designed to keep the evictees as rent-paying tenants while still freeing for large-scale sheep farming the lands the tenantry had formerly held; sheep farming had become highly profitable at that time thanks to a new breed of foot–rot–resistant sheep and a good market for wool (Adam 1972: xxvi–vii, xxxii). The evictees were resettled beside the sea, at first on plots of land more or less adequate to sustain them, but subsequently, by deliberate policy, on plots too small to permit later arrivals to support themselves by any form of agriculture. Plot size was in fact reduced as soon as local participation in the herring fishery was under way (Loch 1820:104–5). Hooks and lines were distributed, and some expert fishermen from Scots-speaking east coast fishing areas far to the south were induced to settle among the intended fisherfolk of East Sutherland, the newcomers accommodated in one of the newly designated fishing settlements (Helmsdale to the north of Brora) to serve as occupational role models for the evictees. The outlay on the part of the estate was considerable, but the improvers anticipated a good return on their investment, first from the large sheep farms they had brought into being and second from the new fishing enterprise, which was expected to grow steadily in profitability. As the House of Sutherland did in connection with the fishing settlements of Helmsdale, Brora, and Golspie, the much smaller estate of the Gordons (lesser kin to the House of Sutherland) apparently did in connection with the fishing settlement at Embo, just to the south of Golspie. Estate records are extensive for the House of Sutherland at this period, while they are unavailable for the Gordon estate; the patterns of settlement, the timing, and the outcomes are so similar that one can reasonably assume parallel histories.

3 FISHING AS A WAY OF LIFE IN EAST SUTHERLAND

Necessity is a powerful adaptive force, as the Sutherland estate clearly recognized in its policy of limiting evictees' landholdings to a size inadequate for the support of a family. The resettled inlanders learned to fish because they had to. Those who survived the transition period became expert at it, but it remained a difficult and dangerous livelihood and it never became a reliably remunerative one, let alone the highly profitable industry that estate managers had confidently predicted.

Fishing in Eastern Sutherland was of two kinds—the small-scale local fishery in which men in open boats used mostly long lines with baited hooks, and the large-scale seasonal herring fishery, in which men followed the migratory herring around the coasts of Britain, fishing by net from considerably larger boats. Both kinds had a great impact on the fisher family as a whole, but in quite different ways. The description that follows depicts fisherfolk life as it was in the very late nineteenth and early twentieth centuries, which is to say in the childhoods of the most proficient fisherfolk Gaelic speakers of the 1960s, the time at which I first came to know them. The account given is based on extensive oral history interviewing; see Dorian (1985) for a fuller presentation.

3.1 The Local Fishery: Line Fishing

Line fishing had the great advantage of feeding the family in the most immediate day-to-day sense, but it was particularly laborious and offered no real chance of economic prosperity. The work never ended. Only extremely strict observance of the injunction against labor on the Sabbath or the arrival of a spell of desperately bad weather offered respite, with the latter sort very unwelcome because there would be no income until the boats could go out again. The efforts of an entire family were needed to make the line-fishing enterprise pay at a merely subsistence level, given the very low price that fish commanded. In long-line fishing, hundreds of hooks had to be baited for each fishing trip. The baits in use were various, according to the type of fish the men were after and according to the seasonal availability of the bait itself. Mussels and cockles were prime varieties of bait, but both required "sheeling" (opening the shells to get at the meat); cockles, which had to be dug for, were unusable between May and August. Lugworm, a long sea worm that burrowed in the sand, was available year-round and needed no laborious opening, but as with cockles it had to be dug for, using a special implement to get down to it when traces of its presence were spied on the surface of the sand. Speed was important, since the lugworm could burrow out of digging range if the digger was slow. Gathering various baits, extracting meat from shellfish baits, and attaching bait to the hooks were all part of the unending cycle of work that line fishing required. The baiting would often be done in the wee hours of the morning, if the tides made a pre-dawn departure necessary, and children were roused from bed to do their part. Children were involved in bait gathering and preparation, too, as soon as they were capable of carrying a basket or pail and could be trusted with a sheeling knife. Children also had responsibility for the daily gathering of bentgrass from the shore, for use as a buffer between the coils of baited hooks (so that hooks did not catch and tangle the line as it was paid out of the line basket). The job of gathering pinecones in the nearby woods, for use, wetted-down, as fuel in smoking white fish (those with white flesh), was assigned to children as well.

In the process of hauling the lines swiftly enough to be sure of preserving all of the catch, the fishermen unavoidably tangled the lines, on which some empty hooks would be dangling, so that untangling lines was a tedious but necessary job that followed each trip. Sometimes bait not taken by the fish was fresh enough and intact enough to be left on the hooks for the next trip out, but when it wasn't it had to be removed by hand, another laborious task to be undertaken before the next round of baiting could begin.

Fish processing and marketing occupied the family equally intensively. Adults did most work connected with the smoking of white fish—stringing up the fish, getting the fire going, and judging the length of time needed for the job—but children were expected to check that the smoky fire was still burning and alert their parents if more fuel was needed or if fish had fallen down onto the fire as the smoking softened their flesh. Men packed and transported to the railhead such fish as were being sent to southern British markets, but women did all of the extensive local marketing. Each woman had the exclusive right to a particular marketing route, normally one inherited from her mother or another older female family member. With great loads of fish, both fresh and smoked, in creels on their backs, they walked daily through various local districts or took the train to slightly more distant districts, where they then walked from house to house, selling directly to housewives and to the hotels that had become common in these scenic parts by the twentieth century. The hotels paid cash, but otherwise payment was more typically in kind (oats, apples, or butter, for example), so that the women came home nearly as heavily laden as when they had left.

In the long absences of the mother on these marketing trips, the older girls in the family were in charge of the household and took over the care of their younger siblings. Older boys were responsible for the animals (hens and often a pig or two, bought as piglets from farmers and raised for later consumption or sale) and for help in any heavier work. As soon as they could manage the weight, children went as needed to the nearest pumps or springs for buckets of water, carried home in pairs with the aid of a wooden yoke, and they walked daily with pails to the nearest farms for a supply of milk. Late arrival at school was a common phenomenon among the children of fishing families, who might have been up in the night opening shellfish and baiting hooks and might also have been required to go to the woods for the day's pinecone supply before being allowed to leave for school. The older children in the family often got limited schooling because of heavy responsibilities at home while their mothers were out selling fish from creels. This applied above all to the oldest girl in the family, whose child care duties could be very nearly those of a parent.

In the local fishery, the family was the fundamental workforce. The fisherman, his wife, and their children were all essential to the enterprise. A man who did not marry might have the help of a widowed mother or grandmother and of an unmarried or widowed aunt or sister, but he would probably be limited in the number of lines he could put out by the lesser amount of support work on shore.

3.2 The National Fishery: Herring Fishing

The timing of the Scottish herring fishery, and its success, depended on the arrival of large shoals of herring in waters they had been known to frequent in previous years. But herring will go wherever their own preferred food sources are to be found. The imperfect predictability of arrival times, of the places where herring would turn up in a given year, and of the size of the shoals all made the herring fishery a far less guaranteed success than Sutherland estate managers grandiosely predicted when planning and implementing the eviction programs. The market was good, at the beginning of the nineteenth century, and the herring were plentiful, but neither remained true invariably enough to make fishing for herring a dependably good livelihood. Still, the very large-scale herring fishery was the one fishing enterprise that offered a chance of real profit rather than mere subsistence, and the men went to it regularly in hopes of securing that chance.

In the years before World War I, East Sutherland men fished for herring from sailing boats, larger than the open boats used for line fishing and with a design geared to speed and maneuverability. Local men fished from locally owned boats, usually bought collectively by a boat's crew and acquired secondhand from Scots-speaking fishermen farther south along the coast; each crewman would own a single share in one of these sailing boats. After World War I, British herring fishing boats were increasingly powered by steam, and the cost of these more modern boats rose beyond what the East Sutherland fishermen could readily afford to own a share in. They signed on, usually singly, as hired hands with "south side" fishermen (Scots speakers from the Morayshire, Banffshire, and Aberdeenshire coasts), sometimes returning for several seasons to a particular crew, sometimes fishing each season from a different boat as the opportunity offered. There were two herring fishing seasons, the first beginning in May and running through the summer, the second beginning in September and carrying on for another month or two. Depending on the success of the fishery and on his family circumstances, a fisherman might work one or both seasons.

The herring fishery moved along the coasts of the British Isles in synchrony with the anticipated migratory movement of the herring. For the East Sutherland fisherman, it usually began either off Northern Ireland or off the Outer Hebrides, moving into Inner Hebridean waters and into the fjord-like west coast sea lochs, then up into the waters around the Orkneys and Shetlands and down along the eastern seaboard of Scotland and England, with the eastern English coast the focus of the second season from September on. Fishing for herring took adult males away from their home villages for months at a time. Since it was net fishing, the labor required for fishing with bait was eliminated, but the shooting and hauling of nets went on in a steady rhythm that kept the fishermen constantly short of sleep. They were also farther from shore and in that respect more than ever exposed to risk. In a good season the strong national and international market for herring compensated them for their work and its risks, sending them home at season's end with the greater part of the family's cash income for the entire year. In a bad season they came home with very little to show for their trouble, and their families' existence during the line fishing season became more hand-to-mouth than ever.

During the herring fishing season, many of the adult women and girls were also away from the home village, having hired out as herring gutters and packers. Women from each village signed on in crews of three, two gutters and a packer, contracting for the season with a particular curer. Like the men, they migrated along with the herring. They might start in fishing stations in Northern Ireland, move to a station in the Outer Hebrides (sometimes Barra, but usually Stornoway in the Isle of Lewis), on to ports on the west coast, up into the Orkneys and Shetlands, and down again to Wick, on the extreme northeast mainland coast, and then down the east coast of Scotland, and, if they signed on for the second season, down the east coast of England. Some women made this entire circuit of the western isles and coasts, the northern isles, and the east coasts of Scotland and England, while others, especially married women with families, might sign on only for the season in the Orkneys and on the east coast of Scotland. A woman might rent a room in Wick or Helmsdale, the ports nearest home, for the relevant part of the herring season and take her younger children with her, especially if she had cooperative kinfolk in that port or could also take along an older daughter responsible enough to care for the youngest children. Alternatively, children might be left with kinfolk in the home village while a mother worked for part of the herring season. At some stations the gutting and packing crews were housed in small huts, spartan accommodations that they made as welcoming as possible for the duration of their occupancy. On the eastern English coast they usually took lodgings. The gutting and packing was piecework, so that whenever fish were landed, day or night, the pace of work was frenzied as each crew tried to increase its earnings by getting as many barrels packed as possible while still maintaining a standard of work that would pass inspection at the end of the stint. Despite the fluctuations between heavy landings and light landings (or even no landings, in the occasional disastrous season) the women had one advantage over the menfolk in the herring fishery. They got their lodgings and food paid, and apart from what they could earn per barrel, they also received a weekly wage, very small but guaranteed, so that they never went home completely empty-handed at the end of the season. The men, by contrast, had at season's end only what their crewman's share entitled them to. If the boat's gear and operating costs outran the profit in a bad season, a fisherman might go home with nothing at all from the herring fishery he had hoped would give him most of his annual income.

4 THE EAST SUTHERLAND FISHERFOLK AS A SOCIALLY AND LINGUISTICALLY DISTINCTIVE POPULATION

As this brief sketch of the fishing livelihood indicates, the fisherfolk in the late nineteenth and early twentieth centuries lived a life sharply different from that of other village dwellers in East Sutherland and equally different from that of the crofting population in the countryside. (Crofters were sub-subsistence agriculturalists who by the late nineteenth century had guaranteed tenancy but who required some additional source of income to supplement what they could earn from part-time farming and stock raising.) The rhythm of fisherfolk lives was dictated by their occupation: by the need to adjust working hours to the tides during the line fishing season and by the necessity of leaving home to follow the herring migration during the herring fishing season. Some of the distinctive life patterns entailed by their history and their livelihood are noted here.

4.1 Separateness and Poverty

From the time of their forced resettlement, the people who became the fisherfolk of Brora, Golspie, and Embo were isolated residentially, as required by the Sutherland Estate's plan for recouping their investment in the new fishing settlements. Settlement density was part of that plan, since density was the inevitable result of land allotments intentionally kept too small, after the very first settlement wave, to allow reversion to an agricultural way of life. The estate created what amounted to fisherfolk ghettoes at the beginning of the nineteenth century, and ghettoes they remained until the watershed years between the world wars of the twentieth century, when fishing faltered in this region and social mobility began to increase. In this sense, the Gaelic-speaking fishing communities were enclaved even in earlier times, when surrounding crofting populations in the Embo area and fellow villagers in Brora and Golspie still spoke Gaelic.

Less obvious is the process by which the emerging fisherfolk of east coast Sutherland became not just a distinctive occupational group but also a stigmatized one. Their arrival as destitute evictees surely played a part in that development, especially in combination with the residential separateness that estate plans decreed. The early poverty of the fishing communities was never to be overcome so long as fishing remained the local livelihood, since, contrary to the expectations of the estate planners, herring fishing was not a reliable route to prosperity.

Wealth may not always bring high social standing, but poverty (or at least involuntary poverty) nearly always guarantees low social standing. The poorest occupational groups resident in East Sutherland, throughout the nineteenth century and into the twentieth, were the agricultural laborers and the fisherfolk. As late as the 1960s and 1970s, interview responses in Brora and Golspie indicated that local opinion ranked fishermen lower than agricultural laborers in the occupational and social hierarchy that prevailed until after World War I. People pointed out that farm laborers might have had a pitifully low wage, but they did at least have that wage reliably, and they also had certain food resources deriving from their work on the land. The fishermen, by contrast, might do very well in an unusually good year for herring, but in an average year they simply managed to get along, and in a bad year they toppled into a poverty more extreme than that of the farm laborers. A good many of the shortcomings that negative local stereotypes attributed to the fisher-folk were directly related to their poverty: wearing seasonally inappropriate cloth-ing (light clothes in winter as well as summer), buying food in very small quantities, getting into debt, and so forth. Only the tinkers, traveling people with no perma-nent residence, ranked below the fisherfolk in village opinion.

A cluster of adverse features taken together—their arrival as impoverished evictees, their enforced residential separateness, their coerced occupational dis-tinctiveness, their continuing poverty, and their enduringly low social standing—make intelligible the remarkable degree to which the fisherfolk constituted a group apart, a population whose members passed their social and occupational lives mostly among themselves. The bulk of all fisherfolk contact with non-fisherfolk was commercial: fish were carried for sale to villagers, hoteliers, and crofters in the countryside; milk was bought from local farmers; oats were taken to the mill; wood for the construction of sheds and smoking kilns was bought from the saw-mill; land rents were paid in estate offices. In Brora and Golspie (though not in Embo, which had its own primary school) young children from the fishing com-munities attended school with the children of other social groups, but after-school play was effectively segregated by the separateness of fisherfolk residential areas. The school years ended early for fisherfolk children, in any case; with rare excep-tions they left school at age fourteen, the earliest school-exit age allowed by law.

A modest practical command of English was required for adult fisherfolk interactions with non-fisherfolk and also for non-local occupational undertakings, such as both men and women hiring on with English-speaking employers for the seasonal herring fishery. Both local and herring fishery jobs were at the laboring level, however, with no opportunity for occupational advancement, and by vari-ous oral accounts a rough and ready English was sufficient in the late nineteenth century and early twentieth century (see chapter 1, §8.2, for an anecdotal account of fisherfolk difficulties with English). Even somewhat beyond that time, fisher-folk social interaction continued to be primarily with other local Gaelic speakers, whether at home or in the curing stations around the coasts.

4.2 Separateness and Language

At the time when the fishing communities were established, nearly all people of eastern Sutherland-shire birth were mother-tongue speakers of Gaelic, most of them also Gaelic monolinguals. Functionaries connected with the House of Sutherland might be, like the aristocratic family itself, English monolinguals, and the clergy were by necessity bilinguals, but ordinary people spoke Gaelic. The Clearance period, which changed so much in this region, changed the language equation as well. Cattle had been the dominant animal in Highland husbandry, and Highlanders at this period had relatively little experience with sheep; they had none at all with the new sheep farming methods developed in the southern part of Scotland. Lowland farmers taking up the new sheep farms created by the evictions therefore brought their own shepherds with them, and in doing so introduced into eastern Sutherland for the first time a working-class population that was monolingual in English. The English language, already associated with the high-born and the professional class, now came to be associated with the new class of prosperous sheep farmers and their economic dependents.

4.2.1 Settlement History and Dialect Distinctiveness

Materials that could shed light on the degree of dialect differentiation in the Gaelic spoken along the eastern coast of Sutherlandshire are lacking for the nineteenth century. Oral testimony in mid-twentieth century suggests, however, that it must have been considerable: elderly Highlanders in quite different parts of the country agreed that as recently as the time of their youth every glen and hamlet could be said to have had its own Gaelic, at least to the extent that certain telltale words or grammatical features distinguished the spoken Gaelic of each individual location. With scarcely any roads worthy of the name at the beginning of the nineteenth century, with no transport except the Highland pony, with a harsh climate and difficult terrain, households were immobile to a degree difficult even to imagine two centuries later. In these conditions, local linguistic features were easily maintained or developed anew, and it is reasonable to assume that in eastern Sutherland, as elsewhere, Gaelic was distinctive at least to some small degree in every locality. This was certainly true in mid-twentieth century, when the Gaelic Division of the Linguistic Survey of Scotland was conducting its East Sutherland fieldwork in those locations where Gaelic had survived, and the Survey's twentieth-century findings make the assumption of distinctive local features a century and a half before more nearly a certainty than a likelihood.

How uniform the Gaelic spoken in the fishing communities was at the time of their inception is impossible to know. Full identification of the particular hillsides and glens from which each of the start-up fishing populations was removed is not readily available, although it is at any rate certain that the evictees resettled in Brora, Golspie, and Embo were not (as their descendants came to believe) victims of the particularly infamous early nineteenth-century Sutherland clearances in Strathnaver and Kildonan: the 1851 census gives the birthplace of all enumerated adults, and of all those entered as "fisher(man)" or "fisherwife" or the like for the three communities in question, only one individual was born in Kildonan and none in Strathnaver. Most likely the fisherfolk-to-be were cleared from nearby, from glens in the mountainous terrain looming up just behind the narrow coastal shelf. Whether any attempt was made to keep populations cleared from a single area together in the resettlement area is again unclear.

Two sorts of evidence, patronymic and linguistic, make it certain that some admixture of population took place early on. Clan names still had distinct geographic significance in the late eighteenth century and early nineteenth century. Families bearing the name of the locally dominant clan clustered strongly in the district where that clan had been rooted, and the presence of an extraneous clan surname could be taken as a reliable indicator of in-migration. Family names in the East Sutherland fishing communities demonstrate above all the independent character of the eviction-and-resettlement programs of each of the estates, the Sutherland estate (Brora, Golspie) and the Gordon estate (Embo), but in addition they indicate the presence of non-local elements in the fisherfolk populations.

Three dominant family names were shared in the 1960s, as they were in the 1851 census, by the fisherfolk populations of Brora and Golspie: Sutherland, MacRae, and MacDonald. Only the first of these is a strictly local clan name; the two others represent west coast clans and consequently also a west coast dialect presence, at least at the time of in-migration. Two additional non-local surnames are present among the fisherfolk descendants of Brora today: Dempster and Jack. The former but not the latter was already in evidence among the Brora fisherfolk in the 1851 census; a Lowland name, it may have come to East Sutherland via the Lowland fisher families recruited by the Sutherland estate as models for the newly created East Sutherland fisherfolk (chapter 1, §3.1). Possibly the name Jack has the same history, moving southward from Helmsdale (the biggest of the newly created East Sutherland fishing villages) at a date after the 1851 census was complete. Golspie's fisherfolk descendants have remained, as their forebears were in 1851, almost entirely Sutherlands, MacRaes, and MacDonalds. Only one man appears in the 1851 census as a Golspie-born fisherman and yet bears a different clan surname, namely, Urquhart; there are no fisherfolk descendants in the village today who bear that surname.

The family names among the present-day fisherfolk population of Embo, on the former Gordon estate, are different altogether: MacKay, Ross, Fraser, Grant, and Cumming. Only the first of these is a Sutherland-shire clan name (though a name originally from northern rather than eastern Sutherland-shire), but all of the others were already present in Embo at the 1851 census. That census indicates in fact an unusually high proportion of village fisherfolk born elsewhere, mostly in neighboring Ross-shire. The Tarbat Ness peninsula of eastern Ross-shire is very close to Embo by water (though it was not at the time by road), and some of its villages were as strongly dependent on fishing as Embo was. One 1851 Embo fisherman surnamed Ross had been born in Ross-shire, as had one surnamed Fraser, but particularly significant is the presence of nine wives (out of thirty-four spouses of head-of-household fishermen entered for Embo in 1851) born in Ross-shire, together with the widow of another. The presence of so many Ross-shire–born wives makes it certain that a substantial Ross-shire linguistic influence was present early on in Embo Gaelic. The additional surnames Fraser, Grant, and

Cumming represent clans based in more southerly and central areas of Highland Scotland, in various parts of present-day Inverness-shire. All of the non-local surnames indicate incoming population strains associated, at least at the outset, with distinct regional forms of Gaelic.

4.2.2 Geographically Based Differences in the Gaelic of the Fishing Communities

The linguistic divide between the fisherfolk of Brora and Golspie and those of Embo was much less extreme than the patronymic divide, with its complete lack of overlap. The patronymic division does have a linguistic counterpart, however, in that the Gaelic of the Brora and Golspie fisherfolk was more nearly alike than either was like the Gaelic of the Embo fisherfolk in mid-twentieth century. There were between 250 and 300 words whose phonological form was identical in Brora and Golspie Gaelic but different in Embo Gaelic, compared with only a half a dozen or so that were identical in the Gaelic of any other combination of two villages but not in the third; even fewer words had distinct forms in all three villages (Dorian 1978:151–58). In grammar, too, Brora and Golspie fisherfolk speakers had more in common than either group had with Embo speakers. Even so, there remained enough differences between Brora and Golspie Gaelic to disfavor (though not to disprove) the notion that the Sutherland estate peopled both fishing communities from a single group of evictees, dividing them between the Brora and Golspie settlements.[1] The phonological and morphophonological differences between Brora and Golspie Gaelic are quite high in frequency, pervasive enough so that any dialectologist familiar with the Gaelic of both villages would know within seconds whether an unseen local speaker on one end of an overheard Gaelic conversation came from Brora or from Golspie. Brora and Golspie Gaelic speakers made no mention of the differences between them, however, and spoke only of the linguistic chasm they perceived between their own Gaelic and that of Embo. Embo Gaelic speakers, for their part, were much more familiar with Golspie Gaelic than with Brora Gaelic, but insofar as they knew anything of Brora Gaelic they considered it essentially the same as Golspie Gaelic and quite different from their own.

4.2.3 The Church as a Potentially Unifying Institution

Church allegiance would at one time have encompassed both fisherfolk and non-fisherfolk, especially in the second half of the nineteenth century when repugnance at the treatment of the small tenantry by clan chiefs and other large property owners led most Highland clergy to secede from the established church (the Church of Scotland) and found the so-called Free Church. Denominational schism gave rise to additional sectarian subdivisions later on, but most fisherfolk families remained firmly outside the Church of Scotland.

During the latter part of the nineteenth century and still more so during the early twentieth century, most segments of the general East Sutherland population moved gradually away from Gaelic, first toward Gaelic-English bilingualism and then English monolingualism. Free Church ministers who had served large Gaelic-speaking congregations in the nineteenth century confronted growing numbers of monolingual English-speaking parishioners, and an additional service in English came to be offered as well. Over time the relatively prosperous local tradesmen and craftsmen who had remained Free Church adherents but no longer spoke Gaelic went over to attendance at the English service, leaving the fisherfolk, a scattering of crofters, and a few Gaelic-speaking incomers from western parts of Scotland the only remaining Gaelic-speaking congregants. In East Sutherland, the largest Gaelic-speaking congregation consisted chiefly of Embo fisherfolk who attended the Gaelic service at the Free Church in Dornoch, but they found that their social segregation extended even to religious services, where the non-fisherfolk sat apart from the fisherfolk. An Embo bilingual described her own experience in what would have been the 1920s and 1930s as follows (see Dorian 1981:64 for fuller quotation): "The Dornochs sat on the other side, far away. We sat there [gesture], and they were on the other side of the church... You'd never see them sitting beside us."

With congregations increasingly made up primarily of a dwindling and aging population of fisherfolk, regular Gaelic services were discontinued first in Brora and Golspie and eventually even in the Dornoch Free Church that served Embo villagers. The informal religious segregation that had come into being with the rise of a better-off monolingual population in East Sutherland disappeared in the end because the fisherfolk themselves were disappearing as a distinctive group.

4.3 Separateness and Endogamy

The occupational distinctiveness of the fisherfolk, the poverty associated with it, and the stigma in turn associated with that poverty produced other social effects besides residential separateness and unusually long-lasting maintenance of Gaelic. Most notably, they produced a social group whose members married only among themselves, chiefly within the same village but occasionally across villages, so that most fisherfolk families also had at least a few kinfolk in one or both of the other villages. Fisherfolk young people were not viewed as potential marriage partners by the rest of the local population, with the result that fisherfolk out-marriage with non-fisherfolk seems to have been non-existent locally during the nineteenth century; it was very rare on the local scene before World War I, but increased gradually after that war ended.[2] That is to say, the beginnings of out-marriage coincide with the decline of the east coast fisheries and with the gradual entry of fisher-family young people into other occupations.

Since both occupational diversification and marriage between fisherfolk and non-fisherfolk met with considerable local resistance born of social prejudice, emigration proved an attractive alternative to many young people of fisherfolk background. Emigration has a long history in the Highlands, and each Highland economic or political disaster has produced great waves of departures—the two Jacobite defeats and the Clearance period most conspicuously. In East Sutherland World War I seems to have been the twentieth-century catalyst for emigration. Voluntary enlistment was very high among the young fishermen of the area. Those who survived the war (and many did not) came home to an outmoded, technologically backward fishing industry; lacking any means of upgrading their boats and gear, many opted to leave the area in search of a better livelihood. Lowland Scotland, England, and overseas English-speaking countries were all frequent destinations, and in the mid-twentieth century it was a rare fisherfolk family that had no kinfolk in one or more of those locations.

4.3.1 Maintenance of Kin Ties

Both consanguineal and affinal ties were given great weight in the fishing communities. They were extremely dense, however, which meant that keeping track of them was a complex matter. Fisherfolk families ran large. Even in the early twentieth century families of seventeen or eighteen children were not unheard of, if not common. Childlessness was considered a pitiable affliction, both because of a genuine, culturally deep-seated love of children and because of the valuable contribution that children made to the vital on-shore support work of line fishing. Infant and childhood mortality was high, however, making the number of children who reached marrying age considerably smaller than the number born. Emigration also reduced the number of kinfolk in residence, but many overseas kinfolk were kept well informed and well integrated within the kin network. This was especially true if the emigrant had made a fisherfolk marriage either before or after emigration, but could also be the case even if the emigrant had married out in the new location. Many local families had what amounted to a designated correspondent, that is, one member who took on the task of writing to distant family members and keeping the lines of communication open. Such a correspondent could be either male or female and could be kin to the distant recipients by either blood or marriage. If the correspondent died or was incapacitated, another correspondent was quickly settled on, by common consensus as to who was best able to handle letter writing responsibilities (or who disliked them least, in some cases), and took up the task. The oldest generation still resident in the village was expected to be knowledgeable about consanguineal and affinal ties, in particular where their own siblings, parents, grandparents, and cousins were concerned, whether in local residence or elsewhere, but also for the village at large.

4.3.2 Naming Practices and the Maintenance of Kin Ties

There was real need of good genealogical knowledge. The small number of family names in each fishing population, combined with the large number of children in most families and with endogamous marriage, produced a shortage of distinctive names. This problem was greatly increased by traditional naming practices, still largely observed well into the twentieth century among East Sutherland fisher-folk. The first child born would be given the first name of the father's father, if a boy, or of the father's mother, if a girl. The second child was given the first name of the mother's father or the mother's mother, in similar fashion. The third child would be given the first name of whichever grandparent had not supplied the name for the first grandchild, as gender-appropriate, and the fourth child would be given the first name of whichever grandparent had not supplied the name for the second grandchild, as gender-appropriate. After that, the first names of the father's and mother's (great-)uncles and (great-)aunts were usually drawn on. As a conse-quence of this practice, a man named Simon MacAngus, married to Flora MacPherson (to take as a neutral example two names with no East Sutherland connections whatever), if he happened to have four sons and two daughters, would in due course most likely have four grandsons bearing the name Simon MacAngus after their father's father, assuming that all his sons had sons of their own. He might have two others with the given name Simon (though not MacAngus, of course), if his daughters had more than one son. He would also have four grand-daughters bearing the given name Flora after their mother's mother, if his sons all had daughters as well as sons, and he might have two more, if each of his daugh-ters had at least two daughters.

As a result of the constant replication of given and family name combina-tions, official names ceased to have any practical value in the local setting. People referred to each other instead by what are locally known as by-names (/aʃin´ɛn/). These were of various sorts, the most common of them genealogical (hypercoris-tic forms of given names plus a parent's or grandparent's by-name) but some of them were nonsensical and a good many of them mocking.[3] Because of the fre-quent element of mockery, by-names were never used in address, even though they were in constant and universal use as terms of reference. Indeed, by-names were used so nearly exclusively that villagers sometimes needed to confer exten-sively among themselves to retrieve the official name of a fellow villager if some-one inquired about it. The oldest village residents were always looked to for expert knowledge of by-names, their history, and their application. They were expected to be able to track a given individual by by-name through a number of generations and to link the bearer of a particular by-name with an "official" family name when the need arose—in rare dealings with officialdom, for example, or in the much more common case of descendants of émigrés, visiting the village in search of relatives.

4.3.3 Maintaining Less Familiar Degrees of Kinship

Older residents would be relied on, too, when questions arose about half-siblings and the degree of relationship among their offspring. Men whose wives had died early (this having been generally more common than the reverse) usually married again and had additional children, so that half-sibling relationships were relatively frequent, complicating the genealogical lines. Degrees of cousinship at a somewhat greater remove than usual were also especially well tracked by older people, as were cross-village kin ties.

Permissible marriages, not just in the fishing communities but among people native to the region generally, included marriage between cousins. Marriages between third or second cousins were more common, but first-cousin marriages were not ruled out, either among the fisherfolk or among the *tuathanaich* of the area. But a century and a half of enforced endogamy for the fisherfolk meant that by mid-twentieth century fishing community kin ties were dense and convoluted, with two individuals often multiply connected to one another. It was, for example, possible for an individual to be simultaneously cousin, in-law, and aunt or uncle to another. All these relationships were kept track of and valued, at least potentially, for the multiple bonds they created (with the actual social value of the ties depending of course on the continuing amity of the relationships).

4.3.4 Focus on Kinship

Preoccupation with kin ties was very marked in this part of the Highlands (as in others). Two people of fisherfolk descent, meeting for the first time or meeting after the passage of many years, would attempt before any other topic was broached to settle the question of whether they were related to one another and, if so, exactly how. An individual's closest friends and most reliable sources of support in case of need were drawn from within the kin network, and most regular visiting between households was likewise among kin. Large and varied though the circles of callers across households might appear to be, close inquiry usually revealed that the particularly frequent social callers were kinfolk (including affines). Non-kin (or distant kin, as it probably more often was) might be on very good terms with one another, but the level of regular interaction and mutual support was normally a good deal lower. For most people, the kin circle was large enough to offer a wide pool of potential intimates. Especially close ties were often cross-generational. The fact that an older woman usually anchored a crew with two younger women at the herring stations, and that boat crews included both older and younger men, may have encouraged cross-generational ties, but the large size of families and the wide age-range encompassed by sets of siblings (and therefore also by sets of close degrees of cousins) formed the essential basis for close and long-lasting friendships across considerable age gaps.

5 THE FISHING COMMUNITIES AS FACE-TO-FACE COMMUNITIES

The East Sutherland fishing communities, with their relatively small populations but high settlement density and multiple kin relationships, were classic face-to-face communities in which everyone knew everyone else on a personal basis. Like shared occupation and common local language, personal knowledge of fellow villagers contributed to overall social cohesion. Some of the notable features of these cohesive communities are highlighted here.

5.1 Geographic and Demographic Characteristics

In the villages of Brora and Golspie, the fisherfolk lived originally in particular parts of the village that had historically been designated as fisherfolk residential areas. In each case the fisherfolk were a Gaelic-speaking population that ultimately came to be enclaved within a larger English-speaking village. In Brora the fisherfolk section of the village was a low-lying point of land just at the mouth of the river Brora, separated from the upper village by a short but rather steep hill. The fisherfolk themselves took the hill as the boundary and spoke of themselves as living "down the hill" and of the non-fisherfolk as living "up the hill." A neutral term for the down-the-hill section of town was Lower Brora, but the designation "Fishertown" was probably more widely used by up-the-hill villagers. Fisherfolk considered this label derogatory and resented its use, pointing out that there was no such place as Fishertown on the map.

In Golspie there was less obvious spatial separation between the fisherfolk and the non-fisherfolk. Golspie village is laid out along a long thoroughfare (Main Street) paralleling the sea, and originally there were only a few streets intersecting with Main Street. The fisherfolk lived directly beside the sea along a considerably shorter street (Shore Street) on the seaward side of Main Street at the southwestern end of the village, and along another street (Church Street) that makes a right angle with Shore Street by extending some distance along the eastern side of the arm of land that encloses the north side of Loch Fleet, the body of water lying between Golspie and Embo. Small houses, typically with an internal wall making them into two-family residences, accommodated the fisherfolk along Shore Street, Church Street, and Sutherland Street (this last a very short street paralleling the near end of Church Street). This section of Golspie was as much reserved to fisher families as was Lower Brora in Brora village, and again the term Fishertown was sometimes applied (and always resented). More widely and neutrally, it was also called the West End, with the other two-thirds of the long line of Golspie village correspondingly known as the East End. Since fisherfolk at the easternmost point of Shore Street lived directly behind a part of Main Street that was considered more or less part of the East End, there was little physical separation between the easternmost fisherfolk residences and the westernmost non-fisherfolk residences. Small as the physical distance may have been, the social division was just as complete in Golspie as it was in Brora, where the short but steep hill served as a boundary marker. In mid-twentieth century, the historically fisherfolk residential areas still housed a good many people of fisherfolk descent in Brora and Golspie, but occupational and residential segregation had broken down by then, and a good many fisherfolk descendants were also dispersed, living scattered among the non-fisherfolk in various parts of both villages.

Embo, by contrast with the other villages, had been wholly a fishing village. It represented in its entirety a satellite settlement to nearby Dornoch, a larger village in which no fisherfolk resided. Dornoch, with its cathedral and its royal burgh status, served historically (along with Dunrobin and its castle outside Golspie) as a major point of entry for English cultural influence and language in the eastern part of Sutherland. Dornoch replaced Hallkirk as the diocesan seat of the bishopric in the thirteenth century, when the original Dornoch Cathedral was built, and the Dornoch village population demonstrated its strong historic connection to the De Moravia family via the presence of an unusually large number of families with the surname Murray. (Mirroring the utter social separation between the royal burgh and the impoverished fishing village, no Murrays at all were to be found among the Embo fisherfolk.) A zone of farmland, pasturage, and moorland separates Embo from Dornoch, and though each was economically important to the other from the early nineteenth century through at least the first quarter of the twentieth, they could scarcely have been more different from one another in the crucial respects of lifeways and language.

The heart of Embo as a fishing village consisted of five straight parallel streets near the sea with some interconnecting cross-streets. The houses were of the same general type as in the other two fishing communities—largely two-family dwellings with an internal dividing wall. Very large families were routinely accommodated in rather small houses, and in all three communities it was taken for granted that some older children would leave the family home as they became old enough to take jobs or to marry, vacating places for the younger children still coming along. The compactness of the original core of Embo village was such that people could call to one another across an intervening street or two and converse perfectly audibly in this fashion. As late as the 1960s and 1970s, with the adult population of the village still strongly Gaelic-speaking, such conversations were typically conducted in Gaelic. This was very much contrary to bilingual behaviors in Brora and Golspie, where by this time Gaelic speakers were a tiny minority and Gaelic conversations on the streets were more likely to be conducted in a subdued, private fashion among small clusters of people. By this same time, however, Embo had expanded geographically beyond the original five fishing village streets, with a new residential area (known in village parlance as /nə tʰroːr uːr/ 'the new houses') developed farther back from the sea. More in-married or non-local people lived in this part of the village, and Gaelic was less often heard on the street there.

There had long been some people in Embo who did not fish for a living (English speakers who served the village population in some specialized capacity, such as teachers, nurses, or railwaymen who staffed the tiny local railway line that served Embo until the late 1950s or early 1960s).[4] But the village had come into existence as a fishing village, and thanks to the distinctive language and lifeways shared by most of its adult residents during their childhoods, it continued to have the unique character of a Gaelic-speaking "fishing village" even after fishing had disappeared as a viable livelihood.

Brora and Golspie were major population centers by Sutherland-shire standards, with populations of about 1,186 and 1,167 respectively in 1961.[5] As noted in chapter 1, Gaelic speakers constituted just 3.6 percent of Brora's population (forty-three individuals) and 4.6 percent of Golspie's (fifty-four individuals) in the initial speaker census that I conducted in 1963–64. The fact that death had claimed twenty-one Brora speakers, or very nearly half of Brora's speaker population, and fourteen Golspie speakers by the time I conducted a follow-up speaker census in 1972 indicates the aging character of the Gaelic-speaking population in these two villages. In mid-twentieth century these two villages were the most populous in the county. Sutherland, unlike other counties in the Highlands, had no single village or town that served as administrative or commercial center. Brora had the most significant industries (a distillery, a woolen mill, a coal mine, a brickworks, plus in the non-industrial sector a government radio station), while Golspie housed the Sutherland estate offices, the county's only newspaper, a small hospital, and a few county offices. Dornoch, though smaller than Brora and Golspie, was home to the county courthouse and to Dornoch Cathedral, as well as a number of county offices. Eastern Sutherland enjoys beautiful scenery and salmon-rich rivers, and the narrow sandy coastal shelf has provided all three villages with well-known and well-patronized golf courses (a source of after-school caddying work for local children, including a good many from fisherfolk families, in the early twentieth century). All three villages had large and reputable hotels catering to the substantial tourist trade. The local fishing industry had died out in all of the villages by the 1960s, and the one boat that still fished out of Brora belonged to an incomer rather than to a descendant of local fisherfolk. With fishing eliminated as a means of earning a living, Embo had only about 275 residents in 1961, down by some hundreds since the busy fishing industry years of the early twentieth century, but with about 105 Gaelic-speaking residents the village nonetheless retained its Gaelic character.

By the 1960s most of the remaining Gaelic speakers in Brora and Golspie were at retirement age or close to it. They had generally had direct experience with the fishing industry when young, but had held a great variety of other jobs during their working lives (domestic service, hotel work, woolen mill work, construction work, etc.). Among Embo's population of Gaelic speakers, the tradition of following the sea had continued after the fishing industry went into decline, with first whaling and then the merchant navy providing work for a good many men. Domestic service and hotel work provided jobs for Embo women, while the Forestry Commission's local plantation offered work for both men and women. Work on road crews and in construction supplied additional jobs for men.

A substantial number of Embo couples (plus some unmarried individuals) connected to one another by kin ties had gone to the London area to find work before World War II, taking up a variety of jobs but remaining a remarkably cohesive "London-Embo" group in and around the city. Some of the women in this group returned to the home village with their young children (or to have their children) during the war years, after which they went back to London. These exiles returned to Embo otherwise only for their annual vacations and the occasional wedding or funeral, but Embo remained the compass point that focused their social lives. Each weekend saw them gathered in varying but always considerable numbers at the home of one of their group, and their social interests continued to revolve strongly around the home village and its people. They remained solidly Gaelic-speaking, but very few of their children developed any active knowledge of Gaelic.

5.2 Egalitarianism as a Fishing Community Norm

Fishing for a living might seem to require at least a minimally hierarchical social structure, since someone after all must be at the tiller, determining the course of the boat and making the most crucial seamanship decisions in tight spots. Those of the remaining East Sutherland fishermen who had spent the most time at sea nevertheless steadfastly maintained that no hierarchy had existed and that boats' crews decided on their course of action by consensus.[6] The oldest and most experienced man among the crew was listened to most deferentially, on the universally accepted principle of *urram do'n aois* 'honor to age', but every man had his say and the choice of fishing grounds under whatever weather conditions prevailed was made by mutual agreement. Since each crewman had a share in the boat, there was no one owner with a greater stake or larger say. The catch was shared by a method designed to ensure the greatest possible degree of impartiality. It was laid out in a number of piles as equal in size as could be contrived, one for each man in the crew and one "for the boat" (that is, one share whose market price would be used to buy gear and supplies). Each crew member devised a one-time-only token—a bit of stick, a knife, a piece of rock, a cap—and all of these were handed over to some one of the many bystanders on the shore; while the crew turned their backs, the happenstance participant tossed each token in succession onto one of the piles of fish. Each man took the pile his token had been tossed onto, marketing it for the benefit of his own family. Quarrels over division of the catch were avoided, preserving amity among the crew.

Each man provided his own gear, a good deal of it homemade during the winter months, and each man and his family gathered bait for his own lines and baited his own hundreds of hooks, laying them out in his own line baskets. Untangling the lines from the previous day's fishing, removing old bait, and rebaiting the lines was also the work of the individual fisherman and his family, so that most of the heaviest routine work was done on an individual basis before the boat put to sea. There were however also whole-crew responsibilities for upkeep of the boat: removing growths of weed and barnacles from the hull, patching any leaks, and barking the sails and sheets (treating them with bark, a resin-like substance rendered liquid by boiling it in huge kettles full of water) to retard rotting of the fabric and lines. These necessary maintenance activities were undertaken by the full crew, all gathering on one or more designated days for that purpose. Participants' accounts of these activities and of crews' responses to crises of weather or failed gear regularly stress the cooperative nature of the fishing life: every man did his part, in acute awareness that he or any other fisherman might abruptly find himself dependent for his life on the quality of the whole crew's workmanship and the mutuality of their aid and support. The same sense of mutuality was said to prevail within the full village fishing fleet, and for the same reason: on a given day a man might curtail his fishing to come to someone's aid, but a few days or weeks later that same man might need another to do the same for him.

A similar absence of hierarchy prevailed in other aspects of fisherfolk life. Differences in wealth were small and usually temporary, so long as livelihoods depended on fishing, and there were no representative or administrative offices to be filled in connection with village social life—no mayor or king was recognized, even informally. (One self-anointed mid-twentieth-century claimant of such a title in Embo was quietly mocked for his presumption.) Only the church offered special roles that were open to fisherfolk, though only to males: the roles of precentor and elder. Young boys were often trained in special classes as potential precentors for Free Church services, where musical instruments were not permitted. Ability to carry a tune was essential, of course, but no other special qualifications were required. Most boys who were sent to the class in precenting did not actually become precentors, but the young attendees later provided a pool of men who knew the texts of the metrical psalms and were familiar with the lead-out lines of the most frequently used tunes. Females were not offered training as precentors, but in the Dornoch Free Church (where Gaelic services persisted longest) and also in the once-a-week evening prayer services in Embo's village hall, a gradual drop-off in the number of musically adept Gaelic-speaking males led to one or two Embo women taking on the precentor's role; precenting skills in these few cases were acquired by a combination of musical gifts and frequent exposure.[7]

Special qualifications were required for the role of elder, but they were moral and spiritual rather than secular. Only men could serve as elders, and there were separate elders for the English-speaking and the Gaelic-speaking congregations. They were expected to be not only devout but also clean-living, that is, unblemished in the conduct of their lives. Such men had a certain moral authority, but they enjoyed no special secular authority as a consequence of their position. Asked whether an elder was any more likely than another man to be able to prevent or break up a fight, for example, people said that they were not. Insofar as they led, elders led by example and not by authority, except in special spheres where the church took a punitive stand (the public shaming of out-of-wedlock mothers at church, for example, in the days when church attendance was still universal).

In terms of overall social structure, a well-established egalitarianism prevailed within each fishing community so long as fishing continued to provide the livelihood. Although the fisherfolk were treated as social and economic inferiors by the greater part of the non-fisherfolk population, among themselves they recognized no social or economic hierarchies. Some individuals enjoyed a higher degree of respect or liking than others, of course, but rather on the basis of personal character, behavior, or skills than on wealth, occupational standing, or structured leadership role in these communities of remarkably undifferentiated social structure. Only after the decline of the fishing industry propelled villagers into occupationally more diverse roles did egalitarian norms begin to change in the former fishing communities. Even after this development, few individuals achieved an economic success that elevated them to any notable degree above their fellows, and such differences in wealth as were evident by the later decades of the twentieth century appeared to be largely the result of good fortune in the form of legacies from émigré relatives who had done exceptionally well for themselves in some distant location.

5.3 Gender-Distinctive Work Roles

Occupational and domestic roles in the fishing communities were strongly differentiated by gender. Women (and older girls) were responsible for child care, cooking, cleaning, and clothing repair, and by most accounts the management of the family's earnings also fell to the wife. She retained whatever cash derived from her fish marketing, and she took charge of income from the gathering and sale of periwinkles as well as the children's caddying wages, these last usually spent on school clothing. Husbands often turned over the bulk of their earnings to the wife's management as well.

Most of the work connected with fishing was clearly gender-specific. Men alone made fishing gear: creels, bait baskets, floats, and tippets (the part of the line the hooks were attached to, made of horsetail hair). Men maintained and repaired the boats, sails, and sheets, and all were adept at mending nets. Both sexes gathered bait, but in digging for lugworm men and women used different tools. Men readied fish and winkles for transport to the railhead, but they did no local marketing; only women went out with creels to sell fish. Only men went to sea. Women were not welcome aboard the sort of working boat their husbands owned or had a share in; having women on board was considered unlucky.

Fishing-related work was gender-distinctive, but another important kind of work was much less so. Getting in the annual potato crop, vital to the family's subsistence, involved a number of tasks shared by whatever family members were available and fit for the work. The gathering and transporting of seaweed as fertilizer, for example, was an annual event in which everyone participated, and lifting the potatoes at season's end was also a shared task.

5.4 Multiplex Roles

The combination of uniform occupation, residential segregation, affiliation with one religious denomination (or two, each historically based in the Free Church, in cases of schism), and a long-standing socially enforced endogamy meant that the residents of any one fishing community typically stood in multiplex social roles to one another. It was more nearly the rule than the exception that any two men who were fellow crew members in a boat would also be kinsmen (brothers, cousins, father and son, uncle and nephew, say) and fellow congregants at a local church. They would go together to gather hazel and willow for creels and line baskets, would fish together, lend each other gear, live fairly close by one another, spend social time in one another's homes, attend the same church services, and perhaps in due course see some of their children marry into each other's families. Two women who went to the herring fishery together as part of a gutting and packing crew were just as likely as the men to fill multiple roles with reference to one another: to be kin to one another, live near one another, go gathering bait together, offer occasional help with household or child-care needs, share an unexpected windfall in the food line (a gift of rabbits or game birds, say), spend social time in each other's homes, attend church services together, and have a number of children attending school together.

Uniplex social roles were non-existent in these communities. The members of any social network were at the same time relatives, workmates, fellow congregants, and often neighbors, as well as those with whom most voluntary social time was spent. Gaelic as the common home language served as the linguistic medium for the full variety of roles which community members filled for one another. All registers that their form of Scottish Gaelic offered them would be fully in play among the members of any social network within the community, with the exception of a rather formal variety of church-influenced Gaelic cultivated by men who were especially active in religious life. Those who served as elders in particular, but also such other men as were able to offer extemporaneous prayers, tended to use for that purpose a Bible-influenced lexicon that women were familiar with but had no occasion to use actively. Apart from this, no differences in the command of register were apparent among speakers, at least as of mid-twentieth century.

5.5 Community Membership

Given the number of distinctive features of fisherfolk life—place of residence, occupation, deeply interwoven kin ties, a locally distinctive Gaelic—membership in the fisherfolk communities was clear-cut as long as fishing provided the livelihood and endogamy prevailed. Because "fisher" was a stigmatized identity locally, awareness of community membership was acute on the part of both segments of the population, that is, among *maraichean* (fisherfolk) and *tuathanaich* (non-fisherfolk) alike. Three quotations from Brora residents, recorded in the 1970s, demonstrate the strength of local prejudices where the fisherfolk were concerned. A well-to-do, university-educated English monolingual who had lived for some time in Brora said in a 1978 interview, "A 'fisher' was a term of abuse, there's no question about that." He was a native of East Sutherland, though not of Brora, and had a very finely tuned sense of the local social hierarchy. A Brora native from a crofting family, the monolingual daughter of one monolingual parent and one who was a Gaelic-English bilingual, gave a view which supported the affluent man's judgment in another 1978 interview: "It was just that kind of feeling that was among the children when they were in school. And it lived with them...from their parents. Their parents taught them, 'Well, you mustn't go with [i.e., associate with] a fisher.'" A woman who had grown up in a Lower Brora fisherfolk family, a semi-speaker whose Gaelic was much less fluent than her English, agreed with their perceptions in terms of her own experience. In a 1974 interview she said: "The upper village looked down on the Lower Brora people...There was always animosity between them...They looked on us as a race apart."

Where such biases prevail, people are keenly aware of who belongs to the stigmatized community and who does not. Even after endogamy weakened and out-marriage became a reality in East Sutherland, active maintenance of kin ties tended to preserve a sense of fisherfolk community membership, both among the fisherfolk and among nonfisherfolk villagers, as did any continuing use of the Gaelic language. In fact, since all other segments of the East Sutherland population had gone over to English monolingualism by mid-twentieth century bar a very few elderly and scattered crofters, continuing use of Gaelic had in itself become a form of active kin-tie maintenance in Brora and Golspie, where speakers were few. Social interaction was high within Gaelic-speaking Brora and Golspie kin networks; opportunities to use Gaelic therefore arose most often along kin-network lines. Simply residing in Embo had some of the same membership-marking effect during most of the twentieth century, with the village population predominantly of fisherfolk descent. Once outsiders began to buy or build houses in Embo late in the century, local Embo birth and continuing use of Gaelic came to serve as markers of fisherfolk identity.

There was for all these reasons little indeterminacy about community membership during the period of this study (1963–2008). Who was "of the fisherfolk", as the local expression put it, was generally clear and was certainly so for the people who served as sources for this study, both the Gaelic-English bilinguals who provided linguistic data, information on fisherfolk lifeways, and accounts of their personal experience, and the English monolinguals who provided information on local history, social structure, and linguistic and social attitudes. Community membership was by and large more readily determinable than precise speaker status, which because of age-based proficiency differences and long- or short-term emigration experiences posed somewhat greater interpretive complexity. While local Gaelic speakers were all unambiguously community members, consequently, individual linguistic histories were various and levels of proficiency differed accordingly. The proficiency outcomes resulting from various life histories are discussed in the account of sources, which is given in chapter 4.

Dimensions of Linguistic Variation in a Socioeconomically Homogeneous Population

1 INTRODUCTION: THE RESIDUAL FISHERFOLK POPULATIONS IN THE 1960S AND AFTER

The fisherfolk of Brora, Golspie, and Embo became fisherfolk involuntarily, but the transformation was very thorough. The livelihood forced on the evictees early in the Clearance period was the only one available to them, and simple survival required that they master it as quickly and completely as possible. Their lives and those of their descendants were shaped by the need to gain a living from the sea, as this population did for more than 100 years. By the end of World War I, however, the best years of the east coast fishing industry were past, and during the next four decades older men from fisherfolk families gradually retired from the sea, while the younger men who did not emigrate shifted to onshore work, as this became available to them, or took up other seafaring occupations, such as service in the merchant navy.

By 1963, the date of my initial arrival in East Sutherland, little remained of the fishing village character of Lower Brora, Golspie's West End, or Embo. No one from the Gaelic-speaking fishing communities still fished full-time for his livelihood, and in Brora and Golspie a scattering of people who had grown up in Lower Brora or the West End now lived in other parts of the villages. Even Embo, despite its physical isolation, had by then acquired a modest number of monolingual English-speaking residents who were not of fisherfolk descent.

Still, every locally born Gaelic speaker in the three villages had grown up under conditions dictated by the history sketched out in the last chapter and in the social environment that history had brought into being. Most of the older speakers, and even a few of Embo's imperfect youngest speakers, had been involved in the herring fishery in their young days, and only the youngest imperfect speakers in Brora and Embo had no direct experience of their families' intensive rounds of labor in connection with the local line fishing. The equation between speaking the local Gaelic and being of fisherfolk descent still held, and despite a growing number of marriages between fisherfolk descendants and others, no locally born people on either side of the social divide had yet forgotten the days of fisherfolk separateness in the occupational, residential, and social spheres.

2 VARIETIES OF VARIATION IN EAST SUTHERLAND GAELIC

Although the fisherfolk had formed a separate group in each village, distinct from the rest of the local population in a great many respects and following the same lifeways in each location, their Gaelic was far from uniform. For a start, village-by-village differentiation was as pronounced in East Sutherland as in the Highlands generally, each village exhibiting certain distinctive local features. Beyond this, Gaelic was a retreating language locally, spoken by an aging bilingual population and unsupported by active Gaelic literacy, so that the obsolescent state of Gaelic in East Sutherland always had to be taken into consideration when sources did not agree on the form that a particular element should take. Age differences among speakers were potentially of great significance.

Another potential source of variability was diversity of speaking styles. As an unwritten, unstandardized vernacular, fisherfolk Gaelic was put to few formal uses. But it was possible all the same for speakers to adjust their style of speaking according to interlocutor or according to discourse purpose: to speak more casually when speaking to particularly good friends or gossiping, say, and less casually when speaking to less good friends or extending condolences. The bilingualism of local Gaelic speakers also had some effect on speech style, as did their exposure to more mainstream varieties of Gaelic. Many speakers showed some degree of self-consciousness about the English loanwords liberally used in local Gaelic conversation, and for some an attempt at a more formal or "proper" style of speech included an effort to reduce the number of obvious English loanwords. All speakers had some familiarity with more mainstream varieties of Gaelic via sermons, broadcasts, work experience in the fishing industry, and occasional interaction with non-local speakers settled in East Sutherland. In conversation with speakers of other Gaelic dialects, some local speakers made occasional lexical substitutions, replacing local words with lexicon they believed to be more mainstream. They might or might not avoid other localisms as well, depending on their own degree of linguistic awareness and flexibility.

In addition to the variation associated with locality, with age-related change processes, and with speech style, there was, finally, the conspicuous idiosyncratic variation described in chapter 1, with even same-sex speakers of similar age and proficiency using different variants, in some instances even when they were members of a single household, nuclear family, and social network. Depending on the variable in question, individual speakers might themselves use only a single variant, or they might equally well use more than one variant without any apparent linguistic conditioning that could explain the variant selections. Another individual within the same household or social network might use a different variant or set of variants in the same linguistic environments. This sort of idiosyncratic inter-speaker and intra-speaker variation, which I am terming *personally patterned* (or *personal-pattern*) *variation*, could be seen to intersect in some cases with geographically based variation or with age-related variation. In the former cases, idiosyncratically patterned variation associated with a particular lexical or grammatical form might turn up in one or two of the villages but not in the other(s), as in the case of ('on her'), which shows personal-pattern variation only in Golspie. In the latter cases one variant of two or more originally in use for a particular variable might fall off in use or, more rarely, drop almost entirely out of use among younger speakers, while one or more others came to be favored by younger people. In cases where one personal-pattern variant represented analogical change and the other(s) did not, the greater regularity and transparency of the analogical variant offered an obvious reason for favoring of that variant by younger speakers, but in other cases where younger speakers seemed inclined to favor one variant over others there was no clear-cut motivation of this sort.

Absence of any obviously motivated directionality in variant choice was in fact a pronounced feature of personal-pattern variation. Whereas a preference for analytic over synthetic grammatical marking and for paradigmatic consistency could explain the gradual decrease in inflectional expression of the first-person singular conditional in age-related variation, and a desire to reduce the obviousness of English lexical influence could explain the avoidance of English loanwords in attempts at a more formal Gaelic style, there were often no such explanatory factors for the diverse variant choices that appeared in personal-pattern variation, whether in a single speaker's repeated uses of the same variable or in different speakers' uses.

In the sections that follow, a brief introduction is provided to each of the main types of variation. Two of them, geographically based variation and age-related variation, constituted major parts of earlier investigations (Dorian 1978, 1981) and were important precursors to the present investigation in that the delineation of these very prominent sources of variability in the local Gaelic ultimately allowed another kind of variation, the idiosyncratic personal-pattern variation at issue here, to emerge more clearly.

3 GEOGRAPHICALLY BASED VARIATION
IN FISHERFOLK GAELIC

Though I had known before my arrival in East Sutherland that Scottish Gaelic was highly differentiated according to location, I was still surprised by the extent of village-by-village differences in the local fisherfolk Gaelic (and for that matter by the differences between fisherfolk Gaelic and the Gaelic of nearby crofters, still evident in the speech of a very few elderly bilingual crofters who lived near Brora and Embo). There was no ancient centuries-long settlement history involved in the formation of the fishing populations, after all, and the evictions and the 150 years that followed took very much the same course in each location. The villages were not very distant from one another, especially by sea, and their general occupational and social patterns were virtually identical. The Gaelic in each fishing community was distinctive, all the same, with small differences even between Brora's Gaelic and Golspie's. The most striking of these was in morphophonology. These two populations shared most family names and were part of the same estate, but Golspie Gaelic nevertheless had one morphophoneme (/γ/) that Brora Gaelic entirely lacked. Less surprising, in view of the fact that they belonged to different estates and were separated by Loch Fleet and a greater distance in road miles, were the considerably more numerous differences between Embo's Gaelic and the Gaelic of the other two villages.

The greater part of the variation by village was lexically based and easily recognized. The problem for an investigator lay in the fact that there was so much of it. Every newly encountered lexical item was potentially dialect-differentiated and needed cross-checking. Though it was less immediately obvious to a fieldworker, the same was true of grammatical structures: morpho-syntactic differences by village were also present and required the same thorough cross-checking.

3.1 An Example of Geographically Based Variation

The gerund 'taking' offers a typical example of geographically based variation in fisherfolk Gaelic, and freely spoken and elicited instances are presented in table 3.1. The pattern that appears is classic for this dialect area, with identical Brora and Golspie forms (/koal/) contrasting with a distinctive Embo form (/ka:l/).

In the tables here and throughout the volume, speakers are identified by letter and number. The letters B, G, and E represent Brora, Golspie, and Embo, and 1 indicates the oldest source in a given village, with progressively higher numbers representing decreasing age. (Same-age speakers are numbered randomly relative to one another except in the few cases where I happen to know the month of birth as well as the year of birth, where they are numbered accordingly.) Age-related levels of proficiency are indicated by shading and formerly fluent status is

TABLE 3.1. Freely spoken and elicited instances of the geographical variable ('taking') from Brora (B) speakers of two age-and-proficiency levels, from Golspie (G) speakers, and from Embo (E) speakers of three age-and-proficiency levels

speakers	koal free	koal elic	ka:l free	ka:l elic	
B1 81 f.	--	1			
B3 80 f.	3	13			
B4 79 f.	1	--			
B6 69 f.	--	4			
B7 66 f.	1	1			
B8 57 f.	--	1			
B10 43 f.	--	1			
G2 75 f.	4	12			
G3 72 m.	1	9			
G4 68 f.	2	4			
G5 68 m.	--	1			
E3 [85] m.			--	1	
E4 82 m.			9	6	
E7 ?74 f.			1	--	
E9 70 f.			--	1	
E10 70 m.			4	3	
E11 70 f.			--	1	
E12 ?68 f.			--	1	
E13 [67] f.			1	3	
E16 64 m.			--	1	
E17 64 f.			35	2	
E22 58 f.			--	5	
E23 57 m.			--	1	
E25 57 f.			--	2	
E26* 54 f.			31	9	
E27 54 m.			10	7	
E29* 50 f.			9	4	
E30 49 m.			5	3	
E33 45 m.			--	2	
E34 45 f.			5	3	OFSs
E38 40 f.			--	1	YFSs
E40 36 f.			13	3	SSs

Free = freely spoken, elic = elicited; older fluent speakers = OFSs, younger fluent speakers = YFSs, semi-speakers = SSs. Asterisks indicate formerly fluent speakers.

indicated by an asterisk, but for a purely geographical variable of this sort proficiency levels have no role to play.

Table 3.1 represents the most straightforward kind of geographically based variation, the same word appearing with different phonological realizations in different locations. East Sutherland fisherfolk Gaelic offers more than 250 instances of this sort (presented in Appendix A in Dorian 1978:151–58). As noted in chapter 1, however, it also offers both some sharper lexical differences and some differences that are grammatical rather than lexical. For example, the Brora/ Golspie term for 'untangling the fishing lines' is /rɔ:čax/, while the Embo term for the same activity is /re:xu/. The very high-frequency noun /kʰu:pʰ/ 'cup' is feminine in Brora and Golspie but masculine in Embo. Both of these instances exemplify the most common alignment—Brora and Golspie versus Embo. This is not the only possible alignment, however. The word for 'sea', a very central lexical item in these former fisherfolk villages, goes against the trend in that it is identical in Brora and Embo (/mur/) but different in Golspie (/mwir/), and the same is true of gender assignment in the case of the high-frequency noun /pu:/ 'shop', which is feminine in Brora and Embo but masculine in Golspie.

3.2 Establishing the Existence of Geographically Based Variation

Determining that an item varies purely by geographical location requires that the investigator have several sources per village, but it does not require that each of the sources provide a large number of instances of the item in question. In the canonical case, several speakers from a single village produce identical forms of a given word, while several speakers from another village also give identical forms for that word, but the forms given by the two sets of speakers are different from one another. The combination of reliable agreement within each of the villages and reliable difference across the two villages is sufficient to make the case, assuming that no contrary evidence subsequently appears. Many high-frequency items are characterized by geographically based variation of this sort in the East Sutherland fisherfolk communities; for these, copious documentation is easily achieved. For rarer, low-frequency items, including those documented only by elicitation techniques, a consistent even though infrequent finding of multiple-speaker convergence in combination with cross-village difference is evidence enough to allow provisional identification of geographical variation.

4 AGE-RELATED VARIATION IN FISHERFOLK GAELIC

A second source of variability became apparent only with my return visits to East Sutherland in 1965 and after, as my work sessions gradually drew in additional participants, particularly in Embo. The new participants were often younger kin to my original sources, and their translation responses to a given stimulus sentence were not necessarily the same as those of the original sources. In the most striking cases, they seemed to deviate a good deal from what I could recognize, on the basis of prior work with older speakers, as relatively conservative norms for the local Gaelic. I had not been actively looking for such differences, but they were certainly interesting enough to draw my attention when they emerged. It seemed that conditions in Embo offered an outstanding opportunity to explore directions of linguistic change in a small, isolated language community with a high density of interaction but weakening language transmission, and I was eager to take advantage of the opportunity.

I took it as a sign of change in progress if the incidence of a particular form or structure was high at the upper end of the Embo age range but dropped off among younger speakers, either disappearing or being replaced by some modified version of that same form or structure (or in a few cases by a quite different form or structure). Older speakers tended to produce the more conservative forms or structures with good to moderate frequency, but as age decreased, so did the incidence of the items in question. In the case of apparently innovative forms or structures, including blended structures derived from two different conservative models and simplifications such as analogical regularization, the opposite was true: older speakers tended to produce them relatively infrequently, but as age decreased the incidence of the innovative form or structure rose. Incidence did not necessarily fall or rise in perfect correlation with age along the entire age continuum, but overall the fall or rise was in line with age differences.

4.1 An Example of Age-Related Variation

Conservative East Sutherland fisherfolk Gaelic offered contrasting locational and directional forms of four common adverbs: 'out' (locational /mwĩ(ç)/ versus directional /max/), 'up' (/hurəd/ versus /no:rd/), 'down' (/stã:n/ versus /vã:n/), and 'over' (/hau:ł/ versus /nũ:ł/). One similarly contrasting adverbial pair found in most Gaelic dialects, locational and directional 'in,' had disappeared from the local Gaelic at some time in the past; variants representing both original locational and original directional forms of 'in', recognizable on the basis of their resemblance to equivalents in other dialect areas, remained in the local Gaelic as variants of the variable adverbial ('in') but without any current semantic distinction. Absence of the locational/directional distinction in the high-frequency adverb 'in' probably paved the way for ongoing loss, mainly in Embo, of the locational/directional distinction in connection with other adverbs, but in all these other cases the directional form was gradually ousting the locational form, with the latter disappearing from use altogether rather than remaining in the dialect as another variant of the adverb. This process was particularly advanced in the case of 'out'. A number of Embo speakers preserved the locational variant /mwĩ(ç)/ only in the phrase 'the outside' (as opposed to 'the inside'), and some showed no trace of it even there. Table 3.2 sums for all four adverbs the instances of locational forms that a speaker provided in an environment that called traditionally for the locational form, as opposed to all instances of directional forms that the speaker used in those same environments. That is, the "traditional" totals and percentages include all instances of /mwĩ(ç)/, /hurəd/, /stã:n/ and /hau:ł/ that the speaker offered, apart from relic instances of /mwĩ(ç)/ and Golspie/Brora /həu:ł/ (Embo /hau:ł/) in the phrases 'the outside' and 'the over-side' (the latter an expression used for the Tarbat Ness peninsula in Easter Ross, just to the south of Embo).

Movement away from a conservative norm is evident across the age-and-proficiency continuum in table 3.2. Fluent speakers in Brora and Golspie continued to maintain the locational/directional distinction with only a few exceptions (mostly

TABLE 3.2. Locational adverb forms used traditionally versus directional adverb forms used non-traditionally in place of locational forms

speaker	paired advs: traditional locational forms				paired advs: directional forms used locationally				
	fr	el	tot	%	fr	el	tot	%	
B2 80 m.	--	3	3	**100**					
B3 80 f.	3	11	14	82.4	3	--		17.6	
B4 79 f.	2	--	2	**100**					
B6 69 f.	--	2	2	**100**					
B7 66 f.	4	3	7	**100**					
B8 57 f.					2	2	4	**100**	
B9 57 f.	1	--	1	33.3	--	2	2	66.7	
G1 77 f.	--	1	1						
G2 75 f.	67	26	93	**98.9**	1	--	1	1.1	
G3 72 m.	1	7	8	88.9	1	--	1	11.1	
G4 68 f.	9	2	11	**100**					
G5 68 m.	3	1	4	**100**					
E3 [85] m.	3	--	3	**100**					
E4 82 m.	56	1	57	**96.6**	--	2	2	3.4	
E6 75 m.	1	3	4	**100**					
E7 ?74 f.	1	--	1						
E8 ?71 f.	2	-	2	**100**					
E9 70 f.	--	2	2	**100**					
E10 70 m.	2	1	3	**100**					
E13 [67] f.	5	6	11	**91.7**	1	--	1	8.3	
E14 65 f.	--	2	2	**100**					
E15 65 m.	--	2	2	**100**					
E17 64 f.	30	1	31	47	34	1	35	53	
E20 58 f.	--	2	2	**100**					
E22 58 f.	15	6	21	**95.5**	1	--	1	4.5	
E23 57 m.					--	3	3	**100**	
E24 57 f.	--	6	6	85.7	--	1	1	14.3	
E26* 54 f.					55	6	61	**100**	
E27 54 m.	30	18	48	**92.3**	4	--	4	7.7	
E28 51 m.					--	1	1		
E29* 50 f.	5	2	7	3.6	162	27	189	**96.4**	
E30 49 m.	4	--	4	**100**					
E32* 47 m.	6	--	6	66.7	3	--	3	33.3	
E33 45 m.	--	1	1						
E34 45 f.	2	--	2	13.3	8	5	13	86.7	
E37 41 m.	4	--	4	20	10	6	16	80	
E38 40 f.	6	3	9	27.3	8	16	24	72.7	
E39 38 f.	6	2	8	42.1	8	3	11	57.9	
E40 36 f.	[2]	--	[2]		99	12	111	**100**	OFSs
E41 31 f.					--	1	1		YFSs
E42 30 f.	--	1	1	3.2	26	4	30	**96.8**	SSs

Fr = free, el = elicited, tot = total, * = formerly fluent speaker. Percentages 90 and above boldfaced, other 50+ percentages underlined. Square brackets indicate direct echoes of a previous speaker's usage, omitted as otherwise non-occurrent in reckoning a percentage.

semantically ambiguous instances, such as 'fishing out of Wick' with /max/ rather than /mwĩ/ and 'we were [off] down the road' with /vã:n/ rather than /stã:n/); but Brora semi-speakers showed substantial substitution of directional forms for locational forms. With the sharp exception of E17 (one of the Embo speakers who no longer showed any locational/directional distinction at all for the adverb 'out'), older Embo speakers produced mostly locational forms in environments that traditionally called for them, with directional forms in lieu of locational forms beginning to appear more frequently among the younger fluent speakers. Nine of the ten older fluent speakers favored the traditionally appropriate forms, but only six of the eleven younger fluent speakers and none of the four semi-speakers did so. English adverbs of course show no difference in form according to whether they express location or direction, and "negative borrowing"—the loss of features in a retreating language that do not correspond to anything in the expanding language (Sasse 1992:65; Thomason 2001:231; "indirect transfer" in the terminology of Silva-Corvalán 1994:4)—can be invoked to account for a growing tendency toward loss of this distinction in Embo Gaelic. As a result of its loss Gaelic structure is brought into closer conformity with English structure, and the bilingual speaker has fewer language-specific distinctions to maintain.

Age-related variation is a prominent feature of East Sutherland fisherfolk Gaelic, and of Embo Gaelic considerably more than Brora or Golspie Gaelic, at least in the sense that it emerged in Embo among fully fluent speakers much more often than it did in the other two villages. A remarkably large number of grammatical structures were showing signs of change in progress, especially in Embo. A partial list would include the following: nominal case, two different gender-marking features, the passive voice, prepositional relative clauses, pronominal objects of complex prepositions, irregular adjective comparison, and the negative imperative (see, e.g., Dorian 1973, 1981, and 2006).

Lexical variation could also show an age-related pattern of innovation. One prominent case peculiar to Embo involved, as most lexical innovations did, introduction of an English element. Whereas Brora and Golspie Gaelic speakers used the form /n´ɛx/ for 'any-/no-body, a person', Embo speakers used either their own village equivalent /n´ax/ or an English-derived form /pɔ(r)di/ (*body*). Older fluent speakers in Embo made some use of /pɔ(r)di/, but by and large they favored /n´ax/, in some cases very heavily. The reverse was true of younger fluent speakers, who showed a growing preference for /pɔ(r)di/ and a correspondingly decreasing use of /n´ax/. The two youngest made exclusive use of /pɔ(r)di/, in fact, as did all of the semi-speakers who provided freely spoken instances, with the exception of the youngest semi-speaker, who though favoring /pɔ(r)di/ produced a single conversational instance of /n´ax/ as an immediate echo of my usage.

In age-related variation the bilingualism of the local Gaelic speakers was always at least a latent factor, although complete replacement of a Gaelic element by an English element, as in the replacement of /n´ax/ by /pɔ(r)di/ among the youngest Embo speakers, was less common than might have been expected. Even without direct borrowing, the influence of English was clear in many age-related changes, as in the gradual loss of feminine pronoun replacement, with English *it* serving as a model for the extension of Gaelic /a/ 'he, it' to use with grammatically feminine nouns. The bilinguals in whose lives English had played the largest role, the formerly fluent speakers and the semi-speakers, were particularly likely to show pronounced patterns of change, with conservative structures giving way to innovations, but Embo fluent speakers were far from exempt from this process.

Continuing use of Embo Gaelic into a period of ever greater isolation from other forms of Gaelic—as participation in the herring fishery decreased, attendance at Gaelic church services grew less universal, and the crofters in the nearby countryside passed over into English monolingualism—at the same time that the ranks of the oldest and most Gaelic-dominant speakers thinned presumably accounts for this phenomenon. These conditions and the accompanying intrusion of English into village life made themselves felt not only in the sheer number of age-related changes under way in Embo Gaelic but also in the frequency with which Gaelic features without an English parallel were involved in such changes.

The general effect of age is immediately apparent in a visual sense in a presentation such as that of table 3.2, where most of the bold percentage figures are on the "traditional" left for all three villages, and a greater density of entries appears in the lower right of the Embo part of the table. But at the same time, age necessarily interacts with the particularities of individual lives, producing more typical results in some cases and less typical results in others. An elderly parent's presence in the household could keep a younger couple speaking Gaelic more frequently than was usual for their generation, as could childlessness; a job alongside older Gaelic-dominant men could do the same for a younger man. Contrariwise, a large family of children who passed through English-language schooling and remained in the village, gradually speaking more English among themselves and even with their parents, could reduce the amount of Gaelic used by an elderly person and also reduce the older speaker's conservatism. Because of such individual factors, the directionality of age-related variation is most apparent across the age-and-proficiency continuum as a whole, and more apparent for speaker *groups* than for individual speakers.

4.2 Establishing the Existence of Age-Related Variation

As with geographically based variation, no especially large number of instances of the item under investigation is needed from each individual speaker to establish that a change is in progress. The need instead is for a relatively large number of sources, sorted according to a generous spectrum of age and proficiency, so that whatever correlation may exist between deviations from a conservative norm and the age and proficiency of individual speakers will be highlighted by differing frequencies of occurrence across the age-and-proficiency continuum.

5 STYLE-RELATED VARIATION IN FISHERFOLK GAELIC

Style-related variation, in East Sutherland Gaelic as in other speech varieties, tended to appear with changes in such factors as genre, audience, and speaker's topic- or context-related mood or purpose. Older fisherfolk speakers had generally had longer and more intense exposure to religious use of Gaelic than their juniors, and they had usually also had more exposure to other dialects of Gaelic during their working lives in the herring fishing industry. Such cross-register and cross-dialect exposure seems to have made older speakers more conscious than younger speakers of written-language norms and of the forms used in more nearly mainstream dialects; their greater age may also have inclined them toward a slightly greater linguistic conservatism or formality, prompting some of them to try to shift on occasion toward mainstream or written-language forms. It was the case, in any event, that the more conspicuous style shifters among my sources were older speakers.

5.1 An Example of Style-Related Variation

Style shifting in East Sutherland fisherfolk Gaelic was manifested above all in relative frequency of borrowing and code switching (see §7.2.6 and chapter 7). It was much less common for style shifts to involve variant forms of personally patterned variables. One striking instance is available, however, in the case of E10, a shy man who did not converse easily. E10 had an unusually large store of proverbial lore, traditional rhymes, and jokes from which he frequently (and sometimes rather abruptly) produced an example by way of holding up his end of a conversation. For E10, entering the proverb-, rhyme-, or joke-performance style seemed to favor the emergence both of non-local elements and conservative local elements. In this style, for example, he used a negative-imperative particle relatively uncommon in East Sutherland Gaelic (two instances), and he preserved an initial /hr-/ consonant cluster, more often reduced to /r-/ in the local Gaelic (also two instances). In addition to using conservative forms of age-related variables, E10 showed a striking change-over in his choice of variants for the personal-pattern variable conjunctional ('when') in the performance of proverbs and rhymes as compared with his other spoken material.[1] In a description of the games played during his boyhood and in a tape-recorded letter to an emigrant sister, for example, he used the variant /tə/ eight times for ('when') and the variant /nu(ə)rə/ only once; but in performing proverbs and rhymes he used /nu(ə)rə/ ten times and /tə/ just three times, a change from just over 11 percent /nu(ə)rə/ in other freely spoken material to just under 77 percent /nu(ə)rə/ in his performance style.

Other speakers, too, showed some change of variant preference for ('when') in connection with proverb recitation (see chapter 5, §11.1), but none of them made as radical a shift as E10's move from an otherwise preferred variant in initial /t-/ to a variant in initial /n-/. E17, six years younger than E10, was also a notable master of proverbs and traditional rhymes. Like him she showed a preference for /tə/ in conversation, and like him she showed a pronounced shift to a disyllabic variant of ('when') in reciting proverbs, but she shifted only from one variant in initial /t-/ to another. In conversation she used monosyllabic /tə/ at a 58.2 percent level (78 of 134 instances) and disyllabic /tənə/ at a 34.3 percent level (46 of 134 instances), with scattered instances of /tərə/, /nə/, and /nərə/ making up the rest of her conversational variant selections. In giving proverbs E17 reversed her variant use for ('when') sharply, rendering the conjunction as /tənə/ in seven out of eight instances (87.5 percent) and as /tə/ only once (12.5 percent). In conversation both E10 and E17 made very occasional use of /nu(ə)rə/; in proverb recitation, both speakers shifted to a disyllabic variant, but E10's shift from a /t/-initial to an /n/-initial variant was unique, and it was significant for this at least passively literate male in that it moved his variant usage closer to written-language norms.

5.2 Establishing the Existence of Style-Related Variation

In order to plumb the dimensions of style shifting fully, fairly copious material would be needed for individual speakers, with clear changes of interlocutor, genre, topic, and/or purpose. The material I have available is moderately rich and diverse, but it has serious limitations in terms of any full-scale undertaking of that sort. More often than not I was the sole audience when recordings were made, eliminating any change of interlocutor. Tapes recorded with several speakers present, so that people were speaking more nearly among themselves than to me, are useful in terms of offering samples of very informal style. But because I worked in the same setting over many years and was generally well acquainted with the speakers, most tapes for which I was the only audience, especially after the first year or two, were nearly as likely to represent casual speech as recordings made among same-village friends. Consequently the informal end of the style spectrum is reasonably well represented in my materials, but the formal end is not.

Performance styles (storytelling and/or proverb reciting) are on record for a few speakers among my sources, but E10 was unusual in showing major stylistic change between performed material of a relatively fixed type and more routine conversation. For him, and to a lesser extent for one of his sisters, performed materials offer some insight into stylistic range. For a small number of others, interviews undertaken with speakers of other Gaelic dialects (two with fieldworker colleagues of mine and three with radio broadcasters) provide evidence of certain adaptations East Sutherlanders were inclined to make to narrow the gap between their own Gaelic and more mainstream dialects. For a few speakers, some contrast appeared over the course of very lengthy recordings or sequential recordings, with the later material growing more casual in style as the task of recording grew more comfortable. In addition, one especially frequently recorded Golspie speaker produced material in which the narrative style clearly differed according to topic and affect (Dorian 1994a). The limited effect of performance style, interlocutor, genre, and narrator's purpose and affect on personally patterned intra-speaker variation will be discussed further in chapter 5, §11, but it must be said that during my years of work on fisherfolk Gaelic I did not undertake an investigation of style as such and that nothing resembling a full-dress treatment of stylistic variation in East Sutherland Gaelic would be possible on the basis of my data.

With the weaknesses of my materials for a proper study of style duly acknowledged, however, I now can claim that these weaknesses are in one very important sense an advantage rather than a disadvantage. Precisely because the stylistic spectrum encompassed by my materials is relatively narrow, stylistic differences are an unlikely explanation for the abundant inter-speaker and intra-speaker variation to be found in those materials. Personal-pattern variation is in fact largely independent of both style and syntax, with different variants appearing in identical stylistic and syntactic environments, as will emerge in the course of this study.

6 PERSONALLY PATTERNED VARIATION IN FISHERFOLK GAELIC

In age-related variation, competing variants arise from change processes in which innovation is recognizable and movement is prompted by such familiar phenomena as negative borrowing, structural blending, and analogical leveling. In personally patterned variation, competing variants most typically arise from dialect mixing. Since different variants have an originally independent history in one north-mainland dialect area or another, it is not a straightforward matter to identify one variant as "conservative" and another as "innovative". Where younger speakers appear to be using a particular variant more frequently than their elders, there may be no familiar explanatory factor such as negative borrowing or regularization that accounts for the apparent change. Without a particular direction of change in evidence, speakers are less likely to show whole-group agreement on variant preferences and more likely to demonstrate individual patterns of variant use. In personal-pattern variation, accordingly, it is possible for very young speakers to show the same variant preferences as very senior speakers, by definition an uncommon phenomenon in age-related variation.

6.1 An Example of Personal-Pattern Variation

Four variants of the variable ('family') were in use in Embo Gaelic, no one of which was a perfect candidate for the designation "conservative" (or even "original"). Two of the four showed what might be considered a conservative final syllable, since the ending /-ax/ coincides with a historically nominative case ending, while two others showed a historically oblique final syllable /-iç/. But the forms in /-ax/ are not particularly strongly associated with older speakers, nor are the forms in /-iç/ used solely or primarily by younger speakers. The Embo variants of ('family') also include two forms with affricated initial consonant and two with unaffricated initial consonants. The latter are the more unusual in terms of dialect geography, and in this case there is an apparent preference on the part of the younger speakers for one of them, as table 3.3 indicates. (Brora and Golspie forms are omitted in this instance because this lexical item was invariant in Brora—affricated initial consonant, /-ax/ as final syllable—and had only two variants in Golspie—affricated initial consonant, either /-ax/ or /-iç/ as final syllable with inter-speaker but no intra-speaker variation—so that cross-village data are not fully comparable.)

Whereas negative borrowing played a role in the gradual decrease of locational adverb forms in Embo, it does not come into play here. Instead, it is the particular local distribution of features familiar from Gaelic dialect geography that accounts for the multiple variant forms of ('family').

Appearance of a historically oblique form as citation form is a recurrent feature of fisherfolk Gaelic, particularly of Embo Gaelic. It is found in all three villages, for example, in /fegil'/ 'fear' and /pʰuːɫiʃ/ 'pot-hook', and in Embo /strõːn'/ 'nose' and /fagiʃ/ 'near' (with the palatal final consonant reflecting a historically oblique form in each case, along with the associated front vowel in three of the

TABLE 3.3. The Embo personal-pattern variable ('family'), showing variants with and without initial affrication and with and without a historically oblique ending in the citation form

speakers		čʰ ə:rɬax				čʰ ə:rtiç				tʰ ə:rtiç				tʰ ə:rɬax		
		fr	el	tot	%	fr	el	tot	%	fr	el	tot	%	fr	el	tot	%
E4	82 m.					7	3	10	**100**								
E10	70 m.					2	4	6	**100**								
E13	[67] f.					--	1	1	33.3	--	2	2	66.6				
E14	65 f.					--	2	2	**100**								
E15	65 m.	--	2	2	**100**												
E17	64 f.	1	8	9	28.1	2	7	9	28.1	9	4	13	40.6	1	--	1	3.1
E20	58 f.	--	3	3	**100**												
E22	58 f,									--	5	5	**100**				
E23	57 m.					--	1	1									
E24	57 f.									--	11	11	**100**				
E26*	54 f.					--	1	1	9.1	4	6	10	**90.9**				
E27	54 m.	4	5	9	_50_	1	2	3	16.7	3	1	4	22.2	2	--	2	11.1
E28	51 m.					--	1	1									
E29*	50 f.	[1]	--	[1]		17	6	23	_85.2_	2	2	4	14.8				
E32*	47 m.									5	--	5	**100**				
E33	45 m.	--	1	1													
E34	45 f.	1	--	1	33.3					--	2	2	_66.7_				
E37	41 m.					--	1	1		--	1	1					
E38	40 f.					--	1	1	4.3	--	22	22	**95.7**				
E39	38 f.					1	13	14	**100**	--	[1]	[1]					
E40	36 f.					--	3	3	13.6	11	8	19	_86.4_				
E42	30 f.									6	--	6	**100**				

OFSs	
YFSs	
SSs	

Fr = free, el = elicited, tot = total, * = formerly fluent speaker. Percentages 90 and above boldfaced, other 50+ percentages underlined. Square brackets indicate a unique instance that was an echo of a previous speaker or a unique elicited variant after a prompt from another speaker; these are not included in reckoning percentages.

four cases). But how "innovative" a historically oblique form used as citation form can be considered appears to differ from case to case. The Gaelic dialect survey happens to have included both 'family' and 'nose' in their questionnaire, and while its results show that Embo's historically oblique citation form for 'family' was highly unusual, they show that Embo's historically oblique citation form of 'nose' was the norm for the entire northeast mainland region, with the non-oblique forms of Brora and Golspie representing the regional anomaly (Ó Dochartaigh 1997, vol. V: 250–51 and 314–15).

Absence of initial affrication or palatalization in an initial dental where more mainstream dialects show one or the other is likewise an occasional feature of East Sutherland fisherfolk Gaelic in other instances besides ('family'). All local Gaelic speakers showed this feature in the high-frequency interrogative /te:/ 'what?' (more commonly affricated or palatalized in other dialect areas), and Brora and Golspie speakers showed it variably in the verb /tʰilig ~ čʰilig/ 'throw' (as opposed to invariant Embo /čʰilig/). Although the Gaelic dialect survey records no forms of 'family' without either affricated or palatalized initial consonant (the lone Embo Survey source, E11 in my sample, having given a form that corresponds to /čʰə:rɬiç/), an unaffricated and unpalatialized form is attested for Easter Ross fisherfolk Gaelic just to the south, so that this appears to be a narrowly local regionalism (Ó Dochartaigh, 1997, vol. V: 832–33; Watson 2007:xxxxiv).

In terms of regionally dominant features, it seems that Embo speakers were in line with established regional dialect trends in making use of a historically oblique form as the citation form, but out of line with regional dialect trends in favoring such a form for the particular lexical item ('family'). In this instance younger Embo speakers were also moving against apparent regional dialect norms when they showed an increasing preference for a variant with an unaffricated initial dental, even though other lexical items with an unaffricated or variably affricated initial dental were already in use both locally and regionally. In a very limited sense, then, younger speakers' increased preference for the variant /tʰə:rɬiç/ might be considered innovative, but such innovation as appears in this case reflects neither English influence nor decreased knowledge of Gaelic.

6.2 Cases of Age-Related Variation and Personal-Pattern Variation Compared

Where there are multiple coexisting variants, the multiplicity can of course always give way to a simpler pattern in which one or two forms are increasingly favored, whether the variation is age-related or personally patterned. Although the historically more conservative /ax/-final forms of ('family')—at least those with initial affricate—were still in scattered use among Embo's younger fluent speakers, E27 was the youngest speaker to show a (weak) preference for them, and no one younger than E34 used them at all. And although unaffricated forms were not altogether absent among the older fluent speakers and affricated forms did not drop out of use altogether among the younger speakers, younger speakers were showing an apparently increasing preference for the unaffricated (as well as /iç/-final) variant. Rather late in this study E32* and E39 entered the speaker sample as additional relatively young sources; the former preferred the unaffricated variant, while the latter, despite her youth, preferred the affricated variant. The very different variant-use patterns shown by these two young speakers demonstrates the impossibility of predicting variant-use preferences for any given individual in personal-pattern variation. Why the majority of younger speakers in the Embo speaker sample should have shown an increasing preference for the unaffricated variant with historically oblique ending is not clear, at least to me, but an absence of such explanatory factors is as characteristic of changes in personally patterned variant use as their presence is in age-related changes in variant use.

6.2.1 Contrasting Cases Involving Analogical Regularization

More surprising than an apparently unmotivated directionality in the variant-use patterns of some personal-pattern variables, as with Embo ('family') among younger fluent speakers, is the opposite phenomenon: resistance to what would seem to be a particularly obvious opportunity for well-motivated age-related change. A striking instance of such resistance appears in the case of the variable ('wasn't/weren't'), the negated past tense of the verb 'to be'. All regular verbs and nearly all irregular verbs other than 'to be' require the presence of the preterite particle /t(ə)/ in the surface structure of the negated past tense. Introduction of the particle into the negated past tense of this verb would therefore bring ('wasn't/weren't') into line with the negated past tense of all regular verbs and most other irregular verbs. Despite the apparent attractiveness of such an analogical regularization, resistance to this development extends into the youngest reaches of the fluent speaker group and even into the semi-speaker ranks.

Cases like that of ('wasn't/weren't') are ambiguous by comparison with cases like ('family') or locational ('out'). As in the latter case, a non-traditional variant is readily identifiable; as in the latter but not the former case, an explanatory factor that might be expected to motivate a clear-cut direction of change is available. The fact that the seemingly predictable direction of change does not develop according to the prediction persuades me to consider ('wasn't/weren't') (and the somewhat similar cases of ('came') and ('saw'); see chapter 5) a case of personally patterned change rather than age-related change. To highlight the surprising features of the variable ('wasn't/weren't'), it is useful to look at the profile of variant use for this variable side by side with that of a very similar-seeming age-related variable, the first-person singular conditional. Both variables offer the attractive possibility of analogical regularization: in each case a simpler, more consistent verbal pattern could be achieved by the elimination of a grammatical feature that represents a clear irregularity.

The variable (first-person singular conditional), representing age-related variation, shows a change in progress from synthetic to analytic structure across the age-and-proficiency continuum. All the other person-and-number forms in the conditional paradigm have analytic structure: the initial consonant mutation of lenition combines with the suffix /-u/ to mark the conditional of the verb, and a free-standing personal pronoun follows to express person, for example, /xanu ʃīn'/ 'we would say' from the root /kʰan-/ 'say'. Only the first-person singular combines lenition with the suffix /-īn'/ to mark person and number as well as conditional, for example, /xanīn'/ 'I would say'. System pressure thus encourages the spread of the analytic structure into the first-person singular, and this is exactly what appeared in materials from the one Brora semi-speaker who controlled the conditional and also increasingly among the younger Embo speakers, including all of the semi-speakers.

The variable ('wasn't/weren't') is equally anomalous. Not only is 'to be' one of very few verbs for which the preterite particle /t(ə)/ is traditionally omitted in the negated past tense, but for the great majority of fisherfolk speakers the verb 'to be' itself calls for the preterite particle in other "dependent" environments (as called for by certain particles or conjunctions; see chapter 5, §9.1.3) such as the interrogative and the negative interrogative. System pressure would therefore encourage the emergence of the preterite particle in the negated past tense, too, because with the particle introduced into ('wasn't/weren't') the verb 'to be' would be brought into conformity with nearly all other verbs in dependent environments.

Table 3.4 shows the variant selection patterns for the variables (first-person singular conditional) and ('wasn't/weren't') across the age-and-proficiency continuum.

Each of the two variables has one clearly traditional variant and one clearly innovative analogical variant, making each appear to be a candidate for steadily increasing use of the innovative variant among younger speakers. This pattern pertains much more to (first-person singular conditional) than to ('wasn't/weren't'), however. Brora and Golspie fluent speakers showed little deviation from the conservative norm in either instance, though a minor scattering of innovative negated preterites with /t(ə)/ attests to the attraction of the analogical formation in that case. The only Brora semi-speaker who was able to produce verbs in the conditional showed 100 percent innovative forms for (first-person singular conditional), but only one of the three Brora semi-speakers showed 100 percent innovative forms for ('wasn't/weren't'), and one actually maintained 100 percent conservative forms without the particle. Among Embo speakers the highest retention of the conservative first-person singular inflection appears for the most part in the ranks of the older speakers, and the highest incidence of the innovative construction appears among younger speakers and semi-speakers. Only one older fluent speaker favored the innovative form,[2] but four younger fluent speakers did so and so did all five of the semi-speakers. The ('wasn't/weren't') figures for Embo speakers offer the main surprises: 100 percent maintenance of the conservative structure appears across the full age-and-proficiency continuum, with a very strong showing among younger fluent speakers, including two of the four formerly fluent speakers; one semi-speaker also shows 100 percent use of the

TABLE 3.4. Age-related and personally patterned variables with an analogically leveled variant, compared; first-person singular conditional and negated past tense of 'to be'

speaker	age-related traditional: 1 sg cond. suffix /-īn'/				age-related non-traditional: 1 sg cond. suffix /-u/ + pron. /mi/				pers. pattern traditional: wasn't/weren't /(x)a rɔ/				pers. pattern non-trad: wasn't/weren't /(x)a t rɔ/			
	fr	el	tot	%	fr	el	tot	%	fr	el	tot	%	fr	el	tot	%
B1 81 f.					--	1	1									
B2 80 m.	--	5	5	100									--	1	1	
B3 80 f.	--	31	31	91.2	--	3	3	8.8	14	32	46	100				
B4 79 f.	--	2	2	100					1	6	7	100				
B6 69 f.	--	11	11	100					--	9	9	100				
B7 66 f.	3	3	6	100					22	--	22	62.9	11	2	13	37.1
B8 57 f.	a												5	2	7	100
B9 57 f.	a								14	1	15	100				
B10 43 f.					--	6	6	100	--	2	2	50	1	1	2	50
G1 77 f.	--	7	7	100												
G2 75 f.	26	94	120	100					55	29	84	95.5	3	1	4	4.5
G3 72 m.	--	17	17	81	--	4	4	19	4	22	26	92.9	--	2	2	7.1
G4 68 f.	--	4	4	100					12	11	23	97.1	1	--	1	2.9
G5 68 m.	2	3	5	100					29	3	32	97	1	--	1	3
G6 67 f.	--	2	2	100												
G7 64 m.									--	1	1					
E3 [85] m.									3	--	3	100				
E4 82 m.	11	12	23	100					49	6	55	74.3	19	--	19	25.7
E5 77 f.	--	1	1						--	1	1					
E6 75 m.	3	8	11	91.7	--	1	1	8.3	--	2	2	25	2	4	6	75
E7 ?74 f.									4	--	4	100				
E8 ?71 f.	1	--	1													
E9 70 f.	--	11	11	91.7	--	1	1	8.3	--	2	2	100				
E10 70 m.	8	8	16	88.9	--	2	2	11.1	5	10	15	100				
E12 ?68 f.					--	1	1									
E13 [63] f.	7	1	8	80	1	1	2	20	13	5	18	94.7	1	--	1	5.3
E14 65 f.									--	3	3	100				
E15 65 m.	--	2	2	66.7	--	1	1	33.3	--	2	2	20	--	8	8	80
E17 64 f.	11	5	16	32	34	--	34	68	441	23	464	99.1	4	--	4	.9
E18* 60 f.									4	--	4	100				
E20 58 f.					--	1	1		--	8	8	100				
E21 58 f.					--	2	2	100	--	4	4	100				
E22 58 m.	8	17	25	86.2	1	4	4	13.8	12	13	25	100				
E23 57 m.	--	5	5	71.4	--	2	2	28.6					--	1	1	
E24 57 f.	--	1	1	50	--	1	1	50	1	9	10	76.9	--	3	3	23.1
E25 57 f.	--	2	2	18.2	--	9	9	81.8					--	1	1	
E26* 54 f.	6	8	14	63.6	2	6	8	36.4	88	42	130	94.2	7	1	8	5.8
E27 54 m.	11	21	32	84.2	2	4	6	15.8	88	28	116	83.5	18	5	23	16.5
E29* 50 f.					28	6	34	100	17	3	20	7.2	219	39	258	92.8
E30 49 m.	4	1	5	83.3	1	--	1	16.7	29	2	31	100				
E31 48 m.									--	1	1					
E32* 47 m.									12	--	12	100				
E33 45 m.					3	2	5	100	--	1	1	20	--	4	4	80
E34 45 f.	5	20	25	80.6	3	3	6	19.4	8	4	12	24	24	14	38	76
E36 41 m.					--	1	1		--	1	1					
E37 41 m.	1	9	10	90.9	--	1	1	9.1	1	11	12	100				
E38 40 f.					--	19	19	100	26	69	95	100	--	[1]	[1]	
E39 38 f.					2	5	7	100	29	14	43	91.5	1	3	4	8.5
E40 36 f.					42	15	57	100					94	86	180	100
E41 31 f.					--	2	2	100					--	3	3	100
E42 30 f.					--	4	4	100					127	17	144	100

OFSs	
YFSs	
SSs	

Fr = freely spoken, el = elicited, tot = total, * = formerly fluent speaker. Square brackets indicate a unique instance resulting from a sibling's prompting, omitted as otherwise non-occurrent in reckoning a percentage. Percentages in the 90–100 percent range boldfaced, other 50+ percentages underlined. [a] Brora semispeakers B8 and B9 were unable to form verbs in the conditional.

traditional structure. Only two older fluent speakers and three younger fluent speakers (including one formerly fluent speaker) favored the innovative structure, along with three of the five semi-speakers.

In theory the analogical form of ('wasn't/weren't') would seem just as irresistibly attractive as the analogical form of the first-person singular conditional, and the fact that two Embo older fluent speakers actually favored this innovative form (while only one favored the innovative conditional form) attests to the strength of system pressure in that direction. But if we compare the usage of the two younger speaker groups in each case, we find that nine speakers out of twenty-one for whom a percentage of use could be reckoned used no innovative negated past tense forms of 'to be' at all, whereas *none* of the eighteen comparable speakers for whom a percentage of use could be reckoned proved wholly resistant to innovative forms of the first-person singular conditional.

6.2.2 A Single Variable Demonstrating Both Age-Related and Personal-Pattern Variation

A particularly useful demonstration of the distinction between age-related variation and personal-pattern variation is to be found in connection with the variable locational ('out'), with Embo variants /mwĩ/ and /mwĩç/. This variable was introduced in chapter 1 as an illustration of within-the-village variation that speakers seemed not to notice, even when they interacted constantly in Gaelic, as the Embo sister and brother who were next-door neighbors did, and mentioned again as an advanced case of age-related change in §4.1 in this chapter. Age-related change affected the *incidence* of this variable greatly, because the ongoing loss of a distinction between locational and directional adverbs was reducing the number of Embo speakers who made any use at all of the variable locational ('out'). But for those who did still use the locational form of ('out'), both variants of ('out') remained in use across the available Embo age-and-proficiency continuum. In fact, the variant preferences of the oldest speaker and the youngest speaker were identical—not a likely variant-preference distribution for an age-related variable. (See table 5.24 in chapter 5 for a full display of variant use for ('out').)

6.3 Age-Related and Personally Patterned Variation Compared: Summary

In age-related variation both the effect of Gaelic-English bilingualism and the effect of the recessive state of the local Gaelic are in evidence. The features in connection with which age-related variation appeared were typically features without a match in English (locational versus directional forms of adverbs, conditional verb inflection for person), and the speakers in whose lives English had played the largest role (formerly fluent speakers and semi-speakers) were particularly likely to make use of innovative structures. Individual speakers might be out of line in the progressive spread of an innovative age-related change: the relatively young speakers E27, E30, E34, and especially E37 were quite conservative in their relatively persistent use of the synthetic first-person singular conditional inflection, for example. But direction of change away from the traditional variants was clear overall, and the formerly fluent speakers and the semi-speakers showed quite pronounced use of the innovative variant: the formerly fluent speaker E32* was the only member of either of these speaker groups to have shown so much as 67 percent use of the traditional variant of either of the age-related variants presented here.

By contrast, the role of English in personal-pattern variation is negligible. The issue of negative borrowing does not arise in the same direct sense, for example. One might argue that the absence of an array of comparably distinctive variants for English *family* exerts some pressure toward reduction of variants for Gaelic ('family'), but in view of the lack of even the slightest phonological similarity between the lexical items in the two languages any such pressure would be indirect indeed. "Traditional" usage is not as clear-cut in most personal-pattern variation as it is in age-related variation. The most obviously conservative variants of ('family'), those in /-ax/, were not associated with the oldest Embo speakers, for example, and did not therefore constitute a convincing "conservative" model for the variable. Even where a personal-pattern variable offers the possibility of an analogical leveling very much like the leveling often seen in Embo's age-related variation, neither system pressure nor the speakers' bilingualism produces the clear directionality typical of age-related variation: some of the clearly English-dominant formerly fluent speakers, and even one of the semi-speakers, made use of the traditional, non-analogical variant of ('wasn't/weren't') at the 100 percent level.

6.4 The Idiosyncratic Variant-Use Patterns of a Key Embo Sibling Pair

The close-in-age sister and brother who were living next door to one another when I began to work in Embo in the early 1960s were key figures in forcing me to confront the nature and extent of idiosyncratic variant use. Because this pair, plus the siblings of the brother's wife, appear repeatedly in this study, they are given pseudonyms, as are members of other key family-based networks. I had worked with the sister, Elspeth (E22), and with the brother's wife, Lexie (E34), during my initial fieldwork year, but Murdo himself (E27) first entered my pool of sources during a second field trip in 1965. The family profile of Elspeth and Murdo was unusual in several respects that made their sometimes sharply different usage especially surprising. A fisherfolk family with only two children was very uncommon when they were born, in 1912 and 1916, respectively, but there were no other siblings in this case. Both of them had married fellow Embo Gaelic speakers, the sister twice over, since she married a second Embo Gaelic speaker after being widowed. They had also stayed in the home village all their lives, apart from some intermittent migratory work experience (in the herring fishery for Elspeth and in construction work for Murdo). When I met them in the 1960s, and over the more than three decades that each of them survived after that time, they lived in the separate halves of a two-family house with inner dividing wall, interacting on a regular basis. By the time they were young adults, the conservative pattern they had each followed in marrying endogamously and settling for the modest economic rewards likely to be available in East Sutherland was no longer to be taken for granted, and in these social respects each of them had made consistently traditional choices.

The customary language of interaction between these siblings was Gaelic. In terms of age and proficiency, both of them fell into the younger fluent speaker (YFS) category. Despite a small-family background, a small difference in age, a thoroughly local life pattern, and long-continued use of Gaelic between them, the two showed what seemed to me a remarkable set of differences in their Gaelic usage. A number of the items on which they differed were common words that were used often enough to make them very conspicuous, at least to anyone whose business it was to study Embo Gaelic. It was also striking that the items in question did not fall into any one or two structural categories. On the contrary, they included a conjunction, two adverbs, two irregular-verb past tense forms, a noun, a preposition, and the appearance or non-appearance of a grammatically significant particle.

6.4.1 Variables for Which the Siblings Favored Different Variants

The following are some of the variables on which Elspeth and Murdo differed as to which variant they typically used, in addition to their different forms of locational ('out'), already instanced earlier. For conjunctional ('when'), Elspeth overwhelmingly favored /tə/, while Murdo equally strongly favored /nərə, nu(ə)rə/, or /nə/. Elspeth used /stɛ/ almost exclusively for adverbial ('in') in her conversational Gaelic, whereas Murdo heavily favored /sčax/ in his. He used the form /sčɛ/ very occasionally as well, but he only once used the form /stɛ/ that Elspeth regularly used in conversation. Elspeth favored a monosyllabic form of the irregular past tense ('came'), /hã:n/, though she used the conservative disyllabic form as well, /hã:nig/, and she used both disyllabic and monosyllabic forms of the irregular past tense ('saw') (/hũnig/, /hũn/). Murdo used only the disyllabic form of ('saw'), and he heavily favored the disyllabic form of ('came'). Elspeth used the form /tʰə:rłiç/ for ('family') (though for this word only elicited forms are available for her); Murdo used four different forms of the same word in his freely spoken materials, but among them he favored /čʰə:rłax/, a form that Elspeth did not produce. Though they shared two variants of ('along with'), each used at least one variant that the other did not. Murdo's freely spoken and elicited negated past tense forms of the verb 'to be' included a fair number that had the analogically introduced preterite particle. Elspeth used no analogical forms with preterite particle at all.

None of the forms on which the siblings differed was out of line with Embo Gaelic generally, since the forms that each used were also used by other Embo Gaelic speakers. Although Elspeth was older than Murdo, the variant choices she favored were not necessarily those favored by senior siblings in other Embo families. Neither was it the case that Elspeth's variant choices were simply those of a female Embo speaker and Murdo's those of a male Embo speaker, since in most cases of inter-speaker variation the use of certain variants as opposed to others did not show any reliable correlation with the sex of the speaker. Age and sex combined also failed to account for the differences: it was not the case that any female within a few years of Elspeth's age would prove to share her variant choices, or that any males within a few years of Murdo's age would prove to share his.

In many Embo families, the siblings still in the village represented only one or two scattered points along a larger age continuum of siblings, quite a few of whom were unavailable to me because of emigration or early death. If the siblings still in the village differed on the variants they used, it was possible that something like a linked chain of variant choice had prevailed among the full sibling set and the absence of some of the siblings was preventing the linked chain from emerging. It was also often true that the oldest children in a large family had already finished school and left Sutherland in search of work by the time the youngest children came along, so that the considerable age difference among siblings, together with lack of extended personal contact, might explain some differences in variant usage. The importance of Elspeth and Murdo lay in the facts that there were no missing siblings and there was also no large age gap. They had grown up as the only children in the household, just four years apart in age, and yet their variant choices were sometimes startlingly different. Occasionally I asked them whether they had noticed that they weren't saying quite the same thing, when each of them produced a translation for one of my test sentences and the translations did not coincide. They nearly always replied with some surprise that they hadn't. In the case of their different renderings of the locational adverb ('out'), they seemed to have a hard time hearing the difference when I pointed it out. I found this extraordinary, since to me the forms were blatantly different.

Nothing in my professional training suggested an explanation for variation within the closest of kin relationships and without any obvious social explanations in terms of age, sex, education, socioeconomic background, or ethnic group, but my professional training did persuade me to record it and report on it (especially where grammatical forms were concerned) when I produced a descriptive study of East Sutherland fisherfolk Gaelic some years later. Echoes of my own surprise at finding conspicuous differences between the forms used by high-interaction, close-in-age relatives have proven to be a recurrent feature in linguists' accounts of high levels of variation in homogeneous populations. In the long run, encountering that surprise has been a useful indicator of the presence of personal-pattern–like variation in other similarly constituted social settings (see chapter 6, §1).

6.5 Establishing the Existence of Personally Patterned Variation

As with the investigation of stylistic variation, adequate investigation of idiosyn-cratic inter-speaker and intra-speaker variation in fisherfolk Gaelic requires a large and varied database. Because this variation is by definition an individual matter, in fact, a thoroughgoing investigation would require large amounts of both freely spoken and elicited data for every speaker in a given village. Only then could one expect to gain a reasonably complete picture of variability of this sort, giving due consideration to speakers' ages, proficiency, and sex, and to stylistic factors, possible interlocutor effects, social networks, and possible linguistic changes in progress. Not surprisingly, I do not have such thoroughgoing, fully comprehensive data.

For my earliest descriptive and dialect-geographical work, a handful of good sources from each of the villages was sufficient to provide a solid account. For subsequent work on language change, the relatively broad age range of sources available in Embo village was essential. For the individually patterned variation that I ultimately wanted to study, my speaker pool, though reasonably good-sized by general fieldwork standards, had serious shortcomings. For Brora and Golspie, the speaker pool was simply not large enough, even though the seven sources I worked with in each of those two villages constituted 16 percent and 13 percent, respectively, of their entire 1964 Gaelic-speaking populations. There were also too few Brora and Golspie families in which multiple siblings were still available, making it impossible to get a good sense of usage within original nuclear house-holds. In Embo there were plenty of speakers available at the start of my work, and there were at that time still a number of good-sized families in which multiple sib-lings were represented, and even a few parent–child pairs in which both parent and child were fully fluent speakers. I could not foresee the need to recruit my sources along such lines, however, nor anticipate just which linguistic items or structures would prove to be variable in the idiosyncratic, personal-pattern fashion. Sibling sets were not taken to be a central locus of speaker variation at that time, and in any case I would not have known at that early stage what forms I needed to be tracking, since awareness of the variables that showed individual patterns of variation was something acquired only gradually, through slowly accumulating experience. I do consider it certain, however, that I would have identified still more such variability in the 1990s and after, with my attention fully focused by then on the issue of inter- and intra-speaker variation, if the pool of Embo speakers had not been so sharply and sadly dwindling just as I began to be able to work intensively on Embo Gaelic again and gather additional material. Even with the handicaps of long-distance work and a much reduced speaker pool, in fact, heightened awareness of person-ally patterned variation as a pervasive feature of East Sutherland fisherfolk Gaelic led me to recognize a number of variables that I had not previously tracked.[3]

Social factors related to the history of the fishing villages also played a role in skewing my speaker sample. Generally speaking, but most especially in Embo's more isolated fisherfolk population, older women were less self-confident in dealing with outsiders than were older men, many of whom had gained considerable experience of the English-speaking world by serving in the military during World War I. Relatively few of the oldest Embo women were initially comfortable confronting a question-asking outsider, and since elderly men happened to be plentiful in Embo, their greater initial ease with the undertaking led to their becoming overrepresented in my speaker sample. As a result, lack of enough material (most especially freely spoken material) from older Embo women makes it difficult in some cases to rule out gender as a factor in variant choice, though other cases in which gender is clearly not a significant factor at least make it evident that gender is not routinely important to variant choice.

7 THE CHALLENGES OF INVESTIGATING PERSONALLY PATTERNED VARIATION IN THE FISHERFOLK COMMUNITIES

Two major challenges faced anyone who might propose to investigate idiosyncratic inter-speaker and intra-speaker variation in East Sutherland fisherfolk Gaelic: assembling a large enough corpus to allow the full range of individual variation to emerge for at least a fair sampling of speakers, and establishing with a reasonable degree of certainty that most of the variation so prominent within a given village was not socially evaluated by community members. My attempts to meet these challenges are discussed in the next sections.

7.1 Assembling a More Adequate Database

Though I began to recognize the potential importance of personally patterned variation within these communities in the early 1980s, that decade was virtually lost to me for research purposes as a result of severe health problems. In the 1990s, though I was still unable to undertake field trips to Scotland, research possibilities opened up again thanks to the great increase in private telephones in the northern Highlands and likewise in the ownership of tape recorders. By this time, only Embo had any fully fluent speakers of fisherfolk Gaelic remaining; some semi-speakers or formerly fluent speakers remained in Brora and Golspie, but neither village had more than a thin scattering of speakers even at those proficiency levels. Because of the more positive situation in Embo, I was able to send letter-tapes to friends there and receive similar tapes in return, and even send out for responses by tape elicitation tasks that now concentrated on variables that showed personally patterned variation. Several exceptionally good-hearted siblings in one Embo family went around the village making recordings on my behalf, both with those of my long-established sources who remained and with other speakers whom I had long known but with whom I had seldom or never done linguistic work.

A generous colleague who had worked among Easter Ross fisherfolk to the south of Embo, Dr. Seòsamh Watson, began to pay visits to Embo, too, on my behalf and his own, sharing the resulting tapes with me.

Most important, I began to make phone calls to a number of my long-term Embo sources beginning in 1994 to record (with their permission) our general Gaelic conversation. In that way I gained a good corpus of conversational data for four of the five old friends with whom I spoke, and for a sixth individual as well, a returned-from-exile sister to two of the others. The same set of six speakers also supplied a fair amount of elicited material over the phone. In 1987, furthermore, the youngest active Embo Gaelic speaker, a low-proficiency semi-speaker from the London-Embo exile community, began a series of visits to me in the United States, a happy custom terminated only by her sudden and very premature death in 1999. On three of her six visits, a passive-bilingual cousin accompanied her. Both the semi-speaker friend and her passive-bilingual cousin did elicitation work with me, the former a great deal and the latter a very modest amount. The semi-speaker, an eager speaker deeply attached to her Embo heritage, also undertook a number of extensive interviews in Gaelic. The passive bilingual cheerfully undertook what was within her capacity, namely, an extended linguistically asymmetrical interview during which I spoke East Sutherland Gaelic and she spoke English. In 1998, a high-proficiency Embo semi-speaker came for a visit, in this case one of my telephone conversation partners, and again I had a chance to pursue some additional matters, especially a few aspects of her grammar that involved phonetic detail somewhat difficult to check on by phone.[4]

As the possibility of creating a more adequate database emerged, I went back to my field materials from the 1960s and 1970s and scoured them more thoroughly for freely spoken material I might previously have overlooked, as well as for any relevant elicited data I might have missed. There was a fair bit of both.[5] The additional freely spoken material included short direct quotes entered here and there in the margins of field notebooks; parenthetic conversational remarks in the midst of taped elicitation material that friends had sent me during the winter when I was writing my dissertation; Gaelic asides during supposedly English-language interviews I had taped in those earlier decades; a good deal of incidental Gaelic material in extensive oral-history taping sessions; and even a fairly extensive Gaelic interview recorded by a fieldwork colleague with one of my Golspie sources after he had finished asking oral history–related questions on my behalf. These materials frequently provided important instances of a variable I was either newly interested in or trying to document more fully.

7.2 Establishing Lack of Social Weighting in Connection with Individual Variant Selections

The absence of any social weighting attached to differences in variant choice is, above all else, what distinguishes the idiosyncratic variation exhibited by the socioeconomically unstratified minority-language speakers of the East Sutherland fisherfolk communities from the individual variation exhibited by socially stratified speakers of standardized languages in New York City (Labov 1966), Montreal (Sankoff and Sankoff 1973), Norwich (Trudgill 1974), and so forth. In stratified, standardized-language settings such as these urban centers, any variant a speaker uses is inevitably set against norms created by the process of standardization and contrasted with forms used by speakers from different social classes. Variants that do not coincide with standard-language usage are devalued, as are the class-differentiated speakers who use them frequently. In his Lower East Side study, accordingly, Labov was able to demonstrate a powerful linkage between stylistic variation and social variation. Certain variants were considered better, or more correct, than others by most New Yorkers; they shifted toward those variants in formal styles; and those favored variants were likewise the variants used in *all* styles by New Yorkers who ranked high on an objective socioeconomic scale (Labov 1966:405). Since the variables investigated consisted of the phonetic realization of phonemes, Labov was able to devise lively reading passages that featured a particular variable and present them in various renditions that speakers could evaluate in social terms (the subjective evaluation test). The results of these tests indicated that the speech community as a whole shared common perceptions of the social significance attached to various realizations of the phonological variables (1966:450).

The absence of occupational diversity and social stratification, together with an absence of community-external Gaelic-language norms, created within the homogeneous East Sutherland fishing villages a very different sort of social environment for Gaelic (though not for English; see chapter 1, §3.1). In this isolated and classless setting, idiosyncratic variant-use choices for Gaelic variables evoked almost no social judgments at all. (For the one exception, see §7.2.5.) Within the fishing-village communities there was no higher social stratum whose Gaelic usage was admired and favored, there were no highly educated local speakers who could serve reliably as models of "proper" Gaelic speech, and there was of course no reading style for the unwritten local vernacular. Differences in the phonological realization of phonemes were surprisingly few,[6] but even the acoustically quite salient differences that appeared in the phonemic make-up of various lexical items within each village did not call forth contrasting social evaluations.

Making a claim of neutral social value for the variants of nearly all personal-pattern variables in East Sutherland fisherfolk Gaelic confronts the investigator with the difficult challenge of proving the *non*-existence of something—social evaluations—rather than the existence of something. Fortunately a number of arresting indications are available to demonstrate that people in these originally homogeneous communities generally did not make social judgments in response to different variant selections in their local vernacular. I introduce these sources of evidence here for their cumulative as well as their individual value.

7.2.1 Evidence from Apparent Unawareness of Alternative Forms

There was, to begin with, the seeming unawareness of inter-speaker variation within a given village (Embo /mwĩç/ versus /mwĩ/, Golspie /kɛruax/ versus /kɛrəvax/), even when the speakers using different variants of these variables were, as in these two cases, in constant verbal contact (the Embo sister and brother and the Golspie wife and husband, respectively).

One factor that might be supposed to account for community members' apparent lack of awareness is the structural level of some of the variable items. A number of personally patterned variables are free-standing lexical items such as nouns or adjectives, and a few involve free-standing irregular verb forms. The free-standing lexical status and grammatical independence of these variables might conceivably give them a certain salience for speakers, and the same might be supposed in the case of several adverbs among the variables. But many of the items that show within-the-village individual-speaker variation are function words or other elements that fall into grammatical classes with typically low salience for speakers (cf. Silverstein 1981 on "the limits of awareness"): several conjunctions and prepositions, a few syntactic structures involving particles, and a good many alternations involving initial consonants ("consonant mutations", a distinctive and pervasive feature of the Celtic languages).[7] Most ordinary speakers in any speech community lack an adequate metalanguage for talking about language, making it difficult for them to conceptualize grammatical features for which they lack names. When the speaker population is illiterate in their own language, this problem is compounded. The few speakers of East Sutherland Gaelic who tried to talk with me about Gaelic structure usually did so in terms of English grammar, since that was the only kind they had ever been taught. But mostly people made comparisons between Gaelic and English in terms of "words for things" that were available in one language but not the other, those being the differences that struck them most and could most easily be spoken about (see Hinskens 1996:240). It might reasonably be supposed that they faced similar problems in recognizing differences between forms where personal-pattern variants were concerned—that is, they might recognize the different variants of free-standing nouns like ('sand'), ('family'), and ('potato') but fail to notice the variants of the prepositions ('along with') or ('from, off, of'), or, still more understandably, the initial consonant alternations of the variable demonstrative ('that'), /ʃɔ̃n/ ~ /hɔ̃n/. The problem with this explanation is twofold. In the first place, as was demonstrated by the Golspie husband who ignored the ('sand') variant /kɛrəvax/ despite using it himself, people generally took no notice of within-the-village variation even in connection with free-standing elements like nouns. And in the second place, they were not at all unaware of grammatical variation, provided the variation was *geographically* based.

Where the first kind of evidence is concerned, the Golspie speaker who failed to mention within-the-village variation for ('sand') while pointing to cross-village variation for the same word did so in more than one case. Some years earlier he had volunteered the information that Embo speakers said /mədaːtʰ/ for 'potato', and again he was quite correct in identifying an Embo form that Golspie did not share. Yet while making a point of Golspie versus Embo variation with regard to ('potato'), he once again failed to mention the fact that Golspie speakers themselves used two different forms of the word, /mətʰaːtʰ/ and /pətʰaːtʰ/.

Where the second kind of evidence is concerned, the stereotyping so typical of volunteered discussions about cross-village variation was not apparent in speakers' reactions to *actual* cross-village usage. Speakers' volunteered examples of cross-village variables did indeed consist almost entirely of free-standing nouns and adjectives. But though they did not bring them up spontaneously as stereotypes, people responded unhesitatingly and accurately when confronted with other-village grammatical structures. An Embo speaker immediately noticed and commented on my use (with Golspie usages dominating in my speech at the time) of the particle /tə/ after /tuɫ/ 'going' in the construction 'going to' + verb complement; Embo Gaelic uses the particle /ə/ rather than /tə/ in the same construction. In similar fashion a Brora community member reacted sharply to the "Embo" use of a particle and the buffering consonant it produces in the phrase 'pleased to see you', where Brora speakers used no particle and no buffer consonant: Brora /ʃiːçiǰ ɛkən u/, Embo /ʃiːčʰ ə y ɛkən u, 'pleased to see you'/ (with geographically based variants of 'pleased'—Brora /ʃiːçiǰ/, Embo /ʃiːčʰ/— introducing the verb complement). The Brora speaker rejected as unacceptably "Embo" the possibility of /*ʃiːçiǰ ə y ɛkən u/).

Since speakers are quite capable of explicit and strong reactions to grammatical structures when geographically based (cross-village) variation is at issue, the fact that many of the personally patterned, within-the-village variables involve grammatical structures and function words does not make a convincing explanation for speakers' lack of reaction in this latter case.

7.2.2 Evidence from Dyadic Conversational Material: Repetitions Using Different Variants

Dyadic conversational material provided additional evidence. In conversational interactions, speakers who repeated all or part of what another speaker had just said sometimes replaced the original speaker's variant choice with a different variant choice of their own. These substitutions appeared to be quite unconscious. Prosodic features in such cases did not indicate any intention on the repeater's part of making a correction to the original speaker's version, and the original speaker never made any objection or indeed gave any indication that the substitution had been noticed. In one instance, for example, Embo husband Murdo (E27) strongly endorsed his wife (E34) Lexie's opinion of a village character from their young days, and in doing so he repeated the sentence she had just said. But his repetition substituted his own version of the variable ('from, off, of') for hers:

Wife (Lexie): /tɔ̃n´ tʰrikal ə v ãũn č̆ɛ p_____./
Husband (Murdo): /o:, ʃ e tɔ̃n´ tʰrikal ə v ãũn tə p____./

Lexie: '[It's] a sly man that was in it OF B____', i.e., 'B____ was a sly man.'
Murdo: 'Oh, it's a sly man that was in it OF B____', i.e., 'Oh, B____
        was a sly man.'

In another instance two Embo friends, E13 (Flora) and E22 (Elspeth), discussed how one of Flora's family members was spending her days:

Flora (E13): /s ãũn kʰɔ̃:ɫə ri [tu:aɫ] s a:viʃ či vi./
Elspeth (E22): /ɔx, wɛl, xɔ fad s ha i kʰɔ̃nri [tu:aɫ], ha u kʰom./

Flora: 'It's WITH [Dugald] she usually is.'
Elspeth: 'Och, well, so long as she's WITH [Dugald], you don't mind'
        (i.e., 'that's fine').

As a further example, two Embo sisters, both high-proficiency semi-speakers, each in succession made the same comment in the process of video-taping for me the view from a window in another sister's house. Each used her own variant of the variable that headed the clause, the demonstrative ('that'):

First sister (E38): /hɔ̃n ə vyu./
Second sister (E40): /nĩʃ, ʃɔ̃n ə vyu ɛs ə—n ĩn´ag./

First sister: 'THAT['s] the view.'
Second sister: 'Now, THAT['s] the view out of the—window.'

In the first of these cases, the husband and wife were the only people present. They were making the recording, a lengthy reminiscence about the Embo of their young days, as a gift for me, but they were past the slight awkwardness of starting a tape-recording and well into their absorbing subject before they reached the passage cited. In the second case, there were six people present and again the recording session was well under way; the speakers were by this point speaking at least as much to each other as to me. In the third case, there were three other people present, namely, the other Gaelic-speaking sister and her monolingual son and daughter-in-law; the interaction was lively and the focus of attention was the filming rather than what was being said. In none of the three cases was there any reason to suppose that the second speaker was trying to put the first speaker right or otherwise promote a different variant choice. Rather, each speaker was simply using her or his favored variant, and no apparent notice was taken of the differences.[8] This indifference to variability, while typical of nearly all personal-pattern variation, does not extend to all cases of variable speech behavior. See §7.2.5 and

7.2.6 for contrasting cases indicating that people are by no means always so unresponsive to their interlocutors' speech patterns.

7.2.3 Evidence from Intra-Speaker Variant Alternation

A third source of evidence is offered by speakers' own unconstrained alternation between variants in cases where the variants follow one another in quick succession, even though there has been no apparent change in topic, audience, affect, or general syntactic environment.

At my request, E22 (Elspeth) described some of the games that Embo children had played in her childhood while I recorded her account. She briefly described three games in rapid succession, and as she concluded each description she produced a closing formula: 'That/this is [name of game] (for you)'. In two instances she then added a little more information about the game and produced the closing formula once again, so that there are five instances of her concluding formula in all, spoken within a matter of a few minutes.

1. /ʃɔ̃n ad marəgi torlax./
2. /agəs hɔ̃n marəgi torlax./
3. /agəs hu ad kʰĩn′arn:./
4. /agəs ʃɔ̃n ad kʰĩn′arn:./
5. /s hɔ̃n ad tikʰ takʰ er nəh ĩn′agən ig nə ʃũ:n xre:tarn:./

1. 'THAT's Margaidh Dollach for you.'
2. 'And THAT's Margaidh Dollach.'
3. 'And this is Cinnearn'n for you.'
4. 'And THAT's Cinnearn'n for you.'
5. 'And THAT's Dioc-Dac on the windows of the old folks for you.'

Apart from one instance in which she used a form of 'this' instead of 'that', all of the formulas included the demonstrative ('that'), usually with the personalizing prepositional form /ad/ 'at-you' added. This is the same variable on whose variants the two semi-speaker sisters differed in the preceding example. Although in this case only a single speaker is involved, the variation is just as conspicuous. Variation in the use of the two variants is also as typical of Elspeth as a speaker as the decided preference for one particular variant is for each of the semi-speaker sisters. Whereas E40 used just over 97 percent /ʃɔ̃n/ in eighty-five freely spoken and elicited instances of the variable, and her sister E38 used just over 89 percent /hɔ̃n/ in her fifty-six instances, Elspeth used 58.3 percent /ʃɔ̃n/ (seven instances) and 41.7 percent /hɔ̃n/ (five instances) in her twelve examples of ('that') overall. The mixture of /ʃɔ̃n/ and /hɔ̃n/ in her four closing formulas is therefore consonant with her general pattern of variant use for this variable.

7.2.4 Evidence from Traditional Material

A fourth source of evidence was traditional material such as proverbs, sayings connected with folk beliefs, and children's rhymes or other ditties. Originally I had not expected to be able to consider such material "freely spoken" for purposes of variant documentation, because I assumed that it would appear in fixed form, with all speakers giving identical or nearly identical renditions. But as it turned out, speakers used their own favored variants in these traditional materials, too.

A well-known proverb supplied by three different Embo speakers included two personally patterned variables, conjunctional ('when') and adverbial ('in'). Each of the three speakers used different variants in this one familiar saying, 'WHEN hunger/want comes IN (at) the door, love goes out (at) the window':

> E10: /**nuərə** hig ən d akərəs ə **stɛ** er ən darəs, he:ǰ ə gə:ɬ ə max ən´ĩn´ag./
> E17: /**tənə** hig ə xɔrʃtʰ ə **sčax** er ə darəs, [he:ǰ] ə xə:rl ə max er ən ĩn´ag./
> E40: /**tə** hig ə d akərəs **sčɛ** darəs, he:ǰ ə xə:rl max ən´ĩn´ag./

The three speakers show small grammatical differences in their renditions as well (including E10's anomalous rendering of 'love' /kə:(r)ɬ/ as a masculine noun; E17 and E40 render the same noun more traditionally as a feminine, the initial consonant mutations indicating gender in each instance), but apart from E17's choice of /kɔrʃtʰ/ 'want' in place of /akərəs/ 'hunger' the most obvious differences lie in the variable forms of ('when') and ('in').

In the case of a little ditty that various Embo speakers recited, two of the ditty's four lines featured first the variable conjunctional ('when') and then the variable past tense ('saw'), both of which can appear in either monosyllabic or disyllabic form. Three Embo older fluent speakers offered their versions of the ditty, one of them twice. Style shifter E10 and his slightly younger sister, E13, offered identical versions, both of them using /nuərə/ twice and /hũnig/ twice in the four relevant lines. E17, nearly as rich in traditional lore as E10, gave her version of the ditty twice; she had omitted the second line on her first attempt and, evidently sensing that her rendition was not quite on target, she produced it again. She used the variant /tə/, one of the two she favored generally, in all four instances of ('when'), but she varied considerably on ('saw'), even though she made her second attempt within minutes of the first attempt. She used two disyllabic versions of ('saw') the first time, but the first was a much less common disyllabic variant without the final consonant (/hũnə/),[9] while the second was /hũnig/. In her second rendition she used first a monosyllabic variant /hurn/ and then the variant /hũnə/ again.

In sum, personally patterned variation is very nearly as typical of traditional material as it is of general conversational material, quite apart from the conspicuous style shifting of a performance specialist such as E10 (see §5.1).

7.2.5 Evidence from Responses to One Pair
of Socially Weighted Variants

Convincing evidence of the socially neutral status of most idiosyncratic intra-village and intra-speaker variant use comes from the very different response evoked by the one variable certain of whose variants actually *do* carry strong social weighting, at least for some speakers. The very high-frequency gerund-forming suffixes /-u/ and /-al/ were not negatively weighted in and of themselves, but their analogical extension to verbs that traditionally had gerunds formed by other suffixes (or by some process other than suffixation) was. Not all speakers were critical of the analogical formations, but among older fluent speakers and younger fluent speakers alike some individuals strongly condemned any speaker whom they heard saying, for example, /kʰəi:l´u/ or /kʰəi:l´al/ 'losing' (that is, root /kʰəi:l´/ 'lose' + gerund allomorphs /-u/ or /-al/) instead of conservative /kʰəu:ł/ with internal vowel change plus final consonant change.[10] A high-proficiency semi-speaker who regularly formed the gerund of the verb /kʰan/ 'say' with /-u/ rather than the traditional allomorph /-tən/ was the subject of much negative comment from her elders, younger as well as older fluent speakers. She was aware of this and claimed that she persisted in this habit partly for the pleasure of scandalizing more conservative speakers. More indignation about careless speech habits seemed to attach to analogical use of /-u/ than to analogical use of /-al/, perhaps because East Sutherland Gaelic was already famous for the ubiquity of its /-u/ endings: where words in more mainstream Gaelic dialects have word-final /-əɣ/ or /-əv/, East Sutherland Gaelic has /-u/, and since such words are legion, East Sutherland's Gaelic seems to non-local ears to consist stereotypically of words ending in /-u/.

Some gerund-formation purists also expressed disapproval of a very wide-spread re-formation affecting the substantial class of verbs with roots ending in /-iç/, the gerunds of which were traditionally formed by internal vowel change and final consonant change, giving a gerund in /-ax/. The root /furiç/ 'wait, stay, live', for example, had a traditional gerund /furax/; but for quite a number of speakers it had developed an alternative gerund /furiçal/, formed by suffixing /-al/ to the unaltered root. Although the gerund-formation purists claimed that these offenses against conservative usage were typical of younger speakers (believed them to be purely age-related variation, that is), even my earliest observations of actual speech habits indicated that it was a very rare older speaker who did not make use of non-traditional gerund formations him- or herself. E4, eighty-two years of age in 1970 and the oldest Embo speaker for whom I have extensive freely spoken texts, produced eight instances of /furiçal/ and only one of /furax/, for example, and for another verb of this class, /kʰyɔ̃rniç/ 'buy', he produced two traditional gerunds in /-ax/ but three innovative ones in /-içal/.

The analogical variants of this variable were indeed recognizably innovative, like negated past tense forms of ('wasn't/weren't') that included the preterite particle /t(ə)/, but as in that case, use of the analogical forms did not correspond as predictably as might have been expected to the speaker's age, except that the semi-speakers showed a strong tendency to form most of the variable gerunds along analogical lines. Gerund formation was an area of considerable idiosyncrasy in fisherfolk Gaelic, with individual speakers differing as to which particular set of verbal roots they made into gerunds via which suffix (and/or other process), either regularly or variably. The same was true to a lesser extent of noun plural formation, with high-frequency plural suffixes analogically extended to various nouns whose plurals were traditionally formed by other suffixes or by non-suffixing processes; but idiosyncrasy with regard to plural formation did not attract comparable attention or censure. That is to say, this one curious outcropping of purism among speakers of fisherfolk Gaelic was as eccentric in its specificity as linguistic purism usually is.

The strength of the censure evoked in this one case is very useful, however, in that it highlights more sharply than anything else could the total absence of social judgments in the many other cases of personal-pattern variation and even in most cases of age-related variation, including other analogical reformations such as the first-person-singular conditional (/-u mi/ for /-ĩn′/; see §6.2.1). In the example cited in §7.2.2, Lexie showed no reaction whatever when her husband repeated her comment about the "sly man" almost word for word but substituted his own variant /tə/ ('from, off, of') for her variant /čɛ/. By contrast, she reacted very strongly when she heard him give an analogically formed gerund one evening in response to a translation task. I had asked for the Gaelic for 'They might leave', to which he replied /fə:dəs aĭ fa:gu/, giving the gerund for /fa:g-/ 'leave' the suffix /-u/ in place of the /-al/ that was traditional for this verb's gerund (/fa:gal/). Even though this was only a substitution of /-u/ for /-al/, rather than the more stigmatized /-u/ for /-tən/, /-ax/, internal vowel change, and so on, Lexie reacted with surprise and disapproval. Her immediate remark, made in English and sharply enough to cause me to write it verbatim in the margin of the notebook page, was "It's not often *you* say /fa:gu/, [Murdo]!" Both husband and wife were younger fluent speakers, and she was the younger of the two by a little more than eight years. Still, puristic censure of analogical gerund formation was clearly alive and well in Lexie's case, despite her relative youth.

7.2.6 Evidence from Reaction to Gratuitous English Loanwords

Reaction to gratuitous English loanwords offered another contrast with lack of reaction to most intra-village personal-pattern variation. Self-consciousness about loanwords was so strong that it could actually interrupt conversational interaction. Contrasting Lexie's sharp reaction to Murdo's use of /fa:gu/ with her lack of reaction to his use of /tə/ in place of her own /čɛ/, it might be supposed that her negative response to the analogical gerund was provoked by its appearance in an elicitation session, highlighting Murdo's usage, whereas their ongoing conversational interaction inhibited any potential response to the difference between her usage and his in the case of the reminiscence about the "sly man". But negative reactions to the gratuitous use of English loanwords or short English phrases in an otherwise Gaelic interaction demonstrate clearly that interactional constraints (level of formality or informality, the need for politeness, the need to display mutual attentiveness) did not deter Embo speakers from displaying negative responses if the offense was one that was significant for this speaker community.

Early in 1965, while I was back in the United States writing my dissertation, Flora (E13), Elspeth (E22), and Lexie (E34) put a great many phonologically contrastive words and phrases onto tape for me at my request; after finishing that task, they settled down to a lengthy interaction in Gaelic, which they also recorded. Several additional speakers were present to whom I will also give pseudonyms, since they constitute another important social-network grouping: older fluent speaker E3 (Dugald), husband to E13 (Flora); younger fluent speaker E24 (Una), younger sister to Flora; and formerly fluent speaker E18* (Eilidh), home in Embo on a visit after thirty-seven years in Australia, also a sister to Flora (and of course to Una as well). Because of the number and variety of people present, the give and take of the interaction was considerable and the conversation was very informal. Despite the informality of the lively six-person interaction, the appearance of a short high-frequency English phrase in the general Gaelic conversation brought things to a sudden embarrassed halt:

E22 [reminiscing]: oː, wɛl, a kʰwĩːn am tə viu ʃĩn′ kʰɬi—čʰĩmĩçal ə bal.

E13: haː, *that's right.*—[short silence, followed by an embarrassed mutter quoting herself:] *"That's right!"*

E34 [providing the Gaelic equivalent]: **a ʃɔ̃ n kʰyɔrʃtʰ.**

E13 [correcting her original response to E22]: **a ʃɔ̃n—a ʃɔ̃n kʰyɔrʃtʰ,** [ɛlspɛtʰ].

Elspeth: Oh, well, I remember when we would be playing—around the village.

Flora: Yes, *that's right.*— *"That's right"!*

Lexie (in Gaelic): That's right.

Flora: That's—that's right, [Elspeth].

The use of English discourse markers such as *well, oh,* and *so* appeared to be exempt from criticism and did not provoke the same sort of embarrassment. Among semi-speakers even adverbs and conjunctions such as *anyway* and *but* were sometimes borrowed and used erratically along with their Gaelic equivalents /kə yuː/ and /ax/; this, too, passed without censure and was not among the failings that their elders objected to in their Gaelic. Whole English phrases were a different matter, however, and among fluent speakers so was the use of an English adverb well known in Gaelic. Two years after the session just quoted, with Dugald and Flora both dead and Eilidh once again in Australia, I helped Una and her older brother E10 (Duncan) record a long message in Gaelic for the absent Eilidh. Una, not generally an especially conservative younger fluent speaker, was the first to speak on the tape. Only seven sentences into her message, she reacted with conspicuous self-consciousness to her own use of an English loanword in place of a familiar high-frequency Gaelic adverb:

ha [tɔnəxu] *stəl* ig ə dɛ. *"stəl"*! vel u kʰɬĩːnčən!
[Duncan] is still at home. "Still"! Are you hearing!

From Una, this was an unusual degree of self-consciousness about using English *still* as a substitute for Gaelic /haːstʰ/ 'still', since she was not as much of a style shifter as her older siblings Duncan and Flora and was by comparison with them a natural and fairly unselfconscious speaker.[11] In its departure from her usual lack of self-consciousness, this self-critical comment reflects the tension of speaking into the microphone for an absent listener, in front of a non-family member at that, but it also indicates the stigma, even for a relatively young and not especially conservative speaker, of pressing a loanword into service when the Gaelic equivalent is familiar and ready to hand.

In a much less formal interaction within an English-language recording session, an Embo man raised an instant objection to his wife's use of an English loanword in place of a Gaelic word, even though the wife was quoting someone else. Both were YFS members of the London-Embo exile group, and the recording was being made at their home in London. In giving some reminiscences of life in Embo at an earlier time, the wife repeated in Gaelic another man's invitation to her father, a notable singer, to perform some of his songs for a gathering:

Wife (E21L): "Come on, /ilʹam! čʰɛ̃n agəs hor tai anari *čʰũnəxən* tən a d
        ãũːran ad/!"
Husband (E23L) [objecting to the borrowing /čʰũn/ and insisting on the Gaelic
        equivalent]: /pʰɔrʃtʰ. [anʹ ẽː] "*čʰũn*". pʰɔrʃtʰ/.

wife: "Come on, William! Come and give them a few tunes from your singing! "
husband: /pʰɔrʃtʰ. [Not] "/*čʰũn*/". /pʰɔrʃtʰ/.

The original invitation to the singer is just as likely to have contained the English loanword as the Gaelic word, but that did not prevent the husband from objecting to it in his wife's quotation. For all their ubiquity, loanwords were still linguistic bad form in this community if there was a well-known Gaelic equivalent; as with the analogically formed gerunds, some individuals took a puristic stand toward them, as the husband did here.

7.3 Summary: Absence of Social Evaluation in Personally Patterned Variation

Despite the inherent difficulty of demonstrating the *absence* of a social attitude, it proves possible to muster a fair amount of evidence for an absence of social evaluation of most personally patterned variation in Embo. Several sources of evidence

indicated that such variation was not itself a matter for vigilance or social evaluation on the part of community members: speakers' general failure to notice differences between their own variant choices and those of fellow villagers; speakers'
general lack of reaction to conversational repetitions with variant substitutions by
the repeating speaker; speakers' own use of different variants in rapid-succession
repetitions of the same variable; and the persistence of idiosyncratic variants even
in traditional material (proverbs, ditties) that might have been expected to appear
in fixed form. Two sources of evidence indicated that no general indifference to
linguistic usage prevailed, but that, contrariwise, some kinds of linguistic behavior
had an extremely high profile for local speakers: sharply unfavorable reactions to
one disfavored instance of individual within-the-village variability (analogical
extension of /-u/ and /-al/ to verbs that traditionally made use of other gerund-
forming elements or processes) and equally unfavorable reactions to the use of
English words or phrases in instances where there was a perfectly familiar Gaelic
equivalent available.

A General Introduction to Speakers and Variables

1 INTRODUCTION

Few of the fifty-nine individuals who served as sources for this study were recruited with an eye to studying individual variation, because the research undertaken during the first three decades of my engagement with East Sutherland Gaelic always had some other focus. The original speaker sample was enlarged twice, first by happenstance in the mid-1960s and then intentionally in the late 1960s and early 1970s, with the second enlargement aimed at adding more older speakers and a sampling of semi-speakers (the former in Embo and the latter in Brora as well as in Embo) so as to shed light on changes in progress. Later in the 1970s, additional semi-speakers were consulted, and from time to time a few near-passive bilinguals as well, again for purposes of looking at change processes. But it was not until the 1990s, a very late date in view of the thinning ranks of fisherfolk Gaelic speakers, that individual variation became the direct focus of my study.

If the fishing communities and their Gaelic speech had still been fully vigorous, and the investigator likewise, a new research project building on prior work but expanding the speaker sample for overall balance in terms of age, sex, proficiency, and network composition would have been the obvious next step. Nothing of this sort was possible at that point, however, and consequently the present study relies strongly on such augmentation of the speaker sample and the database as could be achieved for Embo at the beginning of the 1990s. By 1990, sadly but naturally enough, many individuals who had been part of the original speaker sample were no longer alive. I was able to draft into the sample a certain number of Embo acquaintances who had either never previously acted as sources or had served as sources only on rare occasions, but long-standing sample imbalances were not correctable at that stage. The original pool of Embo sources was assembled without any thought of providing for statistical balance, and with a very limited number of new sources available in the 1990s there was no possibility of crafting such a balance belatedly. It would not have been possible, for example, to fill a set of cells with size-matched groups of same-sex individuals in various age groupings. In terms of sheer duration, the scope of the study offers some qualitative compensation for this quantitative shortcoming, in that the investigator and a good number of sources interacted over multiple field trips and a good many years, yielding a considerable volume of data and lending a degree of ease and depth to many of the verbal interactions. A statistically well-designed study of individual variation in a socioeconomically undifferentiated minority-language population will nonetheless have to be left to a researcher who has that purpose in mind from the outset.

The new line of inquiry that got under way in the 1990s shifted the focus of my East Sutherland Gaelic investigation very specifically to variables that showed socially unweighted idiosyncratic inter-speaker and intra-speaker variation. Earlier material remained fully relevant, even though it was gathered to other ends; and thanks to the high frequency of many of the variables, even small scraps of material recorded in earlier decades often proved valuable for present purposes. Scouring through early tapes and notebooks for previously overlooked data added welcome instances of many variables, with the newly retrieved material sometimes critical to filling out the evidence for personal-pattern variation and its workings. The next section introduces the body of data ultimately available for this study.

2 THE DATABASE

The material on which the present investigation relies is extremely varied. It encompasses both elicited and freely spoken data gathered from 1963 through 1978 and from 1991 to the present. Although interpretive work continued in the 1980s, physical incapacity on my part ruled out the active gathering of data during that decade.

2.1 Elicited Material

My study of East Sutherland's fisherfolk Gaelic has thus far extended over the forty-five years from 1963 to 2008. The elicitation materials that constituted much of the original 1963–78 database are copious, filling many field notebooks. These elicitation materials were supplemented by additional elicitations gathered via Embo, Golspie, and Brora recordings in 1964–65, via further Embo recordings in 1992, and also by translation task materials designed by me but recorded in Embo on my behalf in 1993 by my colleague, Dr. Seòsamh Watson of University College Dublin. Considerable additional translation task material was elicited via telephone beginning in 1993 and was recorded over the phone, with speakers' knowledge and permission, from mid-1994 forward. Two semi-speakers who visited me in the United States between 1987 and 1998 added during their visits to the elicited material they had previously provided. In addition to the fifty-nine speakers identified as sources for this study, one additional Brora semi-speaker was interviewed and tested in limited fashion, as were two additional Embo semi-speakers and two Embo (near-)passive bilinguals. Elicited material is at least moderately extensive for about thirty speakers, but limited for others who either died at an early stage of my work or were consulted only on occasions when I was working on highly variable age-related structures and in special need of auxiliary sources.

2.2 Freely Spoken Material

The freely spoken materials in the database were gathered over the same lengthy period and consist of the following: tape-recorded interviews; tape-recorded narratives; letter tapes with from one to six Gaelic-speaking participants sending messages (usually to me, but on one occasion to an overseas sibling) and conversing among themselves; reminiscences tape-recorded in my absence but for my benefit; oral history taping sessions including varying amounts of Gaelic (with one session conducted chiefly in Gaelic); traditional lore (proverbs, prognostications, short sayings, tongue-twisters, children's rhymes, and other ditties); comic anecdotes and jokes (at least a few of them traditional, though probably not local in origin); Gaelic asides during English interviews with bilingual sources; Gaelic asides during the recording of material for phonological analysis; one recipe taken down by dictation; one short autobiographical anecdote taken down by dictation; two free retellings of a short, invented story that I had read aloud in East Sutherland Gaelic to the two speakers; short comments or phrases taken down verbatim, both during work sessions and during social interactions; letters, postcards, and a few journal entries written by an ingenious semi-speaker in an invented but perfectly intelligible orthography; the audio track of a 1998 videotape made in Embo; and many dyadic telephone conversations recorded between 1994 and 2007 with seven Embo Gaelic speakers.[1] Two colleagues, David Clement, formerly of the Linguistic Survey of Scotland, and Dr. Seòsamh Watson of University College Dublin, shared with me recorded Gaelic interviews that they conducted in Golspie and Embo, respectively, with speakers who were among my sources. Several Embo speakers were interviewed in Gaelic by radio broadcasters in the 1990s. Radio nan Gaidheal, a Gaelic radio service, made the full text of one of these interviews available to me, with the permission of the interviewee. The broadcast texts of two other programs were sent to me by the individuals interviewed in the program, and these materials are also drawn on with their permission. Four Embo speakers were interviewed for a Gaelic radio program in 2004, and the BBC

Gaelic service generously made the full interview texts available to me, again with the interviewees' permission.

Freely spoken material recorded in the 1960s and 1970s is available for three of the seven fully fluent Brora speakers in the study, for all three of three Brora semi-speakers, and for four of the fully fluent Golspie speakers. Diverse sorts of freely spoken material are available for twenty-four of the thirty-seven fully fluent Embo speakers in the study, although for nine of the twenty-four the materials are very limited. Very substantial freely spoken material is available for two of the five Embo semi-speakers, one of high proficiency and one of low proficiency; more limited material is available for two others of high proficiency. At least some freely spoken material is thus available for thirty-nine of the fifty-nine speakers who served as sources for this study. For the twenty others, only elicited material can be drawn on.

3 FOCUS ON EMBO GAELIC

The fully fluent Brora and Golspie speakers who contributed to this study represented something approaching a conservative local norm for grammar and phonology.[2] With respect to most grammatical and phonological features, they were at least as conservative as most Embo older fluent speakers and in a number of cases more so, while they were less conservative on just two grammatical features. Since Embo Gaelic was a distinct speech variety with its own local history and character, it cannot be assumed that the features in regard to which Brora and Golspie Gaelic were more conservative were once also the prevailing norm in Embo; it cannot be assumed, that is, that any Embo difference represented a recent development. Especially in cases where the oldest fluent speakers in Embo themselves showed different forms of a grammatical feature variably, it is perfectly possible that the variation was well established and long persistent. When increased variation appeared among younger Embo speakers in particular, however, with signs of a distinct direction of change, the development in question was more likely to be a recent one related to isolation, obsolescence, or both.

In spite of the lesser conservatism of the Gaelic spoken there, Embo was a much more vigorous environment for the use of Gaelic in the 1960s and 1970s than were Brora and Golspie. Fully fluent Gaelic speakers in Embo had far more conversation partners available than their counterparts in Brora and Golspie, and many more people in Embo had the opportunity to use Gaelic most of the time if they cared to, as a good number of them did. The geographical isolation of Embo village kept the number of English-monolingual "incomer" residents low, so long as private car ownership was still relatively rare, as it was throughout the 1960s and into the 1970s, and Gaelic speech still generally prevailed on the Embo streets as well as in homes, provided no English monolinguals were present.[3] An absence of speakers under age thirty indicated that effective transmission of Gaelic had ceased in Embo some time in the 1930s, but the presence of fluent speakers in their thirties and forties testified to a good twenty-five years of continuing transmission in Embo beyond the time when transmission had petered out in the other two villages.

Though fluent-speaker Gaelic in Brora and Golspie was relatively conservative grammatically, personal-pattern variation was as prominent a feature of Brora and Golspie Gaelic as of Embo Gaelic. Central focus on Brora and Golspie Gaelic was ruled out, however, by the small number of surviving bilinguals in those two villages. The heavy absence of family members through emigration or death made it impossible even in the 1960s and 1970s to investigate usage within Brora and Golspie kin networks, and in all of these fishing communities, it was kinship ties that underlay the chief social networks. In the case of Brora, for example, all but one of my sources (fluent speakers and semi-speakers alike) were actually kinfolk who formed quite a strong social network; but as a small remnant population, only a few of them still had a Gaelic-speaking sibling, spouse, or parent alive in the village. Many of their siblings had emigrated, while others had died, and since nearly all remaining speakers were themselves elderly, their parents were not available as sources. Only one pair of speakers had a child living in the village who had acquired any Gaelic at all. It was not possible in Brora to get a sense of within-the-family usage by working with a number of close kin, as was still possible in Embo. Because of the relative intactness of Embo as a Gaelic-speaking village, Embo Gaelic will necessarily be to the fore in this study, with discussion of Brora and Golspie Gaelic introduced where possible.

4 SOURCES

In this section the sources for this study are introduced in terms of (1) village of origin, (2) age, (3) sex, and (4) proficiency level. In the list of sources that follows, B, G, and E stand for Brora, Golspie, and Embo, with the number 1 representing the oldest source in each village.

4.1 Village of Origin

Fisherfolk sources resident in East Sutherland at the outset of my study were all born in the same village where they were living when I encountered them, with the single exception of E33, an Embo-born man resident in Brora. In most cases their parents or childhood care-givers were also born in the same village.[4] Members of the London-Embo group, an extended kin group of exiles living in the general vicinity of London as well as in the city itself, are entered with an L after the identifying number. As far as I know, all were Embo-born and spent the formative period of their childhoods in Embo. E15L, whom I had known while he was still part of the London-Embo group, became an OFS source in my study only after he had retired to live in Embo again. Since he had spent his long working life among the London-area Embo exiles, he is identified here as a London-Embo speaker. E25L, also part of the London-Embo group, was usually consulted in London, but during one summer he voluntarily joined a number of my Embo-based work sessions while home on vacation. E12, a neighbor of husband and wife E3 and E13, likewise voluntarily joined work sessions while at home on vacation over two field trips in succession. Her proficiency was superb, but so far as anyone knew, there was no coherent group of Embo speakers in her exile area, so she is entered purely as an Embo speaker.

4.2 Age

Ages are normed for all speakers to the rough midpoint of my on-site fieldwork, 1970, but are entered in square brackets for those speakers who had died before that date. The ordering of speakers is as accurate as available sources of information could make it. Those sources included autobiographical statements, family records, obituaries, gravestone inscriptions, and in some cases the best guesses of a number of fellow villagers.[5] Where the ordering of a speaker relative to other villagers is assessed by fellow speakers' estimates but the chronological age is uncertain, age is entered with a preceding question mark. Individuals born in the same year are chronologically ordered relative to one another only if I happened to know month as well as year of birth; otherwise they are randomly ordered.

4.3 Sex

In Embo, the critical location for this study, males are somewhat overrepresented among the older speakers. As mentioned earlier, older fisherfolk men had nearly always had wider experience outside the home area than their female counterparts, and this generalization held most particularly in Embo's more isolated village setting. Whether from military service or from extended periods of work away from East Sutherland, the older Embo men had acquired a social self-confidence that made it relatively comfortable for them, compared with older women, to handle questions from an unfamiliar person, especially in the earliest period when I was originally recruiting speakers.

Among the imperfect speakers, by contrast, men are underrepresented. Both in Brora and in Embo, females were more in evidence than males among those who continued to make some use of Gaelic despite imperfect speaker skills, perhaps because of women's particularly good integration within kin circles.[6] The seven semi-speakers whose active control of Gaelic I was able to assess by means of translation tasks in 1974 and 1976 were all female and all strongly connected with their kin networks, interacting regularly and warmly with older kinfolk. In 1978 I made a concerted effort to locate male equivalents, and I did find several men who could be considered semi-speakers, one in Brora and two in Embo, though I did not have the opportunity to test them extensively, as I had done with the earlier imperfect-speaker sample. Embo semi-speaker E39 provided tape-recorded variation-targeted material in 1992 but became a regular source only in

2004. The full extent of her grammatical proficiency remains less fully assessed than that of the other Embo semi-speakers, all of whom participated in extensive translation task batteries in 1974 and 1976.

4.4 Proficiency: Descriptive Proficiency-Level Labels

Two of the labels that designate proficiency level here are largely descriptive, reflecting the speaker's linguistic history and observable level of language use: *formerly fluent speaker* and *(near-)passive bilingual*. The formerly fluent speakers were raised in homes where Gaelic was the normal language of family interaction. They had siblings (including, in all of the Embo cases, siblings younger than they) whose full fluency reflected the family's regular use of Gaelic, but these individuals had married English monolinguals and all but one of them had spent a major part of their lives in an entirely English-speaking environment. Their fluency had suffered as a result, and they frequently struggled with lexical retrieval; less commonly used grammatical constructions tended to elude their grasp, and English influence could be seen not just in borrowings but sometimes also in the way they put Gaelic sentences together.

(Near-)passive bilinguals were non-speakers who nevertheless demonstrated essentially full understanding of any Gaelic spoken in their presence. Their social responses were perfectly in accord with what was said in Gaelic in their vicinity: they laughed at sly remarks, produced appropriate exclamatory sounds at surprising or shocking information, and shook their heads in sorrow or wonder at equally appropriate junctures in a narrative. If asked to, they could and did supply English translations for a particular remark. Very early in my fieldwork, in fact, one such passive bilingual translated a brief conversation for my benefit, yet when she was asked to say simple things in Gaelic, it was evident that she could not pronounce Gaelic sounds accurately. Another near-passive bilingual undertook a long interview with me in which I spoke the local Gaelic and she spoke English; during the whole session she asked for a translation of only one word, an old-fashioned irregular plural I had used for which a more transparent diminutive and its plural are frequently substituted by younger speakers. I was also able to do some limited translation testing with one or two (near-)passive bilinguals in Embo, establishing that they had modest lexical resources but only very limited ability to construct sentences with them.

4.5 Proficiency: Evaluative Proficiency-Level Labels

Three other proficiency labels used in this study are more nearly evaluative than descriptive: *older fluent speaker*, *younger fluent speaker*, and *semi-speaker*. These labels were chosen to reflect the fact that grammatical change was under way in

East Sutherland fisherfolk Gaelic, giving rise to observable differences in certain grammatical structures, and that the degree of change was correlated to a considerable extent with age. In Brora (and almost certainly also in Golspie, though I did not explore the issue there), there were only two proficiency groupings, fully fluent speakers and semi-speakers. The latter were chronologically younger than the former, and the grammar of their Gaelic differed from that of their elders in quite conspicuous ways. In Embo, with its much broader age span of speakers, the amount of grammatical change in progress was large; the combination of much change with a broad age range of speakers called for recognition of an additional age-based proficiency level.

Whereas in Brora there was a sharp demarcation line between fully fluent speakers whose grammar was conservative and semi-speakers whose grammar was markedly deviant, Embo speakers differed on a more individual basis. The younger speakers taken as a whole were certainly less conservative than their elders, but at the same time it was possible for a very young fluent speaker to be more conservative on some particular point of grammar than someone many years his or her senior. In the case of some grammatical constructions, it was evident that a structure was moving from a conservative near-consensus among older speakers to a regularized form or even disappearance among the youngest speakers, as with the gradual elimination of the first-person singular conditional inflection (see table 3.2). In many cases, however, the change in question was neither as rapid nor as complete as that, so that the resulting picture was more complex overall.

Dividing the fully fluent Gaelic speakers of Embo village into an older and a younger fluent-speaker group, as I do in this study, serves above all to recognize that speakers at the upper end of the age range were, by and large (and not surprisingly), more conservative in their usage than speakers at the lower end. Extensive translation task testing, especially the large test batteries of 1974 and 1976, identified many cases of grammatical change in progress, and freely spoken materials as well as additional translation task materials confirmed those findings. Even so, the age-based line I draw between older and younger fluent speakers in Embo is to some extent an arbitrary one, appropriate to this very particular pool of sources rather than to any receding-language setting with a fairly broad age range of speakers. The community at large considered E17 and E16 to be excellent speakers (though to be sure community judgments in this matter did not rest mainly on grammatical intactness; see chapter 7). E18*, next in age below them, was a formerly fluent speaker of markedly reduced skills, and the cluster of speakers who fell immediately below her in age (E19 through E25) seemed in village social life to represent a somewhat different generation from that of E16 and E17.

The positioning of the OFS/YFS dividing line reflects both social and chronological factors, therefore, as is appropriate in my view. Same-age speakers did not reliably produce uniform grammatical usage, however, and even speakers at the top end of the age scale did not necessarily altogether agree on the grammatical forms they used. Any non-arbitrary use of grammatical conservatism as the basis for dividing speakers into distinct proficiency groups would therefore require working out transitional zones for each of the many grammatical structures that showed change in progress. Ultimately each speaker would have to be evaluated and treated separately in connection with each grammatical usage; indeed, in future treatments of grammatical change in Embo Gaelic I expect to find it necessary to do this. But for overall views of the general effect of age as a factor, a rough division between older and younger fluent speakers can be useful, and the dividing point adopted here, between speakers age sixty-four and older and speakers sixty and younger, is reasonably realistic in terms of this Embo speaker sample and the social life of Embo village. Group findings obscure individual performances, however, and since the focus in this study is on individual variation, much of the discussion remains centered on individual speakers.

A distinction between older and younger fully fluent speakers is not necessarily a usual or even a useful feature of speech communities in which a language is passing out of use. Even in the East Sutherland setting Embo is unusual in this respect. Brora and Golspie Gaelic did not—at least within their small remaining speaker populations—show evidence of such a distinction. In other settings where a large amount of grammatical change accompanies the linguistic obsolescence process, researchers may or may not find it useful or appropriate to divide the fluent-speaker ranks into age groups or other proficiency-related rankings that recognize the cumulative effect of ongoing change processes.

All of the fully fluent fisherfolk Gaelic speakers were highly proficient, comfortable, and frequent users of Gaelic. But fluent Embo speakers recognized a group of imperfect speakers whose Gaelic contained deviations that they explicitly considered mistakes. All such imperfect speakers were among the youngest active users of the local Gaelic in their respective villages (ages forty-three to fifty-seven in Brora and ages thirty to forty in Embo, with ages normed as usual to 1970). Though these individuals were considered imperfect speakers, the community had no designation for them as a group; the term *semi-speaker* is a label I apply purely for descriptive and analytic purposes. Within the semi-speaker group itself, proficiency differed considerably (see the discussion in chapter 7, §8.1), so that the label indicates community-recognized deviation rather than such matters as ease of self-expression, control of lexical resources, or even overall degree of grammatical intactness.[7]

Whatever their individual level of Gaelic proficiency, the semi-speakers possessed a remarkable degree of sociolinguistic skill in the deployment of their linguistic resources. Like the (near-)passive bilinguals, they reacted with thoroughgoing appropriateness to the Gaelic interactions going on around them, but unlike the (near-)passive bilinguals they were able to contribute a greater or lesser amount of Gaelic of their own to these interactions. Most of them tended to be short-burst speakers rather than sustained conversationalists, but on occasions when the motivation was sufficient, a number of them proved themselves capable of producing more continuous and connected Gaelic than they ordinarily did. E40 in particular underwent what amounted to an upsurge in her conversational skills over the years of our phone conversations, and by 2004, when she participated in a Gaelic radio broadcast recorded in Embo, she had emerged as a remarkably comfortable conversationalist.

5 SPEAKERS

Introduced here are the speakers who served as sources for this study. Formerly fluent speakers are indicated with an asterisk. The one Golspie speaker so entered chose to identify herself in those terms. On the occasions when I asked her to do translation tasks, her responses were indistinguishable from those of fully fluent Golspie speakers, but in the 1960s and 1970s she was not a regular speaker, and she did not supply any freely spoken texts. It was not clear from her statements or those of her habitual-speaker husband G3 how much Gaelic they used together in the home, and therefore I am accepting her self-designation in assigning her formerly fluent status.

Two Embo speakers designated formerly fluent, E26* and E29*, considered that they had fallen away from fully fluent status by reason of extended residence outside the Highlands after their marriages to English monolinguals. E26* was Lexie's oldest sister, Sheila. She made annual two-week vacation trips to Embo for many years but was otherwise wholly in an English-speaking environment, except that she stayed in close touch with Embo relatives by phone after private phones came into wider use. She claimed (both to her relatives and to me) no longer to be able to converse freely in Gaelic, but in 1995 she began doing so during our long-distance phone conversations and reported that she was also using more Gaelic in phone conversations with kinfolk in Embo. Though clearly rusty and somewhat halting at first, she declared herself dedicated to recovering as much fluency as she could. She was a voluble speaker, conversing with gusto, and she used Gaelic during a good many phone conversations thereafter, gradually speaking more easily despite occasional memory problems caused by age and ill health, until failing health impaired her speaker skills in the last year or two of her life.

E29* returned to Embo to live in 1993. Health problems caused her to make several temporary returns to an area of England where she had previously lived, but she made a permanent return to Embo, along with a monolingual son and daughter-in-law, in 1998. Married to a monolingual military man, she had lived in various parts of the world; but during periods of residence in England she had sometimes had a sister living nearby with whom she regularly spoke Gaelic. Two other sisters with whom she occasionally spoke Gaelic had also lived with her in England for at least some years. She had therefore been less completely cut off from daily use of Embo Gaelic than Sheila had been, but E29*, too, was rusty and experienced retrieval problems. She also showed perhaps somewhat more influence from English in her Gaelic than did the slightly older Sheila. In addition to permitting the recording of extensive free conversations, both women cheerfully and even enthusiastically undertook many translation exercises, giving me an additional measure of their control of Embo Gaelic after long disuse.

A third formerly fluent Embo speaker, E18* (Eilidh), had emigrated to Australia at age eighteen. In 1965 she returned to Embo, for the first time in thirty-seven years, making a very extended stay with her sister E13 (Flora) and her brother-in-law E3 (Dugald). Two unmarried siblings of Flora's, E10 (Duncan) and E24 (Una), lived in the same household, and Gaelic was the normal family language. Eilidh was eager to revive her Gaelic and made a considerable effort to do so during her lengthy stay. She had been more isolated from Gaelic than either E26* or E29*, however, and had suffered a good deal more loss of fluency than either of them had. She conversed rather haltingly, lapsing into English with some frequency, and she had a very noticeable Australian accent in her Gaelic (as in her English). She provided some freely spoken material for this study through her participation in a long letter tape made primarily by Flora, Elspeth, and Lexie early in 1965 (with Dugald and Una also present and participating minimally; see chapter 5, §11.3.2), before I actually met her in person in the summer of 1965.

One other formerly fluent speaker, E32* (Stuart), was a younger brother to Sheila and a slightly older brother to Lexie, but was never one of my sources. He was raised in a thoroughly Gaelic-speaking family and married a wife said to be a passive bilingual, but though he lived locally he declined to speak Gaelic in adult life. His recorded freely spoken material emerged as a unique response to the presence of a radio broadcaster anxious to interview Embo Gaelic speakers; the tape was made available to me with his permission through the cooperation of the broadcaster. Otherwise Stuart's routine practice was to reply in English when spoken to in Gaelic, even when the person speaking to him was an older member of his own kin circle—a highly unusual, though not entirely unique stance for someone known to have grown up in a fully Gaelic-speaking household.

Most semi-speakers (and also the handful of near-passive Embo bilinguals whom I interviewed and tested) were living locally at the time I worked with them, though most of them had left the area at some point to take up work elsewhere and had then returned. The non-resident exceptions were a pair of cousins from the London-Embo group, one the semi-speaker E42L and the other a near-passive bilingual. They had spent some of their earliest childhood years in Embo during World War II and had subsequently also spent long summer vacations there, exposed to a great deal of Gaelic (as they were at home, for that matter). The near-passive bilingual cousin represented by far the more common outcome of such a history for the London-Embo second generation; the semi-speaker cousin became an active if imperfect speaker very much by an act of will (Dorian 1980b).

The full list of speakers and their ages according to proficiency-level groupings follows. Members of the London-Embo group are identified by an L after their codings.

OFSs	YFSs	SSs
B1 [81] f.	E18* 60 f.	B9 57 f.
B2 80 m.	E19 59 m.	B10 57 f.
B3 80 f.	E20 58 f.	B11 43 f.
B4 [79] f.	E21L 58 f.	E38 40 f.
B5 [73] m.	E22 58 f.	E39 38 f.
B6 69 f.	E23L 57 m.	E40 36 f.

B7 66 f.	E24 57 f.	E41 31 f.
G1 77 f.	E25L 57 m.	E42L 30 f.
G2 75 f.	E26* 54 f.	
G3 72 m.	E27 54 m.	
G4 68 f.	E28L 51 m.	
G5 68 m.	E29* 50 f.	
G6* 67 f.	E30 49 m.	
G7 [64] m.	E31 49 m.	
E1 [88] m.	E32* 47 m.	
E2 [88] m.	E33 45 m.	
E3 [85] m.	E34 45 f.	
E4 82 m.	E35 43 f.	
E5 77 f.	E36 41 m.	
E6 75 m.	E37 41 m.	
E7 ?74 f.		
E8 ?71 f.		
E9 70 f.		
E10 70 m.		
E11 70 f.		
E12 ?68 f.		
E13 [67] f.		
E14 65 f.		
E15L 64 m.		
E16 64 f.		
E17 64 f.		

Some of the speakers entered in this list make no appearance at all in the chapters to follow. Much of my early work on East Sutherland Gaelic focused on phonology or grammar, and the limited materials collected from certain speakers in pursuit of those interests did not always include items of significance for the study of personal-pattern variation. In luckier cases, whole sets of grammatically oriented translation tasks turned out by pure good fortune to include one or more of the variables of interest here. To take just two examples, translation tasks aimed at investigating change in progress in the expression of passive voice in East Sutherland Gaelic happened to include many instances of the variable adverbial ('in'), and translation tasks intended to track the spread of an initial consonant mutation from shibilant-initial nouns to shibilant-initial verbs included many instances of the variable ('tomorrow').

5.1 Factors in Gaelic-Language Social Interaction Patterns

Quite conventional features are used to classify the speakers in this sample: age, Gaelic-language proficiency, and speaker's sex. Socioeconomic class is conspicuously absent, however, because of the exceptional homogeneity of these originally single-occupation and single-class Gaelic-speaking communities. Additional factors typically related to class, such as income, housing type, and education, go unregarded for the same reason.

Residential area, or neighborhood, is another familiar factor of little or no significance here, since the fisherfolk parts of Brora and Golspie, and the whole village in the case of Embo, originally constituted a single Gaelic-speaking neighborhood. Because of the multiplicity of kin relationships and the large size of families, age differentiation actually played a smaller role in determining fishing village interactional patterns than is typical in the urban and suburban settings with which contemporary linguists are most familiar. Older siblings might be very nearly of another generation compared to the youngest children in the family, and cousins, aunts, and uncles also frequently crossed what would be considered typical generational lines in terms of age. Kinfolk constituted each speaker's most significant interactional group, and close, high-interaction relationships routinely included kinfolk of widely different ages. Autobiographical recollections indicate that children fairly near in age also played together without regard to school-year class.

Social organizations in which participation was voluntary, such as the Women's Rural Institute for women and the Masonic Lodge for men, were pallid in their social impact when compared with the primary social impact of ascribed social status as *maraichean* ('fisherfolk') and the pervasive social effect of the kin network (and such organizations were of course also settings for the use of English rather than Gaelic). Residual social stigma tended to produce patterns of joint ethnic group interaction even outside (sub)community boundaries. Men from the fishing communities were likely to patronize a particular pub, for example, and women often made their shopping trips together and hired on in groups for agricultural field work at harvest time. Where Gaelic church services were still available, family members attended as a group; fisherfolk parishioners also sat together, with other Gaelic-speaking attendees (incomers and the few remaining bilingual crofters) sitting separately.

It can be said, in summary, that class-based groupings were absent in the Gaelic-speaking fisherfolk communities and that age-based groupings were a weaker factor and kin-based groupings a stronger factor than in larger and more complex social environments, while the uniform *maraichean* ethnic identity deeply linked the entire community.

6 VARIABLES: INTRODUCTION

The focus of attention in this study is the reverse of that in most sociolinguistic studies of variation: not a collective abstraction from group linguistic practice in the spirit of Saussure's *langue*, but rather the usage of individual speakers; not the "'shared' system...that is of interest only insofar as it can be treated as identical from individual to individual" (Johnstone 2000:408) but the individual differences that remain once the common patterns are known (Hymes 1979:36). Speakers' *parole* is plumbed for the idiosyncratic speech patterns that are not, in this community, deviance or aberration, nor in-group/out-group markers, but are instead part of the intrinsic linguistic character of local speech. A number of different levels of individual variation might be considered, from phonetic variation in the realization of certain phonemes to syntactic variation such as the ordering of subordinate clauses relative to main clauses. The forms of variation I have chosen to concentrate on here—variation in the phonological realization of morphemes and variation in the use of morphological alternatives—have the advantage of being highly salient. This is just what made them so interesting to me in the first place: the differences between variant forms seemed so blatant that I found it difficult to credit community members' apparent obliviousness to the contrasts in their variant selections. In the longer run the salience that drew my attention to variation in the realization of morphemes proved to have great practical value, in addition to its intellectual interest, in that most of the data gathered from 1993 on was collected over the phone. The telephone is a notoriously difficult acoustic environment, but working with relatively unmistakable variant forms made transcription a feasible exercise. In their turn, of course, more reliable transcriptions made the sorting and tallying of data more reliable.

6.1 Selection of Variables for Presentation

Within the chosen sphere of variation I have been concerned not to narrow the field of variables unduly. In particular, I have wanted to avoid selecting just two or three variables and following only that tiny selection, because it has seemed to me (as also to some critics; see Hinskens 1996:87–89) that sociolinguistic studies have sometimes selectively treated too few variables of too few sorts, and those few in too little relation to each other. I made a point therefore of considering the larger part of the morphological variation of which I was aware, plus some phonological and syntactic variation, working my way systematically through my field notebooks and the recorded materials in my possession twice, tallying freely spoken instances of selected variables separately from those that were either elicited by translation tasks or offered by sources in a metalinguistically self-conscious fashion during discussions about usage. Inevitably I became belatedly aware during this process of additional variables (as just two examples, the displacement in Embo of /nˊax/ 'person, somebody' by /pɔ(r)di/, described in chapter 3, §4.1, and the gradual favoring, also in Embo, of the contracted form /pɔːr/ 'ought' over fuller /pə xɔːr/). Since it was impractical to revisit my mountain of field notebooks yet again to complete the record for such items, some variables remain incompletely tracked. In most such cases, these belatedly recognized variables are tracked chiefly in freely spoken materials (not always completely, in the case of the overwhelmingly voluminous phone materials) and in the uncharacteristically tidily organized elicitation notebooks in which I pursued questions of grammatical change from 1970 onward; in some cases they are tracked only for Embo. As a result they come under discussion here only to a limited extent.

Other variables were ruled out as cases for extended presentation for quite different reasons. Some forms of variation were so ubiquitous that listing them would have been an endless undertaking, tripling or quadrupling an already daunting tracking task. This is the case with the dropping of initial consonants in certain high-frequency function words (for example, /ax/ for /nax/ in three dependent negative morphemes; /a/ or /ha/ for /xa/ as independent 'not'), and with the dropping of final consonants, especially liquids, in other high-frequency words (/tu/ and /kʰu/ for the verbs /tuɫ/ 'going' and /kʰur/ 'putting,' for example).

In certain other cases there were simply not enough useful instances, especially freely spoken, from enough speakers to make a good case for individual patterns of variation across the sample (e.g., initial sibilant plus lateral as opposed to initial shibilant plus lateral in the relatively few nouns with these initial clusters; the conjunction ('before') with or without change in the initial consonant of a following verb). In still other cases there were a great many instances available, but not enough to produce an adequate number of instances for each of a variety of syntactic conditions in which the variant forms appeared (and so to check for the possible effect of syntactic environment as such on variant choice); this was true in the case of variants of the two irregular verbs 'see' and 'get' in nasalized environments, where they can appear in Embo with initial /f/, /b/, or /v/. In one case, an auditory shortcoming of my own (a curious difficulty in distinguishing between initial /b/ and initial /v/ in a word that frequently occurred unstressed at the beginning of sentences or clauses) seemed so likely to have biased the tallies that the wiser course was to exclude the variable from discussion. In another unusual case the pattern of variation was oddly skewed by a single Embo semi-speaker who produced three variants unique to herself, an exceptionally high variability with very limited relevance to Embo Gaelic overall.

There were still a number of possible candidates for presentation, even after cases such as those just mentioned were eliminated, and the particular variables selected for discussion here constitute a subset, though a relatively generous one. Variables were not dismissed out of hand, at any rate, and most morphological and morphophonological variables I was aware of were at least considered for inclusion.

6.2 Particular Variable Features Selected for Discussion

In some instances, the variants of a variable selected for presentation differ in several respects, only one of which is considered here. The past-tense forms of the irregular verbs 'come' and 'see' are looked at here in terms of monosyllabic or disyllabic structure, for example, because this is the variable feature the two past-tense forms share. Past-tense ('came') has in fact only the two variants disyllabic

/hã:nig/ and monosyllabic /hã:n/.[8] Past-tense ('saw'), however, has not only variants differing in syllabic structure by presence or absence of the final /-ig/ syllable
but also a disyllabic variant that lacks the consonant /-g/ even though it retains an
unaccented second vowel (see chapter 3, §7.2.4). In addition, all of the variants of
('saw') may show an /r/ before the medial /n/ for some (but not all) speakers. For
present purposes the variable ('saw') is considered only in terms of monosyllabic
versus disyllabic variants. That variable feature is what links it to the variable
('came') and also to a third variable, the regular verb /čʰilig/ 'throw', which in the
usage of a few younger, mostly male Embo speakers shows the same past-tense
loss of final syllable. Another reason for focusing on the difference in syllable
count is that syllable count disparity appears in geographically based variation as
well as in personally patterned variation. In a high-frequency case of geographical
variation, Brora and Golspie speakers used a monosyllabic verb root /prĩ:n/
'speak' while Embo speakers used a disyllabic root /prĩ:niç/ for the same verb,
even though speakers from all three villages shared a monosyllabic gerund /prĩ:n/.
This is therefore another case demonstrating that it need not be a difference in *type*
of variation that distinguishes within-the-village variation from cross-village variation: syllable count difference comes into play both across villages (Brora and
Golspie /prĩ:n/ versus Embo /prĩ:niç/ 'speak') and within Embo village (/hã:n/
versus /hãnig/ 'came').

6.3 Choices in the Identification of Variant Forms

In most cases, the variants of the variables introduced here were easily identified
and represented. In some cases, however, questions arose about the number of
distinct variants that merited recognition, and in others there was one variant
among several with distributions uniquely limited by phonological or structural
properties. The variable ('when') offers an instance of the first type and the variable ('along with') an instance of the second type.

    In the case of ('when'), it seemed possible in some cases to posit an underlying
disyllabic form even for a speaker who actually used only the monosyllabic variant
/tə/. This was at least arguably possible, for example, if the speaker in question supplied the negative conjunction ('when not') in the form /tənax/. Speakers who used
the variants /tərax/ and /nərax/ for ('when not') were clearly dropping the initial /n-/
of the negative element /(n)ax/ in compounding the conjunction, and the variant
/tənax/ might therefore represent /tən/ + /ax/ as easily as /tə/ + /nax/. This would be
a possible interpretation for a speaker such as E24, for example, who used only /tə/
for ('when') but used /tənax/ for ('when not'). The same might be assumed for E22,
who favored /tə/ strongly in freely spoken material, used both /tə/ and /tənə/ heavily
in elicited material, and occasionally made use of the variant /tərə/: since her two
instances of ('when not') were both /tənax/ rather than /tərax/, one might (on that
slender evidence) assign all her /tə/ variants to an underlying / tənə/. This assumption cannot be made so easily in the case of E17, however, since she used both

/tənax/ and /tərax/ for ('when not') (and /nərax/, as well, for that matter), eliminating any basis for assigning her favorite /tə/ variants to /tənə/ rather than to /tərə/. In view of cases such as E17, as well as those of /tə/-users for whom no instances of ('when not') are available (E5, E14, E20), it seems necessary to recognize /tə/ as a variant in its own right, distinct from /tərə/ and /tənə/. Although there are again few cases and the number of tokens is small, there were also a few speakers who used /nə/ without providing any instances of /nu(ə)rə/, /nərə/, or /nərax/, and /nə/ is therefore also recognized as a distinct variant. At the same time, I have chosen to lump the forms /nərə/, / nurə/, and /nuərə/ into a single variant, treating them as phonological alternates of an underlying /nV(V)r(ə)/ structure (with the final vowel normally appearing before consonant-initial elements, as is true for all of the disyllabic variants of ('when')). There is a degree of arbitrariness involved in this decision, however, and at least for such older fluent speakers as were also style shifters the relatively uncommon form /nuərə/ might be considered a separate variant associated with careful or formal speech. Speakers of this sort were at least passively literate and were therefore aware that the pronunciation /nuərə/ would accord best, among the various /nV(V)r(ə)/ variants in use in Embo, with the written rendering *nuair a*. The variant pattern exhibited by E10 in his performance style certainly suggests this interpretation: he used the form /nuərə/ almost entirely in proverbs (just one freely spoken and one elicited non-proverbial instance) and he rarely used any /nV(V)r(ə)/ forms other than /nuərə/ (just one instance of /nərə/, also in a proverb, and one of /nur/ in a comic ditty). But this interpretation works less well for younger fluent speakers such as E27 and E34, husband and wife Murdo and Lexie, who were indeed passively literate to a limited extent but who used a wider selection of / nV(V)r(ə)/ variants in their speech and who offered in the putatively more formal elicitation condition not just /nuərə/ but also others of the /nV(V)r(ə)/ variants. I opt for recognition of the shared phonological structure /n + V(V) + r(ə)/ in identifying just one variant here, with the result that variants /nə/ and /nV(V)r(ə)/ parallel the variant forms /tə/ and /tərə/. If it had been possible to revisit earlier sources and pose additional questions about variant choices, however, a different tack might have seemed more appropriate.

In the case of the conjugating preposition ('along with'), the variants display an assortment of assimilative processes involving liquids and nasals. All of the variants have the same potential distributional privileges except one, namely, /kʰɔi/, the most abbreviated form. The initial consonant of this compound preposition's second element (/ri/, the preposition 'to') is missing altogether from this variant, leaving only the unvarying vowel /i/ and precluding any conjugation for person. Thus, while any of the variants can take nouns or personal names as objects (/kʰɔ̃:ɬa ri maːri, kʰɔra ri maːri, kʰɔ̃na ri maːri, kʰɔ̃rna ri maːri, kʰɔi maːri/ 'along with Mary'), only the first four can be used with a pronoun object (/kʰɔ̃:ɬa rəm, kʰɔra rəm, kʰɔ̃na rəm, kʰɔ̃rna rəm/ 'along with me'). The fifth form, /kʰɔi/, cannot appear conjugated for person as the other forms can, since no inflected form of the preposition /ri/ 'to' is available as a second constituent element. One Embo source showed 100 percent use of the variant /kʰɔi/ (see table 5.4 in chapter 5), but this was possible only because none of his instances of ('along with') happened to involve personal pronouns. The presence of a variant like /kʰɔi/, with distributional privileges that differ from those of the other variants of the same variable, has an obvious impact on the overall pattern of variant distribution.

Cases like that of /kʰɔi/, where variant choice is constrained by structure, are very rare. Cases like that of ('when'), in which the precise identification of the relevant variants might be arguable, are considerably more common. It is important to note, however, that the identification choices made here do not necessarily operate to increase the appearance of variation in Embo Gaelic. In some cases they may instead reduce it, as with the focus exclusively on syllable count for ('saw'). In any case, the key question for the present discussion is not one of precisely how many variants are to be identified but whether it can be convincingly demonstrated that more than a single form is in use, both by various same-village speakers and by one and the same speaker. The central argument begins with that demonstration: that clearly identifiable variation occurs from speaker to speaker within the community and also within the speech of individual community members, to an extent that cannot be explained away as the result of linguistic conditioning or strictly social or socioeconomic factors, and also very largely without any social significance attaching to the use of particular variants.

6.4 Representation of the Variables

Other issues of overall presentation remain to be dealt with, quite apart from phonemic representation of variants: how to represent the variables themselves and how to tabulate them without giving unwarranted preference to any one variant.

6.4.1 Adopting English Glosses

The variables introduced so far have been written within the parentheses used by variationists to set off the variables featured in correlational sociolinguistic studies; but rather than represent them in Gaelic orthography or in phonemic writing, I have represented them by English glosses. This is an admittedly awkward solution to a troublesome problem. A close look at one typically problematic case, the variable ('on her') introduced in chapter 1, can illustrate the problem. The standard Gaelic writing of this word is *oirre*, and the Golspie variant /ɔir/ can reasonably be considered a local representation of that form; the other Golspie variants, /ɛr, ɔi, ɔiç/ correspond less well. If I were to choose to represent the variable as (*oirre*), those who know Scottish or Irish Gaelic would be grateful for an immediately interpretable signpost. But those who are unfamiliar with the peculiarities of Gaelic orthography (which is arguably as loosely linked to phonological values as that of English) would not be equally well served—and the disservice would only grow larger with the addition of variables like ('family'), which according to this principle would be rendered as (*teaghlach*), a form without an obviously interpretable pronunciation for readers of English.

This second case, ('family'), raises another question of representation that had to be confronted in this study. Fisherfolk Gaelic speakers in East Sutherland frequently used a retroflexed lateral in place of the velar lateral of more main-stream Gaelic dialects. Some speakers showed only velarization, some showed both retroflexion and velarization, and some showed only retroflexion. Embo speakers were somewhat more likely to use a retroflexed lateral than were Brora and Golspie speakers, generally speaking, or at least to use it in more lexical items. Younger Embo speakers also increasingly used retroflexion even in initial position, as Brora and Golspie speakers did not. I opted not to routinely represent the /r/ that appeared variably in Embo usage before the /n/ of ('saw') (/hũ(r)n, hũ(r)nig/, but contrariwise I *am* opting to write the /r/ that appeared in Embo usage before the /ɬ/ or /l/ of ('family'). The reason for treating these two cases differently is a simple one of local usage: while some Embo speakers never pro-duced an /r/ in /hũn, hũnig/, scarcely anyone in my Embo sample ever produced any of the variants of ('family') without the prelateral /r/. As in certain lexical items in which an immediately postvocalic and preconsonantal /r/ is not historical (as it more probably is before what was historically a velarized nasal in *thunnaig* 'saw', despite the erraticness of the /r/ in Embo renderings), a strongly retroflexed /r/—never the flapped, lightly trilled, or fricative allophones of /r/—seems to have become an immutable part of the word 'family' in Embo Gaelic (though not so universally in Brora or Golspie Gaelic). This was true also before /ɬ/ in /me:rɬɔ/ 'midday', to take another example, and before /v/ in /sə:rvə(r)ɬ/ 'world'. Compare also Embo /pɔ(r)di/ 'anybody, somebody, a person', identifiable with English *body*, discussed in chapter 3, §4.1: most Embo speakers introduced a retroflexed /r/ before a likewise retroflexed /d/. A similar retroflexed /r/ was invariable, although so far as I know ahistorical, before /d/ and /t/ in /kʰɔrdərl/ 'sleep' and /ɔrtərl/ 'a small amount (of a liquid)'. As these examples indicate, the use of English glosses offered a way of avoiding difficult problems of phonemic repre-sentation (and of phonetic opaqueness for English-speaking readers) and there-fore seemed the simplest solution.

6.4.2 Avoiding a Main-Variant Nomination

A particularly problematic issue for this study was selecting any one of a variable's variants to represent that variable, since the selection would create a subtle claim to some sort of primacy for the chosen variant. In a speech variety with a history of dialect mixing in the wake of forced evictions, primacy is not easy to assign, and any such assignment can prompt readers—a category of people inescapably conditioned by standardization—to consider the namesake variant of an item its "main" variant and any others as somehow secondary or lesser. The temptation to nominate a main variant is greatest when just one of a pair (or set) of local variants happens to coincide with the written-language form. Anyone whose habits of mind have been shaped by a life-long experience of language standardization will be inclined to assume not only that the form that is phonologically closest to the written-language form represents the main or original form but also that any more dissimilar form is somehow a less valid or less correct form of the language in question. All of these interpretations (that some one variant is the "main" variant, that the variant closest to the written-language form is the "right" or "original" variant, and that any more dissimilar variant is a deviation) must be strenuously avoided in the East Sutherland case. Contemporary dialect forms are not necessarily reflexes of the forms that served as antecedents to the written standard. In the first place, the standard language forms will often have developed out of a very different regional variety of the same language; in the second place, they may have undergone some leveling or other reformation during the process of standardization.

To take as a concrete example of these issues a case already introduced, it would certainly be unwise, without a good deal of additional historical and dialectological evidence, to assume that /ɔir/ is the "original" form of 'on her' for Golspie. Two Golspie speakers did appear to have /ɔir/ as their dominant (though not sole) variant, and one Golspie speaker who provided only a single instance of the variable used /ɔir/ in that solitary instance. But in the three East Sutherland fisherfolk communities overall, the dominant form of 'on her' is /ɛr/, not /ɔir/. Two Golspie speakers used /ɛr/ as their sole variant, two others used it as a rare variant (along with /ɔir/, in one case, and along with both /ɔir/ and /ɔi/, in the other), and *all* Brora and Embo speakers used /ɛr/ exclusively for 'on her.' Consequently it seems least misleading to avoid taking any written Gaelic form or any one phonological form as the representation of the variable. Use of the English gloss may be awkward, but it has the virtue of being neutral in a way that Gaelic orthography with its historical and regional biases cannot be.

A parallel problem involving primacy arises in presenting the full array of variants for the most variant-heavy variables. Placing a variant in the left-most position in tabular arrays inevitably seems to create a suggestion, however slight, that that variant is somehow more primary or fundamental than the others. In the case of Embo variables with only two variants, I automatically placed the variant used by the largest number of speakers to the left, but in the case of Embo variables with multiple variants, I discovered to my considerable chagrin that in developing my original handwritten tables I had unconsciously yielded to linguistic egocentrism, placing my own dominant variant in the left-most position in nearly every case. I let this bias stand, ultimately, both because there was no solid basis for any more rational ordering and because my variant preferences represented variants shared across villages, in particular across Golspie (where I lived) and Embo (where I worked most frequently), so that the variant placed left-most represented a common East Sutherland Gaelic form. It should be kept in mind, however, that Golspie and Embo belonged to different estates, so that the original population of each village was bound to have been drawn from different glens and hillsides; subsequent in-migration was likewise from different points of origin (from other Sutherland Estate coastal villages to the north of Golspie, in the case of that village, and especially from nearby coastal Ross-shire in the case of Embo). In the twentieth century, despite the existence of a number of cross-village kinship ties resulting from fisherfolk marriages, the social worlds of Golspie and Embo were quite separate; they must have been even more so in the nineteenth century, when social contact across villages was harder to achieve. There are no firm grounds, therefore, for assuming that forms that happen to coincide in the two villages must be "original"; they are shared, currently, but in one or both of the villages they may not have been the form most in use among the earliest local speakers.

6.5 Inclusion of Repetitions and Broken-Off Variants in Token Counts

One question that arose with considerable frequency was how to reckon immediate repetitions of a variant after a momentary hesitation: should they be counted as single instances or separate instances? This question was easily resolved thanks to the presence of a good many repetitions that used a second variant that differed from the first, despite occurring in immediate succession to the original. It happened with some frequency, for example, that ('when') as a clause-initiating conjunction was followed by a momentary pause and then repeated as the clause was begun over again. In the course of E17's rather copious phone-conversation materials, she produced fifteen sentences in which a clause-initiating variant of ('when') was followed after a momentary pause by a second instance of the same variable. In eleven of those cases, another instance of the same variant followed the pause: /tənə/ in eight cases, /tə/ in two, and /nərə/ in one. But in addition to these variant-consistent cases, E17 also produced four sentences in which a first variant of ('when') was followed by a different variant: /tənə/ by /tə/ in three cases, and in one especially striking case /tənə/ by /nərə/ (/tənə va—nərə va.../ 'when was—when was...'). No one else produced so dramatic a change of variants after a slight pause, but one instance of repeated ('when') from E29* demonstrated that the sequence of variants could run in more than one direction: she provided a case of /tə/ followed after a momentary pause by /tənə/, a variant sequence the opposite of the three instances from E17 cited already. E17 herself produced one instance of /tə/ followed by /tərə/, in fact, though the repetition was less immediate than the ones instanced so far:

> tə va—va—[ɛlspɛtʰ] s mĩ ĩan, **tərə** va sĩ ãnə ələpul,...
> '_WHEN_ [Elspeth] and myself were—were—, _WHEN_ we were in Ullapool,...'

Another variable particularly likely to be repeated several times in a row was ('wasn't/weren't'). In Gaelic, which has no direct equivalents to English 'yes' or 'no', repetition of the finite verb is conventionally used to express agreement or disagreement with a conversation partner's statement. The irregular past-tense form ('wasn't/weren't') traditionally appears without the preterite particle otherwise required in negated past-tense verbs (/(x)a rɔ/ or /(h)a rɔ/), but as table 3.4 showed, many local speakers produced at least a few forms with an analogically introduced preterite particle, to give /(x)a t rɔ/ or /(h)a t rɔ/. Relatively fervent agreement with a statement or question that itself used a dependent negative or negative-interrogative form of the verb 'to be' often led to a number of instances of ('wasn't/weren't') in a row. Most speakers used the same variant in each repetition, but exceptions occurred, as these two conversational instances indicate:

NCD: /xa rɔ moːran čʰĩãm [ə] vi kʰɬi, ig ə xɬɔ̃ĩːn'/.

E4: /oː, **xa rɔ. a t rɔ. a rɔ**—**a rɔ** mi kʰeːr pliərn čiəg—**a t rɔ**—**a t rɔ** mi kʰɬi er ə skɔl.../

NCD: 'there wasn't much time to be playing, for the children.'

E4: 'Oh, there WASN'T. There WASN'T. [I] WASN'T—I WASN'T 14 years—[I] WASN'T—I WASN'T playing at the school...'

NCD: /ən d rɔ əʃəːrɬax ul mər ʃɔ̃n?/

E27: /**a rɔ, ha rɔ, ha rɔ. ɔːx, ha d rɔ.**/

NCD: 'Was the whole family like that?'

E27: 'No (='WASN'T'), no, no. Och, no.'

Since immediate repetitions of the same variable can appear with different variants, as these instances with ('when') and ('wasn't/weren't') demonstrate, each instance of a variable was counted in tallying occurrences of a variable's variants, whether after a brief hesitation or in a string of repetitions.

What was true of repetitions in conversational material was equally true of repetitions in elicited material. In most cases, immediate repetition of a variable resulted in a rendering exactly like the original rendering, but occasionally a speaker unaccountably changed variants across repetitions. On one occasion E38, momentarily stuck for the word 'shouting', repeated the first clause of a translation task sentence six times in rapid succession before /k eːax/ 'shouting' finally popped into her memory and let her complete the translation of the sentence 'Why didn't you get up when I was calling/shouting to you?' In her first six immediate-repetition renderings of the opening clause, she gave the negative-interrogative verb phrase 'didn't get up?' as /ax č eːriç/, and in the final (successful) seventh translation she gave it as /ax tə y eːriç/ instead. E38 was one of just seven speakers who used the unaffricated and uncontracted form of the preterite particle /tə/ in combination with a buffer consonant /y/ before a front vowel in such phrases (see table 5.12), but it was the least frequent of her three variants. There was no apparent reason for the sudden switch away from the variant she most frequently used, the contracted and affricated variant /č/, to a variant less commonly used, even by her, on a seventh repetition. Such a change of variants is always possible across repeated elicitations, however, and for that reason all instances of a variant are counted separately, even if they occurred in immediate repetitions.

Fragmentary and faulty instances of a variable—instances broken off partway through, or distorted slightly at word's end, for example, instances of ('along with') consisting only of /kʰɔ̃n-/ or /kʰɔ̃rn-/)—were counted for tabulation here provided the variable feature was clearly produced in the fragment.

7 SELECTION AND PRESENTATION OF VARIABLES: SUMMARY

The very nature of the variation under investigation here poses a dilemma for the researcher who wishes to give an account of it. Because each variable shows its own unique pattern of variant distributions among speakers and instances, no one variable or set of variables stands out as inherently more deserving of exposition than another. That is, there is no particular set of variables the exposition of which can adequately represent the personal-pattern variation phenomenon of East Sutherland fisherfolk Gaelic. There is likewise no particular reason to begin with one variable rather than another, and there are rarely obvious grounds for following the presentation of one variable with that of any other particular variable. What a realistic depiction of this sort of variation requires instead is that a fairly large number of variables be presented, so that the typical lack of simple correlations between variant and age, sex, social network, and often proficiency level can come to light, and so that variables' divergent manifestations under similar syntactic and stylistic conditions can be appreciated.

In the absence of any obvious group of especially significant variables, I present a selection that includes a structurally broad variety, from full lexical item ('family,' 'needing') to conjunction ('when') and from preposition ('along with', 'from, off, of') to grammatical particle (preterite particle before front vowel). I also deliberately include a number of variables with a relatively large number of variants, since the array of individually distinctive variant-selection patterns is particularly striking in such cases. The result is a suitably miscellaneous collection of variables for consideration of personally patterned variation in East Sutherland fisherfolk Gaelic, the miscellaneousness of the items being itself a characteristic of the phenomenon in this dialect cluster.

A Close Look at Some Embo
Variables and Their Use

PART I: THE VARIABLES

1 INTRODUCTION

In the first section of this chapter, data on the use of eighteen variables' variants by individual speakers are presented in tabular form. Freely spoken and elicited instances are entered separately, then totaled, with the totals for each variant given as percentages of variant use. The table or pair of tables presenting each variable records the number of speakers who provided any instances at all of the variable; the number who provided at least three instances of the variable; the age, sex, and proficiency level of each speaker; the number of speakers who used each variant; the number who favored any particular variant of the variable; and the number who used any variant at a 100 percent level. Intermittent tabulation for multivariant variables groups the speakers who agreed on a variant preference in the case of a first variable in such a way that their subsequent agreement or disagreement on variant preferences in the case of other variables can be tracked by a rapid visual scan.

Tabulations of this sort are contextless, necessarily, and they are most interesting when there is a relatively large number of instances from which to calculate percentages of use. For the researcher actually at work in the field, a more indelible impression of variability arises from the process of eliciting one-at-a-time responses to a translation task from an age-stratified sample of speakers and watching the variant divergence characteristic of the community emerge in the elicited data. Single-speaker data from a 1970 translation exercise of this sort, testing for the preservation of case and gender in two masculine /kʰ/-initial nouns, /kʰɫɔːr/ 'lid' and /kʰɔr/ 'kettle', in the usage of seventeen fully fluent Embo speakers, can serve as an example. The stimulus sentence 'Take the lid off the kettle!' produced the following seventeen responses:

E4 (82, m.)	hor ən gɫɔːr tən ə xɔr
E5 (77, f.)	hor ə gɫɔːr yɛn ə xɔr
E6 (75, m.)	hor ə gɫɔːr tən ə xɔr
E9 (70, f.)	hor ə gɫɔːr yɛn ə xɔr
E10 (70, m.)	hor ə gɫɔːr tən ɔ xər
E11 (70, f.)	hor ə gɫɔːr tən ə gɔr
E17 (64, f.)	hor ən gɫɔːr yɛn ən gɔr
E 21L (58, f.)	hor ə gɫɔːr tən ə gɔr
E22 (58, f.)	hor ə gɫɔːr yən ə xɔr
E23L (57, m.)	hor ə gɫɔːr tən ə gɔr
E24 (57, f.)	hor ə gɫɔːr čɛn ə xɔr
E27 (54, m.)	hor ə gɫɔːr yɛn ə xɔr
E30 (49, m.)	hor ə gɫɔːr tən ə xɔr
E33 (45, m.)	hor ə gɫɔːr yɛn ə xɔr
E34 (45, f.)	hor ə gɫɔːr čɛn ə gɔr
E36 (41, m.)	hor ə gɫɔːr yɛn ə gɔr
E37 (41, m.)	hor ə gɫɔːr čɛn ə xɔr ~ čɛn ə gɔr

What I was chiefly interested in at the time was the perfect retention, across the age-and-proficiency continuum, of the initial consonant mutation (known as nasalization) of /kʰ-/ to /g-/, marking masculine gender in the noun /kʰɫɔːr/ 'lid' when it appeared as direct object after the definite article, versus the variable retention of the initial consonant mutation (known as lenition) of /kʰ-/ to /x-/, signaling imperfect retention of the dative case in the masculine noun /kʰɔr/ 'kettle' after the preposition 'from, off, of' plus the definite article. With E11, the presence of the preposition and article failed for the first time to produce the expected dative form /xɔr/, and the subject/direct object form /gɔr/ appeared instead; /gɔr/ was used by one other older fluent speaker and by five subsequent younger fluent speakers, including the three youngest.

Because of the particular test sentence I used, more emerged from these responses than the gender and case information I was looking for. The prepositional phrase 'off the kettle' turned out to offer an excellent example of grammatically unmotivated inter-speaker variation, eliciting from the seventeen speakers three different variants of the preposition ('from, off, of')—the same preposition on which husband and wife E27 and E34, Murdo and Lexie, differed in their mutually ratified account of a certain

Embo fellow as a "tricky man" (see chapter 3, §7.2.2).[1] A much larger database than this would of course be necessary to sort out the full inter-speaker and intra-speaker patterns of variant use for ('from, off, of'). For example, the apparent correlation in the array just presented of the variant /čɛ/ with younger speakers represents a modest apparent-time trend, and yet the variant proved to be neither universal among younger speakers nor exclusive to them; semi-speaker E39 did not use it at all, while very senior speaker E4 made occasional use of it in his freely spoken material.

Still, any fieldworker who gathered this array of responses from seventeen fully fluent speakers would feel very little doubt that the preposition ('from, off, of') had at least three different variant forms among fluent Embo Gaelic speakers. It would not yet be clear whether the differences in speakers' variant choices were likely to be consistent, whether the apparent favoring of different variants by older men as opposed to older women would persist in a larger sample, and whether these particular variant choices were or were not influenced by something in the syntax or semantics of the sentence presented for translation, but the existence of different variant forms would be apparent enough to invite further exploration.

Single-speaker arrays of translation task responses are not featured in the discussion of variables in this chapter. Suggestive as they are, they represent only lone-instance responses from each speaker, whereas establishing personal-pattern variation as a recurrent inter-speaker and intra-speaker phenomenon requires that the largest possible number of instances be gathered together for each variable and from each speaker; and in any case, freely spoken data, where available, are more persuasive than elicitation responses, since they are arguably less susceptible to self-consciousness and artificiality. All the same, repeated encounters with such results is experientially persuasive and plays an important part in heightening an investigator's awareness of variation, and therefore also in sparking interest in learning how extensive variation may be and what its limits are.

2 ORDER OF PRESENTATION AND PERCENTAGE OF USE

The discussion of Embo variables begins with those that offer the largest number of variants, since the potential for individually distinctive variant choices is highest in such cases. Among the eighteen variables presented in this chapter, ('in'), ('along with'), and ('when') have five variants each in Embo Gaelic; while ('would go') and ('family') have four; and ('from, off, of'), (preterite particle before front vowel), and ('potato') have three. After these multivariant variables have been presented, a number of two-variant variables will be introduced.

A second important consideration in presenting the variables is that the maximum number of individual preference patterns should be discernible. Variables with the same number of variants are therefore presented according to the number of speakers who produced three or more instances of the variable (the number taken here to allow a percentage of use to be reckoned; see next paragraph), from highest number of speakers to lowest. In conformity to this principle, the variable ('in'), with three or more instances from twenty-five speakers, is introduced first among the five-variant variables, followed by ('when') from twenty-four speakers and ('along with') from twenty-two speakers. The same principle prevails in the presentation of subsequent sets of four-, three-, and two-variant variables, except that the variable ('near') is treated last despite the fact that more speakers provided instances of ('near') than of the immediately preceding variable ('out'). The final position of ('near') reflects the fact that this variable was added belatedly to those already under consideration, for reasons discussed in §9.10.

In representing patterns of variant use by percentages, I took three instances of a variable as the minimum for reckoning percentage of variant use so as to eliminate cases in which a single use of a variant, or one instance each of just two variants, would result in the seemingly very high percentage-of-use scores of 100 percent or 50 percent. Tables show all instances of any variant, however, with or without percentages of use, since one- and two-instance cases of a variant are useful in tracking the persistence of variants across the age-and-proficiency continuum and in establishing which variants are shared within kin or peer circles.

With only a few exceptions, the variants discussed here are not linked to one another structurally or functionally. The few that do show such links are explored in terms of possible parallels in variant-use patterning.

3 FEATURES OF VARIANT USE

Tables for each variable show who uses which variant, and which variant, if any, an individual speaker favors, permitting the tracking across tables of the extent to which speakers who share an initial variant preference continue to do so from variable to variable. Issues to be looked at include: which speakers and how many use more than one variant in the case of each variable; to what extent the use of just one variant or of more than one variant is characteristic of particular individuals; to what extent the use of more than one variant is characteristic of any particular age-and-proficiency group or of any pair or set of age-and-proficiency groups (e.g., of semi-speakers and formerly fluent speakers as the two less than fully fluent groups); to what extent particular individuals show a preference for less widely used variants; to what extent the variant preferences of males and females may differ from one another; and whether certain pairs or clusters of individuals can be seen to share variant preferences more frequently than others. Such similarities or differences as exist in patterns of use among individuals or groups will emerge as the tabulations proceed, though given the composition of the speaker sample, an effect deriving from a speaker's age is more likely to be evident than an effect deriving from his or her sex.

Attending to these matters will make it possible to gauge how general personally patterned variation is within the speaker population as a whole, whether it rises or falls within particular age-and-proficiency groups, whether certain individuals are particularly given to either variation or invariance, and whether some individuals are out of step with their fellow-villagers in favoring less widely used variants.

3.1 The Significance of Personal-Pattern Variation Ubiquity: Brora and Golspie Parallels

In the case of each variable, note is taken of any Brora and Golspie parallels to the Embo variables. Although all of the fluent Brora and Golspie speakers were the equivalent of Embo's relatively conservative older fluent speakers, and therefore less change in progress was to be found in the fluently spoken Gaelic of those two villages than in Embo's, Brora and Golspie Gaelic were characterized by the same personally patterned variation prevalent in Embo. If the change processes characteristic of obsolescence accounted for this sort of fluent-speaker variation, it should have been less prominent in Brora and Golspie than in Embo. If it is instead a long-established product of early dialect mixture in these small and isolated minority-language communities, the phenomenon should be as prominent in Brora and Golspie Gaelic as in Embo Gaelic, as is the case, though the variables are not always the same.

Further evidence that personal-pattern variation is independent of obsolescence as such is to be seen in the fact that Embo's semi-speakers do not show a whole-group, imperfect-speaker profile in the degree of intra-speaker personal-pattern variation they display, but instead differ a good deal among themselves in degree of variation. The two most proficient Embo semi-speakers, for example, each offering data for seventeen of the eighteen variables, show very different levels of intra-speaker variation: E39 used more than one variant for seven of the seventeen variables, E40 for thirteen of the seventeen, giving a 41.2 percent level of variation for the former and a 76.5 percent level of variation for the latter. On this measure of variability, the results for the relatively high-proficiency E39 are closer to those of the low-proficiency semi-speaker E42L (more than one variant for five of sixteen variables, or 31.3 percent variation) than to those of her fellow high-proficiency semi-speaker E40. (See table 5.26 in §12.1.)

3.2 Absolute Numbers versus Percentage of Use

The stretch of time over which the materials that underpin this study were gathered was very long, and the purposes to which material was gathered differed considerably from period to period. Many early sources did not survive into the later periods; some new sources came into the study very late and all too briefly. The total number of instances available for any given variable differs greatly from person to person, and the mode or genre of speech involved is also often imperfectly comparable (translation tasks, interviews, narratives, letter tapes, and telephone conversations providing the largest array of data). The significant comparisons, therefore, are not absolute numbers of variant use from speaker to speaker, but first the percentage of use for each variant within an individual speaker's overall use of the variable, and second an individual's patterns of variant selection by percentages compared with other speakers' equally individual patterns of variant selection, also in terms of percentages.

3.3 Elicited versus Freely Spoken Variants and Other Possible Stylistically Cued Patterns of Variant Use

Some speakers provided only elicited material for this study, others provided both freely spoken and elicited material, and three individuals provided either only freely spoken material or very nearly so. In the case of those who provided both, differences between the variants an individual used in elicitation and those he or she used in freely spoken material might conceivably reveal social evaluations that go otherwise unexpressed. Absence of a particular variant in elicitation, contrasted with its frequent or at least moderate presence in freely spoken material, might indicate some conscious or unconscious level of purism regarding the variant absent in elicitation, whereas the opposite pattern, if it was pronounced enough, might suggest that the speaker had developed a sense that one particular variant was "best" and was making a point of producing the preferred variant in the more self-conscious mode. This possibility is considered in §10. Just as elicitation might have some effect on patterns of variant use, other sorts of differences in discourse function are potential sources of corresponding differences in variant use. Such possibilities will be considered in §11.

4 MULTIVARIANT VARIABLES: FIVE-VARIANT VARIABLES

Following the principles set out in §2, five-variant variables are taken up first, followed by four-variant variables and three-variant variables.

4.1 The Variable Adverbial ('in')

Thirty-four speakers provided instances of the variable ('in'), of whom twenty-five produced three or more instances. Table 5.1 shows Embo speakers' variant selections for adverbial ('in'), with freely spoken and elicited instances tallied separately before being totaled. Ideally, percentages for variant use would be given in the same table, as will be the case for variables with fewer variants, but space limitations dictate that a separate table repeat the variant-use totals and give the percentages of variant use for the totaled variant scores.

TABLE 5.1. Freely spoken and elicited variants of the variable adverbial ('in') from Embo speakers of three age-and-proficiency levels

total # of speakers: 34	stɛ			stɛx			sčax			sčɛx			sčɛ		
	fr	el	tot	fr	el	tot	fr	el	tot	fr	el	tot	fr	el	tot
E3 [85] m.	1	--	1												
E4 82 m.	5	2	7	25	6	31				1	--	1			
E5 77 f.				--	1	1									
E6 75 m.							1	5	6	1	2	3			
E8 ?71 f.							--	1	1						
E9 70 f.	--	5	5							--	1	1	--	2	2
E10 70 m.	4	11	15^a												
E13 [67] f.	5	7	12	3	1	4	--	2	2						
E14 65 f.	--	4	4												
E15L 65 m.	--	1	1	1	--	1				--	4	4			
E16 64 m.										--	1	1			
E17 64 f.	4	--	4	1	--	1	2	--	2	33	5	38	22	20	42
E20 58 f.	--	1	1										--	1	1
E21L 58 f.	--	1	1												
E22 58 f.	15	9	24				--	8	8	1	--	1			
E23L 57 m.										--	4	4			
E24 57 f.	--	9	9												
E25L 56 m.										--	3	3			
E26* 54 f.	2	1	3							9	2	11	122	18	140
E27 54 m.	1	1	2				34	29	63				3	1	4
E29* 50 f.	4	1	5							8	2	10	47	25	72
E30 49 m.							3	5	8						
E 31 49 m.													--	1	1
E32* 47 m.													1	--	1
E33 45 m.										--	3	3	--	2	2
E34 45 f.							6	19	25	--	1	1			
E35 43 f.							--	1	1						
E36 41 m.													--	3	3
E37 41 m.							3	12	15						
E38 40 f.							--	1	1	7	13	20	1	13	14
E39 38 f.				2	13	15				--	6	6			
E40 36 f.	1	2	3							1	--	1	62	39	101
E41 31 f.							--	4	4	--	1	1			
E42L 30 f.										14	22	36	1	1	2
# speakers using variant	16			6			12			18			13		

OFSs	
YFSs	
SSs	

Fr = free, el = elicited, tot = total. ^a E10 also used three non-local forms.

Adverbial ('in') had only two variants in Brora and Golspie, /stɛ/ and /sčax/.[2] In freely spoken material there was no intra-speaker variation, but when elicited materials are considered as well a few instances of intra-speaker variation emerge: in each village two speakers out of six used both variants. More speakers used /sčax/ than /stɛ/ in each village, but two in each village favored /stɛ/.

TABLE 5.2. Variant selections for the variable adverbial ('in') as number (freely spoken and elicited totaled) and percentage from Embo speakers of three age-and-proficiency levels

total # speakers: 34	ste		stex		sčax		sčex		sče	
spkrs with 3(+): 25	tot	%	tot	%	tot	%	tot	%	tot	%
E3 [85] m.	1									
E4 82 m.	7	17.9	31	79.5			1	2.6		
E5 77 f.			1							
E6 75 m.					6	66.7	3	33.3		
E8 ?71 f.					1					
E9 70 f.	5	62.5					1	12.5	2	25
E10 70 m.	15	100								
E13 [67] f.	12	66.7	4	22.2	2	11.1				
E14 65 f.	4	100								
E15L 65 m.	1	16.7	1	16.7			4	67.7		
E16 64 m.							1			
E17 64 f.	4	4.6	1	1.1	2	2.3	38	43.7	42	48.3
E20 58 f.	1								1	
E21L 58 f.	1									
E22 58 f.	24	72.7			8	24.2	1	3		
E23L 58 m.							4	100		
E24 57 f.	9	100								
E25L 56 m.							3	100		
E26* 54 f.	3	1.9					11	7.1	140	90.9
E27 54 m.	2	2.9			63	91.3			4	5.8
E29* 50 f.	5	5.7					10	11.5	72	82.8
E30 49 m.					8	100				
E31 48 m.							1			
E32* 47 m.							1			
E33 45 m.							3	60	2	40
E34 45 f.					25	96.2	1	3.8		
E35 43 f.					1					
E36 41 m.									3	100
E37 41 m.					15	100				
E38 40 f.					1	2.9	20	57.1	14	40
E39 38 f.			15	71.4			6	28.6		
E40 36 f.	3	2.9					1	1	101	96.2	OFSs
E41 31 f.					4	80	1	20			YFSs
E42L 30 f.							36	94.7	2	5.3	SSs
use of variants:										
# of speakers using	16		6		12		18		13	
# favoring	6		2		6		6		5	
# using exclusively	3		0		2		2		1	

Tot = total. Results in 90–100 percent range boldfaced, results favored to a lesser degree underlined.

4.1.1 Use of Multiple Variants

The single most striking fact about the variable adverbial ('in') is the heavy individual use of multiple variants. Among the twenty-five speakers who provided three or more instances of ('in'), only eight individuals used just one variant, while seventeen (68 percent) used more than one. Of those seventeen, eleven

(64.7 percent) used three or more. Most of the seventeen speakers who used more than a single variant showed a preference for some one variant to at least the 51 percent level, but one did not: E17 used all five variants without favoring any one of them to that level.

Noteworthy is the fact that older fluent speakers were more given to multiple-variant use than younger fluent speakers: five older fluent speakers (males E4 and E15L, females E9, E13, and E17) made use of three or more variants, while four younger fluent speakers (male E27, females E22, E26*, and E29*) did likewise, as did the semi-speakers E38 and E40. It was clearly not an age-related decline in language skills that gave rise to the use of many variants among Embo Gaelic speakers, therefore. Rather, the use of multiple variants was characteristic of the Embo speech community as a whole, with particular individuals differing in the extent to which they demonstrated the phenomenon.

Of the eight speakers who used a single variant to the 100 percent level, six were male and two female. Among the speakers who used three or more variants, contrariwise, six were female and three male. For this variable, then, women showed heavier multivariant use than men.

4.1.2 Patterns of Variant Preference by Age and Sex

The variant preference patterns of OFS males showed no clustering; E4, E6, E10, and E15L each favored a different variant. YFS males' preferences clustered either around /sčax/ (E27, E30, E37) or around /sčɛx/ (E23L, E25L, E33), with E36 the exception in his preference for /sčɛ/. OFS females showed a preference for /stɛ/ (E9, E13, E14), whereas YFS females' preferences were thoroughly diverse, the only shared preferences being those of E22 and E24 for /stɛ/ and of E26* and E29* for /sčɛ/. The semi-speakers, all females, favored four different variants; the only shared preference was that of E38 and E42L for /sčɛx/.

The closest table 5.2 comes to offering a block of preference-sharing speakers is the group of speakers E9 through E14, in which one male and one female showed 100 percent use of /stɛ/ and two other females much lower percentages of use of that same variant (62.5 percent and 66.7 percent). There is an occasional pair of same-sex speakers close in age who showed some tendency to favor the same variant: females E22 and E24; males E23L and E25L (who shared their variant preference with two other London-based Embo speakers, furthermore); but males E36 and E37, who were the same age, favored different variants.

4.2 The Variable Conjunctional ('when')

Twenty-nine speakers provided instances of the variable conjunctional ('when'), of whom twenty-four produced three or more. Tables 5.3 and 5.4 present Embo speakers' variant selections for ('when').

TABLE 5.3. Freely spoken and elicited forms of the variable conjunctional ('when') from Embo speakers of three age-and-proficiency levels

total # of speakers: 29	tərə			tə			tənə			nu(ə)rə, nərə			nə		
	fr	el	tot	fr	el	tot	fr	el	tot	fr	el	tot	fr	el	tot
E4 82 m.	1	--	1	53	4	57									
E5 77 f.				--	2	2									
E6 75 m.	7	13	20	1	1	2									
E7 74 f.	1	--	1	1	--	1									
E9 70 f.				--	1	1	--	4	4						
E10 70 m.				11	3	14				11	1	12			
E13 [67] f.	1	1	2				2	--	2	18	2	20	5	--	5
E14 65 f.				--	4	4									
E15L 65 m.							--	9	9						
E16 64 m.				--	1	1									
E17 64 f.	2	2	4	86	15	101	53	14	67	7	3	10	2	--	2
E20 58 f.				--	6	6									
E21L 58 f.	--	1	1												
E22 58 f.	1	1	2	16	16	32	2	16	18				1	1	2
E23L 57 m.										--	1	1	--	2	2
E24 57 f.				5	11	16									
E26* 54 f.				2	--	2				130	26	156	25	1	26
E27 54 m.	2	2	4	1	--	1				28	20	48	30	4	34
E29* 50 f.				32	3	35	133	33	166				1	--	1
E30 49 m.				8	--	8	3	--	3	1	1	2	3	2	5
E32* 47 m.										2	--	2	2	--	2
E33 45 m.										--	1	1	--	2	2
E34 45 f.	1	--	1	1	--	1				6	7	13	26	2	28
E37 41 m.				1	--	1	3	6	9				--	1	1
E38 40 f.				1	--	1	11	75	86						
E39 38 f.				--	1	1	4	9	13						
E40 36 f.				219	63	282	3	1	4						
E41 31 f.										--	4	4			
E42L 30 f.				1	--	1[a]							1	--	1[a]
# speakers using variant		9			22			11			11			13	

OFSs	
YFSs	
SSs	

Fr = free, el = elicited, tot = total. [a] E42L used an idiosyncratic variant unrelated to established Embo variants in twenty-eight instances.

In Brora and Golspie, the variable ('when') had only the variants /tərə/ and /tə/, except for a single unexplained instance of the otherwise non-occurrent variant /nə/ (one instance out of twenty-one from Brora speaker B7). There was a strong preference overall for the variant /tə/; six Brora and Golspie speakers favored that variant, and just two (unrelated) Golspie speakers, female G2 and male G3, favored /tərə/. Both of the speakers who favored /tərə/ also made some

TABLE 5.4. Variant selections for the variable conjunctional ('when') as number (freely spoken and elicited totaled) and percentage from Embo speakers of three age-and-proficiency levels

total # speakers: 29	tərə		tə		tənə		nu(ə)rə , nərə		nə		
spkrs with 3(+): 24	#	%	#	%	#	%	#	%	#	%	
E4 82 m.	1	1.7	57	**98.3**							
E5 77 f.			2								
E6 75 m.	20	**90.9**	2	9.1							
E7 74 f.	1		1								
E9 70 f.			1	20	4	80					
E10 70 m.			14	<u>53.8</u>			12	46.2			
E13 [67] f.	2	6.9			2	6.9	20	<u>69</u>	5	17.2	
E14 65 f.			4	**100**							
E15L 65 m.					9	**100**					
E16 64 m.			1								
E17 64 f.	4	2.2	101	<u>54.9</u>	67	36.4	10	5.4	2	1.1	
E20 58 f.			6	**100**							
E21L 58 f.	1										
E22 58 f.	2	3.7	32	<u>59.3</u>	18	33.3			2	3.7	
E23L 57 m.							1	33.3	2	66.7	
E24 57 f.			16	**100**							
E26* 54 f.			2	1.1			156	<u>84.8</u>	26	14.1	
E27 54 m.			1	1.1			48	<u>55.2</u>	34	39.1	
E29* 50 f.			35	17.3	166	<u>82.2</u>			1	.5	
E30 49 m.			8	<u>44.4</u>	3	16.7	2	11.1	5	27.8	
E32* 47 m.							2	50	2	50	
E33 45 m.							1	33.3	2	66.7	
E34 45 f.	1	2.3	1	2.3			13	30.2	28	65.1	
E37 41 m.			1	9.1	9	<u>81.8</u>			1	9.1	
E38 40 f.			1	1.1	86	**98.9**					
E39 38 f.			1	7.1	13	**92.9**					
E40 36 f.			282	**98.6**	4	1.4					
E41 31 f.							4	**100**			OFSs
E42L 30 f.			1 [a]						1 [a]		YFSs / SSs
use of variants:											
# of speakers using	9		22		11		11		13		
# favoring	1		9		6		4		3		
# using exclusively	0		3		1		1		0		

Results in the 90–100 percent range boldfaced, results favored to lesser degrees underlined. [a] E42L used an idiosyncratic variant unrelated to established Embo variants in twenty-eight instances.

use of /tə/, but only one of the speakers who favored /tə/ ever used /tərə/ (B3), and then only once in thirty instances of the variable.

4.2.1 Use of Multiple Variants

Once again, a large number of speakers used more than one variant of the variable. Of the twenty-four speakers who provided more than three instances of the variable, nineteen (79.2 percent) used more than one variant, as did two speakers who provided only two instances of the variable. Eight of the nineteen who used more than one variant (42.1 percent) used three or more variants. Most of the multiple variant users showed a preference for some one variant to at least the 51 percent level, but again one individual did not: E30 used four variants, but his highest usage level was 44.4 percent for /tə/. E32*, who provided only four instances, used /nu(ə)rə ~ nərə/ and /nə/ equally at 50 percent. Multiple variant use is more apparent among the younger fluent speakers than among the older fluent speakers in this case: E13 used four variants and E17 all five, but as many as seven of the younger fluent speakers used three or more variants. No semi-speaker used more than two of the five variants, and each had a strongly preferred variant. E42L aberrantly favored a curious variant /kə/ for ('when'), entirely unique to herself and unrelated to any other Embo form of the variable (and therefore untabulated). She used established Embo variants only twice, a different variant on each occasion.

4.2.2 Patterns of Variant Preference by Age and Sex

Older fluent speakers showed a diverse set of preference patterns, with one favoring /tərə/ (male E6), four favoring /tə/ (male E4 and female E14 strongly, male E10 and female E17 much less so), two favoring /tənə/ (female E9 and male E15L), and one favoring /nərə/ (female E13). Except for /nə/, all variants were used by older fluent speakers of both sexes. Among younger fluent speakers, several same-age or close-in-age duos shared a favored variant, but a different variant in each case: females E20 and E22 /tə/, female E26* and male E27 /nu(ə)rə/, male E33 and female E34 /nə/. Semi-speakers E38 and E39, close in age and of the same sex and proficiency group, favored /tənə/, but so did younger fluent speaker E37, of the opposite sex and the next higher proficiency level. E6's preference for /tərə/ was not shared by any other speaker, of his own age or younger, and no older fluent speakers or semi-speakers shared the mild preference shown for /nə/ by three younger fluent speakers.

For the variable overall no preference patterns by sex of speaker emerged, except where invariance is concerned: whereas most of the single-variant users in the case of ('in') were male (six of eight), most of the single-variant users in the case of ('when') were female (four of five). Single- versus multiple-variant use is therefore not routinely linked to either sex.

4.3 The Variable ('along with')

Thirty-one Embo speakers provided instances of the variable ('along with'), of whom twenty-two provided three or more. Tables 5.5 and 5.6 present Embo speakers' variant selections for ('along with').

TABLE 5.5. Freely spoken and elicited variants of the variable ('along with') from Embo speakers of three age-and-proficiency levels

total # of speakers: 31	kʰɔ̃:ɫa ri			kʰɔr(a) ri			kʰɔ̃n(a) ri			kʰɔ̃rn(a) ri			kʰɔi		
	fr	el	tot	fr	el	tot	fr	el	tot	fr	el	tot	fr	el	tot
E4 82 m.				1	--	1	11	6	17						
E6 75 m.				1	--	1	--	1	1	--	8	8			
E7 ?74 f.	2	--	2												
E9 70 f.				--	1	1	--	5	5	--	2	2			
E10 70 m.													3	1	4
E13 [67] f.	6	2	8	--	1	1	1	1	2				6	3	9
E14 65 f.								2	2						
E15L 65 m.	--	3	3				--	2	2						
E17 64 f.	1	3	4	1	--	1	10	3	13	38	11	49			
E18* 60 f.													1	--	1
E20 58 f.				--	1	1									
E21L 58 f.				--	1	1									
E22 58 f.				4	1	5	2	4	6	--	6	6	--	5	5
E23L 57 m.				--	1	1	--	1	1	--	4	4			
E24 57 f.							1	9	10						
E26* 54 f.							42	12	54	3	2	5			
E27 54 m.	1	1	2				3	8	11	2	18	20			
E29* 50 f.	1	--	1	43	5	48	44	22	66	3	--	3			
E30 49 m.							2	2	4						
E31 49 m.										--	1	1			
E32* 47 m.										1	--	1			
E33 45 m.							--	3	3	--	4	4			
E34 45 f.	2	3	5				3	2	5	1	8	9	--	3	3
E35 43 f.										--	1	1			
E36 41 m.				--	2	2									
E37 41 m.							2	13	15	--	1	1			
E38 40 f.							1	36	37	1	14	15			
E39 38 f.				4	6	10	2	3	5				--	1	1
E40 36 f.							45	13	58	5	7	12			
E41 31 f.										--	4	4			
E42L 30 f.				14	9	23	5	3	8	--	7	7			
# speakers using variant	7			13			21			18			7		

OFSs	
YFSs	
SSs	

Free = free, el = elicited, tot = total.

In Brora and Golspie, the dominant variants were /kʰɔ̃:ɫa ri/ and /kʰɔr(a) ri/, although /kʰɔi/ was also used by three of nine speakers. The variant /kʰɔr(a) ri/ was favored by three Brora speakers and one Golspie speaker, the variant /kʰɔ̃:ɫa ri/ by two Brora speakers and two Golspie speakers. As with the variable ('when'), there was a lone unexplained instance of an otherwise absent variant, one /kʰɔ̃n(a) ri/ among G2's eighty-four instances of the variable. Otherwise the variants /kʰɔ̃n(a) ri/ and /kʰɔ̃rn(a) ri/ were non-occurrent in Brora and Golspie.

TABLE 5.6. Variant selections for the variable ('along with') as number (freely spoken and elicited totaled) and percentage from Embo speakers of three age-and-proficiency levels

total # of speakers: 31	$k^h\bar{\mathrm{o}}$:ta ri		k^hɔr(a) ri		$k^h\bar{\mathrm{o}}$n(a) ri		$k^h\bar{\mathrm{o}}$rn(a) ri		k^hɔi	
speakrs with 3(+): 22	#	%	#	%	#	%	#	%	#	%
E4 82 m			1	5.6	17	**94.4**				
E6 77 f.			1	10	1	10	8	80		
E7 75 m.	2									
E9 70 f.			1	12.5	5	62.5	2	25		
E10 70 m.									4	**100**
E13 [67] f.	8	40	1	5	2	10			9	45
E14 65 f.					2					
E15L 65 m.	3	60			2	40				
E17 64 f.	4	6	1	1.5	13	19.4	49	73.1		
E18* 60 f.							1			
E20 58 f.			1				1			
E21L 58 f.			1							
E22 58 f.			5	22.7	6	27.3	6	27.3	5	22.7
E23L 57 m.			1	16.7	1	16.7	4	66.7		
E24 57 f.					10	**100**				
E26* 54 f.					54	**91.5**	5	8.5		
E27 54 m.	2	6.1			11	33.3	20	60.6		
E29* 50 f.	1	.8	48	40.7	66	55.9	3	2.5		
E30 49 m.					4	**100**				
E31 48 m.							1			
E32* 47 m.							1			
E33 45 m.					3	42.9	4	57.1		
E34 45 f.	5	22.7			5	22.7	9	40.9	3	13.6
E35 43 f.							1			
E36 41 m.			2							
E37 41 m.					15	**93.8**	1	6.3		
E38 40 f.					37	71.2	15	28.8		
E39 38 f.			10	62.5	5	31.3			1	6.3
E40 36 f.					58	82.9	12	17.1		
E41 31 f.							4	**100**		
E42L 30 f.			23	60.5	8	21.1	7	18.4		
use of variants:										
# of speakers using	7		13		21		18		7	
# favoring	1		2		9		7		2	
# using exclusively	0		0		2		1		1	

(right margin group labels: OFSs, YFSs, SSs)

Results in 90–100 percent range boldfaced, results favored to a lesser degree underlined.

4.3.1 Use of Multiple Variants

Of the twenty-two speakers who provided more than three instances of ('along with'), eighteen (81.8 percent) used more than one variant, as did one speaker who provided only two instances. There were fewer speakers who made 100 percent use of any one variant for ('along with') than for ('in') or ('when') (four speakers, versus eight and five, respectively, for the other two variables), but three of the four who used only one variant of ('along with')—E10, E24, and E30—also used just one variant of ('in'), and E24 likewise used only one variant of ('when'). In this recurrence of invariance we see a first suggestion that some speakers may be less inclined than others to intra-speaker variation.

Eleven speakers of the eighteen who used more than one variant (61.1 percent) made use of at least three variants (compared to 64.7 percent for ('in') and 42.1 percent for ('when')). For ('along with'), three or more variants were used by a male and three female older fluent speakers (male E6, females E9, E13, E17), and five younger fluent speakers (females E22, E29*, E34, and males E23L and E27), plus one semi-speaker, E39 (or alternatively two semi-speakers, if E42L's use of a completely idiosyncratic variant is taken into consideration). Again the distribution of multivariant use across the three age-and-proficiency levels demonstrates that use of a large number of variants was not simply an age-related consequence of declining language skills.

Two female speakers, E13 and E22, used multiple variants of ('along with') to such an extent that they did not favor any variant to the 51 percent level. The one speaker (E17, likewise female) who showed a similarly diverse pattern of variant use for ('in')—multiple variants, none used to a 51 percent level—did not repeat this pattern in the case of ('along with'), nor did the one speaker, male E30, who did so in the case of ('when'). Although women again appear as greater multivariant users than men for this variable, it should be noted that two of the four speakers who used only one variant for ('along with') were also female.

4.3.2 Patterns of Variant Preference by Age and Sex

There is an overall Embo convergence around two variants of ('along with'): of the thirty-one Embo speakers who produced instances of ('along with'), twenty made some use of /kʰɔ̃n(a) ri/ and eighteen some use of /kʰɔ̃rn(a) ri/; of the twenty-one speakers who showed a preference for one variant, sixteen preferred one of these same two variants, including all of the younger fluent speakers. Falling outside this variant-preference consensus were only one OFS male who showed a relatively weak preference for /kʰɔ̃:ɫa ri/, one male and one female older fluent speaker who preferred /kʰɔi/ (the female very weakly), and two semi-speakers who weakly favored /kʰɔr(a) ri/.

5 GENDER AND MULTIPLE- OR SINGLE-VARIANT USE PATTERNS FOR THE FIVE-VARIANT VARIABLES

The question of a possible gender effect in the use of multiple variants can be raised at this point, though it does not prove easy to answer. The same core set of individuals tends to re-emerge as multiple variant users for each of the five-variant variables, with females predominating among those who used three or more variants in at least two cases.

('in')	('when')	('along with')	age, sex
E9		E9	70, f.
E13	E13	E13	[67], f.
E17	E17	E17	64, f.
E22	E22	E22	58, f.
E26*		E26*	54, f.
E27	E27	E27	54, m.
E29*	E29*	E29*	50, f.
	E34	E34	45, f.
	(E42L)	E42L	30, f.

Every speaker in this listing is female except for E27.

The list of those who used only a single variant in at least two of the three cases (using that variant therefore at the 100 percent level) is shorter, but females predominate slightly in this list as well.

('in')	('when')	('along with')	age, sex
E10		E10	70, m.
E14	E14		65, f.
E24	E24	E24	57, f.
E30		E30	49, m.
	E41	E41	31, f.

In this listing two males appear, E10 and E30. The latter is a cross-over speaker where these variables are concerned in that he used multiple variants for ('when') but a single variant each for ('in') and ('along with'). Only one other speaker, also male, showed a similar pattern, but to a more limited extent: E15L used multiple variants for ('in'), but only a single variant for ('when'). (He ran to neither extreme for ('along with'), using two variants in that case.)

The fact that largely separate lists can be made of speakers who tended to use three or more variants and speakers who tended to use only one variant again suggests the distinctiveness of individual speakers' patterns of use, a distinctiveness residing not just in their particular variant selections—that is, whether they used /stɛ/ or /sčax/, /tənə/ or /nərə/—but also in the extent to which they made use of one variant or many. It is difficult to say whether gender as such plays any role in such differences. Certainly females predominate among the speakers who used the greatest number of variants of all three variables examined so far. OFS females E13 and E17 and YFS females E22 and E29* used three or more variants in every case, as against the one YFS male who did so, E27. At the same time, the only speaker to use a single variant in all three cases was also female, younger fluent speaker E24; and two other females, older fluent speaker E14 and semi-speaker

E41, used a single variant in two of the three cases. Two males used a single variant in two of the three cases, E10 and E30; E30 is the cross-over speaker who used multiple variants in the case of ('when').

If the wholly female semi-speaker sample is left aside, there is very nearly the same number of males and females represented in the speaker samples for these three variables, theoretically allowing men at least as good an opportunity as women to demonstrate multiple-variant use. But five of the nine speakers who appear as multivariant users survived into the period when I was recording large amounts of material by phone or during visits from overseas, four of them females (E17, E29*, E30*, and E42L), so that females provided an exceptionally large amount of material; three other females (E13, E22, and E34) were the chief speakers on the very early and extensive multispeaker letter tapes sent to me from Embo while I was writing my dissertation. If the amount of material provided by a speaker has any bearing on the number of variants that appear, then females were disproportionately represented among those who provided a large amount of material and therefore had the greater opportunity to produce multiple variants. At the same time, the fact that E4 provided a large amount of material without pro-ducing extremes of either high or low variant use for these variables, as was also true of semi-speaker E40, indicates that a large volume of material does not *nec-essarily* correlate with a very high level of multivariant use.

6 ALIGNMENT OF INDIVIDUAL VARIANT PREFERENCES: THREE FIVE-VARIANT VARIABLES

Table 5.7 provides a direct comparison between Embo speakers' variant-use pref-erences for ('in'), ('when'), and ('along with'). The tabulations show proficiency level by the usual differences in shading. Age is represented by the numbers assigned to each speaker, and gender is indicated for each individual. Percentages of variant use are for freely spoken and elicited instances totaled.

A common typeface is established for each set of speakers who shared a var-iant preference for ('in'), the variable for which percentage-of-use preferences can be established for the largest number of speakers. Typeface is then carried over from the groupings for ('in') into the tabulations for ('when') and ('along with')—as it will be carried over also into subsequent tabulations for four- and three-variant tabulations—so that groupings of typeface patterns track the degree to which the same speakers' variant preferences did or did not coincide for subsequent variables. E20, the one speaker who appears in the tabulation for ('when') without having appeared in the tabulation for ('in') (because she did not provide three instances of the latter variable), is identified by a distinctive type-face of her own, among the other speakers who favored /tə/, so as to avoid making an arbitrary choice between placing her with the group E10, E14, E22, E24, or with the pair E17 and E40, each already sharing a typeface based on their ('in')

TABLE 5.7. Embo variant preferences for ('in'), ('along with'), and ('when') by percentage of use

stɛ		stɛx		sčax		sčɛx		sčɛ	
m. E10	100	m. E4	79.5	m. E30	100	m. E23L	100	m. E36	100
f. E14	100	f. E39	71.4	m. E37	100	m. E25L	100	f. E40	96.2
f. E24	100			f. E34	96.2	f. E42L	94.7	f. E26°	90.9
f. E22	72.7			m. E27	91.3	m. E15L	67.7	f. E29°	82.8
f. E13	66.7			f. E41	80	m. E33	60	f. E17	48.3
f. E9	62.5			m. E6	66.7	f. E38	57.1		

tərə		tə		tənə		nərə		nə	
m. E6	90.9	f. E14	100	m. E15L	100	f. E41	100	m. E23L	66.7
		f. E20	100	f. E38	98.9	f. E26°	84.8	m. E33	66.7
		f. E24	100	f. E39	92.9	f. E13	69	f. E34	65.1
		f. E40	98.6	f. E29°	82.2	m. E27	55.2	m. Æ32*	50
		m. E4	98.3	m. E37	81.8	m. Æ32*	50		
		f. E22	59.3	f. E9	80				
		f. E17	54.9						
		m. E10	53.8						
		m. E30	44.4						

kʰɔ̃:ta ri		kʰɔra ri		kʰɔ̃na ri		kʰɔ̃rna ri		kʰɔi	
m. E15L	60	f. E39	62.5	f. E24	100	f. E41	100	m. E10	100
		f. E42L	60.5	m. E30	100	m. E6	80	f. E13	45
				m. E4	94.4	f. E17	73.1		
				m. E37	93.8	m. E23L	66.7		
				f. E26°	91.5	m. E27	60.6		
				f. E40	82.9	m. E33	57.1		
				f. E38	71.2	m. E34	40.9		
				f. E9	62.5				
				f. E29°	55.9				

Type faces are assigned according to preferences shared for ('in'). Proficiency level is indicated by shading: OFSs no shading, YFSs light gray, SSs darker gray. Asterisks indicate formerly fluent speakers.

preferences, or with either E4 or E30, each of whom already has a typeface based on a variant preference for ('in'). Where two or more speakers' use of a given variant was identical by percentage, they are entered according to their age-and-proficiency numbering.

6.1 Variant-Preference Distributions

It is immediately evident from the tabulation that variant preferences for ('in') were more evenly divided than for ('when') and considerably more so than for ('along with'). Only the variant /stɛx/ is rarely a preferred variant; /stɛ/, /sčax/, and /sčɛx/ were preferences for equal numbers of individuals, with /sčɛ/ lagging only slightly behind. For ('when'), preference distributions were somewhat less well balanced. Two of the /t/-initial variants are more often preferred, both singly and as a pair, than the /n/-initial variants, whereas /tərə/ was extremely rare as a preference. For ('along with'), the general Embo favoring of the variants /kʰɔ̃n(a) ri/ and /kʰɔ̃rn(a) ri/ leaves the other three variants unusual as preferences.

A variant can be in moderately heavy use without appearing prominently as a preferred variant. The semi-speakers E39 and E42L were the only individuals who showed an actual preference for the variant /kʰɔr(a) ri/, but it was well represented among E22's very mixed variant choices for this variable and was the second most common variant for E29*. Seldom preferred, it was nevertheless used by as many as thirteen speakers. Whereas the tables for each variable display the full range of variant use, table 5.7 displays only the preference convergences and divergences of the speakers. Carrying forward the typeface shared by E9 and E13 because of their similar levels of preference for the same variant of ('in') makes it easy to track the subsequent divergence of their preferences for ('when') and ('along with'), but it does not reveal a different feature of their variant use, highlighted by table 5.2, namely, that the other two variants each speaker used for ('in') showed no overlap at all.

6.2 Variant-Preference Clusterings

The predominance of no shading in the first column of the ('in') tabulations reflects four older fluent speakers' shared preference for /stɛ/ and the relative rarity of that preference among younger fluent speakers and semi-speakers. The four older fluent speakers who favored /stɛ/ do not reappear as a group in either of the subsequent tabulations, however. For ('when'), E10 and E14 continued to share a variant preference, but E9 and E13 differed both from them and from each other. For ('along with'), E10 and E13 again shared a variant preference (again at very different levels); E9 favored a different variant, the one also used by E14, even though the latter did not produce enough instances to allow for the establishment of a percentage of use. This is a typical pattern for Embo variant use: whatever grouping of speakers is established by a shared variant preference for one variable generally breaks into different subgroupings, or breaks apart beyond any groupings at all, when their preferences for some other variable are tallied.

The semi-speakers do not show high variant-use consensus as a group despite the fact that all of them fell at the low end of the age range, shared a common history of incomplete acquisition, and showed a relatively low level of active Gaelic use. The five women favored four different variants of (in'), with only E38 and E42L sharing a variant preference. They favored three different variants for ('when'), with only E38 and E39 sharing a variant preference; E42L disappeared from the tabulation in this case because of idiosyncrasy. All five are again represented for ('along with'), but they favored three different variants. E38 and E40 shared a variant preference, as did E39 and E42L. No pairing of semi-speakers by shared variant preferences occurs twice across the three variables; each is unique.

6.3 Clusterings by Sex of Speaker

Groupings by the speaker's sex appear in table 5.7, but they are neither exclusive nor very persuasively patterned. The strongest grouping appears once again in connection with the variant /stɛ/ for ('in'), where five of six speakers who favor that variant are women; for /sčɛ/ the ratio is almost as strong, with four women to one man. In each of these cases the lone male used the variant in question at the 100 percent level, but several of the females also used the variant at an identical or similar level. Reversals of this pattern appear for /sčax/ and /sčɛx/, with twice as many men favoring these variants as women. In the latter case, the only women who favored the variant were semi-speakers. Given these preference patterns, it is tempting to propose that the variants /stɛ/ and /sčɛ/ were associated with women and the variants /sčax/ and /sčɛx/ with men. The overall picture presented in table 5.2 makes this proposition hard to sustain, however, since a fair number of men used the former and women the latter, even if they did not prefer them or did not provide enough examples for a percentage-of-use figure.

The same is true for the other two variables. Although twice as many women as men favored the variant /tə/, and two males but only one woman favored /nə/, table 5.4 indicates that several additional males used /tə/ without preferring it and several additional females used /nə/ without preferring it. Table 5.6 shows considerably more women favoring /kʰɔ̃n(a) ri/ than men, but table 5.5 indicates that five additional men used it without favoring it. Gender-related preferences may be suggestive, but overall variant-use distributions present a complex mix that makes any strong association of particular variants with males or females unlikely.

6.4 Invariance

In the tabulation for ('in'), males appear very prominently among those who use one or another variant at the 100 percent level: six of the eight invariant speakers are males. The prominence of males as invariant speakers did not reappear with the other two variables, however: two males and two females showed invariance for ('along with'), and only one male was among the five individuals who used any variant of ('when') at the 100 percent level. Invariance reaches 32 percent (eight of twenty-five speakers) for ('in') but is less prominent for the other two five-variant variables: five of twenty-four speakers (20.8 percent) showed invariant use of a single variant for ('when'), and four of twenty-two (18.2 percent) for ('along with').

6.5 The London-Embo Speaker Group

The four London-Embo speakers' striking variant-preference consensus on ('in') disappears in the two subsequent tabulations. The two who provided enough instances of ('when') to establish a variant preference favored different variants, and for ('along with'), where three of the four are represented, each of the three favored a different variant.

6.6 Patterns of Atypical Variant Preference

With three tabulations available, it is also becoming apparent that the speakers who demonstrate the least typical variant-selection preferences are different individuals in each case: for ('in') E4 and E39, for ('when') E6, and for ('along with') E15L, E39, E42L, E10, and E13. Only E39 appears twice in this list. If the same pattern of occasionally atypical variant preferences shown by a variety of individual speakers appears in subsequent cases, any explanation of inter-speaker variation as the result of atypical speech habits on the part of a recognizable subset of maverick speakers will be ruled out, just as heavy multiple variant use on the part of older fluent speakers rules out the possibility that intra-speaker variation can be explained as the result of declining language skills (see §4.1.1).

7 MULTIVARIANT VARIABLES: FOUR- AND THREE-VARIANT VARIABLES

7.1 The Variable ('would go')

Four conditional forms of the irregular verb 'go' are in use in Embo, all of them well formed. They show the conditional suffix /-u/ and, except in the environments that call for dependent forms of the verb (see next paragraph), those with susceptible initial consonants show lenition, the initial mutation which together with the suffix /-u/ marks the conditional.

Tables 5.8 and 5.9 present Embo speakers' variant selections for ('would go'). The parentheses around the aspiration of the initial consonant in the first and last of the four variants in these two tables, /č⁽ʰ⁾ɛu/ and /č⁽ʰ⁾eːju/, reflects the fact that in this irregular verb (as in one other with initial /č⁽ʰ⁾-/ and one with initial /t⁽ʰ⁾-/) the underlying root from which the conditional is formed has an initial consonant that is aspirated in the so-called independent forms but unaspirated in the so-called dependent forms (the latter being those which follow the negative particle and a good many conjunctions, especially those with a negative component).[3] The actual independent conditional forms of ('would go') are /hɛu/ and /heːju/ for these two variants, deriving from underlying forms /čʰɛu/ and /čʰeːju/, with normal initial-consonant lenition of /čʰ-/ to /h-/ for conditional aspect. The corresponding dependent negative conditional forms 'wouldn't go' are /(x)a čɛu/ and /(x)a čeːju/, however, deriving from underlying forms /čɛu/ and /čeːju/, with *un*aspirated initial consonant.

TABLE 5.8. Freely spoken and elicited variants of the variable ('would go') from Embo speakers of three age-and-proficiency levels

total # of speakers: 27		č(h)εu			rεu			raxu			č(h)e:ju		
		fr	el	tot	fr	el	tot	fr	el	tot	fr	el	tot
E4	82 m.							7	4	11			
E6	75 m.	2	3	5							--	2	2
E9	70 f.							--	7	7			
E10	70 m.	4	5	9	--	1	1	--	2	2			
E13	[67] f.				--	2	2	3	3	6			
E15L	65 m.	--	1	1	--	2	2						
E17	64 f.							23	8	31			
E20	58 f.							--	2	2			
E21L	58 f.				1	3	4						
E22	58 f.							4	5	9			
E23L	57 m.	--	1	1	--	3	3						
E24	57 f.				--	12	12						
E25L	56 m.				--	2	2						
E26*	54 f.							2	2	4	5	8	13
E27	54 m.							8	11	19			
E29*	50 f.	1	1	2	5	2	7				5	9	14
E30	49 m.	1	--	1									
E32*	47 m.							1	--	1			
E33	45 m.										--	4	4
E34	45 f.							5	15	20			
E36	41 m.										--	1	1
E37	41 m.				--	9	9						
E38	40 f.	1	12	13							1	12	13
E39	38 f.										2	5	7
E40	36 f.	5	18	23							6	14	20
E41	31 f.										--	3	3
E42L	30 f.				--	4	4						
# of speakers using variant			8			10			11			9	

OFSs
YFSs
SSs

Fr = free, el = elicited, tot = total.

The conditional of the irregular verb 'go' was not variable in Brora and Golspie. All speakers used /č(h)εu/.

7.1.1 A Case of Linguistic Variation Together with Linguistic Change

In the case of the variable ('would go'), there is a convergence of established East Sutherland Gaelic inter-speaker and intra-speaker variation on the one hand and of grammatical change in progress on the other. As with the emergence of first-person-singular conditional forms with /-u mi/ (/xanu mi/ 'I would say') beside traditional /-ĩn'/ (/xanĩn'/ 'I would say'), the emergence of a variant /č(h)e:ju/ represents an analogical regularization. In the extremely irregular verb 'to go', none of the traditional local forms of the conditional—/č(h)εu/, /rεu/, and /raxu/—bears any obvious resemblance to the independent and dependent preterite forms /xa/ (Golspie /ɣa/) and /čax/,

TABLE 5.9. Variant choices for the variable ('would go') as number (freely spoken and elicited totaled) and percentage, from Embo speakers of three age-and-proficiency levels

total # speakers: 27	č(h)ɛu		rɛu		raxu		č(h)e:ju		
spkrs with 3(+): 22	#	%	#	%	#	%	#	%	
E4 82 m.					11	**100**			
E6 75 m.	5	<u>71.4</u>					2	28.6	
E9 70 f.					7	**100**			
E10 70 m.	9	<u>75</u>	1	8.3	2	16.7			
E13 [67] f.			2	25	6	<u>75</u>			
E15L 65 m.	1	33.3	2	<u>66.7</u>					
E17 64 f.					31	**100**			
E20 58 f.					2				
E21L 58 f.			4	**100**					
E22 58 f.					9	**100**			
E23L 57 m.	1	25	3	<u>75</u>					
E24 57 f.			12	**100**					
E25L 56 m.			2						
E26* 54 f.					4	23.5	13	<u>76.5</u>	
E27 54 m.					19	**100**			
E29* 50 f.	2	8.7	7	30.4			14	<u>60.9</u>	
E30 49 m.	1								
E32* 47 m.					1				
E33 45 m.							4	**100**	
E34 45 f.					20	**100**			
E36 41 m.					1				
E37 41 m.			9	**100**					
E38 40 f.	13	50					13	50	
E39 38 f.							7	**100**	
E40 36 f.	23	<u>53.5</u>					20	46.5	OFSs
E41 31 f.							3	**100**	YFSs
E42L 30 f.			4	**100**					SSs
use of variants: # of speakers using	8		10		11		9		
# favoring	3		6		7		5		
# using exclusively	0		4		6		3		

Results in 90–100% range boldfaced, results favored to lesser degrees underlined.

to the independent and dependent future forms /he:ǰ/ and /če:ǰ/, or to the gerund /tuł/. Using the forms /he:ǰu/ and /če:ǰu/ as the independent and dependent forms of the conditional reduces the irregularity of the verb, since each of those forms is recognizably built on the corresponding future forms /he:ǰ/ and /če:ǰ/.

A few speakers—E33, E39, and E41—appear to have carried through this simplification process fully, producing conditionals of 'go' based exclusively on /č(h)e:ǰ/. None of these speakers produced a great many instances of the variable, however, and a larger number of instances might have presented more variation. Slightly more speakers appear to have adopted an analogical variant for ('would go') without having eliminated the more traditional, non-analogical variants from their usage, as is true of E6, E26*, E29*, E38, and E40. Since even older fluent speakers such as E10, E13, and E15L, who never made any use of /č(h)e:ǰu/ at all, drew on more than one variant of ('would go'), it is less surprising in Embo than it might be elsewhere to find resistance to complete displacement of an irregular variant by a more regular analogical variant. Even much younger speakers demonstrated resistance to the analogical variant: E37 and E42L used 100 percent /rɛu/, for example, and the single instances of the variable produced by E30 and E32* were non-analogical variants.

7.1.2 The Role of Acoustic Salience

The variable ('would go') is of special interest for another reason, namely the acoustic salience of the differences between its variants. Not only do the traditional conditional forms for ('would go') not resemble the preterite, future, and gerund forms of the same verb, they do not resemble one another. The differences between the variant forms /čʰɛu/, /rɛu/, /raxu/, and /čʰeːǰu/ seem so great that it is hard to imagine speakers failing to notice divergent variant choices. If they did notice, they seldom commented on it, a remarkable fact in view of the endless comment about much less salient cross-village variation, such as—to take one among many examples—the Embo versus Golspie forms of the word for 'fire', /čʰĩn/ and /čʰɔ̃n/, respectively. Only two speakers in my Embo sample ever remarked on inter-speaker variation in connection with ('would go'). One was E24, the single individual least given to intra-speaker variation; while giving her own invariant elicitation responses with /rɛu/, she volunteered that some people said /čʰɛu/. The other was E27, contrariwise a speaker very much given to intra-speaker variation; while giving his uniform elicitation responses with /raxu/, he volunteered that some Embo speakers would say /čʰɛu/. Since it was quite unusual for anyone to comment on within-the-village variability at all, perhaps the acoustic distinctiveness of the variant forms did have some effect here. But E24 made no mention of E27's variant /raxu/, he did not mention her variant /rɛu/, and neither of them pointed out that there were actually four different variants, not just two. Of course, most Embo speakers made no comment at all on the sharply different variants in use in their village.

7.1.3 Use of Multiple Variants

Nine of twenty-two speakers (40.9 percent) who provided three or more instances of ('would go') used more than one variant. Conspicuous in this case as compared with the previous three variables is the high number of speakers who used only a single variant (thirteen individuals, 59.1 percent) and the very low number of speakers who used three or more (just two individuals, E10 and E29*). The highest number of speakers using only a single variant in the previous cases was eight, for ('in'), and the lowest number of speakers using three or more variants was eight, for ('when'). To be sure, ('would go') has only four possible variants instead of the five available for the previous three variables, but a smaller number of variants by no means guarantees a larger number of single-variant speakers or a smaller number of multiple-variant speakers, as the case of the variable ('potato') in §7.5 will demonstrate. For ('would go') speakers also tended to have more pronounced preferences for their favored variants. Only semi-speaker E40 had a preferred-variant level below 60 percent, and only semi-speaker E38 showed no clear-cut preference for a single variant, using /č⁽ʰ⁾ɛu/ and /č⁽ʰ⁾eːǰu/ equally.[4]

Despite the relatively high number of invariant speakers, more older fluent speakers used two or more variants than used only one: three OFS males and an OFS female used two or more, while one OFS male and two OFS females used only one. The opposite was true of the younger fluent speakers, however: seven of them, five females and two males, used only one variant, while only three, one male and two females, used two or more. The semi-speakers were more evenly divided, with three using only a single variant and two using two variants apiece.

7.1.4 Patterns of Variant Preference by Age and Sex

Two age-related trends are evident in tables 5.8 and 5.9: first, younger speakers were making a good deal less use of /raxu/ and somewhat less of /č⁽ʰ⁾ɛu/; second, they were making more use of /č⁽ʰ⁾eːǰu/ than their elders. The latter development represents, as noted, increasing adoption of an analogically regularized variant. Only one of seven older fluent speakers used /č⁽ʰ⁾eːǰu/, but four of fifteen younger fluent speakers did so and so did four of five semi-speakers. At the same time, with even semi-speakers continuing to produce non-analogical variants, the analogical form had not prevailed altogether. If the age-and-proficiency continuum could be followed further, by testing near-passive bilinguals for example, one might expect a more complete adoption of the analogical variant. But one of the difficulties of following change processes in an obsolescent language is that the structure sometimes disappears from use before it is clear whether the change will go to completion (see Dorian 1997b for a Pennsylvania German case of this sort). E41 and E42L, the youngest semi-speakers, could not reliably produce the conditional form of Gaelic verbs, as many failed translation tasks demonstrated. Only the fact that 'go' is a very high-frequency verb enabled them to dredge up a few intact variant forms in the conditional.

In this sample of speakers, males were more frequent users of the variant /č⁽ʰ⁾ɛu/ than were females, and two OFS males were two of only three speakers who favored that variant. Both males and females made use of, and favored, the variants /rɛu/ and /raxu/, but /č⁽ʰ⁾eːǰu/ was favored almost exclusively by women (E33 being the only exception). This last variant-selection pattern essentially reflects the greater adoption of /č⁽ʰ⁾eːǰu/ by formerly fluent speakers and semi-speakers, since the two well-represented formerly fluent speakers and all five of the semi-speakers were women.

For ('would go'), males showed more intra-speaker variation overall than females did. Four of eight fluent-speaker males used more than one variant (50 percent of all males who provided three or more instances of the variable), while three of nine fluent-speaker females did so, along with two of the five female semi-speakers. The five women who showed intra-speaker variation constituted 35.7 percent of the fourteen females who provided three or more instances.

7.2 The Variable ('family')

Tables 5.10 and 5.11 present Embo speakers' variant selections for the variable ('family').

Six fluent Brora speakers and a Brora semi-speaker used the form /čʰə:(r)ɬax/ invariably, with all Brora instances elicited. Golspie speakers used two variants, /čʰə:(r)ɬax/ and /čʰə:(r)ɬiç/, both freely spoken or elicited. Only one male among the four Golspie speakers who provided two or more instances of the variable showed intra-speaker variation.

The tabulations for ('family') reinforce the earlier finding that there is no one sub-set of individuals repeatedly favoring less preferred variants. The only two speakers

TABLE 5.10. Freely spoken and elicited variants of the variable ('family') from Embo speakers of three age-and-proficiency levels

total # of speakers: 22	čʰə:rɬax			čʰə:rɬiç			tʰə:rɬiç			tʰə:rɬax			
	fr	el	tot	fr	el	tot	fr	el	tot	fr	el	tot	
E4 82 m.				7	3	10							
E10 70 m.				2	4	6							
E13 [67] f.				--	1	1	--	2	2				
E14 65 f.				--	2	2							
E15L 65 m.	--	2	2										
E17 64 f.	1	8	9	2	7	9	9	4	13	1	--	1	
E20 58 f.	--	3	3										
E22 58 f,							--	5	5				
E23L 57 m.				--	1	1							
E24 57 f.							--	11	11				
E26* 54 f.				--	1	1	4	6	10				
E27 54 m.	4	5	9	1	2	3	3	1	4	2	--	2	
E28L 51 m.				--	1	1							
E29* 50 f.	[1]	--	[1]	17	6	23	2	2	4				
E32* 47 m.							5	--	5				
E33 45 m.	--	1	1										
E34 45 f.	1	--	1				--	2	2				
E37 41 m.				--	1	1	--	1	1				
E38 40 f.				--	1	1	--	22	22				
E39 38 f.				1	13	14	--	[1]	[1]				OFSs
E40 36 f.				--	3	3	11	8	19				YFSs
E42L 30 f.							6	--	6				SSs
# of speakers using variant	7			14			14			2			

Fr = free, el = elicited, tot = total. Square brackets indicate an otherwise absent variant produced as an immediate echo of a previous speaker or following a prompt from another speaker; these are not included subsequently in reckoning percentages.

TABLE 5.11. Variant selections for the variable ('family') as number (freely spoken and elicited totaled) and percentage from Embo speakers of three age-and-proficiency-levels, unique echoed and prompted instances discounted

total # speakers: 22	čʰəːrɬax		čʰəːrtiç		tʰəːrtiç		tʰəːrɬax		
spkrs with 3(+): 16	#	%	#	%	#	%	#	%	
E4 82 m.			10	100					
E10 70 m.			6	100					
E13 [67] f.			1	33.3	2	66.7			
E14 65 f.			2						
E15L 65 m.	2								
E17 64 f.	9	28.1	9	28.1	13	40.6	1	3.1	
E20 58 f.	3	100							
E22 58 f.					5	100			
E23L 57 m.			1						
E24 57 f.					11	100			
E26* 54 f.			1	9.1	10	90.9			
E27 54 m.	9	50	3	16.7	4	22.2	2	11.1	
E28L 51 m.			1						
E29* 50 f.			23	85.2	4	14.8			
E32* 47 m.					5	100			
E33 45 m.	1								
E34 45 f.	1	33.3			2	66.7			
E37 41 m.			1		1				
E38 40 f.			1	4.3	22	95.7			
E39 38 f.			14	100					OFSs
E40 36 f.			3	13.6	19	86.4			YFSs
E42L 30 f.					6	100			SSs
use of variants: # of speakers using	6		14		13		2		
# favoring	2		4		10		0		
# using exclusively	1		3		4		0		

Results in 90–100% range boldfaced, results favored to lesser degrees underlined.

whose percentage-of-use scores indicated a preference for a relatively little used variant of ('family') were E20 and E27, neither of whom was among the speakers who showed less favored variant preferences for any of the previous variables.

7.2.1 Use of Multiple Variants

Eight of sixteen speakers (50 percent) who provided three or more instances of ('family') used more than one variant, as did one of three speakers who provided only two instances of the variable. Only three speakers used more than two variants, OFS female (E17) and female and male younger fluent speakers E29* and E27. The lone instance of a third variant from E29* was an echo of a conversation partner's usage, however, and she is more realistically assessed as a two-variant user. E17 and E27 were the sole users of the variant /tʰəːrɬax/, but each used it in impeccably natural conversational contexts, and in any case they are conspicuous by this time for their general tendency to high intra-speaker variation. E27 used three variants for three of the four previously tabulated variables, whereas E17 did him one better: in three of five cases presented so far (including this one), E17 used all available variants, five for ('in'), five for ('when'), and four for ('family'). In addition she used four of the five possible variants for ('along with'). Her sole departure from multivariant use thus far is her invariant use of /raxu/ for ('would go').

Invariance is not quite as high for ('family') as for ('would go'). Thirteen (59.1 percent) of the twenty-two speakers who provided at least three instances of ('would go') used some one variant exclusively, compared with the 50 percent who did so in this case.

7.2.2 Patterns of Variant Preference
by Age and Sex

Tables 5.10 and 5.11 indicate that Embo speakers' variant selections center on the two forms /čʰəːrɬiç/ and /tʰəːrɬiç/, with nearly equal numbers of speakers using each of the variants. But they also indicate that preferential use shifts from one to the other of these variants over the age-and-proficiency continuum. Five of seven older fluent speakers used /čʰəːrɬiç/, but only six of sixteen speakers in the two younger groups did so. Younger fluent speakers and semi-speakers continued to make some use of /čʰəːrɬiç/, but only two of them favored that variant, while eight of them favored /tʰəːrɬiç/.[5]

Table 5.11 is the first in which the two oldest speakers entered in the tabulation are in complete agreement, both on a variant preference and on its percentage of use. The situation is somewhat simplified for ('family'), however, because several otherwise moderately well-represented older fluent speakers produced no instances of this variable. I was late in recognizing the full degree of variability characteristic of ('family') and therefore in making it the object of inquiry; many of my oldest sources were no longer alive by that time, eliminating the opportunity to make up for chance absences of this item in their materials.

Only four males offered enough instances of the variable to demonstrate a favored variant. The two older fluent speakers among them, E4 and E10, favored /čʰəːrɬiç/, and E32* joined most of the other younger fluent speakers in favoring /tʰəːrɬiç/; E27 was unusual in favoring /čʰəːrɬax/. All but one of the ten speakers who showed a preference for /tʰəːrɬiç/ were female, but gender is not a perfectly clear-cut factor in variant selection. The variant /tʰəːrɬiç/ was the second most frequent variant for male speaker E27 and the sole variant used by E32*, another male, while two females, E29* and E39, both strongly preferred /čʰəːrɬiç/ and female E20 used only /čʰəːrɬax/. Conceivably gender plays some role in variant preference here, but the limited number of speakers who provided more than three instances, plus the age and sex imbalances among the subsample who did, make this difficult to determine.

7.3 The Variable ('from, off, of')

This is the variable featured at the beginning of this chapter in the array of single-speaker responses to the translation task sentence 'Take the lid off the kettle! ', the preposition ('from, off, of') in its non-partitive function. The variation evident in that opening array is also evident in the fuller data presented in table 5.12.

Brora and Golspie speakers used the preposition tabulated here in fewer environments than their Embo counterparts. They preferred the preposition /vɔ/ 'from' and occasionally also /ɛs/ 'out of' in some environments where Embo speakers

TABLE 5.12. Variant selections for the variable preposition ('from, off, of') in non-partitive constructions, as number (freely spoken and elicited totaled) and percentage, from Embo speakers of three age-and-proficiency levels

total # speakers: 31	tə				yε				čε			
spkrs with 3(+): 23	fr	el	tot	%	fr	el	tot	%	fr	el	tot	%
E4 82 m.	9	12	21	84	1	1	2	8	2	--	2	8
E5 77 f.	--	1	1	20	--	4	4	80				
E6 75 m.	1	3	4	100								
E9 70 f.					--	1	1					
E10 70 m.	3	4	7	87.5	--	1	1	12.5				
E11 70 f.	--	1	1									
E12 ?68 f.	--	3	3	100								
E13 [67] f.	1	3	4	57.1	--	1	1	14.3	--	2	2	28.6
E14 65 f.	--	1	1									
E15L 65 m.	--	4	4	100								
E16 64 m.	--	4	4	100								
E17 64 f.	6	--	6	33.3	7	4	11	61.1	1	--	1	5.6
E20 58 f.					--	1	1					
E21L 58 f.	--	1	1									
E22 58 f.	1	2	3	50	--	3	3	50				
E23L 57 m.	--	5	5	100								
E24 57 f.									--	9	9	100
E25L 56 m.	1	9	10	100								
E26* 54 f.					3	9	12	85.7	--	2	2	14.3
E27 54 m.	9	--	9	20.9	5	25	30	69.8	1	3	4	9.3
E28L 51 m.									--	1	1	
E29* 50 f.	2	4	6	18.2	--	1	1	3	6	20	26	78.8
E30 49 m.	--	1	1		1	--	1					
E32* 47 m.					1	--	1					
E33 45 m.	--	1	1	6.7	--	14	14	93.3				
E34 45 f.					--	1	1	5	4	15	19	95
E35 43 f.					--	1	1					
E36 41 m.	--	1	1		--	1	1					
E37 41 m.									2	5	7	100
E38 40 f.	1	3	4	30.8					--	9	9	69.2
E39 38 f.	1	14	15	100								
E40 36 f.	14	4	18	30					10	32	42	70
E42L 30 f.	--	4	4	100								
use of variants: # of speakers using	24				17				12			
# favoring	11				5				6			
# using exclusively	8				0				2			

OFSs	
YFSs	
SSs	

Fr = freely spoken, el = elicited, tot = total. Results in the 90–100% range boldfaced, results favored to lesser degrees underlined.

used /tə ~ yɛ ~ čɛ/. When they did use the same preposition as their Embo fellow speakers, however, they made invariant use of the form /yɛ/. This is apparent in their responses to the test sentence 'Take the lid off the kettle! ', where five Brora and Golspie speakers used the form /yɛ/.

Indeterminacies in the identification of the variable appear in this case. It would be possible on the basis of semantic function to recognize one, two, or even three prepositional variables here for East Sutherland fisherfolk Gaelic, each of which can take the phonological form /tə/ for at least some speakers. For present purposes, I have chosen to recognize two: a partitive preposition that takes the form /tə/ invariably for most (but not quite all) older speakers, /čɛ/ for a certain number of younger speakers, and /yɛ/ only seldom for a few younger fluent speakers; and another preposition that subsumes all nonpartitive functions and takes the forms /tə/, /yɛ/, and /čɛ/ variably across the full age-and-proficiency continuum. More speakers show variation than invariance, where the variable ('from, off, of') is concerned, but the variant /tə/ is the strong favorite among invariant speakers, just as it is for still more speakers in the case of the partitive preposition ('of').

7.3.1 Use of Multiple Variants

Thirteen of the twenty-three speakers (56.5 percent) who provided three or more instances of the variable used more than one variant, as did one speaker who provided only two instances; five speakers used all three. Two of the three-variant users were male and three female; three were older fluent speakers and two were younger fluent speakers. Two of the most conspicuous multiple-variant users thus far, E17 and E27, were among the three-variant users, joined here by two other high-variation speakers, E13 (three or more variants for all three five-variant variables, two variants for each of the four-variant variables) and E29* (three or more variants for all of the five-variant variables, two or more for each of the four-variant variables).

The final speaker who used all three variants of ('from, off, of') was E4, whose pattern of multiple-variant use is rather different from that of most of his fellow villagers. Though he used more than one variant for each of the five-variant variables, in two of the three cases he showed a very strong preference for a single variant, just as he does here; only in the case of the variable ('in') did he show even moderately strong use of a second variant. Moreover he was invariant with respect to the four-variant variables. To anticipate, he will prove to show three different patterns where the three-variant variables are concerned: invariance in one case, a strong preference for a single variant in another case, and quite mixed variant use in a third. E4 resembled most Embo speakers, therefore, in using more than one variant in a good many cases, but he was unlike a good many of his fellow villagers in often preferring one of his variants very strongly and making only marginal use of one or more others.

7.3.2 Patterns of Variant Preference by Age and Sex

Males showed a preference for the variant /tə/, with seven out of the ten who provided three or more instances of the variable favoring that variant. No OFS males preferred any other variant, but two YFS males, E27 and E33, preferred /yɛ/, and E37, the youngest male in that group, used only /čɛ/. OFS females were less unanimous in their variant-use preferences, with two, E12 and E13, favoring /tə/ and two others, E5 and E17, favoring /yɛ/. Although /čɛ/ appeared in both the freely spoken and the elicited materials of a few older fluent speakers, no speaker in that age-and-proficiency group preferred it. The first speaker to show a preference for /čɛ/ was YFS female E24; with the exception of E37, all other speakers who shared that preference were also female. In fact the only other males apart from E37 who used the variant /čɛ/ at all were E4 and E27. This suggests a growing preference for the variant /čɛ/ among younger females, but one or two younger males whose usage is clear in various other cases are either poorly repre-sented here or absent altogether (E30, E32*, E36), weakening the case. Younger women did not uniformly favor that variant, furthermore; E39 and E42L, though both female and young, did not use it at all.

7.4 The Variable (preterite particle) before Front Vowel

The preterite particle /t(ə)/, absent from the surface structure with independent past-tense forms of the verb, is obligatory in the surface structure with *dependent* past-tense verb forms (those that follow the negative particle and a number of other particles and conjunctions) except with the verb 'to be' (see §9.1). If the verb following the preterite particle begins with a front vowel, three outcomes are possible. The particle may (1) appear in its canonical underlying form /t(ə)/; (2) appear in that form and be followed by a buffer element /y/; or (3) assimilate to the buffer, so that underlying /t/ + /y/ produces the affricate /č/. For the verb /ĩ:ʃ/ 'tell', to take a relatively high-frequency example, the preterite particle required after the negative particle /(x)a/ may take the following forms in the phrase 'didn't tell':

1. (x)a t ĩ:ʃ
2. (x)a tə y ĩ:ʃ
3. (x)a č ĩ:ʃ

Table 5.13 presents Embo speakers' variant selections for the variable (preterite particle) before front vowel.

In dependent-verb environments, all Brora and Golspie speakers used /t/ for the preterite particle before verbs with initial front vowels.

TABLE 5.13. Variant selections for the variable (preterite particle) before front vowels, from Embo speakers of three age-and-proficiency levels, as number (freely spoken and elicited totaled) and percentage

total # of speakers: 24	t				tə y				č			
spkrs with 3(+): 15	fr	el	tot	%	fr	el	tot	%	fr	el	tot	%
E4　82 m.	--	5	5	**100**								
E5　77 f.									--	2	2	
E9　70 f.	--	1	1									
E10　70 m.									2	5	7	**100**
E13　[67] f.	--	2	2	14.3	1	--	1	7.1	--	11	11	<u>78.6</u>
E16　64 m.									--	1	1	
E17　64 f.									7	1	8	**100**
E21L　58 f.									--	1	1	
E22　58 f.					--	1	1	14.3	--	6	6	<u>85.7</u>
E23L　57 m.									--	5	5	**100**
E24　57 f.									--	6	6	**100**
E26*　54 f.					1	9	10	<u>66.7</u>	2	3	5	33.3
E27　54 m.									3	7	10	**100**
E29*　50 f.	6	20	26	<u>89.7</u>	--	1	1	3.4	--	2	2	6.9
E30　49 f.									--	1	1	
E33　45 m.									--	1	1	
E34　45 f.									--	7	7	**100**
E35　43 f.									--	2	2	
E36　41 m.									--	1	1	
E37　41 m.									--	3	3	**100**
E38　40 f.	1	4	5	16.1	--	2	2	6.5	--	24	24	<u>77.4</u>
E39　38 f.									--	5	5	**100**
E40　36 f.	3	16	19	<u>45.2</u>	--	8	8	19	--	15	15	35.7
E41　31 f.									--	1	1	
E42L　30 f.					1	1	2					
use of variants:												
# of speakers using	6				7				22			
# favoring	3				1				11			
# using exclusively	1				0				8			

OFSs	
YFSs	
SSs	

Fr = free, el = elicited, tot = total. Results in the 90–100% range boldfaced, results favored to lesser degrees underlined.

For most Embo speakers, the variant with initial affricate was either the only form or the dominant form, but the exceptions are interesting. E4, the oldest speaker to provide instances, produced no freely spoken instances but gave elicited instances that were uniformly /t/. Two other older fluent speakers produced translation task responses with that same variant, although in the case of E13 it was not her favored variant and in the case of E9 it was a sole instance. The single instance from E9 is noteworthy because the three younger speakers who used the variant /t/ were all her daughters, including E29*, the only speaker who preferred this variant. Family usage was not uniform, however: E35 was also E9's daughter and E37 was her son, but both of these speakers used /č/.

7.4.1 Use of Multiple Variants

Six of the fifteen speakers (40 percent) who provided three or more instances of the variable used more than one variant. Only four Embo speakers used all three variants of this variable—three of E9's daughters plus the older fluent speaker E13. They differed on which variant they favored, however: E13 and E38 favored /č/, while E29* and E40 favored /t/. Two speakers, E22 and E26*, used two variants; both used /tə y/ as well as /č/. Again they differed on preferred variants, E22 strongly favoring /č/ and E26* unique in favoring /tə y/.

Although the variant /tə y/ was produced (in a single instance each) by two fully fluent speakers, it may be significant that two formerly fluent speakers and three semi-speakers are otherwise the only users of this variant, one that is likely to have a certain analogical attraction for Embo Gaelic speakers. Use of a buffer consonant before vowel-initial verbs is a dialect-geography feature of Embo Gaelic in contrast with Brora and Golspie Gaelic. In constructions with /tuɫ/ 'going' and verb complement, for example, Brora and Golspie Gaelic speakers did not use a buffer before a following vowel-initial complement, whereas Embo speakers routinely did: Brora and Golspie /ha mi tuɫ t iç/ 'I'm going to eat' corresponds to Embo /ha mi tuɫ tə y iç/.[6] (See chapter 3, §7.2.1, for another instance of Embo use of a buffer consonant where Brora and Golspie Gaelic had none, in the construction 'pleased to'.)

Within Embo Gaelic itself, furthermore, individual speakers show some idiosyncratic differences in making use of a prevocalic buffer consonant. E17 consistently used a buffer in constructing the nonfinite verbal element of passive constructions if the gerund was vowel-initial: /er ə x a:gal/ 'on its leaving' = 'left', /er ə y iç/ 'on its eating' = 'eaten' (with buffer /x/ before back vowel, /y/ before front vowel). No other speaker in my sample did this; the equivalent expressions for other Embo speakers were /er a:gal/ and /er iç/. In similarly idiosyncratic fashion, sister and brother Elspeth (E22) and Murdo (E27) volunteered alternative responses with a buffer consonant in constructing some dependent preterites before an initial back vowel, for example, with the interrogative particle /ən/ in /ən də x oʃkʰ u bɔrʃal?/ 'did you open the package?' (as opposed to much more usual Embo /ən d oʃkʰ u...?/). Elspeth's generous use of buffer consonants reappears, then, when she also emerges as one of only two fully fluent speakers who offered the buffer-using /tə y/ variant for the (preterite particle) variable.

For the imperfectly fluent, such as semi-speakers E38, E40, and E42L, variant forms in /tə y/ may be genuinely analogical, representing the logical prior stage of Embo usage that presumably gave rise to the dominant variant /č/ in the first place: /tə/ + buffer consonant /y/ + front vowel, but without the assimilation that produced palatalization and affrication diachronically. For E26*, who seemed to use both /tə y/ and /č/ unhesitatingly and confidently in both conversational material and elicitation, this is a less reasonable hypothesis. She may, like Elspeth, simply have had a grammar that allowed for both possibilities.

7.4.2 Patterns of Variant Preference by Age and Sex

As noted, age and proficiency level may well have played a role in the production of /tə y/ variants among the semi-speakers; but the use of that same variant by fully fluent speakers such as E13 and E22 (freely spoken from the former), and the general presence of variability in Embo with regard to buffer consonants, indicates that the use of this variant was comfortably within the bounds of acceptable Embo usage.

All of the speakers who used /tə y/ are female, as were all of the speakers who used /t/ except for E4. E4's unusual position as an older fluent speaker who not only used the variant /t/ but used it in 100 percent of the instances he provided would make input from the next most senior male, E6, particularly useful, but unfortunately none is available. The instances of /t/ provided by two OFS females do at least demonstrate that this was not an entirely aberrant usage for a proficient elderly speaker.

7.5 The Variable ('potato')

This variable shows variant-selection patterns quite different from those of the other variables discussed so far. An early loanword from English, this noun is highly aberrant in having second-syllable stress, otherwise rare in Gaelic nouns.[7] Whether for this or other reasons, variability is extraordinarily high in the case of ('potato'), with all but one of the sixteen speakers who provided more than a single instance showing variation. Table 5.14 presents Embo speakers' variant selections for the variable ('potato').

For Brora speakers, the form is /pətʰaːtʰ/, probably invariably despite some indeterminacies in the forms that I recorded. Golspie speakers used both /mətʰaːtʰ/ and /pətʰaːtʰ/, with intra-speaker variation: the three Golspie speakers who provided multiple instances used both variants. Evidently 'potato' was a lexical item with stereotyping value for cross-village differences, because one Brora speaker and two Golspie speakers volunteered an Embo form of the word as a great curiosity; all three claimed that the Embo version of ('potato') was /mədaːtʰ/. This was realistic in the sense that the variant with voiced medial dental is the Embo form most unlike any Brora or Golspie variant. But it was unrealistic at the same time, since one of the three Embo variants coincided with Brora usage and two with Golspie usage. It was distinctly unusual for Brora and Golspie Gaelic speakers to take sharp notice of Embo divergence when at least one Embo variant was the same as a variant that they themselves used. That is, ('potato') was treated by Brora and Golspie speakers as if, like ('sand'), it took an entirely different form in Embo Gaelic, whereas, like ('in'), it actually had variants in common with the same variable in Brora and Golspie.

TABLE 5.14. Freely spoken and elicited forms of the variable ('potato') from Embo speakers of three age-and-proficiency levels, with totaled variant choices as percentages

total # speakers: 19	mətʰaːtʰ				mədaːtʰ				pətʰaːtʰ			
spkrs with 3(+): 14	fr	el	tot	%	fr	el	tot	%	fr	el	tot	%
E4 82 m.	4	3	7	58.3	1	4	5	41.7				
E9 70 f.										1	1	
E10 70 m.	--	1	1	33.3	--	2	2	66.7				
E13 [67] f.	--	10	10	58.8	6	--	6	35.3	--	1	1	5.9
E17 64 f.	5	2	7	31.8	5	10	15	68.2				
E22 58 f.	--	1	1	11.1	4	4	8	88.9				
E23L 57 m.	--	1	1									
E24 57 f.	--	1	1		--	1	1					
E26* 54 f.	3	20	23	60.5	3	9	12	31.6	--	3	3	7.9
E27 54 m.	12	6	18	51.4	12	4	16	45.7	1	--	1	2.9
E29* 50 f.	--	4	4	13.8	5	9	14	48.3	8	3	11	37.9
E30 49 m.	--	1	1									
E32* 47 m.	1	--	1	25	2	--	2	50	1	--	1	25
E34 45 f.	6	4	10	90.9					--	1	1	9.1
E37 41 m.					1	1	2					
E38 40 f.	--	9	9	36	2	13	15	60	--	1	1	4
E39 38 f.	--	6	6	75	--	2	2	25				
E40 36 f.	12	18	30	58.8	5	8	13	25.5	2	6	8	15.7
E42L 30 f.	2	1	3	75					1	--	1	25
use of variants:												
# of speakers using	17				14				10			
# favoring	8				6				0			
# using exclusively	0				0				0			

OFSs	
YFSs	
SSs	

Fr = free, el = elicited, tot = total. Results in 90–100% range boldfaced, results favored to lesser degrees underlined.

7.5.1 Use of Multiple Variants

One hundred percent of the fourteen speakers who provided at least three instances of this variable used more than one variant, as did one of two speakers who provided only two instances. Seven speakers made use of two variants and an additional seven used all three variants; two of the latter seven (E29* and E32*) showed no variant preference to the 51 percent level. Still more than in other cases, variation could be pronounced even with only a modest number of instances available. In his corpus, all freely spoken, E32* produced only four useful instances of the variable (a fifth was unassignable; see the discussion that follows), yet he used all three variants. E24, the individual least given to intra-speaker variability among the well-represented members of the Embo speaker sample, used two variants despite providing only two instances of the variable.

No one favored the variant /pətʰa:tʰ/, and it was produced more than once by only three speakers (E26*, E29*, and E40); nonetheless, ten out of nineteen speakers who provided any form of the variable ('potato') used this variant. For E29*, what is more, /pətʰa:tʰ/ dominated in her freely spoken materials (eight of thirteen instances) even though she produced more instances of /məda:tʰ/ than of /pətʰa:tʰ/ (nine versus three) in elicitation.

Variants in initial /v-/ (/vətʰa:tʰ, vəda:tʰ/) were produced by five Embo speakers: two instances apiece from E10 and E22, and single instances from E27, E29*, and E32*. There is no motivation for an initial mutation here, but initial /v/ is not a permissible base-form phenomenon except in much more recently adopted loanwords; it normally derives only from lenition of /m-/ or /p-/. Because either of those initial consonants can lenite to /v-/, the form /vətʰa:tʰ/ cannot be unambiguously assigned to the /m/-initial or the /p/-initial variant; the four /vətʰa:tʰ/ instances are therefore left out of account here. The variant /vəda:tʰ/ could be considered an alternative form of /məda:tʰ/, but since the parallel form /vətʰa:tʰ/ must be left out of the reckoning, I elected to omit the three instances of /vəda:tʰ/ as well.

7.5.2 Patterns of Variant Preference by Age and Sex

Despite widespread use of multiple variants, there was a modest overall Embo preference for the variant /mətʰa:tʰ/ (Brora and Golspie stereotypes notwithstanding). Speakers favoring this variant included two older fluent speakers (one male and one female), three younger fluent speakers (two females and a male), and three semi-speakers.

The six speakers who showed a preference for /məda:tʰ/ represented each of the three proficiency levels, but only two were male (E10 and E32*). Once again, the data are relatively skimpy for males, especially among younger fluent speakers: E23L, E30, and E37 provided very few instances of the variable. But E27 provided almost as many instances of /məda:tʰ/ as of /mətʰa:tʰ/, and E37's two instances of the variable were also /məda:tʰ/, reducing the likelihood that use of that variant was associated particularly with women.

8 ALIGNMENT OF INDIVIDUAL VARIANT PREFERENCES: EIGHT MULTIVARIANT VARIABLES

We can now compare variant-use preferences for all eight of the multivariant variables introduced so far, following in table 5.15 the conventions adopted in table 5.7.

Two features of the three-variable display of table 5.7 are still in evidence in the more extensive display here. Agreement between a pair of speakers on a variant preference for one variable continues to be no guarantee of agreement in the case of other variables. And there continues to be no obvious subset of speakers who recurrently show unusual variant preferences; the individuals who demonstrate a preference for an atypical variant in one case are seldom the same individuals who do so in other cases.

It becomes more evident in this second, fuller alignment table that the preference profile for each variable is distinctive. Whereas four of the five variants

TABLE 5.15. Embo variant preference tabulations for the multivariant variables ('in'), ('along with'), ('when'), ('would go'), ('family'), ('from, off, of'), (preterite particle), and ('potato')

ste		stex		sčax		sčex		sče	
m. E10	100	m. E4	79.5	m. E30	100	m. E23L	100	m. E36	100
f. E14	100	f. E39	71.4	m. E37	100	m. E25L	100	f. E40	96.2
f. E24	100			f. E34	96.2	f. E42L	94.7	f. E26°	90.9
f. E22	72.7			m. E27	91.3	m. E15L	67.7	f. E29°	82.8
f. E13	66.7			f. E41	80	m. E33	60	f. E17	48.3
f. E9	62.5			m. E6	66.7	f. E38	57.1		

tərə		tə		tənə		nərə		nə	
m. E6	90.9	f. E14	100	m. E15L	100	f. E41	100	m. E23L	66.7
		f. E20	100	f. E38	98.9	f. E26°	84.8	m. E33	66.7
		f. E24	100	f. E39	92.9	f. E13	69	f. E34	65.1
		f. E40	98.6	f. E29°	82.2	m. E27	55.2	m. E32*	50
		m. E4	98.3	m. E37	81.8	m. E32*	50		
		f. E22	59.3	f. E9	80				
		f. E17	54.9						
		m. E10	53.8						
		m. E30	,44.4						

kʰɔ̄:ta ri		kʰɔra ri		kʰɔ̄na ri		kʰɔ̄rna ri		kʰɔi	
m. E15L	60	f. E39	62.5	f. E24	100	f. E41	100	m. E10	100
		f. E42L	60.5	m. E30	100	m. E6	80	f. E13	45
				m. E4	94.4	f. E17	73.1		
				m. E37	93.8	m. E23L	66.7		
				f. E26°	91.5	m. E27	60.6		
				f. E40	82.9	m. E33	57.1		
				f. E38	71.2	m. E34	40.9		
				f. E9	62.5				
				f. E29°	55.9				

č(h)ɛu		rɛu		raxu		č(h)e:ju	
m. E10	75	f. E21L	100	m. E4	100	m. E33	100
m. E6	71.4	f. E24	100	f. E9	100	f. E39	100
f. E40	53.	m. E37	100	f. E17	100	f. E41	100
f. E38	50	f. E42L	100	f. E22	100	f. E26°	76.5
		m. E23L	75	m. E27	100	f. E29°	60.9
		m. E15L	66.7	f. E34	100	f. E38	50
				f. E13	75		

(Continued)

TABLE 5.15. (Continued)

čʰəːrtax		čʰəːrtiç		tʰəːrtliç		tʰəːrtax
f. E20	100	m. E4	100	f. E22	100	
m. E27	50	m. E10	100	f. E24	100	
		f. E29°	85.2	m. E32*	100	
				f. E42L	100	
				f. E39	100	
				f. E38	95.7	
				f. E26°	90.9	
				f. E40	86.4	
				f. E13	66.7	
				f. E34	66.7	
				f. E17	40.6	

tə		yɛ		čɛ	
m. E6	100	m. E33	93.3	f. E24	100
f. E12	100	f. E26°	85.7	m. E37	100
m. E15L	100	f. E5	80	f. E34	94.7
m. E16	100	m. E27	69.8	f. E29°	78.8
m. E23L	100	f. E17	61.1	f. E40	70
m. E25L	100	f. E22	50	f. E38	69.2
f. E39	100				
f. E42L	100				
m. E10	87.5				
m. E4	84				
f. E13	57.1				
f. E22	50				

t		tə y		č	
m. E4	100	f. E26°	66.7	m. E10	100
f. E29°	89.7			f. E17	100
f. E40	45.2			m. E23L	100
				f. E24	100
				m. E27	100
				f. E34	100
				m. E37	100
				f. E39	100
				f. E22	85.7
				f. E13	78.6
				f. E38	77.4

metʰaːtʰ		mədaːtʰ		pətʰaːtʰ
f. E34	90.9	f. E22	88.9	
f. E39	75	f. E17	68.2	
f. E42L	75	f. E10	66.7	
f. E26°	60.5	f. E38	60	
f. E13	58.8	m. E32*	50	
f. E40	58.8	f. E29°	48.3	
m. E4	58.3			
m. E27	51.4			

Typefaces are assigned according to preferences shared for ('in');
subsequent speakers without a preferred variant for ('in') are assigned new
typefaces. Proficiency level is indicated by shading: OFSs no shading, YFSs
light gray, SSs darker gray. Asterisks indicate formerly fluent speakers.

of ('in') are in fairly heavy use in Embo, only two of the five variants of ('along with') and two of the four variants of ('family') are heavily used among this sample of speakers; only one variant of (preterite particle) is in heavy use. Two variables, ('preterite particle') and ('potato'), have variants that, although in moderate use, are not the preferred variant for any of the speakers in the sample. Invariance (use at the 100 percent level) may be typical of several of a variable's variants, as is most noticeably the case with ('in') and ('would go'), or it may be associated chiefly with a single variant, as with ('from, off, of') and (preterite particle). Alone among all the multivariant variables, ('potato') has no variant used at the 100 percent level by any speaker; so variable is ('potato'), in fact, that even 80–90 percent use for any one of its variants is unusual.

At this stage, with eight variables considered, there are a number of pairs of speakers who have agreed on a favored variant for as many as four variables, but some of these pairs did not provide enough instances in all eight cases to determine the extent to which they would have agreed overall. The two men who agreed on a favored variant for all three of the five-variant variables, E23L and E33, proved to agree also in the case of the (preterite particle), while they disagreed on ('would go') and ('from, off, of'). But each man provided only one instance of ('family'), each using a different variant, and E33 provided no instances of ('potato') that could be compared with the one instance available from E23L.

One pair of speakers who showed strong agreement also had a nuclear family connection, sisters E29* and E38, each of whom provided adequate instances of all eight variables. They agreed on variant preferences in four of those cases, or even five, if E38's even 50 percent split between the /č(h)ɛu/ and /č(h)eːǰu/ variants of ('would go') is allowable as an agreement with E29's preference for /č(h)eːǰu/. Three other pairs of speakers provided adequate instances of all eight variables and agreed on preferences for four of them, while disagreeing on preferences for the other four: E10 and E13, E29* and E40, and E38 and E40. The speakers in each of these pairs were also siblings: brother and sister E10 and E13 (Duncan and Flora), sisters E29* and E40 (Emma and Lorna), and sisters E38 and E40 (Elsie and Lorna) (see chapter 6 for complete sets of kin-network pseudonyms). While sibling ties are clearly significant, it should be kept in mind that only one of the sibling pairs, E29* and E38, produced preferences that could be considered to coincide at a better than 50 percent level.

Sibling ties prove to be as interesting for the differences they reveal in variant preferences as for the similarities, in fact. E10, E13, and E24 were not only siblings but also members of a single household. They showed a strong preference for the same variant in the cases of ('in') and (preterite particle), and two of the three—though a different two in each case—shared a strong variant preference for ('when') and ('from, off, of'). But they appear in three different columns for ('would go'), as do the two for whom percentages of use can be reckoned for ('family'). E29*, E38, and E40 were same-sex siblings, with E29* the oldest daughter and E38 and E40 the youngest daughters in a family of seven children; the latter two were co-residents of the same household. All three women agreed on a preferred variant only for ('along with') and ('from, off, of'). The connection between kin relationships, the social interactions they promote, and patterns of variant use will be taken up in chapter 6, but it can be seen by this brief preview that kin ties cannot provide a blanket explanation for variant-preference patterns.

The striking agreement of the London-Embo group on their preferred variant for ('in'), absent for the other two five-variant variables, re-emerges with ('would go'), where four London-Embo speakers strongly favored /rɛu/, and with ('from, off, of'), where a slightly different four shared a strong preference for /tə/. In the latter case, the variant the London-area residents favored was favored by a number of other Embo speakers, but in the case of ('would go') only two speakers who resided in Embo itself showed the same preference for /rɛu/. Unfortunately London-Embo speakers are too poorly represented for ('family'), (preterite particle), and ('potato') to explore how extensive the group consensus might have been overall on variant preferences for the multivariant variables.

9 TWO-VARIANT VARIABLES

Ten variables with two variants each are introduced here, ordered except in the case of the final variable (a late addition; see §9.10) according to the number of speakers who provided three or more instances. In seven of the ten cases, one variant is clearly preferred across the speaker sample as a whole, but the level of use of the other variant differs in each case, as does the roster of speakers who made greater use of the variant less widely preferred overall. The same issues that were raised in connection with multivariant variables are still of interest here: whether speakers who agree on a variant preference in one case will agree on their preferences in subsequent cases; which speakers, and how many, use only a single variant; which and how many make use of more than one; whether the same individuals tend to reappear among the invariant speakers; whether variation is characteristic of all age-and-proficiency groups and both sexes; which speakers show a preference for the variant that is less widely used overall, and whether the same individuals do so repeatedly.

9.1 The Variable ('wasn't/weren't')

Table 5.16 presents Embo speakers' variant-selection patterns for the high-frequency variable ('wasn't/weren't'), the dependent negative past tense of the irregular verb 'to be'.

There were no speakers in Brora or Golspie who actually favored the analogically formed variant /(x)a t rɔ/, but of the eight speakers who provided more than one instance of the variable, five made at least very occasional use of that variant. The youngest of the fully fluent Brora speakers was unusual in making substantial use of /(x)a t rɔ/; fourteen of her thirty-nine instances, or 35.9 percent, were /(x)a t rɔ/. Less material is available for Brora semi-speakers than for Embo semi-speakers, but two of the three provided /(x)a rɔ/ forms, ruling out the possibility that weak semi-speakers might uniformly adopt constructions that included the preterite particle, as the three youngest Embo semi-speakers appear to have done.

TABLE 5.16. Freely spoken and elicited forms of the variable ('wasn't/weren't') from Embo speakers of three age-and-proficiency levels, with totaled variant selections as percentages

total # speakers: 33	(x)a rɔ				(x)a t rɔ				
spkrs with 3(+): 27	fr	el	tot	%	fr	el	tot	%	
E3 [85] m.	3	--	3	**100**					
E4 82 m.	49	6	55	74.3	19	--	19	25.7	
E5 77 f.	--	1	1						
E6 75 m.	--	2	2	25	2	4	6	<u>75</u>	
E7 ?74 f.	4	--	4	**100**					
E9 70 f.	--	2	2						
E10 70 m.	5	10	15	**100**					
E13 [67] f.	13	5	18	**94.7**	1	--	1	5.3	
E14 65 f.	--	3	3	**100**					
E15L 65 m.	--	2	2	20	--	8	8	<u>80</u>	
E17 64 f.	441	23	464	**99.1**	4	--	4	.9	
E18* 60 f.	4	--	4	**100**					
E20 58 f.	--	8	8	**100**					
E21L 58 f.	--	4	4	**100**					
E22 58 f.	12	13	25	**100**					
E23L 57 m.					--	1	1		
E24 57 f.	1	9	10	<u>76.9</u>	--	3	3	23.1	
E25L 56 m.					--	1	1		
E26* 54 f.	88	42	130	**94.2**	7	1	8	5.8	
E27 54 m.	88	28	116	<u>83.5</u>	18	5	23	16.5	
E29* 50 f.	17	3	20	7.2	219	39	258	**92.8**	
E30 49 m.	29	2	31	**100**					
E31 48 m.	--	1	1						
E32* 47 m.	12	--	12	**100**					
E33 45 m.	--	1	1	20	--	4	4	<u>80</u>	
E34 45 f.	8	4	12	24	24	14	38	<u>76</u>	
E36 41 m.	--	1	1						
E37 41 m.	1	11	12	**100**					
E38 40 f.	26	69	95	**100**	--	[1]	[1]		
E39 38 f.	29	14	43	<u>91.5</u>	1	3	4	8.5	
E40 36 f.					94	86	180	**100**	OFSs
E41 31 f.					--	3	3	**100**	YFSs
E42L 30 f.					127	17	144	**100**	SSs
use of variants:									
# of speakers using			28				18		
# favoring			19				8		
# using exclusively			12				3		

Square brackets indicate a unique instance as the result of a direct prompt from another speaker, not included in reckoning percentages. Results in the 90–100 percent range boldfaced, results favored to lesser degrees underlined.

9.1.1 Use of More than One Variant

Of the twenty-seven individuals who provided at least three instances of this variable, thirteen (48.1 percent) made use of both variants, though one of them did so only as the result of a direct prompt. Overall the preference for /(x)a rɔ/ is clear: nineteen of the twenty-seven speakers favored /(x)a rɔ/, with twelve of the nineteen (63.2 percent) using that variant exclusively, including E37, the youngest fully fluent speaker.

9.1.2 Patterns of Variant Preference by Age and Sex

OFS males made more use of /(x)a t rɔ/ than did OFS females, who showed a nearly monolithic preference for /(x)a rɔ/. E13 was the only female speaker to use /(x)a t rɔ/ even to a 5 percent level, but two men in the same proficiency group, E6 and E15L, showed a moderately strong preference for that variant. Exclusive use of /(x)a rɔ/ by males E3 and E10 demonstrated, however, that the speaker's sex was not an absolute factor in variant selection. E17's four freely spoken instances of /(x)a t rɔ/ make an interesting point: with a high number of instances of the variable available, even an overwhelming preference for /(x)a rɔ/ (99.1 percent) did not rule out some use of /(x)a t rɔ/. Conceivably the number of speakers who showed invariance would have dropped, therefore, if a larger number of instances of the variable had been available from more speakers. YFS women showed less uniform variant selections than OFS women, with females E29* and E34 joining male speaker E33 in showing a preference for /(x)a t rɔ/, while three of four males agreed with seven of nine females in favoring /(x)a rɔ/.

The semi-speakers show a pattern very much their own, namely, a tendency to eliminate variation altogether. The oldest and the three youngest of the five semi-speakers used only a single variant each, apart from E38's lone echo-instance of /(x)a t rɔ/. (A unique response during a translation task to a direct prompt from an older sister who heavily preferred /(x)a t rɔ/, that instance cannot be regarded as a reflection of E38's actual usage.) E39, the only semi-speaker to use both variants on her own initiative, used her heavily favored variant /(x)a rɔ/ both in freely spoken material and in elicitation but used /(x)a t rɔ/ only in elicitation. Only E24 shows a similar pattern, but since E24 provided just one freely spoken instance of the variable the parallel to E39's pattern is a weak one.

9.1.3 The Analogical Factor

As in the case of ('would go'), one of the variants of ('wasn't/weren't') involves analogical regularization, as was noted in chapter 3, §6.2.1. The dependent past tense of any regular verb requires that the preterite particle /t(ə)/ appear between whatever particle or conjunction triggers the dependent verb form and the actual verb root that follows, for example, past tense /xur/ 'put' (from verb root /kʰur/), matched by negated past tense /(x)a tə xur/ 'didn't put'. The exceptions are a very few irregular verbs before the past tense of which no preterite particle appears after the negative particle /(x)a/: 'wasn't/weren't', 'went', and 'saw'. Particularly relevant is the fact that the particle appears invariably with the only irregular verb other than 'be' that has an initial /r-/ in the dependent past, namely, /rɔ̃ĩn'/ 'did', the negative past tense of which is /(x)a t rɔ̃ĩn'/ 'didn't do'.

Not only is the preterite particle obligatory in dependent forms of all regular verbs in Embo Gaelic, and in a number of parallel irregular verb forms likewise (including /r/-initial /rə̃ĩn'/ 'did'), it is also present for most speakers in dependent forms of 'to be' after particles and conjunctions other than the negative particle /(x)a/. After the interrogative particle /ən/ and the conjunction /kən/ 'that', two elements that call for dependent verb forms plus the initial mutation known as nasalization, the preterite particle is used with /rɔ/ 'was/were' by the overwhelming majority of speakers (twenty of twenty-two speakers who provided three or more instances, 90 to 100 percent of the time by eighteen of the twenty). The particle is only slightly less frequently used after two other elements that call for dependent verb forms, the negative interrogative particle /(n)ax/ and the negative-relative particle, also /(n)ax/: eleven of fifteen speakers who provided three or more instances used the particle in those two environments, ten of them 95 to 100 percent of the time. Only three individuals never used the preterite particle after /(n)ax/, E13, E24, and E38—all women but at three different age-and-proficiency levels. Male speaker E27 used the preterite particle with /(n)ax/ at the 50 percent level (five of ten instances, with all five of his elicited instances showing the particle). Of the three individuals who never used the preterite particle with /(n)ax/, only E38 never used it in nasalizing environments either (that is, after elements such as /ən/ and /kən/). E13 omitted the particle 70.6 percent of the time in nasalizing environments, but E24 used the particle 100 percent of the time in such environments, completely reversing her pattern with /(n)ax/. E27 made the same shift from a less extreme starting point: he went from 50 percent use of the particle after /(n)ax/ to 100 percent use of the particle in nasalizing environments.

To sum up, the preterite particle was widely and strongly used with /rɔ/ in Embo in all syntactic environments *other* than the negated dependent past with /(x)a/. Only a few speakers failed to use it with /(n)ax/, and fewer still with the interrogative particle /ən/ and the conjunction /kən/ 'that'. The fact that the preterite particle was much more variably present in the negated dependent past with /(x)a/ was of course my reason for choosing that environment as the one to be presented in detail in this chapter. The attractiveness of analogical regularization notwithstanding, the preterite particle had not been adopted wholesale in this especially high-frequency environment, and Embo speakers still favored the negative past tense of 'to be' without the particle by a ratio of more than two to one.

Only the semi-speakers apart from E39 showed nearly complete regularization, but curiously enough the eldest of them, E38, regularized in the opposite direction, always omitting the preterite particle with /rɔ/. She was thoroughgoing about eliminating the particle, furthermore, since she was the one speaker who omitted it in *all* dependent environments for /rɔ/, including all appearances of /rɔ/ after the elements /(n)ax/, /ən/, and /kən/.

9.2 The Variable ('came')

Table 5.17 presents Embo speakers' variant selections for ('came').
Only the disyllabic form /hã:nig/ is in use in Brora and Golspie.

TABLE 5.17. Freely spoken and elicited variant selections for the variable ('came') from Embo speakers of three age-and-proficiency levels, with totaled variant selections as percentages

total # speakers: 33		hā:nig				hā:n				
spkrs with 3(+): 26		fr	el	tot	%	fr	el	tot	%	
E4	82 m.	30	7	37	80.4	7	2	9	19.6	
E5	77 f.	--	2	2						
E6	75 m.	2	1	3	100					
E7	?74 f.	2	--	2						
E9	70 f.	--	2	2						
E10	70 m.	3	12	15	88.2	1	1	2	11.8	
E12	?68 f.	--	2	2						
E13	[67] f.	14	15	29	93.5	2	--	2	6.5	
E14	65 f.	--	5	5	100					
E15L	65 m.	--	12	12	92.3	1	--	1	7.7	
E16	64 m.					1	--	1		
E17	64 f.	41	14	55	68.8	23	2	25	31.3	
E18*	60 f.	2	--	2	33.3	4	--	4	66.7	
E20	58 f.	--	4	4	100					
E21L	58 f.					--	1	1		
E22	58 f.	4	9	13	43.3	8	9	17	56.7	
E23L	57 m.					--	2	2		
E24	57 f.	6	22	28	100					
E25L	56 m.	--	3	3	75	--	1	1	25	
E26*	54 f.	55	15	70	98.6	1	--	1	1.4	
E27	54 m.	18	30	48	96	2	--	2	4	
E29*	50 f.	63	18	81	71.1	23	10	33	28.9	
E30	49 m.	[1]	1	2	18.2	8	1	9	81.8	
E32*	47 m.	11	--	11	100					
E33	45 m.	--	4	4	100					
E34	45 f.	7	14	21	95.5	1	--	1	4.5	
E36	41 m.	--	3	3	100					
E37	41 m.	--	1	1	7.7	4	8	12	92.3	
E38	40 f.	--	5	5	5.9	14	66	80	94.1	
E39	38 f.	--	4	4	30.8	2	7	9	69.2	
E40	36 f.					130	39	169	100	OFSs
E41	31 f.	--	2	2	50	--	2	2	50	YFSs
E42L	30 f.	29	15	44	81.5	7	3	10	18.5	SSs
use of variants:										
# of speakers using		29				22				
# favoring		18				7				
# using exclusively		7				1				

Square brackets indicate a response produced as an echo of a preceding speaker. Fr = free, el = elicited, tot = total. Results in 90–100 percent range boldfaced, results favored to lesser degrees underlined.

9.2.1 Use of More than One Variant

Of the twenty-six speakers who provided at least three instances of the variable, eighteen (69.2 percent) made at least some use of both variants, but the four speakers who provided just two instances used only a single variant each. All but seven of the eighteen individuals who made use of both variants favored the disyllabic variant, and only one speaker, semi-speaker E40, used the monosyl-labic form exclusively. By contrast, seven speakers used the disyllabic form exclusively. Overall, then, use of disyllabic /hã:nig/ far outweighed use of mono-syllabic /hã:n/. Although E40 was unique in using the monosyllabic variant exclu-sively, two of her near-in-age siblings, E37 and E38, also made very little use of disyllabic /hã:nig/. (Their older sister E29* showed the opposite pattern, joining the majority of Embo speakers in favoring /hã:nig/.)

Seven speakers made up the minority that favored the monosyllabic variant of ('came')—E18*, E22, E30, E37, E38, E39, and E40—while eight speakers made up the minority that favored a negated past tense ('wasn't/weren't') with analogical preterite particle—E6, E15L, E29*, E33, E34, E40, E41, and E42L. Only one speaker, E40, appears in both sets. As was the case with multiple-variant variables, the speakers who showed a preference for the less commonly favored variant of these two-variant variables were largely distinct in each case.

9.2.2 Patterns of Variant Use by Age and Sex

Older speakers made less use of the monosyllabic variant than younger speakers, but that may in part reflect the fact that most of them provided relatively few freely spoken instances of the variable. Even so, five of seven older fluent speakers who provided three or more instances of the variable used the monosyllabic var-iant at least once, more often in freely spoken material than in elicited material. Use of the monosyllabic variant was more prominent among younger fluent speakers, with E18*, E22, and especially E30 and E37 (two females and two males) showing an actual preference for that variant. Among the all-female semi-speakers only E42L showed a strong preference for the disyllabic variant, but E41 used both variants equally in elicitation. Although use of the monosyllabic variant was showing an increase among younger speakers, the increase was not so strong as to suggest that variation was fading out of the picture: three younger fluent speakers in their forties still used only the disyllabic variant (E32*, E33, and E36, all males), and all of the semi-speakers except E40 continued to make some use the disyllabic variant (though E38 and E39 in elicitation only).

9.3 The Variable ('tomorrow')

Table 5.18 presents Embo speakers' variant selections for the variable ('tomorrow').

Both variants were in use in Brora and Golspie. In the heavily female Brora sample, three women favored /ma:riç/ while the other two and the one male favored /ma:rax/; among the latter group, the one male and one of the females showed minor intra-speaker variation. Three of the five Golspie speakers who provided more than one instance of the variable favored /ma:riç/, two males and a female, but four of the five showed intra-speaker variation. One female favored

TABLE 5.18. Freely spoken and elicited variants of the variable ('tomorrow') from Embo speakers of three age-and-proficiency levels, with totaled variant selections as percentages

total # speakers: 29	ma:rax				ma:riç				
spkrs with 3(+): 26	free	elic	total	%	free	elic	total	%	
E3 [85] m.	1	--	1						
E4 82 m.	--	2	2	20	1	7	8	80	
E5 77 f.					--	2	2		
E6 75 m.	--	5	5	**100**					
E9 70 f.	--	8	8	**100**					
E10 70 m.	--	1	1	14.3	1	5	6	<u>85.7</u>	
E13 [67] f.	3	4	7	**100**					
E14 65 f.	--	2	2	<u>66.7</u>	--	1	1	33.3	
E15L 65 m.	--	3	3	**100**					
E17 64 f.	13	8	21	**100**					
E20 58 f.	--	3	3	**100**					
E21L 58 f.	--	3	3	**100**					
E22 58 f.	3	13	16	**100**					
E23L 57 m.	--	10	10	**100**					
E24 57 f.	--	6	6	**100**					
E25L 56 m.					--	2	2		
E26* 54 f.	7	8	15	**100**					
E27 54 m.	1	24	25	**96.2**	--	1	1	3.8	
E29* 50 f.	17	11	28	**100**					
E30 50 f.	--	3	3	**100**					
E33 45 m.	--	2	2	33.3	--	4	4	66.7	
E34 45 f.	2	17	19	**95**	--	1	1	5	
E36 41 m.	--	2	2	28.6	--	5	5	71.4	
E37 41 m.	--	4	4	30.8	1	8	9	69.2	
E38 40 f.	5	12	17	**100**					
E39 38 f.	3	5	8	**100**					
E40 36 f.	14	14	28	**100**					OFSs
E41 31 f.	--	5	5	**100**					YFSs
E42L 30 f.	1	10	11	**100**					SSs
use of variants:									
# of speakers using	27				10				
# favoring	21				5				
# using exclusively	18				0				

Elic = elicited. Results in 90–100% range boldfaced, results favored to lesser degrees underlined.

/ma:rax/, and another used both variants despite providing only two instances of the variable.

9.3.1 Use of More than One Variant

Of the 26 Embo speakers who provided at least three instances of ('tomorrow'), only eight (30.8 percent) used both variants. Neither of the two speakers who provided just two instances of the variable did so. Only five of the twenty-six speakers who provided three or more instances of ('tomorrow') favored /ma:riç/, and no speaker used /ma:riç/ at the 100 percent level. By contrast, eighteen speakers used only /maːrax/. This sort of decisive favoring of a single variant was encountered previously only in the case of (preterite particle) before front vowel. Only one of the five speakers who favored /maːriç/, E37, was also among the minority favoring the monosyllabic variant of ('came') and only one, E33, was among the minority favoring ('wasn't/weren't') with analogical preterite particle.

9.3.2 Patterns of Variant Preference
by Age and Sex

All of the speakers who favored the variant /maːriç/ are males, but not all males favored /maːriç/. Five of nine males who provided three or more instances of the variable did so, two of the three oldest males plus the three youngest, yet the fact that the oldest female in the speaker sample, E5, used /maːriç/ in the only two instances that she provided casts some doubt on how strongly associated with males the variable is or originally was. Apart from E5, however, only two female speakers made any use of /maːriç/ at all: E14 and E34, with one instance apiece. Of the eighteen variables considered in this study, ('tomorrow') comes closer than any other except one yet to be introduced (see §9.10.2) to showing variant selection patterns differentiated by the speaker's sex. The fact that the three youngest males all favored /maːriç/ is particularly suggestive, but the evidence remains inconclusive. Only with instances from more older female speakers could E5's position be clarified, either as an exception or perhaps as one of a subset of elderly women who favored /maːriç/. At the other end of the age-and-proficiency scale, data from male (near-)passive bilinguals would be needed to shed light on the extent to which /maːriç/ was becoming associated primarily or exclusively with males. One near-passive bilingual, a younger brother of E37, was asked for this item by telephone during the 1990s and responded with /maːrax/, indicating that within that family, at any rate, the male preference for /maːriç/ did not extend to the youngest and least proficient son. There is no association of the variant /maːriç/ with males in Brora or Golspie, as is evident from the summary given in §9.3.

9.3.3 Variables with Structurally Parallel
Variants in /-ax/ and /-iç/

Of potential interest here is the fact that the variant /maːriç/ is structurally akin to the /čʰəːrɬiç/ and /tʰəːrɬiç/ variants of the variable ('family'). In both cases the variants in /-iç/ are oblique forms that have become citation forms, while the variants in /-ax/ represent a historically primary citation form. In the case of ('family'), however, the formerly oblique forms in /-iç/ have become the dominant variants for Embo Gaelic speakers, whereas in the case of ('tomorrow') the historically primary form remains the dominant variant for most speakers.

Many other historically oblique forms have emerged as citation forms in East Sutherland fisherfolk Gaelic, but only one other has become an intra-village and intra-speaker variable, so far as I am aware. In Embo the term for 'old lady' takes either the form /kʰal´ax/ or the form /kʰal´iç/, the latter historically an oblique form with (for some but not all speakers) a secondary meaning of 'cowardly, womanish man'. Five older fluent speakers provided two or more instances, free and/or elicited; all of them used the variant /kʰal´iç/, although E13 offered one instance of /kʰal´ax/ in addition to three instances of /kʰal´iç/. All YFS instances were elicited, and four of six speakers offered only /kʰal´ax/; a fifth gave one instance of each form, but E27 (Murdo) used only /kʰal´iç/ (eight instances). As with a number of other variables, his older sister, Elspeth (E22), used a different variant, providing three instances of /kʰal´ax/.

This word is somewhat difficult to elicit from younger speakers, despite the fact that the term is extremely familiar. Perhaps because of their own relative youth, the term seemed disrespectful to them for speaking of older women. Older speakers had no such qualms, but avoidance of the word by younger speakers and their sometimes uncertain memory of its use made it ill-suited for close study as an Embo variable, in spite of the potential interest of a third variable with competing variant forms in /-ax/ and /-iç/. In view of the limited data available for ('old lady'), only a tentative comparison of the three structurally similar variables is possible. Given that /čʰə:rɬiç/ and /tʰə:rɬiç/ were favored by most Embo speakers, while /ma:riç/ was favored primarily by a handful of males and /kʰal´iç/ primarily by older fluent speakers, it is unsurprising that the only speakers who favored /-iç/ variants for all three variables were two OFS males, E4 and E10. Two OFS females, E13 and E17, favored /-iç/ variants of ('family') and ('old lady') but used only the /-ax/ variant of ('tomorrow'). Three YFS females, E22, E26*, and E29*, favored the usual /-iç/ variants of ('family'), but the /-ax/ variants of ('tomorrow') and ('old lady'). Male younger fluent speaker E27 was unique in favoring the /-ax/ variants of ('family'), at least if both variants in /-ax/ are summed and opposed to both /-iç/ variants. Like the YFS females, he favored only one of the three possible historically oblique forms, but in his case it was ('old lady'), rather than ('family') for which he favored the /-iç/ variant. Among the speakers who provided instances of these three variables, therefore, diachronically parallel variant structures did not lead to parallel variant-selection patterns.

9.4 The Variable ('saw')

The past tense of the irregular verb 'to see' has disyllabic and monosyllabic variants that are roughly parallel to those of the irregular verb 'to come': /hũnig, hũnə/ vs. /hũn/. The verb 'to see' is still more irregular than the verb 'to come', however, making fewer past-tense instances available for 'saw' than for 'came'. The independent and dependent past-tense forms of the verb 'to come' are both based on the element /hã:n(ig)/, so that both structural environments yield useful data. The dependent past-tense forms of the verb 'to see', by contrast, are formed on the root /akʰ/ rather than on /hũni(g)/, and the many instances of 'saw' in environments calling for dependent forms offered useful data for this study only in the very rare case that a speaker produced an analogical dependent form based on /hũnig/ instead of /akʰ/.[8] Despite this relatively restricted environment of occurrence, however, twenty-seven speakers offered independent past-tense forms of ('saw'), nineteen of them providing three or more instances of the variable. Table 5.19 presents Embo speakers' variant selections for ('saw').

Only the disyllabic form /hũnig/ was in use in Brora and Golspie.

Because ('came') and ('saw') are structural parallels to one another (apart from the absence of /hũnig/ in the dependent past-tense environment), the degree to which they parallel one another in patterns of variant use is of potential interest and patterns for ('saw') will be compared to those already noted for ('came').[9] In

TABLE 5.19. Freely spoken and elicited forms of the variable ('saw') from Embo speakers of three age-and-proficiency levels, with totaled variant selections as percentages

total # speakers: 27	hũnig, hũnə				hũn						
spkrs with 3(+): 19	free	elic	total	%	free	elic	total	%			
E3 [85] m.					1	--	1				
E4 82 m.	8	6	14	**100**							
E6 75 m.	--	4	4	**100**							
E7 ?74 f.	1	1	2								
E9 70 f.	--	3	3	**100**							
E10 70 m.	1	4	5	**100**							
E13 [67] f.	5	7	12	80	3	--	3	20			
E15L 65 m.	--	1	1								
E17 64 f.	6	9	15	37.5	20	5	25	62.5			
E21L 58 f.	--	1	1								
E22 58 f.	2	8	10	76.9	1	2	3	23.1			
E23L 57 m.					--	2	2				
E24 57 f.	--	5	5	62.5	3	--	3	37.5			
E25L 56 m.					--	3	3	**100**			
E26* 54 f.	4	5	9	90	1	--	1	10			
E27 54 m.	8	11	19	**100**							
E29* 50 f.	17	14	31	**93.9**	2	--	2	6.1			
E30 49 m.					--	2	2				
E33 45 m.	--	5	5	**100**							
E34 45 f.	4	7	11	**91.7**	--	1	1	8.3			
E36 41 m.	--	2	2								
E37 41 m.	--	1	1	25	--	3	3	75			
E38 40 f.	8	59	67	**100**	[3]	--	[3]				
E39 38 f.	--	1	1	16.7	1	4	5	83.3			
E40 36 f.	1	3	4	4.4	23	64	87	**95.6**	OFSs		
E41 31 f.	--	1	1						YFSs		
E42L 30 f.	9	12	21	**100**					SSs		
use of variants:											
# of speakers using		23				15					
# favoring		14				5					
# using exclusively		8				1					

Square brackets indicate otherwise absent variants produced in direct response to another speaker's prompts, not included in reckoning percentages. Elic = elicited. Results in 90–100 percent range boldfaced, results favored to lesser degrees underlined.

both cases, the question arises as to whether longer and shorter variant forms are to some extent stylistically cued.

9.4.1 Use of More than One Variant

Ten of the nineteen speakers who provided three or more instances (52.6 percent) used both variants (with the three echo-instances from E38 discounted). None of the four speakers who provided only two instances did so; they differed on their variant choices, however, two using only the disyllabic variant and two only the monosyllabic variant. Invariant speakers preferred the disyllabic variant by eight to one.

Comparison of preference patterns for the variables ('came') and ('saw') indicates that use of monosyllabic /hã:n/ outran use of monosyllabic /hũn/ overall. Two thirds of all speakers who provided instances of ('came')—twenty-two of thirty-three, or 66.7 percent—made some use of /hã:n/, while the comparable figure for /hũn/ is fifteen of twenty-seven, or 55.6 percent. Among older fluent speakers, six of twelve (50 percent) who provided instances of ('came') made some use of /hã:n/, whereas only three of nine (33.3 percent) who provided instances of ('saw') made any use of /hũn/. The comparable YFS figures are eleven of sixteen, or 68.8 percent, and nine of thirteen, or 69.2 percent; and for semi-speakers five of five, or 100 percent, versus two of five, or 40 percent. Only among younger fluent speakers does use of monosyllabic ('saw') very slightly exceed use of monosyllabic ('came'). Among older fluent speakers other than E17 the monosyllabic variant of ('saw') remains rare, and among semi-speakers the disyllabic variant of ('saw') remains unexpectedly strong by comparison with the disyllabic variant of ('came'); only one semi-speaker favored the latter, whereas two semi-speakers used the former 100 percent of the time.

Comparison of the sets of speakers who favored monosyllable variants for ('saw') and for ('came') indicates that overlap appears only at the youngest ages: speakers E18*, E22, E30, E37, E38, E39, and E40 favored the monosyllabic variant of ('came'), but of these seven only three of the youngest—E37, E39, and E40—were among the five speakers who favored the monosyllabic variant of ('saw'). Strikingly absent among the latter is E38, who very strongly favored the monosyllabic variant of ('came') yet never used /hũn/ at all except in echo of a sister's version of a folk-practice rhyme.

9.4.2 Patterns of Variant Preference by Age and Sex

Three OFS males (E4, E6, and E10), plus OFS female E13, showed a preference both for disyllabic /hã:nig/ 'came' and for disyllabic /hũnig/ 'saw'. Female E9 used disyllabic /hã:nig/ exclusively, and the only two instances of ('saw') that she provided were also disyllabic. One female older fluent speaker, E17, showed a moderate preference for disyllabic /hã:nig/ (68.8 percent) but a moderate preference for monosyllabic /hũn/ (62.5 percent). She was in fact the only older fluent speaker who favored a monosyllabic variant for either of these two variables.

For ('came'), two male and two female younger fluent speakers showed a preference for the monosyllabic variant. While two out of four YFS males showed a preference for the monosyllabic variant of ('saw') as well, no YFS females preferred the monosyllabic variant of the latter. One YFS male showed a stronger version of E17's somewhat surprising pattern: E25L strongly favored the disyllabic variant of ('came') yet strongly favored the monosyllabic variant of ('saw'), though the number of instances he provided was small in each case. The opposite pattern was shown by YFS female E22, who favored the monosyllabic variant /hã:n/ at a 56.7 percent level and the disyllabic variant /hũnig/ at a 76.9 percent level. This same pattern was shown to a still greater degree by semi-speaker E38, as noted in the previous paragraph.

The monosyllabic variant of ('came') appears to have been better established in Embo than the monosyllabic variant of ('saw'), but on the evidence of greater use among younger speakers both monosyllabic variants were advancing in tandem, with that of ('came') in the lead. Though age appears to be significant in this development, the use of /hã:n/ by E4 and of /hũn/ by E3 (the latter a single instance, to be sure, but a telling one in view of his seniority) indicates that older speakers did not reject the monosyllabic variants, and indeed, female older fluent speaker E17 actually favored /hũn/. Any apparent-time change that may have been in progress among younger speakers was making only erratic progress, however: five younger fluent speakers continued to use /hã:nig/ to the 100 percent level, as did two younger fluent speakers and even two semi-speakers in the case of /hũnig/.

A male lead in the use of the monosyllabic variants is possible but unlikely. Older males E3 and E4 each made use of one of them, but E6 did not; E10's monosyllabic variant use was limited to /hã:n/, and at that only at an 11.8 percent level. Among the younger fluent speakers, two females and two males (in that age order) favored /hã:n/, but three males used 100 percent /hã:nig/; two males favored /hũn/, but two others used 100 percent /hũnig/. In an unusual third case, involving the *regular* verb /čʰilig/ 'throw', three males showed a striking development that may have represented an incipient change in progress: the emergence of a past-tense variant /hil/ 'threw' in place of traditional /hilig/, apparently on the model of /hã:n/ and /hũn/. Within my sample, the three YFS males E23L, E25L, and E37 used monosyllabic /hil/, with the first of them favoring it strongly (four of five instances) and the youngest, E37, using it exclusively (six instances); on one occasion E37 even eliminated the /-ig/ element from the traditional gerund /čʰiligal/, producing instead a gerund /čʰil:u/ 'throwing'. Until as late as 2006 I believed that only males made use of this innovative variant, but at that date several translation task responses with monosyllabic /hil/ from semi-speaker E39 proved otherwise. E39's use of the monosyllabic form was particularly effective in ruling out an exclusively male link for this variant, because her older brother E36 had *not* been among the monosyllabic variant users.

9.5 The Variable Demonstrative ('that')

The demonstrative /ʃɔ̃n/ occurred in a variety of syntactic environments, but it was characterized by considerable variation only in one of them.[10] When the demonstrative appeared as the head of a verbless sentence or clause, it could appear with initial shibilant, /ʃɔ̃n/, or with the lenited equivalent of that initial shibilant, /hɔ̃n/. Both variants appeared when the sisters in the 1998 Embo videotape each remarked on the view from another sister's window, one saying "/hɔ̃n ə vyu/" and the other saying "/ʃɔ̃n ə vyu/" 'that['s] the view' (chapter 3, §7.2.2). Fully fluent speakers generally used no finite verb in sentences or clauses headed by a demonstrative, but if for some reason (to express particularly strong agreement, for example) one was included, it was almost always /ʃ e/ (the copula /ʃ/ with the so-called extender element /e/ [Oftedal 1956:245]), followed then by an unlenited demonstrative, for example, /ʃ e ʃɔ̃n ən´ ĩːrĩn´/ 'That's the truth'. The demonstrative does not inflect for number or for gender.

TABLE 5.20. Freely spoken and elicited forms of the variable demonstrative pronoun ('that') (serving as head of a verbless clause), with totaled variant selections as percentages, from Embo speakers of three age-and-proficiency levels

total # speakers: 24	hɔ̃n				ʃɔ̃n				
spkrs with 3(+): 15	free	elic	total	%	free	elic	total	%	
E4 82 m.	6	7	13	56.5	8	2	10	43.5	
E6 75 m.	--	1	1						
E9 70 f.	--	1	1						
E10 70 m.					2	8	10	**100**	
E13 [67] f.					1	--	1		
E15L 65 m.					1	--	1		
E17 64 f.	68	2	70	**94.6**	4	--	4	5.4	
E18* 60 f.	1	--	1		1	--	1		
E21L 58 f.	--	1	1						
E22 58 f.	4	1	5	41.7	5	2	7	58.3	
E23L 58 m.	--	2	2						
E24 57 f.					--	1	1		
E26* 54 f.	99	3	102	**96.2**	3	1	4	3.8	
E27 54 m.	8	--	8	34.8	2	13	15	65.2	
E29 * 50 f.	63	3	66	76.7	19	1	20	23.3	
E30 49 m.	36	--	36	**100**					
E32* 47 m.	7	--	7	77.8	2	--	2	22.2	
E33 45 m.					--	2	2		
E34 45 f.	3	1	4	22.2	2	12	14	77.8	
E37 41 m.	2	--	2	66.7	1	--	1	33.3	
E38 40 f.	28	22	50	89.3	6	--	6	10.7	
E39 38 f.	2	5	7	**100**					OFSs
E40 36 f.	2	--	2	2.4	74	9	83	**97.6**	YFSs
E42L 30 f.	16	2	18	**100**					SSs
use of variants:									
# of speakers using		19				17			
# favoring		10				5			
# using exclusively		3				1			

Elic = elicited. Results in 90–100 percent range boldfaced, results favored to lesser degrees underlined.

Table 5.20 presents Embo speakers' variant selections for the variable demonstrative ('that') in the specified environment.

Both variants were in use in Brora and Golspie. Available Brora instances are mostly elicited, with four speakers using /ʃɔn/ exclusively and one using /hɔn/ exclusively. The one Brora speaker who provided freely spoken instances of the variable overwhelmingly favored the variant /hɔn/, but no elicited instances are available from her for comparison. In freely spoken material three Golspie speakers provided multiple instances of the variable. All favored /ʃɔn/, but all made some use of /hɔn/ as well. In elicitation two Golspie speakers used only /ʃɔn/ and a third used /ʃɔn/ in the single elicited response she provided.

9.5.1 Use of More than One Variant

Of the fifteen Embo speakers who provided at least three instances of the variable, eleven (73.3 percent) used both variants; this is the highest rate of dual variant use encountered so far. One of three speakers who provided just two instances of the variable also used both variants.

Apart from the general run of strictly demonstrative uses ('That's her youngest brother', 'That's where I was born'), many high-frequency discourse formulas appear with demonstrative ('that') as their lead-in element, for example, 'That's you!' (to round off the discussion of something), 'That's what I'm saying' (as part of an effort to explain something), 'That's it!' (in triumph over something remembered or found), 'That's all!' (to close out a verbal response). The degree to which speakers used these formulas was very much an individual matter, as was the lenited or unlenited form of the demonstrative in such phrases. Most of the speakers whose personal style included frequent use of formulaic phrases such as 'That's you!', 'That's all!' favored the lenited form /hɔn/ (E40 being the only sharp exception), and most of them also tended to add the element /ad/ 'at-you' as an intensifier and personalizer in such phrases, for example, /hɔn ad ul/ 'That's all (for you)!' However the example of E22's concluding formulas for each description of a game played by Embo children, presented in chapter 3, §7.2.3, demonstrates that it was perfectly possible for /ad/ to occur with /ʃɔn/ as well as with /hɔn/, even though it less frequently did: in her first summing up of the game called Margaidh Dollach, E22 concluded with /ʃɔn ad marəgi torlax/ 'That's Margaidh Dollach (for you)'.

9.5.2 Patterns of Variant Preference by Age and Sex

Data are rather thin for older fluent speakers in the case of this variable, with individuals otherwise fairly well represented, like E6 and E13, poorly represented here. Male E10 showed a clear preference for /ʃɔn/ and female E17 a clear preference for /hɔn/, with male E4 showing only a moderate preference for /hɔn/.

Among the younger fluent speakers, both males and females showed a preference for /hɔ̃n/, with one male (E27) and two females (E22 and E34) as the exceptions, though only the last of these three by a relatively high percentage. The semi-speakers showed strong preferences for a single variant, but while E38, E39, and E42L strongly favored /hɔ̃n/, E40 favored /ʃɔ̃n/ just as strongly. There is thus no wholesale shift to /hɔ̃n/ across the age-and-proficiency continuum, despite the greater number of speakers favoring that variant.

9.6 The Variable Affirming ('is/are')

Like the variables ('that') of §9.5 and ('this') of §9.8, the variable affirming ('is/ are') has variants differing from one another in terms of unlenited or lenited initial shibilant. This variable is structurally binary, consisting of the copula *(i)s*, palatalized before a front vowel, plus the extender element noted in §9.5. The extender has a long vowel in its underlying form, but in casual speech it often appears with a short vowel or even in reduced form with a lax vowel (/ʃ ɛ/). In the affirming function both elements, copula and extender, are always present. In simple statements without this affirming function, the copular element is never lenited, and the extender normally appears as a short but tense vowel. In formulations that begin with the affirming element but then proceed to a simple statement, either variant of the affirming element can appear, /ʃ e(:)/ or /h e(:)/, but the seemingly identical element that begins the statement can take only the unlenited form /ʃ e(:)/:

> E30 /**h** e:, ʃ e miʃ—o:, ʃ e:, ʃ e iʃ [ə] va k iari hẽn [= hĩãn] n ə val.
>
> '<u>YES</u>, it's I—oh, <u>YES</u>, it's she [who] wanted to come to the village.'

Only freely spoken data are presented for this variable, since it belongs fundamentally to spontaneous discourse.[11]

Table 5.21 presents Embo speakers' freely spoken variant selections for the variable affirming ('is/are'):

Examples of the variable are not plentiful for Brora or Golspie, but both variants were in use in both villages. Only two Brora women, B3 and B7, provided instances, but while B3's lone instance was /ʃ e:/, B7 provided two instances of /h e:/ and one of /ʃ e:/. Golspie female G2 provided three instances of /ʃ e:/ and one of /h e:/, Golspie female G4 three instances of /ʃ e:/, and Golspie male G3 a lone instance of /h e:/.

Although the variants of the variable affirming ('is/are') paralleled those of demonstrative ('that') in *form* (unlenited and lenited variant choices), they paralleled those of the variable ('wasn't/weren't') in *function* (the expression of agreement). As with ('wasn't/weren't'), it was common for several repetitions of the variable to occur in rapid succession, or for instances to appear both at the beginning of a statement or a conversational turn and at its end, as a reflection of the strength of the speaker's cordiality or level of agreement.

TABLE 5.21. Freely spoken instances of the variable affirming ('is/are') with variant selections as numbers and percentages, from Embo speakers of three age-and-proficiency levels

total # speakers: 19	ʃe:		h e:	
spkrs with 3(+): 15	#	%	#	%
E3 [85] m.	1		1	
E4 82 m.	14	82.4	3	17.6
E10 70 m.			1	
E13 [67] f.	2	40	3	60
E15L 65 m.	10	90.9	1	9.1
E17 64 f.	4	66.7	2	33.3
E18* 60 f.	4	100		
E21L 58 f.			1	
E22 58 f.	3	100		
E26* 54 f.	3	60	2	40
E27 54 m.	12	85.7	2	14.3
E29* 50 f.	43	49.4	44	50.6
E30 49 m.	3	20	12	80
E32* 47 m.	1			
E34 45 f.	11	91.7	1	8.3
E38 40 f.	30	100		
E39 38 f.	12	100			OFSs
E40 36 f.	12	92.3	1	7.7	YFSs
E42L 30 f.	25	100			SSs
use of variants:				
# of speakers using	17		13	
# favoring	12		3	
# using exclusively	5		0	

Results in 90–100 percent range boldfaced, results favored to lesser degrees underlined.

9.6.1 Use of More than One Variant

Of the fifteen speakers who provided three or more instances of the variable, ten (66.7 percent) used both variants, as did one speaker who provided only two instances. This is almost as high a rate of dual variant use as appeared with the variable demonstrative ('that'), but despite the high use of both variants in the two cases, the overall pattern of variant preference is more lopsidedly in favor of one variant in the case of affirming ('is/are'). Ten of the fifteen speakers who provided three or more instances of ('that'), or 66.7 percent, favored the lenited variant, half of them at the 90–100 percent level; however, twelve of the fifteen speakers who provided three or more instances of affirming ('is/are'), or 80 percent, favored the unlenited variant, three quarters of them at the 90–100 percent level. In the case of the variant /h e:/, as in the case of the variant /kʰɔr(a) ri/ for ('along with'), a good many people used the variant but few of them used it heavily or preferred it.

When affirming ('is/are') appeared several times in succession to indicate cordial agreement, the variant remained the same throughout the string of repetitions.

E37 /či sɔ:rn, ə—a haləwĩ:n/

E15L /o:, ʃ e, ʃ e, ʃ e, ʃ e:. ʃ e, ʃ e.

E 37 'Saturday, uh—is Halloween.'

E15L 'Oh, <u>yes</u>, <u>yes</u>, <u>yes</u>, <u>yes</u>. <u>Yes</u>, yes.'

E27 /ax hurd i, "an el is am te ha n ɛr ʃɔ̃n ra:."

E30 /o, **h e:**, **h e**, **hɛ**/.

E27 'But she said, "I don't know what that fellow is saying."'

E30 'Oh, <u>yes</u>, <u>yes</u>, <u>yes</u>.'

When affirming ('is/are') was used both to begin and to end a speaker's conversational turn, with other material in between, the variant used at the opening and at the close was likewise most often the same one.

E37 /a:i, hɔ̃n ə ǰəiçu łɔ: čɛn ə—čɛn ə ǰia mĩãs.

E30 /ʃ e:. ə ǰiau mĩãs, ʃ e:./

E37 'Aye, that's the tenth day of the—of the six[th] month.'

E30 '<u>Yes</u>. The sixth month, <u>yes</u>.'

But although it was uncommon for different variants of affirming ('is/are') to appear at the opening of a conversational turn and at the closing of the same turn, instances did occur.

E29* /**he:**, du hau:ł, hɔ̃n ad ɛ l´o:s, nax e? stɔrnəwe.—an el u

tʰigal mo:ra[n]—ə—ə—kʰə:bən, ʃ ɛ./

'<u>Yes</u>, the over side, that's from Lewis, isn't it? Stornoway.—You're not understanding much—uh—uh—bits, <u>yes</u>.'

9.6.2 Patterns of Variant Preference by Age and Sex

Only one older fluent speaker favored /h e:/, female E13. One male and one female younger fluent speaker shared her preference. Females outnumbered males among the fluent speakers who preferred /ʃ e:/, but some otherwise well-represented males (E6, E10, E23L, E33, E37) provided few or no data for affirming ('is/are'), making it difficult to get a good sense of male preferences for this variable.

The semi-speakers were nearly monolithic in their preference for /ʃ e:/. Semi-speaker agreement on the variant /ʃ e:/ included, interestingly, the sisters E38 and E40, who differed dramatically both on their preferred variants for ('that'), parallel in variant form, and on their preferred variants for ('wasn't/weren't'), parallel in variant function.

Semi-speakers, especially E42L, showed some tendency to treat affirming ('is/are') as the equivalent of English *yes*, using it with little regard for the special syntactic conditions that apply in Gaelic. This does not explain their near-invariance in using the variant /ʃ eː/, however, since all had exposure to both variants, including E42L, whose mother E21L used /h eː/ in the one instance she provided. E29*, older sister of E38 and E40, was one of the few speakers who favored the variant /h eː/, but this clearly had no effect on her younger sisters' usage.

9.7 The Variable ('needing')

Table 5.22 presents Embo speakers' variant selections for the variable ('needing').
    The gerund ('needing') took the form /ĩmərd/ invariably in Brora and Golspie.

TABLE 5.22. Freely spoken and elicited forms of the variable ('needing') from Embo speakers of three age-and-proficiency levels, with totaled variant selections as percentages

total # speakers: 27		n´ĩmərd				ĩmərd				
spkrs with 3(+): 14		fr	elic	total	%	fr	elic	total	%	
E4	82 m.	2	9	11	**100**					
E5	77 f.					--	1	1		
E9	70 f.	--	1	1						
E10	70 m.	--	2	2	<u>66.7</u>	--	1	1	33.3	
E11	70 f.						1	1		
E12	?68 f.	--	1	1						
E13	[67] f.	--	1	1	10	2	7	9	**90**	
E14	65 f.	--	1	1						
E17	64 f.	12	9	21	**100**					
E18*	60 f.					[1]	--	[1]		
E21L	58 f.					--	1	1		
E22	58 f.	--	10	10	**90.9**	--	1	1	9.1	
E24	57 f.					--	6	6	**100**	
E25L	56 m.	--	1	1						
E26*	54 f.					3	20	23	**100**	
E27	54 m.	1	6	7	<u>77.8</u>	--	2	2	22.2	
E29*	50 f.	7	13	20	**100**					
E30	49 m.	--	1	1						
E32*	47 m.					1	--	1		
E33	45 m.					--	1	1		
E34	45 f.	3	8	11	<u>84.6</u>	--	2	2	15.4	
E36	41 m.	--	1	1						
E37	41 m.	--	1	1						
E38	40 f.	3	12	15	**100**					
E39	38 f.					--	6	6	**100**	OFSs
E40	36 f.	1	--	1	2.2	9	36	45	**97.8**	YFSs
E42L	30 f.					--	7	7	**100**	SSs
use of variants:										
# of speakers using			17				16			
# favoring			8				6			
# using exclusively			4				4			

Elic = elicited. Results in the 90–100 percent range boldfaced, results favored to lesser degrees underlined.

9.7.1 Use of More than One Variant

Six of the fourteen speakers who provided three or more instances of ('needing') used both variants (42.9 percent), but those who favored one or the other variant did so quite strongly: all preferences, for either variant, were at a level of 75 percent or better except for the 66.7 percent preference (two of just three instances) shown by E10. Usage is unusually evenly divided for ('needing'). Nearly as many speakers used /ĩmərd/ as /n´ĩmərd/; only two more favored the latter than favored the former, and exactly the same number used one or the other exclusively.

9.7.2 Patterns of Variant Preference by Age and Sex

The two OFS males who demonstrated a variant preference for ('needing') favored /n´ĩmərd/, while the two OFS females who did so each favored a different variant. YFS females were also divided, three favoring /n´ĩmərd/ and two /ĩmərd/. Only one YFS male provided enough instances of the variable to show a preference, and his preference coincided with that of the two OFS males.

In the case of ('needing'), far more speakers than usual provided only a single instance of the variable. All such OFS cases are females, and once again their usage (all in elicitation) is divided, three using /n´ĩmərd/ and two using /ĩmərd/. Four YFS males who provided only one instance of the variable apiece (all in elicitation) also used /n´ĩmərd/, but two others departed from this pattern by providing a single instance apiece of /ĩmərd/, one freely spoken and one elicited. Three of four semi-speakers favored /ĩmərd/ very strongly, but the one who did not favored /n´ĩmərd/ equally strongly.

In this rather unbalanced array of data (too few freely spoken instances, too many speakers represented by a single token), there seems to be a preference for the variant /n´ĩmərd/ among males but not among females. In the absence of any instances from male speakers such as E6 and E23L, however, and with exceptionally sparse data from others such as E30, E33, and E37, this can be only a possibility rather than a genuinely discernible pattern. E32 and E33, two of the YFS males who provided only a single instance of ('needing') apiece, used /ĩmərd/, and together with the occasional use of the same variant by E10 and E27, their usage indicates at any rate that /ĩmərd/ is not ruled out for males.

9.8 The Variable ('this')

The most direct structural parallel to the variable demonstrative ('that') is the equivalent proximal demonstrative ('this'), which begins with the same consonant and has the same unlenited and lenited variants. Like its counterpart, it often serves as the first element in verbless clauses. In the local fisherfolk Gaelic, demonstrative ('this') takes the three forms /ʃɔ/ (the predominant form), /ʃu/, and

TABLE 5.23. Freely spoken and elicited forms of the variable demonstrative pronoun ('this') (serving as head of a verbless clause and as proffering deictic), with totaled variant selections as percentages, from Embo speakers of three age-and-proficiency levels

total # speakers: 16	ʃɔ, ʃu, ʃɔːrn				hɔ, hu, hɔːrn				
spkrs with 3(+): 13	free	elic	total	%	free	elic	total	%	
E4 82 m.	--	2	2	50	1	1	2	50	
E10 70 m.	--	1	1						
E13 [67] f.	6	2	8	**100**					
E17 64 f.	1	1	2	16.7	10	--	10	<u>83.3</u>	
E22 58 f.	1	5	6	<u>85.7</u>	1	--	1	14.3	
E24 57 f.	--	2	2	<u>66.7</u>	1	--	1	33.3	
E26* 54 f.	2	4	6	46.2	1	6	7	<u>53.8</u>	
E27 54 m.	7	16	23	**92**	--	2	2	8	
E29* 50 f.	2	3	5	<u>62.5</u>	3	--	3	37.5	
E30 49 m.	--	2	2	<u>66.7</u>	--	1	1	33.3	
E33 45 m.	--	1	1						
E34 45 f.	--	10	10	**100**					
E37 41 m.	2	--	2	40	2	1	3	<u>60</u>	
E38 40 f.	4	5	9	<u>69.2</u>	4	--	4	30.8	
E40 36 f.	10	17	27	**100**					
E42L 30 f.					1	1	2		
									OFSs
									YFSs
									SSs
use of variants:									
# of speakers using		15				11			
# favoring		9				3			
# using exclusively		3				0			

Elic = elicited. Results in 90–100 percent range boldfaced, results favored to lesser degrees underlined.

/ʃɔːrn/, but all three of these can appear with either unlenited or lenited initial consonant. Just as differences other than syllable count were left out of consideration in the case of the variable ('saw'), which paralleled ('came') in its potential for mono- or disyllabicity, differences other than the presence or absence of lenition are left out of account for ('this'), which parallels ('that') and affirming ('is/are') in the variability of lenition. Table 5.23 presents Embo speakers' variant selections for demonstrative ('this').

For Brora speakers, only elicited data are available. B3 was the only Brora speaker to use the lenited form of demonstrative ('this'); she used it without exception in every elicited response she provided. This mirrors her equally invariant use of /hɔ̃n/ in elicitation responses for demonstrative ('that'). Golspie speakers used only unlenited forms of ('this'), whether elicited or freely spoken.

9.8.1 Use of More than One Variant

Of the thirteen Embo speakers who provided three or more instances of the variable, ten (76.9 percent) used both variants, the highest percentage of dual variant use yet. Variant-preference patterns parallel those for affirming ('is/are') better than those for demonstrative ('that'), in that a considerably higher proportion of speakers favored the variant with unlenited initial /ʃ-/, even though they made some use of the other, and no speakers made exclusive use of the less favored variant.

9.8.2 Patterns of Variant Preference by Age and Sex

Data are once again scarce for older fluent speakers. Only two speakers in that group, both females, showed preferences, with each favoring a different variant. OFS male E4 used both variants to an equal degree. Younger fluent speakers of both sexes strongly favored unlenited /ʃ/-initial variants, with only female E26* and male E37 weakly favoring the lenited /h/-initial forms. Among the semi-speakers, E40 favored the unlenited /ʃ/-initial variant, as she did also in the case of ('that'), and insofar as she provided instances, E42L likewise remained consistent, using lenited /h/-initial ('this') in addition to lenited /h/-initial ('that'). E38, by contrast, showed different variant preferences for the two variables, moderately favoring unlenited /ʃ/-initial ('this') in spite of her very strong preference for lenited /h/-initial ('that').

9.9 The Variable ('out')

Table 5.24 presents Embo speakers' variant selections for the variable ('out'), the locational member of the adverb pair locational 'out' /mwĩ(ç)/ and directional 'out' /max/.

The locational versus directional distinction was well preserved in Brora and Golspie, with the locational form of ('out') almost invariably represented by /mwĩ/.

In Embo some speakers (E17, E26*, E23L, E34, E37, and E38 in my sample) had lost the distinction between the locational and directional forms of the adverb ('out'), as was true of all East Sutherland fisherfolk speakers in the case of the adverb ('in'). The latter distinction was evidently lost some time ago, with both the original locational and the original directional forms of ('in') remaining in use, though now without semantic distinction. In the case of ('out'), however, the locational form had fallen out of use among those who had lost the distinction, with the originally directional form /max/ remaining as the sole expression of the adverb. Since only the locational form of ('out') shows intra-speaker and inter-speaker variation, speakers who had lost that form of the adverbial pair 'out' could provide no data unless they happened to have retained the locational form of the adverb in the compounded noun phrase /ə du mwĩ(ç)/ 'the outside', as I eventually discovered that a few speakers had.

TABLE 5.24. Freely spoken and elicited variants of locational ('out') from Embo speakers of three age-and-proficiency levels, with totaled variant selections as percentages

total # speakers: 16	mwĩç				mwī				
spkrs with 3(+): 12	free	elic	total	%	free	elic	total	%	
E4 82 m.	11	--	11	**100**					
E6 75 m.	--	1	1	33.3	--	2	2	66.7	
E9 70 f.	--	2	2						
E10 70 m.	--	2	2	25	3	3	6	<u>75</u>	
E13 [67] f.	3	--	3	42.9	1	3	4	<u>57.1</u>	
E14 65 f.	--	4	4	**100**					
E15L 65 m.					--	2	2		
E18* 60 f.	[1]		[1]						
E20 58 f.	--	1	1						
E22 58 f.	6	5	11	**91.7**	1	--	1	8.3	
E24 57 f.					--	3	3	**100**	
E27 54 m.					8	12	20	**100**	
E29* 50 f.	1	2	3	30	3	4	7	<u>70</u>	
E30 49 m.					2	2	4	**100**	OFSs
E39 38 f.	2	3	5	**100**					YFSs
E40 36 f.	3	1	4	**100**	[1]	--	[1]		SSs
use of variants:									
# of speakers using	12				10				
# favoring	5				7				
# using exclusively	4				3				

Elic = elicited. Square brackets indicate instances produced as an immediate echo of a previous speaker, not included in reckoning percentages. Results in the 90–100 percent range boldfaced, results favored to lesser degrees underlined.

9.9.1 Use of More than One Variant

Of the twelve speakers who provided three or more instances of the variable, five (41.7 percent) used both variants. Variant use was relatively evenly divided: about the same number of speakers used each variant, only slightly more favored one than the other, and very nearly the same number used one or the other variant exclusively.

9.9.2 Patterns of Variant Preference by Age and Sex

The variant preference of E4, the only one of the three OFS males with a very strongly favored variant, was not the same as that of the other two OFS men. One OFS female favored /mwĩç/ and E9's two elicited instances also took that form, but E13 used /mwī/ in both modes and preferred that variant in freely spoken material. With the exception of E22, both male and female younger fluent speakers favored /mwī/. The two semi-speakers who provided instances both used /mwĩç/ exclusively, apart from a single echo-instance produced by E40. No clear-cut patterns of age- or sex-related usage emerge.

9.10 The Variable ('near')

In chapter 3, note 1, I mentioned several variables that caught my attention belatedly, including the adjective/adverb ('near') with Embo variants /fagiʃ/ and /faʃkʰ/ and Brora/Golspie variants /fegəs ~ fəgəs/ and /feʃkʰ ~ fəʃkʰ/. I had already completed two extensive reviews of other variable items in my field notebooks at the time, and I did not undertake a third complete review for these late-entry variables. But ('near') was a variable that I had begun to track for its geographical variation in my telephone recordings, and it soon became apparent that it was emerging as the polar opposite of the variable ('potato'): it was rare for a speaker to use only one variant of ('potato'), but it was equally rare for a speaker to use *more* than one for ('near'). Up to this point the variable with the lowest level of intra-speaker variability was ('tomorrow'), for which only 30.8 percent of the speakers used more than one variant (see §9.3). The variability rate was clearly going to be lower still for ('near'); consequently I decided to track this one additional variable as fully as I could without actually attempting a complete notebook review.[12] Though not so full as the accounts of the other seventeen variables, the data given here for ('near') are copious enough to indicate the striking extent to which intra-speaker variation is absent in this case, despite the presence of inter-speaker variation. Table 5.25 presents Embo speakers' variant selections for the variable ('near').

Brora speakers' instances of ('near') included both disyllabic and mono-syllabic variants and also variants with both stressed vowels. The one Brora speaker for whom incomplete review of the Brora data turned up more than a single instance of the variable used the disyllabic variant and the stressed vowel /e/ consistently. In a likewise incomplete Golspie review, female G2 consistently used the disyllabic variant and male G3 the monosyllabic variant; only female G4 offered instances of both. In terms of vowel quality, however, all three Golspie speakers showed intra-speaker variation, using both /e/ and /ə/ as the stressed vowel.

9.10.1 Use of More than One Variant

Of the twelve Embo speakers who provided three or more examples of the variable, only two (16.7 percent) showed any variation at all, and none of the three speakers who provided just two instances of the variable showed variation. All fully fluent speakers used one variant or the other at the 100 percent level; intra-speaker variation was demonstrated only by the two semi-speakers, each of whom diverged just once from an otherwise strongly favored variant.

TABLE 5.25. Variant selections for the variable ('near') from Embo speakers of three age-and-proficiency levels, with totaled variant selections as percentages

total # speakers: 22	fagiʃ				faʃkʰ			
spkrs with 3(+): 12	fr	el	tot	%	fr	el	tot	%
E4 82 m.					3	4	7	**100**
E6 75 m.					1	1	2	
E7 ?74 f.	1	--	1					
E9 70 f.					--	1	1	
E10 70 m.	--	2	2					
E13 [67] f.	--	6	6	**100**				
E17 64 f.	15	--	15	**100**				
E22 58 f.	--	4	4	**100**				
E23L 57 m.	--	1	1					
E24 57 f.	--	4	4	**100**				
E27 54 m.					6	6	12	**100**
E29* 50 f.	9	5	14	**100**				
E30 49 m.					4	--	4	**100**
E31 49 m.	--	1	1					
E32* 47 m.					3	--	3	**100**
E34 45 f.	--	2	2					
E35 43 f.	--	1	1					
E37 41 m.	--	1	1					
E38 40 f.	2	6	8	88.9	--	1	1	11.1
E39 38 f.	--	4	4	**100**				OFSs
E40 36 f.	--	1	1	6.7	--	14	14	**93.3** YFSs
E42L 30 f.	--	1	1					SSs
use of variants:								
# of speakers using	16				8			
# favoring	7				5			
# using exclusively	6				4			

Fr = free, el = elicited, tot = total. Results in 90–100 percent range boldfaced, results favored to lesser degrees underlined.

9.10.2 Patterns of Variant Preference by Age and Sex

At all three age and proficiency levels, more speakers used /fagiʃ/ than /faʃkʰ/. Among those who provided three or more instances of the variable the male preference for /faʃkʰ/ is striking; apart from semi-speaker E40, all of the individuals who favored that variant were male. But OFS female E9 gave one instance of /faʃkʰ/, as did semi-speaker E38, and not all of the men in the sample used /faʃkʰ/. E10 gave two instances of /fagiʃ/, and E23L, E31, and E37 one instance each. Since intra-speaker variation was non-existent for ('near') among all better-documented speakers except semi-speakers E38 and E40, /fagiʃ/ was most likely the preferred variant for at least these four males. The pattern here is somewhat similar to the pattern for the variable ('tomorrow'), with one of the variants used predominantly but not exclusively by men and the other predominantly but not exclusively by women.

Part II : Variant Use by Speech Functions, Variability by Speaker and Variable, and Speakers' Levels of Variant-Preference Agreement and Disagreement

10 THE EFFECT OF ELICITATION ON VARIANT USE

No definitive sample-wide elicitation effects emerge in connection with the variables treated in this study. That is, there are no instances in which the speaker sample can be seen to have shifted as a group away from a disfavored variant or toward a favored variant in elicitation. This realistically reflects the linguistic isolation of an enclaved speaker population with limited exposure to written Gaelic and mainstream varieties of Gaelic; it does not, however, preclude individual variant-use differences in elicitation versus freely spoken material.

The Embo sample that provided material in both modes consists of seventeen speakers, five older fluent speakers (E4, E6, E10, E13, E17), eight younger fluent speakers (E22, E24, E27, E30, E34, E37, plus formerly fluent speakers E26* and E29*), and four semi-speakers (E38, E39, E40, and E42L). Three of these speakers (E4, E17, E30) provided more freely spoken material than elicited; five (E6, E24, E34, E37, E38) provided more elicited material than freely spoken. The materials provided by the remaining nine were relatively balanced across modes.

10.1 Variables with Analogically Formed Variants

High-frequency variables with at least one analogical variant offer the most obvious candidates for avoidance of one variant—the analogical one—in elicitation. This makes ('wasn't/weren't') and ('would go') the likeliest possibilities among the eighteen variables treated here.

The variable ('would go') proved to show low variation, with more speakers than average using only a single variant. Most speakers who used the analogical variant /he:ʝu/ used it in both modes, the exception being, surprisingly, E6, who produced it exactly where an elderly male might have been expected to avoid an analogical variant, namely in elicitation.

The variable ('wasn't/weren't') shows a hint of an elicitation effect for a few older fluent speakers, but this does not hold up across the full OFS group and even less so across the sample generally. Three OFS males used /(x)a t rɔ/ in free speech but not in elicitation, with the disparity especially marked in the case of the oldest of them, E4: 26.9 percent of his freely spoken instances were analogical (eighteen out of sixty-seven) versus *none* of his six elicited instances. E6, the next oldest male, used the analogically formed variant in his only freely spoken instances of the variable, but the fact that his elicited instances were evenly divided between analogical and non-analogical variants suggests that he, too, may have been aware that /(x)a rɔ/ represented traditional usage. But if familiarity with church and Bible Gaelic suppressed elicited use of /(x)a t rɔ/ for E4 and E6, it did not for E15L. All his instances of the variable were elicited, yet he strongly favored the analogically formed variant. Younger fluent speakers E24, E27, E29*, E33, and E34 also did not avoid /(x)a t rɔ/ in elicited material.

Apart from the three youngest semi-speakers, formerly fluent speaker E29* was the heaviest user of the analogical variant; but heavy favoring of the *non-analogical* variant by E26* in both modes (and by E32* in his freely spoken material) indicates that this was not a group-wide development for formerly fluent speakers.

10.2 Variables with Both Disyllabic and Monosyllabic Variants

Five speakers who occasionally used /hã:n/ ('came') in their freely spoken material never offered it in an elicited response: E13, E15L, E26*, E27, and E34. Since all of them offered substantial numbers of elicited responses, always with /hã:nig/, these speakers may have regarded the monosyllabic variant as relatively informal and less suitable for translation tasks. Three speakers who typically used /hã:n/ in freely spoken materials (E30, E37, and E38) nonetheless produced an occasional elicited /hã:nig/, suggesting the same possibility.

As with ('came'), so with ('saw'). Speakers E13, E24, E26*, and E29* made some use of a monosyllabic variant in freely spoken material without using it in elicited material. (Data from E38, whose freely spoken monosyllabic instances all followed immediately on a sister's prompt, are discounted.) These speakers might conceivably have been avoiding a variant with colloquial overtones in elicitation, even though only E13 among them was both passively literate and puristically inclined. Arguing against this interpretation, however, is the fact that the puristically minded E34 offered one elicited instance of /hũn/ despite never using that variant in her freely spoken material; if she had considered /hũn/ overly colloquial, she more than most speakers would have been inclined to avoid it in elicitation. E24, who otherwise used only disyllabic variants of both ('came') and ('saw'), used her freely spoken monosyllabic variants of ('saw') only in a rhyme associated with a traditional folk practice.

In the case of the variable ('when'), no fewer than nine speakers made use of a monosyllabic variant in freely spoken material without making use of that variant in elicitation. Yet seven of those nine, while seemingly avoiding one monosyllabic variant in elicitation, *did* use the other monosyllabic variant in elicitation. More suggestive, therefore, is the fact that thirteen of fifteen speakers who showed a difference in percentage of use for disyllabic variants of ('when') in elicited versus freely spoken material showed at least a slight increase for the disyllabic variants in elicitation. There seems to be some indication of a preference for disyllabic variants in elicitation, then; yet at the same time there were some speakers who strongly preferred monosyllabic variants in *both* modes, such as E4, E24, and E40.

10.3 Other Variables

Generally speaking, other cases of discrepancy in variant use across the two modes appear to be personal rather than general. For the variable ('in'), for example, E17 preferred the variant /sčɛx/ in her freely spoken material but favored /sčɛ/ in elicitation. Since several older fluent speakers used /sčɛx/ in elicitation and most made little or no use of /sčɛ/, there is no reason to suppose that E17's shift to /sčɛ/ in elicitation indicated that it was considered somehow preferable to the variant /sčɛx/, unless idiosyncratically by E17 herself.

E22's striking shift to /sčax/ in elicitation, a variant she never used in her freely spoken material, likewise appears to have been idiosyncratic. Most speakers who used /sčax/ produced it in both modes. E13 joined E22 in using it only in elicitation, but only in a single instance; in sharp contrast to them both, E17 used it only in freely spoken material.

In the case of the variable ('tomorrow'), the three male speakers who generally favored /ma:riç/ (E4, E10, and E37) made occasional use of /ma:rax/, the variant that coincides with standard-language usage, in elicitation, even though they did not produce it in their freely spoken material. The fact that E37 was wholly illiterate in Gaelic makes it unlikely that he at least was avoiding a local, non-standard variant in the elicitation mode. Furthermore, E27 and E34 showed the opposite pattern: each of them strongly favored /ma:rax/ and used that variant in their few freely spoken instances, yet each offered a single instance of /ma:riç/ in elicitation. These last two speakers were both puristically inclined, so that their use of /ma:riç/ in elicitation argues against any generally poor standing for that variant.

E17's deployment of the variants of the variable ('family') offers an example of the personal character of elicitation effects. In her first encounter with my colleague, Seòsamh Watson, he presented her with four translation task sentences that included the word 'family'. She gave a translation of the first of them three times in rapid succession, the first two times with /čʰə:rɫax/ but the third time with /čʰə:rɫiç/. A second sentence with ('family') also produced the variant /čʰə:rɫiç/. The final sentences with ('family') came very much later in the session, and in those final instances, when she was perhaps more comfortable with her interlocutor, she used /tʰə:rɫiç/, her favored variant in freely spoken contexts and in her materials overall. She also self-corrected in elicitation work with me, changing from /čʰə:rɫiç/ to /čə:rɫax/ twice; at other times, too, she seemed self-conscious about her elicitation responses for ('family'). Surprisingly, however, she used /tʰə:rɫiç/ when she was interviewed over the phone by a radio broadcaster in 1998.

She appeared to consider variants in initial /čʰ-/, most especially /čʰə:rɫax/, preferable to /tʰə:rɫiç/; the fact that the telephone interviewer had not told her she was being recorded may account for absence of self-correction on that occasion. Whatever social weighting the variants of ('family') had for E17 was unique to her, in any case, since no other Embo speaker showed self-consciousness about the variants of this variable.

11 OTHER POTENTIALLY STYLE-RELATED PATTERNS OF VARIANT USE

Just as elicited and freely spoken material might be expected to produce somewhat different patterns of variant use, other functionally distinctive varieties of speech might be expected to show somewhat distinctive variant-use patterns as well: discourse stretches with sharply different affect, for example, or the more traditional form of rhymes from folk practice and childhood. Shortcomings in the material on which this study is based preclude any genuinely full consideration of style (see chapter 3, §5.2), but the more limited question of whether the variation characteristic of personal-pattern variables, in particular intra-speaker variation, is to some detectable extent stylistically cued remains open. Some possibilities are considered here.

11.1 Variant-Use Patterns in Traditional Material

E24 produced her lone instances of monosyllabic ('saw') in a folk-practice rhyme, and her brother (E10) likewise produced his one freely spoken instance of monosyllabic ('came') in traditional material. E10's one instance of /hã:n/ appeared when he recited a line from a popular song, a striking instance because the song itself provides a disyllabic model in the line in question. E10's usage in traditional material did not otherwise show monosyllabic variants of ('came') or of ('saw'): he used the disyllabic variant of ('came') in another proverb and in a folk saying, and all of his uses of ('saw') in traditional material were disyllabic. Other speakers who used monosyllabic variants of ('came') in proverbs (E17, E40) or in ditties (E17, E40) showed no pattern of shift, since they made use of the monosyllabic variants in nontraditional material as well.

For the variable ('when') E4 produced what was for him a unique disyllabic variant /tərə/ in reciting a proverb; elsewhere he used the monosyllabic variant /tə/ exclusively. Traditional material likewise produced E22's sole freely spoken instance of the variant /tərə/, in a children's rhyme in her case. Both of these speakers therefore showed in much less striking form the pattern of E10, who shifted from his otherwise preferred freely spoken monosyllabic variant /tə/ for ('when') to disyllabic /n(u)ərə/ in reciting proverbs (see chapter 3, §5.1). But at the same time, there were six speakers who used the same variant in proverbs that they used in free speech outside traditional lore (E13, E17, E24, E27, E34, and E40).

No one showed any shift between nonanalogical and analogical variants for ('wasn't/weren't') in traditional material. E10, E17, and E22 used the same conservative variant without preterite particle in traditional material that they preferred elsewhere, and E34 was equally consistent in using her preferred analogical variant with the preterite particle. To sum up, then, traditional material produced variants unusual for their monosyllabicity for two speakers, variants unusual in their disyllabicity for three speakers, and only variants consistent with speakers' usual patterns in the case of an analogical variable. That is to say, no overall pattern of shift toward either more conservative or less conservative variants can be associated with the production of traditional material.

11.2 Variant-Use Patterns in Stories with Sharp Differences in Tone and Affect

Some speakers who provided material distinctive as to tone and affect did not provide enough contrastive material to allow a useful intra-speaker comparison. E10, for example, told a number of jokes; but his recorded material otherwise (his account of childhood games and his part of a taped message to his sister in Australia) did not include any small set-pieces in a narrative style that might have offered a valid contrast. E13 provided some passages that offered a contrast in tone during the first of the two tapes she made together with E22 and E34, but they were too brief to supply enough material for clear variant-use comparisons.

Among my Embo sources, anecdotalist E17 offered the best instances of recorded discourse distinct enough in topic and tone to make it reasonable to look for variant-use differences related to style even when the audience had not changed. In an April 1996 telephone conversation she told a very light-hearted 444-word story of having taken advantage of being in the hospital for respite care over Leap Year's Day to make a jocular proposal of marriage to an elderly male patient, who by Scottish Leap Year tradition did not have the option of refusing her proposal. In an October 1994 phone conversation with a radically contrasting tone, she told a somber 141-word story of paying a visit to a terminally ill relative, and in a January 1995 conversation she told of that last visit again and of the relative's death, this time in 362 words of equally somber tone. The incidence of variant forms with both longer and shorter variants (including ('when'), ('came'), and ('saw'), plus several variables not included among the ones introduced in this chapter) scarcely differed; the somber stories showed just as much use of shorter forms as the merry story. The most direct contrast in disyllabic versus monosyllabic variants appeared in fact not between merry versus somber stories but across the two somber narratives, as E17 recounted in each of them her relative's happy reaction to news of an impending visit:

tənə xuarl mi kə d rɔ ʃi čʰĩ̃ãn (Oct. '94)

tə̱ xuarl mi kə d rɔ ʃi čʰĩ̃ãn (Jan. '95)

'ᴡʜᴇɴ I heard that you[-plural] were coming…'

The appearance of both variants in identical environments within stories of the same somber tone and affect makes it unlikely that the monosyllabic variant of ('when') was intended to convey more colloquial or informal overtones than the disyllabic variant in E17's usage.

11.3 Variant-Use Patterns in Extended Discourse

A few multispeaker Embo recordings were of exceptional length, offering an opportunity for a somewhat stiff and self-conscious opening style to give way to more relaxed style after the early self-consciousness had passed. In one case the same speaker(s) also made more than one tape in fairly short order, allowing a comparison in style across the successive tapes. In three of four cases I was not present during the recording process.

11.3.1 The "Gift Tape"

In the very long tape-recording about earlier Embo times made by husband and wife E27 (Murdo) and E34 (Lexie) in 1968 as a gift for me, a few variants appeared in both longer and shorter form over the course of the recording. Only in one case, however, was there a shift from longer to shorter variants that suggested increasingly casual style, possibly reflecting an increasing ease with the undertaking. Of the mere seven disyllabic forms of ('when') that E34 used during the recording (versus twenty-one monosyllabic forms), six of the seven appeared in the first twenty pages of a fifty-five-page transcription. This proved to be a unique pattern for the recording overall, however. By contrast, for example, the four disyllabic forms of ('used to') that E27 used (versus sixteen monosyllabic forms) were scattered throughout the long recording.

More than one factor may play a role in variant choice, of course, and their effects may be impossible to distinguish. E27 used both disyllabic and monosyllabic forms of ('when'), but unlike his wife, he used them in nearly balanced numbers, nineteen disyllabic variants and twenty-one monosyllabic variants. With just over half of his disyllabic variants occurring in the last third of the recording, there is no likelihood that transition into a more relaxed style was involved. Instead, E27's disyllabic variants seem to have appeared at least partly in response to the verb with which they appeared: seventeen of his twenty-one monosyllabic variants (81 percent) occurred with forms of the verb 'to be', whereas only six of his nineteen disyllabic variants (31.6 percent) did so. With verbs other than ('to be'), disyllabic variants predominated. For E27, therefore, monosyllabic ('when') may have been context-sensitive in a lexical sense. A reconsideration of E34's forms of ('when') in the light of her husband's usage showed that a similar pattern applied in her case (81 percent of her monosyllabic variants of ('when') occurring with forms of 'to be'); but the fact that more of her instances of ('when') with 'to be' happened to occur in the latter part of the recording made a possible lexical-context effect indistinguishable from a possible relaxed-style effect in her case.

As for the variable ('wasn't/weren't'), E27 produced his few analogical forms in the first half of the gift tape, ruling out a relaxation factor for his use of this variant, while E34 used her very few non-analogical forms later in the session rather than in the early stage where they might have represented more formal speech behavior on her part.

11.3.2 The "Ceilidh Tapes"

During the fall of 1964 and the winter of 1965, while I was writing my dissertation, the Embo friends who put a good deal of phonologically contrastive material on tape for me filled up the remainder of each tape they sent with general conversation about village doings and about people whom I knew. They considered this the equivalent of having a *ceilidh* [kʰeːli], or visiting session, among themselves and with me. E13, E22, and E34 were the chief speakers on both tapes, with E13 (Flora) dominating both sessions. E3 was also present in each case but spoke very little. The second of these tapes was both longer and more casual in style than the first. There were additional people present (E24, and the returned exile E18*, sister to E13 and E24), and while some of the speech was addressed directly to me, quite a lot of it was simply conversation among the people present. This had the effect of making a good many interchanges poorly audible and difficult to transcribe, but key variables emerged clearly as they appeared and reappeared over the course of the very lengthy and lively recording.

The formidably intelligent E13 had had limited schooling of any kind (as an oldest daughter rarely free to attend school; see chapter 6, §2) and none at all in Gaelic, but she had nonetheless taught herself to read Gaelic. She held distinctly puristic views about Gaelic usage and was also, like her brother E10 (Duncan), capable of a style shifting that introduced forms drawn from the written language or from more mainstream dialects. In the ceilidh tapes she used three personal-pattern variables in high enough numbers to allow them to be tracked through and across the two sessions. One of the three, ('came'), showed no significant change, remaining predominantly disyllabic throughout. The other two, ('along with') and ('when'), showed changes that may have reflected the more relaxed style of the second tape.

All three of E13's ('along with') variants in the first tape coincided with the written-language form, /kʰɔ̃ːɫa ri/. In the second tape, two of her first three instances were also /kʰɔ̃ːɫa ri/. Three of these five initial instances were conjugated for person, which ruled out the variant /kʰɔi/ (see chapter 4, §6.3), but in the other two instances any of the remaining four variants of ('along with') was potentially possible. In the remainder of the second tape, no further instances of the variant that coincided with the written-language form appeared. Indeed, five of the second tape's last six instances took the form /kʰɔi/, and overall Flora used monosyllabic /kʰɔi/ in six of seven possible (non-conjugated) environments in the second, more casual, tape.

For ('along with') E13 showed something of the same pattern that E17 showed in her elicitation session with Seòsamh Watson, during which she began with the variant of ('family') that coincided with the written language and shifted first to the variant most typical of older speakers and then to her own preferred variant (see §10.3). In a very stilted recording replete with non-local elements that E13 made for me near the end of my first year of Sutherland residence, she used only the variant of ('along with') that coincided with the written-language form. In the first of the ceilidh tapes sent by mail the following autumn, she did the same. After starting the second ceilidh tape the same way, she soon shifted to monosyllabic forms of ('along with'), and for conjugated instances to a more widely favored Embo form, one built on /kʰɔ̃n(a) ri/ rather than /kʰɔ̃:ɬa ri/. E22 (Elspeth) was the only other speaker to offer instances of ('along with') across both ceilidh tapes. Unlike E13 she showed no change to the monosyllabic variant; she used two disyllabic variants in the first tape and four in the second.

For ('when') E13's shift was less consistently toward a shorter form. Although she moved from 100 percent disyllabic variants of ('when') in the very stilted 1964 recording and from five disyllabic variants out of six in the first of the two ceilidh tapes to one instance of monosyllabic /nə/ in the first tape and four in the second, she also produced her only freely spoken instances of disyllabic /tənə/ and /tərə/ in the second ceilidh tape. While it remains true, therefore, that the only monosyllabic forms of ('when') that E13 produced were freely spoken in the two ceilidh tapes, and that four of the five were in the second of these, she did not go over entirely to monosyllabic variants even during the exceptionally long and informal second ceilidh tape. Once again E22 was the only other speaker who offered instances of ('when') across both ceilidh tapes, and once again she showed no pattern of shift, this time using only monosyllabic variants in each tape, two instances in the first and six in the second.

Neither E22 nor E34 provided instances of ('came') or ('saw') in the first ceilidh tape, eliminating any possibility of cross-tape comparison. As for the analogical variant of ('wasn't/weren't'), E22 made no use of it in the ceilidh tapes or elsewhere. E13 showed a consistent pattern for this variant across tapes (predominant use of the non-analogical variant and a single instance of the analogical variant in each tape). E34 produced only one instance of ('wasn't/weren't') in the first ceilidh tape, a non-analogical variant, whereas two of her four variants in the second tape were her more usual analogical variants. With only one instance in the first tape, however, this can be only faintly suggestive of a shift toward more casual style.

11.4 Variant-Use Patterns with Different Interlocutors

Several quotations from conversations among Embo speakers offered in §7.2.2 of chapter 3 demonstrated absence of accommodation to fellow villagers' variant-use patterns. Drawn from the gift tape, for example, were the contrasting variants of ('from, off, of') used by E34 (Lexie) and E27 (Murdo) in speaking of the "tricky man", and drawn from the second ceilidh tape were the contrasting variants of ('along with') used by E13 (Flora) and E22 (Elspeth) in speaking of how the visiting E18* (Eilidh) was passing her days. In this enclaved bilingual community where local Gaelic conversation partners were all well known to one another, "audience design" (Bell 1984, 2001) scarcely came into play, since the Gaelic-speaking speech community consisted in effect of a single extraordinarily undifferentiated social group. Any realistic expectation of changes in variant-use patterns arising from a change in interlocutors would therefore need to involve Embo people conversing with Gaelic-speaking outsiders. (Chapter 7, §4.3, discusses the same issue in connection with translation tasks conducted by an outsider.)

Among the fully fluent speakers, it is again chiefly for E17 that there are freely spoken materials directed to interlocutors distinct enough to make a difference in formality likely. A number of variables with both longer and shorter forms appeared in her conversations with me over the telephone, in a long interview with Seòsamh Watson, and finally with a radio broadcaster who interviewed her over the phone, but these materials do not make as solid a contrast as they might. While E17 thoroughly enjoyed Seòsamh Watson's visits and he taped his long interview with her on what was perhaps the third such visit (1997), he had brought a Scandinavian colleague along on that occasion, someone completely strange to her. She was uncertain how much Gaelic this second man understood and raised uneasy questions about him toward the end of the taped session. The occasion was therefore marked by a minor social unease on her part; in addition the very high informational content of the session marked it clearly as an interview rather than a conversation.

In this very long interview and in the quite brief phone interview, there were seven instances of the variable ('came') and twenty-two instances of the variable ('when'). Six instances (85.7 percent) of ('came') were disyllabic /hã:nig/, versus only one (14.3 percent) monosyllabic /hã:n/, whereas in her telephone conversations with me thirty of forty-eight ('came') instances (62.5 percent) were disyllabic and eighteen (37.5 percent) monosyllabic. It might be supposed therefore that the greater informality of our frequent phone conversations favored the use of the monosyllabic variant, but this argument is undercut by the corresponding counts for the variable ('when'). In the two interviews with a stranger or with a stranger present, only five of E17's twenty-two instances of ('when') were disyllabic (22.7 percent), with seventeen instances (77.3 percent) monosyllabic. In telephone conversations with me, 76 of E17's 125 instances of ('when') were disyllabic (39.2 percent), with 76 (60.8 percent) monosyllabic. Since it would be difficult to argue that our frequent phone conversations were a more formal linguistic environment than the two interviews, the more tenable position is that the shorter forms of ('when') do not correlate with degree of formality for E17.

Evidence pointing in a very different direction comes from semi-speaker E40, who took part in a short telephone interview with a radio broadcaster in 1997. That interview produced the only three freely spoken disyllabic instances of ('when') ever offered by E40, who used 219 monosyllabic variants otherwise in her freely spoken materials; even in 64 elicited instances she used only one disyllabic variant. It seems highly probable, given her variant-use figures for ('when'), that she was making a shift toward a more formal style in the interview setting, although she is in most circumstances, in common with her fellow semi-speakers, not a style shifter. During their lifetimes exposure to relatively formal styles of Gaelic has been reduced, and perhaps on that account they appear not to have developed as broad a stylistic flexibility as their elders in the matter of variant range. For E40, however, the disyllabic variant of the variable ('when') does seem to have been elicited by a particularly self-conscious speech performance and to have marked a greater formality of style. The self-consciousness may have been somewhat extreme on this occasion, since E40 was masquerading as her older sister, E38. E38, always a reluctant conversationalist, was replaced without the interviewer's knowledge by E40, a much more comfortable talker. Answering to another person's name is not the most relaxing of conversational circumstances, however, even for a good conversationalist. In another interview with a radio broadcaster in 2004 E40 showed no shift toward the disyllabic variant of ('when'); but in this second case she had made the acquaintance of the broadcaster previously and the interview was conducted much more congenially in her own home, rather than over the telephone.

11.5 Conclusion

The findings presented in sections 10 and 11 are inconclusive. Variant-use patterns in traditional material are somewhat distinctive, but the differences do not run uniformly in the same direction for all speakers. E10 and E17 showed a preference for disyllabic variants of ('when') in proverbs, and in the same environment E4 and E22 used variants of ('when') that were unusual for them otherwise. But it was also in traditional material that E10 and E24 used monosyllabic variants of ('came') and ('saw') that were unusual for them otherwise.

Certain other indications of one or another stylistic effect can be detected—or perhaps more nearly suspected—in the patterns of variant selection that speakers showed when they used variables that offered both longer or shorter variants or both non-analogical and analogical variants. E34 used more monosyllabic variants of ('when') in the later part of the gift tape recording session than in the earlier part, and E13 more monosyllabic variants of ('along with') in the second, longer and more relaxed ceilidh tape. E40 used her only instances of freely spoken disyllabic ('when') in a phone interview with a radio broadcaster. E10, E17, and

E22 used a smaller proportion of monosyllabic variants of ('came') in elicitation as compared with their freely spoken materials, while E27 and E34 eliminated the monosyllabic variant entirely in elicitation. E4, almost a quarter of whose freely spoken instances of ('wasn't/weren't') were analogical, used no analogical variants at all in elicitation.

For every such case, however, there were speakers who failed to show corresponding stylistic effects in those same circumstances. E27's monosyllabic instances of ('when') in the gift tape appeared to be lexically rather than stylistically cued, and his disyllabic instances of ('used to') were scattered throughout the recording rather than clustered toward the beginning. E17 showed a novel preference for disyllabic ('when') in her rich proverbial material, but unlike E10 no such preference for a disyllabic variant in traditional rhymes; she also showed no change to disyllabic variants of ('when') in her telephone interview with a radio broadcaster. E4 and E29* used a somewhat higher proportion of monosyllabic variants of ('came') in elicitation than in their freely spoken materials, and E6 preferred the analogical variant of ('wasn't/weren't') in elicitation as well as in his freely spoken material.

By way of a summing up, the following might be said. There appear on the one hand to have been certain stylistic factors that affected the way particular speakers used variants that differed in length and phonological fullness or variants that were analogical rather than traditional in form. There appear on the other hand to have been *no* stylistic factors that affected all speakers the same way under parallel conditions. That is to say, personal-pattern variation remains just that—personally patterned—under stylistically similar conditions just as under syntactically similar conditions.

12 VARIABILITY AS A PROPERTY OF VARIABLES AND OF SPEAKERS

The tables in this chapter document several of the chief features of personal-pattern variation in East Sutherland fisherfolk Gaelic: a wide variety of linguistic forms (noun, pronoun, verb, adjective, adverb, preposition, conjunction, particle) had from two to five variant forms; individual speakers frequently used more than one variant of the same variable; any two speakers whose preferred variants coincided in the case of one variable might disagree on preferred variants in the case of another. Evidence for lack of social significance in the use of one variant form of a variable rather than another was presented in chapter 3. Occasional idiosyncratic exceptions may be suggested by an individual speaker's avoidance of a variant in elicitation (e.g., E4's elicitation avoidance of analogical /a t rɔ/ ('wasn't/ weren't'), a variant he used with some frequency in feely spoken material) or in a speaker's tendency to use an unusual variant in elicitation but move away from it over the course of a translation task session (e.g., E17's early use of /čʰə:rɫax/ and /čʰə:rɫiç/ ('family') with Seòsamh Watson and her change-over later in the session to her more usual form /tʰə:rɫiç/). The occasional style shifter might also prefer a variant in performance style that was not his preferred variant in more conversational styles (e.g., E10's preference for /nu(ə)rə/ in reciting proverbs).

The tables also indicate that level of variation differed both from person to person and from variable to variable. While none of the speakers in the sample used more than one variant for every variable for which they provided three or more instances, only one speaker, E21L, used just a single variant for all variables for which she provided that many instances. (To be sure, she did so for only three variables, but a small number of variables does not guarantee absence of variation: E3, who provided three or more instances of only *two* variables, nonetheless used more than one variant for one of the two.) Variables themselves had distinctive profiles, with ('potato') and ('near') representing the extremes. Every personal-pattern variable had more than one variant form by definition, but some, like ('near'), showed little intra-speaker variation; most speakers used one variant or another, but few used more than one. Other variables, like ('potato'), showed a very high level of intra-speaker as well as inter-speaker variation: nearly every speaker used more than one variant. Consideration of levels of variability for speakers and for variables follows.

12.1 Individual Speakers' Levels of Variation

The number of variables for which each individual speaker made use of more than one variant is presented here. Because speakers sometimes used two different variants even when they produced only two instances of a variable, two- instances cases are included here in reckoning individuals' percentage of intra-speaker variation. Thirty-two Embo speakers can be compared in terms of this measure.

Non-contiguous occurrences of the various shadings for proficiency level in table 5.26 indicate that speakers of a particular proficiency level do not show whole-group profiles of intra-speaker variation. Two formerly fluent speakers show a very high intra-speaker variation rate, for example, but two others show only a middling range. Both full-fluency speakers (such as E13 and E34) and semi-speakers (such as E38 and E40) also show very high intra-speaker variation percentages. At the bottom range of variation a similar mix is evident: older fluent speakers, younger fluent speakers, and one semi-speaker appear among those who show an intra-speaker variation level below 30 percent.

Intra-speaker variation levels above 60 percent are more common among speakers who provided two or more instances of a larger number of variables, naturally enough, and levels below 30 percent are likewise commoner among speakers who provided two or more instances of fewer variables. But this factor does not by any means account for all of the differences evident in the table, since speakers with the same number of variables available can show very different levels of intra-speaker variation. E26* and E24, each of whom provided two or more instances of sixteen variables, had variation levels of 87.5 percent and 25 percent, respectively; E33 and E23L, each of whom provided two or more instances of ten variables, had levels of 60 percent and 30 percent, respectively.

TABLE 5.26. Individual Embo speakers ordered by percentage of intra-speaker variation

speakers	# variables with 2(+) instances	# variables showing variation	% of variation		
E26* 54 f.	16	14	87.5		
E29* 50 f.	18	15	83.3		
E13 [67] f.	17	14	82.4		
E34 45 f.	17	13	76.5		
E40 36 f.	17	13	76.5		
E38 40 f.	16	12	75		
E27 54 m.	18	13	72.2		
E17 64 f.	17	12	70.6		
E22 58 f.	18	12	66.7		
E4 82 m.	18	11	61.1		
E33 45 m.	10	6	60		
E37 41 m.	14	8	57.1		
E6 75 m.	11	6	54.5		
E15L 65 m.	11	6	54.5		
E3 [85] m.	2	1	50		
E10 70 m.	16	8	50		
E18* 60 f.	4	2	50		
E32* 47 m.	6	3	50		
E39 38 f.	17	7	41.2		
E30 49 m.	13	5	38.5		
E9 70 f.	9	3	33.3		
E42L 30 f.	16	5	31.3		
E23L 57 m.	10	3	30		
E41 31 f.	7	2	28.6		
E5 77 f.	4	1	25		
E20 58 f.	8	2	25		
E24 57 f.	16	4	25		
E7 ?74 f.	5	1	20		
E36 41 m.	5	1	20		
E25L 56 m.	6	1	16.7	OFSs	
E14 65 f.	8	1	12.5	YFSs	
E21L 59 f.	3	0	0	SSs	

The presence in table 5.26 of as many as four speakers who showed intra-speaker variation below 40 percent despite providing two or more instances of ten to sixteen variables (E30, E42L, E23L, and E24) demonstrates that a lower level of intra-speaker variation can be characteristic of the speaker rather than the simple outcome of having provided multiple instances of only a small number of variables.

Table 5.26 displays some conspicuous blocks of either male or female speakers. All six of the speakers with intra-speaker variation levels of 75 percent or higher are women. A block of five males accounts for all of the intra-speaker variation levels between 62 percent and 54 percent, and a block of five females appears at the 29 percent to 20 percent level (though one male speaker also shows a 20 percent level). Women are particularly prominent at the highest levels of intra-speaker variation, but they are equally prominent at the lowest levels, since six of eight speakers with intra-speaker variation levels of 25 percent or lower are also women. Women as a group can therefore not be seen as given either to high intra-speaker variation or to low intra-speaker variation but instead perhaps to extremes of variation. Most males—nine of thirteen—appear in the relatively moderate ranges (62–38 percent), but there is nonetheless a scattering of females in the moderate range and a scattering of males at the higher and lower ranges.

Table 5.26 does not offer a means of distinguishing speakers who were particularly given to using several variants in the case of multiple-variant variables from those who used just two variants. E17, for example, is entered with a 70.6 percent rate of intra-speaker variation and E38 with a 75 percent rate. But E17 used five variants of ('in'), five variants of ('when'), and four variants of ('along with'), while E38 used three variants of ('in'), two variants of ('when'), and two variants of ('along with'). On this alternative measure, therefore, where the question is more than just the binary issue of variation/no variation, E17 is much more given to variation than E38. Looking at variant use just for the eight multiple-variant variables, and considering only the fifteen speakers who provided two or more instances of all eight variables, intra-speaker variation levels differ from those of table 5.26: E17 with twenty-five variants for the eight variables, and E13 and E29* with twenty-four, all averaged three or more variants per variable. E27, with twenty-two, averaged 2.8. A block of four speakers (E22, E26*, E38, and E40) used nineteen variants for the eight variables and E34 used eighteen, that is, still better than two variants per variable. The remaining six speakers (E4, E10, E39, E42L, E37, and E24) all used an average of fewer than two variants per variable; E4 used fifteen variants for the eight variables, E10, E39, and E42L used thirteen, and E37 used twelve. E24, with only nine variants for the eight variables, or an average of 1.1 variants per variable, showed the least variation. Two older fluent speakers (E17 and E13) thus showed the highest level of intra-speaker variation and two younger fluent speakers (E37 and E24) the lowest. By this alternative measure, the two formerly fluent speakers showed different levels (an average of three variants per variable for E29*, but 2.4 for E26*), as did two different pairs of semi-speakers (an average of 2.4 variants per variable for E38 and E40, 1.6 for E39 and E42L). This measure brings out additional similarities and differences among speakers of the same age and proficiency level, therefore, but it applies to a smaller number of speakers.

12.2 Variables Compared by the Number of Individuals Using More than One Variant

The number of speakers who showed intra-speaker variation in the use of a particular variable, again including two-instances cases, ranges from a high of 93.8 percent for ('potato') to a low of 13.3 percent for ('near'). Table 5.27 presents the figures for each of the eighteen variables.

Once again it is evident that the level of intra-speaker variation associated with a particular variable is not explained simply by the number of speakers who provided two or more instances of the variable, since the twenty-seven speakers who did so

TABLE 5.27. Degree of intra-speaker variability for eighteen personal-pattern variables by percentage of speakers who used more than one variant of a given variable

variable	# of variants for variable	# speakers providing 2(+) instances	# speakers using more than one variant	% speakers using more than one variant
'potato'	3	16	15	93.8
'when'	5	27	22	81.5
'along with'	5	26	19	73.1
'this'	2	14	10	71.4
'in'	5	26	18	69.2
affirming 'is'	2	16	11	68.8
'that'	2	18	12	66.7
'from, off, of'	3	25	15	60
'came'	2	31	18	58.1
'saw'	2	23	11	47.8
'family'	4	19	9	47.4
'wasn't/weren't'	2	28	13	46.4
'needing'	2	14	6	42.9
'would go'	4	24	9	37.5
'out'	2	14	5	35.7
preterite particle	3	18	6	33.3
'tomorrow'	2	28	8	28.6
'near'	2	15	2	13.3

for ('when') showed an 81.5 percent level of intra-speaker variation, while the twenty-eight speakers who did so for ('wasn't/weren't') showed a 46.4 percent level and the twenty-eight speakers who did so for ('tomorrow') a 28.6 percent level.

The number of variants available for the variable also did not predict degree of intra-speaker variation. All of the five-variant variables showed a relatively high degree of intra-speaker variation, but neither of the four-variant variables did so. Two- and three-variant variables appear both at or near the top of the table and at or near the bottom: ('potato'), with three variants, shows the highest level of intra-speaker variation, and ('this'), with two variants, the fourth highest level, but (preterite particle), with three variants, shows the third lowest level of intra-speaker variation, above only ('tomorrow') and ('near') with two variants each.

13 SPEAKERS COMPARED BY THE TYPICALITY OR ABERRANCE OF THEIR VARIANT PREFERENCES

The possibility that high inter-speaker variation in Embo might have arisen as the result of aberrant variant choices on the part of a distinct subset of speakers, individuals who repeatedly made use of variants seldom used by their fellow villagers, has been raised several times in this chapter. A table such as table 5.6, showing that most Embo speakers preferred just two of the variants of the variable ('along with'), might suggest such a possibility, but for the fact that table 5.2 showed that four of the five variants of ('in') were favored by just about the same number of Embo speakers in each case. An individual who favored a relatively little-used variant in one case could also prove to favor a more typical variant in the next case. E4 showed this pattern, for example, with regard to the variables ('in') and ('along with'): he favored the least commonly preferred variant of the former but one of the two most commonly preferred variants of the latter.

For five of the eighteen variables, there was no marked village-wide variant preference. The number of speakers who favored each variant were fairly similar for ('from off, of'), ('needing'), ('out'), and ('near'); and though one variant of ('potato') was not favored by anyone at all, the other two were favored by similar numbers of speakers. Of the twenty-six Embo speakers who provided two or more instances of at least seven of the thirteen variables for which preferred Embo variants can be identified, most showed only a few atypical variant preferences. Six showed none, five showed one, and seven showed two. E4, E6, E26*, E29*, and E39 preferred atypical variants in three cases each. E10 preferred atypical variants in four cases, E37 in five, and the pinnacle of aberrance was represented by E40, who preferred atypical variants in six cases out of a possible thirteen. One inevitable consequence of atypical variant preferences is that the speaker who displays them will also display relatively high levels of disagreement on variant preferences with a number of fellow speakers, as is demonstrated by E40 and her sister and fellow semi-speaker E38. E38 showed only one atypical variant preference; she appears only once in table 5.29, where relatively low levels of agreement between pairs of speakers are presented. E40 showed six atypical variant preferences; she appears, correspondingly, as many as eleven times in the low-agreement speaker pairs of table 5.29.

14 SPEAKERS' LEVELS OF AGREEMENT AND DISAGREEMENT WITH FELLOW SPEAKERS

In determining both levels of agreement and levels of disagreement on variant preference between speakers, only relatively high and relatively low percentages of preference coincidence or difference were considered (agreement at 60 percent or better, and disagreement at less than 40 percent), and only cases in which the two speakers had provided two or more variants for at least ten of the eighteen variables. Setting the level of agreement at 60 percent or better and disagreement at less than 40 percent avoids the range of 50–59 percent agreement and 50–40 percent disagreement, where differences by only a single instance would have excessive significance: seven shared variant preferences for thirteen variables would give a 53.8 percent agreement level, for example, whereas six shared variant preferences for thirteen variables would give a 46.2 percent level of disagreement.[13] Setting the minimum number of shared variant preferences at ten was intended to exclude statistically strong-looking instances of agreement that were based on a small number of variables. For example, seventeen pairs of speakers actually showed 100 percent levels of variant-preference agreement; but thirteen of those pairs provided data for only two variables in common and the other four pairs provided data for only three variables in common. Similarly, of twenty-two speaker pairs who fell into the 70–79 percent range of variant-preference agreement, fifteen pairs consisted of speakers who provided data for only four variables in common, agreeing on a variant preference in three of the four, or 75 percent. Requiring agreement on variant preference for at least ten variables renders the notion of speaker agreement somewhat more substantial.

Despite these efforts to make variant-preference agreement a reasonably strong concept, it should be kept in mind that "agreement" is reckoned here on the dimension of coinciding variant preferences alone, with the degree of preference not taken into consideration and the presence or absence of shared less-favored variants for multivariant variables also disregarded. In these respects this is therefore still a crude measure of agreement; reference can be made to the tables for each variable to determine the degree to which one speaker's preference level resembled another's and to determine whether, in the case of variables with more than two variants, they did or did not have a second-most-favored variant in common. In chapter 6, where variant use within close kin circles is considered, a more nuanced tabulation of shared variant use is attempted.

14.1 Relatively High Levels of Agreement on Variant Preference

Preferences for ten or more variables are available for twenty speakers, allowing 180 possible coincidences in variant preference. Just sixteen pairs of speakers showed agreement on variant preferences at a 60 percent level or better, and there was no level of agreement higher than 73.3 percent. Table 5.28 presents the relatively high-agreement cases.

14.1.1 High Agreement Levels by Sex and Proficiency Level

Two female speakers showed a high level of agreement on variant preferences with one another in nine instances, and a female speaker with a male speaker in seven instances. The absence of agreement on variant preference among male speakers is striking: there is not a single instance of two male speakers in agreement at a level of 60 percent or above.

Across proficiency levels there are also some striking differences. Older fluent speakers showed a relatively high level of agreement on variant preferences with younger fluent speakers in five instances, younger fluent speakers with each other in five instances, and younger fluent speakers with semi-speakers in six instances. There were no cases in which older fluent speakers showed a high level

TABLE 5.28. Pairs of speakers showing high levels of agreement (60–71 percent) on variant preference for ten or more variables, each with two or more instances available

speaker pair	sex of speakers	# of shared variables with 2(+) instances	# of shared variant preferences	% of preference agreement
E13 & E24	f. & f.	15	11	73.3
E27 & E34	m. & f.	17	12	70.6
E22 & E24	f. & f.	13	9	69.2
E24 & E38	f. & f.	13	9	69.2
E22 & E38	f. & f.	15	10	66.7
E17 & E22	f. & f.	15	10	66.7
E26* & E42L	f. & f.	15	10	66.7
E10 & E22	m. & f.	14	9	64.3
E22 & E34	f. & f.	14	9	64.3
E29* & E38	f. & f.	16	10	62.5
E37 & E38	m. & f.	13	8	61.5
E6 & E34	m. & f.	10	6	60
E13 & E22	f. & f.	15	9	60
E23L & E39	m. & f.	10	6	60
E24 & E30	m. & f.	10	6	60
E33 & E34	m. & f.	10	6	60

of variant-preference agreement with each other or with semi-speakers. There were also no cases in which semi-speakers showed a high level of variant-preference agreement with each other. The younger fluent speakers appear to be the bridge generation in this respect: three of them (E22, E24, and E34) shared variant preferences at a high percentage level with at least one older fluent speaker (E22 with no fewer than three older fluent speakers), and six of them (E22, E23L, E24, E26*, E29*, and E37) shared variant preferences at a high percentage level with one semi-speaker. E22 and E24 formed a bridge in both directions, sharing high-percentage variant preferences both with at least one older fluent speaker and with one semi-speaker.

14.1.2 High Agreement Levels between Spouses

The second-highest level of agreement was between Murdo (E27) and his wife, Lexie (E34), at 70.6 percent. Determining whether coincidence in variant preferences is typical of spouses or is instead a feature of this particular couple is problematic. Many of my sources were widowed, a number were unmarried, and a few were married to an English monolingual. There was a sprinkling of other Gaelic-speaking couples in my East Sutherland sample, but in most cases some factor of personality or relative availability made it difficult to assess both partners adequately. The only realistic candidates for comparison with E22 and E34 were G4 and G5 in Golspie, and E21L and E23L in the London-Embo group, but neither couple is nearly as fully represented in my materials as E27 and E34.

Variant preferences can be compared for G4 and G5 in the cases of nine Golspie variables, however, and they prove to have agreed on a variant preference in three of them—('tomorrow'), ('when'), and ('wasn't/weren't')—and to have disagreed in six. The six cases in which they favored different variants were the gerund ('looking'), the conjugated preposition ('on her'), adverbial ('in'), ('family'), the conjunction ('until'), and the presence or absence of lenition in one prominent environment for the conjugated preposition ('to'). (Several of these variables are either unique to Golspie or are common to Golspie and Brora but not to Embo.) For this Golspie couple, at any rate, variant-preference agreement reaches only a 33.3 percent level as compared with Murdo and Lexie's 70.6 percent level.

In the London environment, E21L and E23L were nearly always both present when I was asking questions about Gaelic. Despite the fact that she had a very strong personality and was a lively and voluble speaker, E21L generally deferred to E23L when it came to responding to translation tasks. Possibly this reflected her awareness that her husband had the passive literacy of a male trained in pre-centing the metrical psalms while she herself was not literate in Gaelic. In the extremely lively social environment of London-Embo group gatherings at their home on weekends, I was seldom able to take useful notes on spontaneous usage, and unfortunately, not foreseeing the great potential value that an interview in Gaelic would have had, I recorded my hosts only in English. While I have solitary instances of many of the Embo variables for E21L, there are only three cases in which she provided at least three instances of a variable; each such variable happens to be invariant in her usage. This is probably the result of the particular variables concerned, however (the three relatively low-variation variables ('would go'), ('wasn't/weren't'), and ('tomorrow')), rather than a reflection of E21L's overall level of variation. Her husband, E23L, shared both her variant preference and her invariance with regard to ('tomorrow'), and though his usage was not invariant he favored the same variant for ('would go'). What little material I have otherwise for E21L indicates that her usage differed considerably from that of her husband. She favored /(x)a rɔ/ for ('wasn't'), while his one instance of that variable was /(x)a t rɔ/. His variant preference for ('in') was /sčɛx/; her one instance was /stɛ/. His variant preference for ('when') was /nə/; her one instance was /tərə/. His variant preference for ('along with') was /kʰɔ̃rna ri/; her one instance was /kʰɔra ri/. His variant preference for ('saw') appeared to be /hũn/ (two instances); her one instance was disyllabic. They agreed (as far as extremely minimal data can indicate) on (preterite particle), ('came'), and ('that'). For ten variables, then, scanty data suggest that they may have agreed in five cases and disagreed in five, for a modest 50 percent level of variant agreement. It seems unlikely that more abundant materials for E21L and E23L would have reached the high level of variant-preference agreement that E27 and E34 demonstrated, and more likely that Murdo and Lexie's level of agreement was unusual for spouses rather than typical.

14.1.3 High Agreement Levels within the London-Embo Group

Though E21L and E23L do not appear to have shown a high level of variant-preference agreement with each other, members of the London-Embo group other than E21L (the most poorly represented of the group) did do so. They do not appear in table 5.28 because there were no cases in which any two of them provided as many as ten variables in common, but it is worth noting that if E21L, who provided two or more variants for only three variables, is left out of account, the six remaining pairs of London-Embo speakers all showed variant-preference agreement with one another that was above the 50 percent level, from E15L and E25L's high of 80 percent (four out of five variables) to E23L and E42L's low of 55.6 percent (five out of nine variables).

14.1.4 High Agreement Levels outside the London-Embo Group

The London-Embo speakers formed a unique social group that may have favored relatively high levels of variant-preference agreement, but there were certain other speaker pairs whose very strong agreement across a modest number of variables makes the lack of further evidence for them regrettable. E20, for example, showed very high levels of variant-preference agreement with E17 and E27 (five of six variables, 83.3 percent, in both cases) and with E9 and E14 (four out of five variables, 80 percent, in both cases). Especially desirable would have been additional instances of well-documented variables for E9 and E14, who showed variant-preference agreement with each other for six of their seven available variables (85.7 percent). With another few variables attested for each, it would have been possible to determine whether these two speakers constituted the otherwise missing phenomenon of two older fluent speakers with a high level of agreement for ten variables. Finally, there were two sibling pairs who showed high agreement levels, sisters E13 and E24 at 60.7 percent and sisters E29* and E38 at 62.5 percent.

14.2 Relatively Low Levels of Agreement on Variant Preference

Although only sixteen pairs of speakers showed agreement on variant preferences at the relatively high level of 60 percent or better for ten or more variables, fifty-three pairs of speakers showed agreement on variant preferences only at the relatively low level of 39 percent or less for ten or more variables. Across the eighteen variables looked at here it was clearly more common for two well-represented Embo Gaelic speakers to prefer different variants than the same variant.

TABLE 5.29. Pairs of speakers showing low levels of agreement (10–39 percent) on variant preference for ten or more variables, each with two or more instances

speaker pair	sex of speakers	# of shared variables with 2(+) instances	# of shared variant preferences	% of preference agreement
E33 & E37	m. & m.	10	1	10
E33 & E39	m. & f.	10	1	10
E13 & E37	f. & f.	12	2	16.7
E6 & E39	m. & m.	11	2	18.2
E10 & E40	m. & f.	16	3	18.8
E4 & E23L	m. & m.	10	2	20
E10 & E23L	m. & m.	10	2	20
E23L & E26*	m. & f.	10	2	20
E23L & E29*	m. & f.	10	2	20
E10 & E26*	m. & f.	14	3	21.4
E10 & E42L	m. & f.	13	3	23.1
E27 & E37	m. & m.	13	3	23.1
E34 & E37	f. & m.	13	3	23.1
E37 & E42L	m. & f.	12	3	25
E4 & E15L	m. & m.	11	3	27.3
E15L & E40	m. & f.	11	3	27.3
E30 & E34	m. & f.	11	3	27.3
E22 & E42L	f. & f.	14	4	28.6
E27 & E39	m. & f.	17	5	29.4
E6 & E17	m. & f.	10	3	30
E10 & E15L	m. & m.	10	3	30
E10 & E30	m. & m.	10	3	30
E17 & E33	f. & m.	10	3	30
E15L & E17	m. & f.	10	3	30
E23L & E27	m. & m.	10	3	30
E23L & E40	m. & f.	10	3	30
E26* & E27	f. & m.	13	4	30.8
E37 & E40	m. & f.	13	4	30.8
E10 & E39	m. & f.	16	5	31.3
E34 & E39	f. & f.	16	5	31.3
E4 & E37	m. & m.	12	4	33.3
E4 & E38	m. & f.	15	5	33.3
E10 & E37	m. & m.	12	4	33.3
E22 & E37	f. & m.	12	4	33.3
E27 & E29*	m. & f.	18	6	33.3
E27 & E40	m. & f.	18	6	33.3
E27 & E42L	m. & f.	15	5	33.3
E29* & E42L	f. & f.	15	5	33.3
E13 & E40	f. & f.	17	6	35.3
E17 & E40	f. & f.	17	6	35.3
E29* & E39	f. & f.	17	6	35.3
E22 & E29*	f. & f.	17	6	35.3
E4 & E24	m. & f.	14	5	35.7
E22 & E26*	f. & f.	14	5	35.7
E24 & E39	f. & f.	14	5	35.7
E4 & E6	m. & m.	11	4	36.4
E6 & E40	m. & f.	11	4	36.4
E13 & E15L	f. & m.	11	4	36.4
E15L & E39	m. & f.	11	4	36.4
E4 & E38	m. & f.	16	6	37.5
E26* & E34	f. & f.	16	6	37.5
E29* & E37	f. & m.	13	5	38.5
E29* & E40	f. & f.	18	7	38.9

Four pairs of siblings appeared among the sixteen speaker pairs who showed relatively high levels of variant-preference agreement, but three pairs of siblings also appear among the fifty-three speaker pairs who showed relatively low levels of agreement in table 5.29.

14.2.1 Low Agreement Levels by Sex and Proficiency Level

Male speakers showed low levels of variant-preference agreement with female speakers in twenty-nine cases and females with females in twelve cases. Whereas high-level variant-preference agreement between any two male speakers was entirely absent, male speakers proved to show a low level of variant-preference agreement with one another in twelve cases. At least within this sample of speakers and for this selection of variables, males for whom at least ten variant preferences were available were overwhelmingly more likely to disagree with one another on variant preference than to agree with one another. Although there are also twelve cases of women showing low levels of agreement with one another, only two of them appear in the 10–30 percent range of variant-preference agreement. In that same particularly low range, fifteen of the twenty-nine (51.7 percent) cases of low male–female agreement are to be found, and nine of the twelve cases (75 percent) of low male–male agreement.

Low percentages of variant-preference agreement appeared between speakers of all age and proficiency levels except one: none of the four semi-speakers with ten or more variables available showed a low level of agreement with another semi-speaker. Since none of them showed a *high* level of agreement with their fellow semi-speakers either, it is evident that shared semi-speaker levels of both agreement and disagreement were always in the moderate range of 40–59 percent. Older fluent speakers, who showed high levels of agreement neither with other older fluent speakers nor with semi- speakers in table 5.28, presented a correspondingly different profile in the case of low variant-preference agreement: they showed low levels of agreement with one another in six cases and with semi-speakers in eleven cases. Given the disparity in age and proficiency, disagreement between older fluent speakers and semi-speakers seems natural enough, but the level of OFS disagreement among themselves is more surprising. Younger fluent speakers show low-level agreement with older fluent speakers in nine cases, with other younger fluent speakers in fifteen cases, and with semi-speakers in fourteen cases.

14.3 Unpredictable Outcomes in Levels of Agreement on Variant Preferences

There was no reason to anticipate that neither older fluent speakers nor males would show any coherence as a group in terms of levels of variant-preference agreement. The older fluent speakers did, however, show a predictable level of variant-preference disagreement with the group most unlike them in terms of age and proficiency, the semi-speakers.

In the tables for individual variables, tables 5.1 through 5.25, there were no fully convincing cases in which a particular variant was associated with males as opposed to females. The variables ('tomorrow') and ('near') showed a pattern that suggested variant differentiation along gender lines, but with a few females using the variant favored chiefly by males, and a few males using the variant favored by females, the differentiation was far from absolute. In table 5.27, no male speakers proved to show a high level of agreement with other males on variant preferences, but in table 5.28 they showed a low level of agreement with other males a dozen times. There was no evidence whatever of strong male–male agreement as opposed to male–female disagreement. In view of the strong gender-based role differentiation described in chapter 2, more gender-based alignment in variant use and variant preference might have been anticipated.

Sibling ties proved in tables 5.27 and 5.28 to be no guarantee of high levels of variant-preference agreement,[14] but the kin group as the single most important basis of social relations in the fisherfolk communities merits further attention. So does the peer group, if only because it has proven to be so important a factor in urban variationist studies. These two groups are examined in chapter 6.

Kin Groups, Peer Groups, and Variation

1 INTRODUCTION

In chapter 1 I recorded my surprise at discovering, early in my East Sutherland work, that members of a small and highly homogeneous community, in particular people who were close kin to one another, might routinely give different forms in response to the same translation task. Neither the discovery nor the surprise is unique to me, as it happens. Trudgill, reporting on the "astonishing variability" he found among natives of a single small community in New Zealand, all near in age and many of them related to one another, gives the following sketch of one pair of speakers:

> Mrs. H. Ritchie and Mr. R. Ritchie...were both born in Arrowtown in 1963, went to school together and became brother-and-sister-in-law. They have lived close to each other, and have remained in close contact, all their lives. Nevertheless, they differ from one another in their phonologies in a way which one would not expect in a more stable situation [i.e., one with less dialect mixture in the parental generation] and in a way which cannot be explained in terms of social-class dialect. (Trudgill 1999:203)

After discussing variability in Arrowtown natives' English phonology with respect to both consonants and vowels, Trudgill acknowledges his surprise at these findings:

> Even in highly stratified and complex urban societies, we would be very surprised indeed to find this degree of variability between nine speakers all from the same area.

It is all the more remarkable, then, that we find this degree of variation in a single small town amongst people all of approximately the same age and social standing. (1999: 204)

In another case, a researcher in the Aran Islands off Ireland's west coast reports on sharp variation in the usage of two siblings:

> I was intrigued further as I examined linguistic data from two friends in Corrúch, a brother and a sister who had lived alone in their family house in Corrúch since they were born [sic], and who had traveled very little outside the area. The amount of linguistic variation in the data was astonishing. (Duran 1992:6)

The East Sutherland fisherfolk can be presumed to have had in common with the Arrowtown New Zealanders a degree of dialect mixture in the founding generation, but, without the pressures of standardization and educational use to induce conformity to a preferred norm, East Sutherland Gaelic did not experience what Trudgill anticipated as the next stage: "the reduction of variants that accompanies focusing" (Trudgill 1999:197). Instead, as in Corrúch, a variation that was presumably of long standing continued to be characteristic even of speakers who shared life-long nuclear family bonds and a single household.

2 THE INFLUENCE OF FAMILY AND PEER GROUP

The received wisdom in sociolinguistics has long been that "the family circle normally provides the first speech models for infants", but that "within a few years it is replaced by a more significant one", namely the speech model represented by a circle of "classmates and close friends" (Chambers 1995:159). The underlying assumption here—that the family circle on the one hand and the circle of classmates and friends on the other will represent identifiably distinct speech patterns, with each showing a certain degree of uniformity—is a highly doubtful one for Embo. In most cases both parents in the family were natives of Embo, but the pronounced inter-speaker variability characteristic of Embo speakers (not to mention the intra-speaker variability) offers no reason to believe that any two Embo adults would have supplied uniform models for their children. Furthermore, any distinction between a family circle in which the parents constituted the main linguistic influence and a peer group in which same-age younger people exercised important linguistic influence was far less absolute in Embo than is typical of urban settings or of middle-class settings generally.

During the months of the local line fishing, marketing the catch took women away from the home for large parts of most days, each woman going out with creels of fish to the district where she had an established sales territory; during the herring fishery season, mothers might be away from home for several months at a time. In the mother's absence, the oldest daughter in the household necessarily became a substitute parent, and as the oldest daughter reached an age where she could take full-time employment, she might be succeeded in this task by a slightly younger daughter. The household responsibilities given over to an oldest daughter included preparing food for her siblings and minding the youngest children. Home duties were so heavy for oldest girls that they were seldom able to attend school with any regularity and got little formal schooling.[1] Under these circumstances, younger children in the family might easily have more exposure to their oldest sisters' speech than to their mother's. The same was true with respect to their father, out at sea many hours a day and likewise away from home for long stretches during the herring season. In addition, as noted in chapter 4, §5.1, children in this small village populated by large families were less sharply stratified by age in their interactions than is typically the case in present-day towns or suburbs. All children near to each other in age played together, except that girls and boys each had some games that the other sex seldom or never played. (Only girls played house, for example, and only boys played soccer.) In this deeply interrelated village made up of a small number of densely populated streets, adults other than the parents frequently had significant roles in children's lives. Children often had strong ties to an aunt or great-aunt, an uncle or great-uncle, or to a grandparent, since a relative older than their own parents (especially someone whose time and energy were no longer completely engaged by work related to fishing) might have more time available for extended interactions with the young. Finally, because of the large size of most families, the sibling set itself might encompass more than the twenty-year span usually reckoned as a generation; the oldest son or daughter might actually be slightly closer in age to the parents than to the youngest child. For all these reasons, the Gaelic speakers of this study are unlikely ever to have confronted, as they grew up, sharp generationally based contrasts between a set of nuclear family speech models offered by their parents and a set of peer-group speech models offered by same-age children.

By the 1960s, direct data on children's Gaelic acquisition was not available, since transmission of Gaelic in the home had ceased well before then. It is presumably relevant, however, that the oldest available speakers as well as the younger fluent speakers showed not just inter-speaker variation but also intra-speaker variation. E4, eighty-two years old in 1970, is the oldest speaker for whom I have extensive freely spoken recordings. Gaelic was his mother tongue and probably still his dominant language,[2] yet he produced both /(x)a rɔ/ and /(x) a t rɔ/, both /hã:nig/ and /hã:n/, both /ʃɔ̃n/ and /hɔ̃n/, both /ma:riç/ and /ma:rax/, both /stɛx/ and /stɛ/, both /mǝda:tʰ/ and /mǝtʰa:tʰ/. At the other end of the age spectrum, where exposure to Gaelic was less extensive and proficiency to some degree limited, variation declined a good deal but did not disappear. E40, thirty-six years old in 1970, was a high-proficiency semi-speaker who likewise provided a large amount of freely spoken recorded material. Gaelic was her first language in a temporal sense, but English was clearly her dominant language. Despite her greater use of English than Gaelic and the increasing prominence of some analogically regularized forms in her Gaelic, her speech patterns are not characterized by wholesale elimination of variation. She used both /kʰɔ̃na ri/ and /kʰɔ̃rna ri/, both

/č⁽ʰ⁾ɛu/ and /č⁽ʰ⁾e:ǰu/, both /č/ and /t/ for the preterite particle, and all three variants of ('potato'). In a number of cases where she had a very strongly preferred variant, she nevertheless made very occasional use of other variants, as with ('in'), ('when'), ('family'), and ('saw'). The still younger and much less proficient semi-speaker E42L, with English as first and dominant language, showed much more reduction of variation; but even she used three variants of ('along with') and two of ('came'), and while she strongly preferred one variant of ('in'), she neverthe-less made some use of another. She used an idiosyncratic form of her own for most instances of ('when'), but on the two occasions when she supplied a tradi-tional form, each was a different variant.

On the evidence of pervasive inter-speaker variation across the entire speaker pool and some degree of intra-speaker variation at all age levels, then, the presence of both kinds of variation was the normal state of affairs in Embo. There is no reason to suppose that either the family or the peer group offered a unitary model for children to acquire. This chapter examines variant-use patterns for the eigh-teen variables of chapter 5 in the usage of Embo family networks to determine the extent to which past or present household membership may have affected those patterns. Sibling relationships will be to the fore, rather than parent–child rela-tionships, since few of the latter were available by the time I came to gather these data. The usage of a spouse is included in one case for possible indications of broader household use. Factors such as age, sex, and proficiency level are of course still at issue.

3 THE CENTRALITY OF KIN GROUPS IN EMBO'S SOCIAL STRUCTURE

The importance of kin ties in the East Sutherland fishing communities was pointed out in chapter 2, especially §4.3.4 and §5.4. People's closest and most frequent social interactions were with consanguineal and affinal kin, whom they also looked to as their most reliable source of support in practical matters. Because the equivalent of a generation could lie between the oldest child and the youngest, the children of the oldest child in a family were sometimes in the same school class with that parent's own youngest sibling, so that an uncle or aunt was the classmate of a niece or nephew. Close ties across considerable age gaps were common among siblings and cousins and also among aunts and uncles and nieces and nephews. The large pool of relatives also made a generous array of kinfolk avail-able as potential intimates. Harmony and cordiality across all the members of large kin groups were not a given by any means, of course, but the sheer number of people within the kin group meant that an individual's chances of finding some particularly compatible people among the group were excellent.

Households often consisted of more than the nuclear family. Unmarried chil-dren who stayed in the area generally continued to live in the parental home; in the absence of surviving parents, they might make their home with a married sibling.

Married children might take an elderly surviving parent into their home or move back into the original parental home to take care of the parent. Children orphaned at a young age were usually taken into the homes of aunts and uncles.

Out-migration from Embo was high between the world wars, as the fishing industry went into decline and the search for work drew a generation of young people away. Most of those who went to England or the Lowlands maintained their ties to Embo and regularly returned to the village to spend their annual two-week summer vacation visiting their parents and those of their siblings who had remained there. Accommodation of visiting siblings was an ongoing responsibility for family members resident in Embo, and this arrangement helped keep family ties strong over many years and considerable distances. By way of such visits home, older brothers and sisters who had left the village as teenagers could become well acquainted with siblings who had been small children or infants at the time of the older children's departure. Reciprocity in the other geographical direction often had the same effect, since older sisters and brothers who had moved away for purposes of work or marriage could be depended on to offer at least initial accommodation to younger siblings who later also went south in search of work. In addition, family members still resident in Embo might head south for an occasional vacation of their own, staying with a sibling (or an aunt, uncle, or cousin) while visiting a large city and taking advantage of favorable urban prices for shopping. In short, interactional kin ties were typically very strong within the village, and even when some kin-group members were living far away from the village, the lines of mutual support could remain intact and powerful.

4 WORKING WITH THE MEMBERS OF KEY SIBLING SETS

Among the forty-two people who acted as sources in my Embo work, there were a number of sets of siblings, a few of them with a parent who was still alive when I first went to the village. In most of these cases some crucial members of the family are inadequately represented because they had died before I embarked specifically on the study of idiosyncratic inter-speaker and intra-speaker variation, but for four sibling sets, one with a surviving parent, I was able to gather enough material from the people in question to make group comparisons possible.

Among my speaker sample four sets of siblings offer the best opportunity for comparison of variant-selection patterns across the family. In each of the four cases, a core group of siblings provided both freely spoken and elicited material, though only elicited material (or in one case only freely spoken material) is available for other members of the sibling set. Speaker identification by age-based number codings, efficient for large-group tabulations like those of the previous chapter, is less useful for present purposes, in which individual identities and relationships are important. In this chapter, then, I again use the pseudonyms intro-

duced in chapter 3 for a few sibling or household groups, and pseudonyms will be
provided for individuals featured here for the first time.

Three sets of siblings were identified in chapter 3, along with affinal members
of two of the families. The first was the household of married couple Dugald (E3)
and Flora (E13), with Flora's unmarried older brother, Duncan (E10), and unmarried younger sister, Una (E24), also in residence. Another sister, Eilidh (E18*),
away for thirty-seven years in Australia, returned for a lengthy visit in 1965. The
second set of siblings was the sister-and-brother pair Elspeth (E22) and Murdo
(E27), unusual for an Embo family of that era in having no other siblings. Murdo's
wife, Lexie (E34), of Group 3, was younger sister to formerly fluent speaker
Sheila (E26*), who had left Embo for England and then the Lowlands in her late
teenage years, returning to Embo only for annual vacations, funerals, and the like;
and to Stuart (E32*), an Embo resident who normally declined to speak Gaelic
but provided material for this study by way of a Gaelic radio interview. The fourth
sibling set consists of four sisters and three brothers: four younger fluent speakers,
two high-proficiency semi-speakers, and a near-passive bilingual. I worked with
the mother of this family and four of the children extensively and with the other
three children minimally, but all provided at least a small amount of material ger-
mane to this study. The established numberings, shadings, and asterisk markings,
with age and sex specified, are combined here with the pseudonyms that will be
used hereafter for easier reference. Boxes indicate the members of Groups 1 and
4 who shared a single household (with visiting sister Eilidh's shared residence
temporary, in the case of Group 1).

Group 1	Group 2	Group 3	Group 4
husband to Flora	siblings:	siblings:	Mother
E3, [85] m., Dugald	E22, 58 f. Elspeth	E26*, 54 f., Sheila	E9, 70 f., Ada
siblings:	E27, 54 m., Murdo	E32*, 47 m., Stuart	children:
E10, 70 m., Duncan		E34, 45 f., Lexie	E30*, 50 f., Emma
E13, [67] f., Flora			E31, 49 m., Angus
E18*, 60 f., Eilidh			E35, 43 f., Euphemia
E24, 57 f., Una			E37, 41 m., Rory
			E38, 40 f., Elsie
			E40, 36 f., Lorna
			(near-passive bilingual Colin, 34 m.)

If infant and childhood deaths are left out of account, there are no missing
siblings in the second and fourth groups; but the brothers and sisters of Groups 1
and 3 are only a subset of an originally larger group of siblings who reached adulthood, some of whom were not available as sources because they had died, were
living elsewhere in Britain, or had emigrated.

The degree to which I drew on the members of these family groupings as sources was not at all equal, partly because of the varying lengths of time that particular individuals survived and partly because personality differences affected the amount and even the type of material an individual provided.

Flora, a woman of exceptional intelligence and strong personality, was my most central Embo source in 1963–64 and again in 1965. Her husband, Dugald, was as quiet as she was lively. He spoke little and in an exceptionally soft voice, making his contributions to group recordings very hard to hear. In elicitation sessions, he nearly always allowed Flora to answer questions and provide translations, chiming in only occasionally. Sadly, by 1967 both had died. Eilidh enters this study only through her participation in a group tape made during her visit home in 1965. Until Duncan retired he was at home only on weekends, and I did not work with him during my first two field trips; he and Una became important sources from 1967 on. Of these two, Una was much more talkative, but Duncan's store of proverbial lore and jokes, which he was quite willing to record, was unique. Una survived into the 1990s and was healthy enough in the early years of that decade to provide some specifically variation-related material via a long elicitation session with my colleague, Dr. Seòsamh Watson.

Elspeth and Lexie, who had kin ties to Flora's household and were often encountered at her home, were also among my earliest Embo sources; Murdo joined them in 1965, outliving them both and becoming one of my regular phone conversation partners. Elspeth was an easy talker, willing both to record freely spoken material and to undertake translation tasks at great length. Murdo relished the translation task challenge of considering ways in which things might be expressed in the local Gaelic, but he was not an easy conversationalist. He saw the value of freely spoken texts as an example of how things were in fact said locally, and he made a great effort to supply such texts, despite the difficulty for him of speaking on tape. He solved that difficulty by recording with Lexie, and after her death on his own, presenting me with the recording after it was finished. He also took part in one three-person recording session in the 1970s.

In the early part of my intensely grammar-focused fieldwork period, I made a serious methodological mistake in working with Elspeth, Murdo, and Lexie, who liked elicitation work best when they could do it in joint sessions, any two of them together or all three at once. During this period, I sometimes coded responses that agreed grammatically (but not necessarily in other respects) from two speakers jointly, not specifying which one of them spoke first, and as a result there are whole stretches of pages in my field notebooks that are not usable for the study of individual variation. I very often "know" who the original provider of the material was by the very inter-speaker variation that characterizes it; but since I have been identifying individual patterns of variant use according to known speakers, reversing tactics and using those same patterns to identify unknown speakers is obviously inadmissibly circular. I made the same mistake at one point in working with Duncan and Una, and again some potentially valuable material had to be disregarded for present purposes.

I note this failing on my part here because it highlights the need for especially meticulous speaker identification in a community where individual variation is rampant and is therefore itself a potential research topic. For grammatical purposes, it was often sufficient to note that "E^{jl}" or "E^{jlk}" had provided a certain construction in common. The joint notation indicated that the speakers whom I was then coding as E^j, E^l, and E^k had repeated the sentence in question one immediately after the other (or in fact, in some cases almost simultaneously, since all three liked the joint elicitation work and sometimes vied to be the first to provide the translation), using the same grammar. But a joint identification of this sort was useless for assigning to one particular speaker any variant of an Embo variable that might also have appeared in the sentence as I took it down. Luckily I continued to work with all of the speakers with whom at one point I took this ill-advised shortcut, and properly attributed material was ultimately gathered from all of them. But with hindsight, needless to say, I deeply regret the patches of unusable material in several notebooks.

I did only elicitation work with Sheila, mostly at her home in the Lowlands, during my years of on-site fieldwork, and initially only elicitation work with her by recording and telephone in the 1990s, since she claimed to be too much out of practice to speak Gaelic freely. But in 1995 she began quite suddenly to use Gaelic conversationally, becoming a fairly regular source of both freely spoken and elicited material until health problems overwhelmed her in 2003–2004. She was a lively and voluble speaker, despite some rustiness. Stuart's contribution to this study came about purely thanks to his Gaelic radio interview and his willingness to let me use it for research purposes; otherwise he would not have been available as a source, since he ordinarily declined to speak in Gaelic. Lexie, quiet and shy, usually said much less than any others who might be present in a taping session. She participated in four multispeaker recordings, however, and cumulatively over the four provided a certain amount of freely spoken material. She did elicitation work without difficulty, and since she entered my sample early and remained a key source until her premature death in 1977, her speech is reasonably well represented.

Ada was one of the two Embo older fluent speakers who served as sources for the extensive sets of translation tasks that I presented in 1974 and 1976 to eight fluent Brora, Golspie, and Embo Gaelic speakers and seven Brora and Embo semi-speakers, with the aim of gathering fully comparable materials for an assessment of grammatical change in their Gaelic. Ada's son Rory was the youngest of the YFS sources for the same study, and her two high-proficiency semi-speaker daughters, Elsie and Lorna, also served as sources (as did Murdo and Lexie, for that matter, representing younger fluent speakers, and Sheila, representing formerly fluent speakers for the first half of the translation task batteries). Three others of Ada's children, Angus, Euphemia, and Colin, participated in a survey of lexical retention that I undertook during the same years, using the 200+ lexicostatistical word list of so-called core vocabulary. Despite the fact that Angus was seriously ill by the time I met him, his siblings pressed him to complete the family record, so to speak, and both he and Euphemia undertook the lexical survey and also provided a small amount of other elicited material.[3] Colin, not an active speaker of Gaelic but fully bilingual in terms of receptive skills, produced what he could of the lexical material and also provided a small amount of elicited material both at that time and in a phone session in 2001. Ada, Angus, and Euphemia did not survive into the 1990s, but Rory, Elsie, and Lorna were the key figures in gathering freely spoken material and elicited material for me from fellow Embo villagers by recording in 1991 and 1992; all also participated in the taping sessions themselves. Rory, noticeably more relaxed and confident when speaking in Gaelic than in English (though his English was entirely fluent), died suddenly shortly before I began doing telephone work. Elsie and Lorna became telephone conversation partners, though of very different temperaments and styles. Elsie was frugal of words in both of her languages. Never a talker, she was cheerful and generous about undertaking elicitations, but she always preferred to minimize purely conversational interaction. Lorna was Elsie's diametric opposite—highly verbal and always ready for a chat. Though she originally claimed not to be able to maintain an extended conversation in Gaelic, she soon did so almost as readily in Gaelic as in English, at least where everyday topics were concerned.

At the urging of Lorna and Elsie, their eldest sister, Emma, began to speak with me over the phone as well, providing both elicited and freely spoken material (see note 3). She had been living in England or overseas during all of my on-site fieldwork years, and we had therefore never met. Living in Embo again, and even while only planning to live there, she was eager to recover as much of her original Gaelic fluency as possible, and, as was the case with all of her exceptionally kindly and generous family, she was simply pleased to be of help with my work. From about 2001 on, Emma and I found ourselves increasingly reliant on one another for regular conversational use of Gaelic, each of us lamenting the losses in our mutual circle of fluent-speaker friends and each grateful still to have the other as a conversation partner, as remained the case until Emma's death in 2005.

Materials from those who remained sources into the 1990s, when my concerted investigation of idiosyncratic variation began, clearly offer the best data for present purposes. For earlier sources, the larger the amount of material available was, the better the chances were that some of the variables considered here would turn up in useful numbers. Despite Flora's lamentably early death, for example, the fact that she dominated two multispeaker recording sessions in 1964 and 1965 meant that a number of variables were available for her in moderate numbers and in a freely spoken context.

5 VARIANT SELECTIONS BY PERCENTAGE OF USE AMONG FAMILY-GROUP MEMBERS: INTRODUCTION

In chapter 5, all Embo sources were compared with one another in terms of variant preferences. Here, questions about variant choices are raised instead for speakers who share not just use of a particular minority-group language but also close consanguineal or affinal ties and in some cases household membership as well. At least in theory, these ties increase the possibility of greater similarities in variant selection, if only because of the greater exposure to one another's usage. The smaller size of these speaker sets within the overall pool of Embo sources allows the question of variant preference to be raised in more finely graded fashion. For each of the eighteen variables treated in chapter 5, six possible levels of variant selection will be compared for each speaker set: 100–90 percent (strongly preferred variant), 89–70 percent (moderately preferred variant), 69–51 percent (mildly preferred variant), 50–31 percent (moderately used variant), 30–11 percent (lightly used variant), and 10 percent or under (rarely used variant). If an individual provides only one or two instances of the variable (i.e., not enough for reckoning a percentage of use), the form(s) used are entered in the first column but in brackets and smaller print, reflecting the limited extent of the evidence for that speaker's usage. Variants produced only in direct response to a prompt from another speaker, entered in brackets in the tables of chapter 5 for completeness' sake, are omitted in the present tables; the prompter in several cases was a sibling and the response is insufficiently independent to stand reliably for the speaker's own variant choices within the family group.

5.1 Group 1

Table 6.1 presents the variant-selection patterns for Group 1, Flora and her siblings Duncan, Eilidh, and Una, plus Flora's husband, Dugald.

Differences in degree of intra-speaker variability are perhaps the most salient feature of patterns of variant use among this group. For each individual, there are a few variables with insufficient instances to work with, but for the cases in which two or more variants are available, sibling differences are conspicuous. (Two-instances cases are considered once again because of the frequency with which speakers showed variation even when they provided only two examples.) Flora was strikingly given to variation, using more than one variant for fourteen of the seventeen variables for which she provided at least two instances, or 82.4 percent. Una was almost as strikingly given to invariance, using only a single variant for twelve of sixteen variables for which she provided two or more instances; only four of her sixteen variables showed variation (25 percent). Duncan fell between the two, using a single variant for eight of the sixteen variables for which he provided at least two instances, a 50 percent level of variation.[4]

For only two of the eighteen cases did the available siblings all favor the same variant at a fairly strong level: /č/ preterite particle and /xa rɔ/ 'wasn't/ weren't'. Their levels of agreement are slightly less uniform for ('out'). It is likely that they agreed on the same variant for /fagiʃ/ 'near', since Duncan's two instances agreed with Flora's and Una's usage, and intra-speaker variation for ('near') is almost entirely absent. All of the siblings agreed on a variant preference for ('came') except Eilidh, who was unique in favoring the monosyllabic variant. Duncan and Flora agreed at rather different levels on variant preferences for ('in') and ('from, off, of'), and Flora and Una agreed on variant preferences for

TABLE 6.1. Variant-selection patterns for the members of kin/household group 1

percentage	100 - 90	89 - 70	69 - 51	50 - 31	30 - 11	10 or less
Variable ('in')						
Dugald	[stɛ]					
Duncan	stɛ					
Flora			stɛ		stɛx	sčax
Una	stɛ					
Variable ('when')						
Duncan			tə	nuərə		
Flora			nuərə		nə	tənə, tərə
Una	tə					
Variable ('along with')						
Duncan	kʰɔi					
Flora				kʰɔi, kʰɔ̃:ta ri		kʰɔ̃na ri, kʰɔra ri
Eilidh*	[kʰɔi]					
Una	kʰɔ̃na ri					
Variable ('would go')						
Duncan		č$^{(h)}$ɛu			raxu	rɛu
Flora		raxu			rɛu	
Una	rɛu					
Variable ('family')						
Duncan	čʰə:rtiç					
Flora			tʰə:rtiç	čʰə:rtiç		
Una	tʰə:rtiç					
Variable ('from, off, of')						
Duncan		tə			yɛ	
Flora			tə		čɛ, yɛ	
Una	čɛ					
Variable (preterite particle)						
Duncan	č-					
Flora		č-			t-	tə y-
Una	č-					
Variable ('potato')						
Duncan			məda:tʰ	metʰa:tʰ		
Flora			metʰa:tʰ	məda:tʰ		petʰa:tʰ
Una	[metʰa:tʰ, məda:tʰ]					

(Continued)

TABLE 6.1. Continued

Variable ('wasn't'/weren't')						
Dugald	xa rɔ					
Duncan	xa rɔ					
Flora	xa rɔ					xa t rɔ
Eilidh*	xa rɔ					
Una		xa rɔ			xa t rɔ	

Variable ('came')						
Duncan		hã:nig			hã:n	
Flora	hã:nig					hã:n
Eilidh*			hã:n		hã:nig	
Una	hã:nig					

Variable ('tomorrow')						
Dugald	[ma:rax]					
Duncan		ma:riç			ma:rax	
Flora	ma:rax					
Una	ma:rax					

Variable ('saw')						
Dugald	[hũn]					
Duncan	hũnig					
Flora		hũnig			hũn	
Una		hũnig	hũn			

Variable ('that')						
Duncan	ʃẽn					
Flora	[ʃẽn]					
Eilidh*	[ʃẽn, hẽn]					
Una	[ʃẽn]					

Variable affirming ('is/are')						
Dugald	[ʃ e:, h e:]					
Duncan	[h e:]					
Flora			h e:	ʃ e:		
Eilidh*	ʃ e:					

Variable ('needing')						
Duncan			n̓ĩmərd	ĩmərd		
Flora	ĩmərd					n̓ĩmərd
Una	ĩmərd					

Variable ('this')						
Duncan	[ʃɔ]					
Flora	ʃɔ					
Una			ʃɔ	hɔ		

Variable ('out')						
Duncan		mwĩ			mwĩç	
Flora			mwĩ	mwĩç		
Una	mwĩ					

Variable ('near')						
Duncan	[fagiʃ]					
Flora	fagiʃ					
Una	fagiʃ					

One- or two-instance variants are entered in square brackets in the leftmost column, representing that speaker's usage insofar as it is available. No shading indicates older fluent speakers, light shading younger fluent speakers. Asterisk indicates formerly fluent speaker.

('family'), ('tomorrow'), and ('needing'), the last two at similar levels. Duncan and Una, at the age extremes, agreed on variant preferences for ('when'). One of the three cases in which Una differed from both Duncan and Flora—('along with'), ('would go'), and ('from, off, of')—seems likely to have been the result of her relative youth: Una is the most senior exemplar of an apparent tendency among younger speakers to favor /čɛ/, the affricated variant of the variable ('from, off, of'), increasingly or exclusively (see table 5.12).

Although Flora was much closer in age to Duncan than to Una, her variant preferences are less like Duncan's than like Una's. Her preference for /tə/ 'from, off, of' is shared with Duncan, her preferences for /tʰə:rɫiç/ 'family', /ma:rax/ 'tomorrow', and /īmərd/ 'needing' with Una, and her preferences for /raxu/ 'would go' and /mwĩç/ 'out' with neither sibling. For the multivariant variables, Flora drew on a wider range of variants than her siblings and tended to produce variants seemingly unique for the household, such as /sčax/ 'in', /tərə/ and /tənə/ 'when', /kʰɔ:ɫa ri/ and /kʰɔra ri/ 'along with', and the preterite particle variant /t/.

Duncan and Flora were only three years apart in age, while Una was a full decade younger than her sister. Nearness in age does not find much expression in coincidence of variant selections for Duncan and Flora; identity of sex appears to find greater expression in coincidence of variant selections for Flora and Una. Eilidh, substantially younger than Duncan and intermediate in age between her sisters Flora and Una, did not provide enough material to shed light on the potential influence of age versus sex as factors in variant preference. There are some indications of family patterns—a general preference for /stɛ/ ('in'), for /-iç/ variants of ('family'), for non-analogical /xa rɔ/ ('wasn't/weren't'), and, with the exception of Eilidh, a fairly strong preference for the disyllabic variants of ('came') and ('saw')—but the siblings as a group do not present a distinctive family-wide variant-preference profile.

Dugald did not produce variants in sufficient number to establish his preferences clearly, except that for ('wasn't/weren't') he agreed with the rest of the household in favoring /xa rɔ/. His single instance of ('in') also agreed with family preferences overall, but his monosyllabic variant of ('saw') was moderately unusual for this household. His single but freely spoken variant of ('tomorrow') departed from the largely male preference for /-iç/ that Duncan shared.

5.2 Group 2

Table 6.2 presents the variant-selection patterns for Group 2, sister and brother Elspeth and Murdo.

A superficial scan of the first three variable entries (five-variant variables) in table 6.1 versus table 6.2 reveals a slight pile-up of variant entries in the last three columns of the latter: Elspeth and Murdo, both high-variation speakers, used a good many variants at a 50 percent level or less as compared with the siblings of Group 1. There is in fact only one case in which both Elspeth and Murdo used only a single variant, namely, /raxu/ for ('would go'). Overall, Elspeth used more

TABLE 6.2. Variant selection patterns for members of kin group 2

percentage	100 - 90	89 - 70	69 - 51	50 - 31	30 - 11	10 or less
Variable ('in')						
Elspeth		stɛ			sčax	sčɛx
Murdo	sčax					sčɛ, stɛ
Variable ('when')						
Elspeth			tə	tənə		tərə, nə
Murdo			nu(ə)r ə	nə		tərə, tə
Variable ('along with')						
Elspeth					kʰɔ̄na ri, kʰɔ̄rna ri, kʰɔra ri, kʰɔi	
Murdo			kʰɔ̄rna ri	kʰɔ̄na ri		kʰɔ̄:ta ri
Variable ('would go')						
Elspeth	raxu					
Murdo	raxu					
Variable ('family')						
Elspeth	tʰə:rɫiç					
Murdo				čʰə:rlax	tʰə:rtiç, čʰə:rtiç, tʰə:rɫax	
Variable ('from, off, of')						
Elspeth				tə, yɛ		
Murdo			yɛ		tə	čɛ
Variable (preterite particle)						
Elspeth		č-			tə y-	
Murdo	č-					
Variable ('potato')						
Elspeth		məda:tʰ			mətʰa:tʰ	
Murdo			mətʰa:tʰ	məda:tʰ		pətʰa:tʰ
Variable ('wasn't/weren't')						
Elspeth	xa rɔ					
Murdo		xa rɔ			xa t rɔ	
Variable ('came')						
Elspeth			hã:n	hã:nig		
Murdo	hã:nig					hã:n
Variable ('came')						
Elspeth	ma:rax					
Murdo	ma:rax					ma:riç
Variable ('tomorrow')						
Elspeth		hŭnig			hūn	
Murdo	hŭnig					

(Continued)

TABLE 6.2. (Continued)

Variable ('that')						
Elspeth			ʃə̄n	hə̄n		
Murdo			ʃə̄n	hə̄n		
Variable affirming ('is/are')						
Elspeth	ʃeː					
Murdo		ʃeː			h eː	
Variable ('needing')						
Elspeth	nĩ̄mərd					ĩmərd
Murdo		nĩ̄mərd			ĩmərd	
Variable ('this')						
Elspeth		ʃɔ			hɔ	
Murdo	ʃɔ					hɔ
Variable ('out')						
Elspeth	mwĩç					mwĩ
Murdo	mwĩ					
Variable ('near')						
Elspeth	fagiʃ					
Murdo	faʃkʰ					

Light shading indicates that both members are younger fluent speakers.

than one variant for twelve of eighteen variables, or 66.7 percent, Murdo more than one variant for thirteen of eighteen variables, or 72.2 percent. Each was therefore closer to Flora's level of intra-speaker variation than to Duncan's, and light years away from Una's low level.

This sister and brother were the original sibling pair I came across whose variant-use patterns were conspicuously different but not explainable by differences in age, missing links in a sibling chain, or lack of regular exposure to each other's Gaelic (see chapter 3, §6.4). Six cases of considerably different preferred-variant choices appear here: ('in'), ('when'), ('family'), ('came'), ('out'), and ('near'); the incompletely investigated variable ('old lady') appears to be another such. Only in the cases of ('out') and ('near'), however, did each sibling use a different favored variant at a very high level; in most cases, their favored variants were separated by less dramatic percentage-of-use figures. Despite the conspicuous disagreements, furthermore, cases in which this sibling pair agreed on a favored variant were actually more numerous. Eight such cases are evident here: ('would go'), (preterite particle), ('wasn't/weren't'), ('tomorrow'), ('saw'), ('that'), ('needing'), and ('this').

At the same time, there is another respect in which these two especially closely linked siblings showed notable variant-use differences: in a rather large number of cases, one of the two made some use of a variant that the other did not use at all. For ('in'), for example, Elspeth alone used /sčɛx/, Murdo alone /sčɛ/. For ('along with'), only Elspeth used /kʰɔra ri/ and /kʰɔi/, while only Murdo used

/kʰɔ́:ɫa ri/. For ('from, off, of'), only Murdo used /čɛ/, and for (preterite particle) only Elspeth used /tə y/. For ('family'), in addition to favoring a variant different from Elspeth's preferred variant, Murdo used two variants not produced by his sister at all: /čʰə:rɫiç/ and /tʰə:rɫax/. Taken together with the six or seven variables on which the siblings showed different variant preferences, these cases of variants used solely by one sibling or the other strengthen the picture of highly distinctive variant-use patterns in the face of extremely close social bonds.

5.3 Group 3

Table 6.3 presents the variant-selection patterns for Group 3, Sheila and her younger brother and sister, Stuart and Lexie.

The core members of Group 3, Sheila and Lexie, both used more than one variant for most variables. Sheila showed variation in fourteen of her sixteen variables, or 87.5 percent, whereas Lexie showed variation in thirteen of seventeen for which she provided at least two instances, or 76.5 percent. In Group 1 only Flora showed such a pattern, whereas in Group 2 both siblings did so. Stuart did not provide enough material for a robust comparison with his sisters. He provided the requisite three instances for only six variables, and he used more than one variant in just two of those six cases, a 33.3 percent variation level. But it is of course impossible to know how representative a single-occasion speech performance from an exceptionally rusty speaker may have been.

There was a difference of nine years between sisters Sheila and Lexie, just one year short of the ten-year difference between sisters Flora and Una. Agreement on preferred variants was considerably higher between the Group 1 sisters. Flora and Una agreed on preferred variants at a fairly similar level in seven cases, Sheila and Lexie in just three. Una, however, was the only YFS member of a household that consisted otherwise of older fluent speakers, and it is possible that this imbalance had the effect of keeping her usage a little closer to that of an older sister who was a dominant household presence. Lexie and her husband had lived in her elderly father's household in his last years, but after his death in the early 1960s she had only YFS husband Murdo in her immediate household plus Murdo's YFS sister Elspeth as next-door neighbor; her older sister Sheila had not been a household presence since Sheila was sixteen and Lexie just seven. Still, in view of the role that oldest daughters played in raising the younger children, more congruence between their variant choices was at least a possibility. No such oldest-sister effect appeared in Lexie's variant usage, however.

Although Stuart did not provide enough material for comparison in most cases, he agreed with both of his sisters in his variant preferences for ('family') and ('came'). For the variables ('wasn't/weren't') and ('that'), his variant preferences coincided with Sheila's and differed from Lexie's, despite the fact that he was closer to Lexie in age. The three siblings did not agree perfectly on their variant choices for ('when'), but they all showed a very marked preference for the /n/-initial variants, /nu(ə)rə/ or /nə/. While both sisters showed high levels of

TABLE 6.3. Variant-selection patterns for members of kin group 3

percentage	100-90	89 - 70	69 - 51	50 - 31	30 - 11	10 or less
Variable ('in')						
Sheila*	sčɛ				sčɛx	stɛ
Stuart*	[sčɛ]					
Lexie	sčax					sčɛx
Variable ('when')						
Sheila*		nu(ə)rə			nə	tə
Stuart*				nu(ə)rə, nə		
Lexie			nə	nu(ə)rə		tərə, tə
Variable ('along with')						
Sheila*	kʰɔ̄na ri					kʰɔ̄rna ri
Stuart*	[kʰɔ̄rna ri]					
Lexie				kʰɔ̄rna ri	kʰɔ̄:rta ri, kʰɔ̄na ri, kʰɔi	
Variable ('would go')						
Sheila*		č$^{(h)}$e:ǰu			raxu	
Stuart*	[raxu]					
Lexie	raxu					
Variable ('family')						
Sheila*	tʰə:rtiç					čʰə:rtiç
Stuart*	tʰə:rtiç					
Lexie			tʰə:rtiç	čʰə:rtax		
Variable ('from, off, of')						
Sheila*		yɛ			čɛ	
Stuart*	[yɛ]					
Lexie	čɛ					yɛ
Variable (preterite particle)						
Sheila*			tə y-	č-		
Lexie	č-					
Variable ('potato')						
Sheila*			mətʰa:tʰ	məda:tʰ		pətʰa:tʰ
Stuart*				məda:tʰ	mətʰa:tʰ, pətʰa:tʰ	
Lexie	mətʰa:tʰ					pətʰa:tʰ
Variable ('wasn't/weren't')						
Sheila*	xa rɔ					xa t rɔ
Stuart*	xa rɔ					
Lexie		xa t rɔ			xa rɔ	

(Continued)

TABLE 6.3. (Continued)

Variable ('came')							
Sheila*	hã:nig						hã:n
Stuart*	hã:nig						
Lexie	hã:nig						hã:n
Variable ('tomorrow')							
Sheila*	ma:rax						
Lexie	ma:rax						ma:riç
Variable ('saw')							
Sheila*	hũnig						hũn
Lexie	hũnig						hũn
Variable ('that')							
Sheila*	hə̄n						ʃə̄n
Stuart*		hə̄n			ʃə̄n		
Lexie		ʃə̄n			hə̄n		
Variable (affirming 'is')							
Sheila*			ʃe:	h e:			
Stuart*	[ʃ e:]						
Lexie	ʃe:						h e:
Variable ('needing')							
Sheila*	īmərd						
Stuart*	[īmərd]						
Lexie		n´īmərd			īmərd		
Variable ('this')							
Sheila*			hɔ	ʃɔ			
Lexie	ʃɔ						
Variable ('near')							
Stuart*	faʃkʰ						
Lexie	[fagiʃ]						

Single-instance variants are entered in square brackets in the leftmost column, representing that speaker's usage insofar as it is available. Light shading indicates that all three members are younger fluent speakers. Asterisks indicate formerly fluent speakers.

intra-speaker variation, each of them made some use of variants the other did not use. Sheila alone used /stɛ/ for ('in'), /č⁽ʰ⁾e:ǰu/ for ('would go'), /čʰə:rłiç/ for ('family'), and /tə y/ for (preterite particle). Lexie made occasional use of distinctive variants a little more often than Sheila did (six cases to Sheila's four), using /sčax/ for ('in'), /tərə/ for ('when'), /čʰə:rłax/ for ('family'), /čɛ/ for ('from, off, of'), /ma:riç/ for ('tomorrow'), and /n´īmərd/ for ('needing').

5.4 Group 4

In this group, too, there is a core group of siblings with whom I worked particularly extensively. I was able to raise questions dealing directly with variability with four of Ada's children: younger fluent speakers Emma and Rory, and high-proficiency semi-speakers Elsie and Lorna. Rory, Elsie, and Lorna had not married, but while Rory had always stayed in the home area, Elsie and Lorna had lived and worked elsewhere in Britain, returning home in the 1950s when their father took ill. All continued to live in their original Embo home after their parents' deaths. Their (near-)passive bilingual youngest brother, Colin, shared this household when on leave from his seagoing work and after retirement.

Table 6.4 presents the variant-selection patterns for Group 4, Ada and her children, including where possible the (near-)passive bilingual youngest.

In the core group of four siblings, the oldest demonstrated the greatest degree of intra-speaker variation, but all of the females showed more intra-speaker variation than the lone male. Emma used one variant exclusively for only the three variables ('tomorrow'), ('needing'), and ('near'); that is, she showed intra-speaker variation for fifteen of eighteen variables, or 83.3 percent. Of the younger siblings, Rory used one variant exclusively for ('in'), ('would go'), ('from, of, of), (preterite particle), and ('wasn't/weren't'), leaving seven of his twelve adequately documented variables, or 58.3 percent, showing intra-speaker variation. Elsie used one variant exclusively for (wasn't/weren't'), ('tomorrow'), ('saw'), affirmative ('is/are'), and ('needing'), with twelve of her seventeen variables, or 70.6 percent, showing intra-speaker variation. Lorna used one variant exclusively for ('wasn't/weren't'), ('came'), ('tomorrow'), ('this'), and ('out'), with thirteen of eighteen variables, or 72.2 percent, showing intra-speaker variation.

With the variant usage of four groups of siblings now considered, the likelihood of a general female lead in intra-speaker variation seems somewhat weaker, despite the fact that females within the Embo sample overall are conspicuous for such variation. In Group 1, oldest sister Flora showed the greatest intra-speaker variation, but youngest sister Una showed considerably less intra-speaker variation than brother Duncan. In Group 2, brother Murdo showed slightly greater intra-speaker variation than sister Elspeth. Only in the last case, Group 4, did brother Rory show less intra-speaker variation than any of his sisters. (Stuart in Group 3 showed a very low intra-speaker variation level, but his data are too scanty for a reliable comparison with his sisters' variation levels.)

To highlight across-the-family variant preferences for the core members of Group 4, table 6.5 presents just the favored variant for each speaker, with degree of use indicated.

There was only one variable for which all speakers shared a preferred variant, namely, ('along with'). Otherwise consensus was greatest on ('when') and ('tomorrow'). Lorna alone had a preferred variant other than /tənə/ for ('when'), and Rory alone a preferred variant other than /ma:rax/ for ('tomorrow'). Particularly striking are the cases in which variant preferences were very strong yet not uniform. Whichever variant they preferred for ('wasn't/weren't'), family members used that variant at a level of 90–100 percent. The same was true for ('needing') and very nearly true for ('came') and ('saw'). Equally striking are the cases in which some one family member made 100 percent use of a variant others

TABLE 6.4.　Variant selection patterns for members of kin group 4

percentage	100 - 90	89 - 70	69 - 51	50 - 31	30 - 11	10 or less
Variable ('in')						
Ada			stɛ		sčɛ, sčɛx	
Emma		sčɛ			sčɛx	stɛ
Angus	[sčɛ]					
Euphemia	[sčax]					
Rory	sčax					
Elsie			sčɛx		sčɛ	sčax
Lorna	sčɛ					stɛ, sčɛx
Colin	sčɛ					
Variable ('when')						
Ada		tənə			tə	
Emma		tənə			tə	nə
Rory	tənə					tə, nə
Elsie	tənə					tə
Lorna	tə					tənə
Variable ('along with')						
Ada			k^hɔ̄na ri		k^hɔ̄rna ri, k^hɔra ri	
Emma			k^hɔ̄na ri	k^hɔra ri		k^hɔ̄rna ri, k^hɔ̄rta ri
Angus	[k^hɔ̄rna ri]					
Euphemia	[k^hɔ̄rna ri]					
Rory	k^hɔ̄na ri					k^hɔ̄rna ri
Elsie		k^hɔ̄na ri			k^hɔ̄rna ri	
Lorna		k^hɔ̄na ri			k^hɔ̄rna ri	
Colin	[k^hɔ̄rna ri]					
Variable ('would go')						
Ada	raxu					
Emma			$č^{(h)}$eːju		rɛu	$č^{(h)}$ɛu
Rory	rɛu					
Elsie				$č^{(h)}$ɛu, $č^{(h)}$eːju		
Lorna			$č^{(h)}$ɛu	$č^{(h)}$eːju		
Variable ('family')						
Emma		$č^h$əːrtiç			t^həːrtiç	
Rory	[$č^h$əːrtiç, t^həːrtiç]					
Elsie	t^həːrtiç					$č^h$əːrtiç
Lorna		t^həːrtiç			$č^h$əːrtiç	

(Continued)

TABLE 6.4. (Continued)

Variable ('from, off, of')						
Ada	[yɛ]					
Emma		čɛ			tə	yɛ
Rory	čɛ					
Elsie			čɛ		tə	
Lorna		čɛ			tə	

Variable (preterite particle)						
Ada	[t]					
Emma		t				č, tə y
Rory	č					
Elsie		č			t	tə y
Lorna				t, č	tə y	

Variable ('potato')						
Ada	[pətʰaːtʰ]					
Emma				mədaːtʰ, pətʰaːtʰ	metʰaːtʰ	
Rory	[mədaːtʰ]					
Elsie			mədaːtʰ	metʰaːtʰ		pətʰaːtʰ
Lorna			metʰaːtʰ		mədaːtʰ, pətʰaːtʰ	

Variable 'wasn't/weren't')						
Ada	[xa rɔ]					
Emma	xa t rɔ					xa rɔ
Rory	xa rɔ					
Elsie	xa rɔ					
Lorna	xa t rɔ					
Colin	[xa t rɔ]					

Variable ('came')						
Ada	[hãːnig]					
Emma		hãːnig			hãːn	
Rory	hãːn					hãːnig
Elsie	hãːn					hãːnig
Lorna	hãːn					

Variable ('tomorrow')						
Ada	[maːrax]					
Emma	maːrax					
Rory			maːriç		maːrax	
Elsie	maːrax					
Lorna	maːrax					

Variable ('saw')						
Ada	hŭnig					
Emma	hŭnig					hŭn
Rory		hŭn			hŭnig	
Elsie	hŭnig					
Lorna	hŭn					hŭnig
Colin	[hŭnə]					

(Continued)

TABLE 6.4. (Continued)

Variable ('that')

Ada	[ʃə̃n]						
Emma		hə̃n			ʃə̃n		
Rory			hə̃n	ʃə̃n			
Elsie		hə̃n					ʃə̃n
Lorna	ʃə̃n						hə̃n
Colin	[ʃə̃n]						

Variable affirming ('is/are')

Emma				ʃeː, heː			
Elsie	ʃeː						
Lorna	ʃeː						heː

Variable ('needing')

Ada	[nˈiːmərd]						
Emma	nˈiːmərd						
Rory	[nˈiːmərd]						
Elsie	nˈiːmərd						
Lorna	iːmərd						nˈiːmərd

Variable ('this')

Emma			ʃɔ	hɔ			
Rory			hɔ	ʃɔ			
Elsie			ʃɔ			hɔ	
Lorna	ʃɔ						
Colin	[ʃɔ]						

Variable ('out')

Ada	[mwĩç]						
Emma		mwĩ			mwĩç		
Lorna	mwĩç						

Variable ('near')

Ada	[faʃkʰ]						
Emma	fagiʃ						
Angus	[fagiʃ]						
Euphemia	[fagiʃ]						
Rory	[fagiʃ]						
Elsie		fagiʃ					faʃkʰ
Lorna	faʃkʰ						fagiʃ

One- or two-instance variants are entered in square brackets in the leftmost column, representing that speaker's usage insofar as it is available. No shading indicates older fluent speaker, light gray shading younger fluent speaker, darker gray shading semi-speaker (and in this kin group also (near-)passive bilingual).

TABLE 6.5. Variant preferences of the core members of kin group 4

varia-ble	('in')	('when')	('along with')	('would go')	('family')	('from, off, of')	pret. part.	('potato')	('wasn't/weren't')
Ada	stɛ	tənə	kʰɔ̃na ri	**raxu**	----	[yɛ]	[t]	[pətʰaːtʰ]	[xa rɔ]
Emma	sčɛ	tənə	kʰɔ̃na ri	č(h)eːju	čʰəːrtiç	čɛ	_t	mədaːtʰ	xa trɔ
Rory	**sčax**	tənə	kʰɔ̃na ri	rɛu	[čʰəːrtiç, tʰəːrtiç]	**čɛ**	**č**	[mədaːtʰ]	**xa rɔ**
Elsie	sčɛx	tənə	kʰɔ̃na ri	č(h)ɛu, č(h)eːju	tʰəːrtiç	čɛ	_č	mədaːtʰ	xa rɔ
Lorna	sčɛ	tə	kʰɔ̃na ri	č(h)ɛu	tʰəːrtiç	čɛ	t	mətʰaːtʰ	xa t rɔ

varia-ble	('came')	('tomor-row')	('saw')	('that')	affirming ('is/are')	('need-ing')	('this')	('out')	('near')
Ada	[hãːnig]	**maːrax**	**hũnig**	[hən]	----	[nˀimərd]	[hɔ]	[mwiç]	[tɑʃkʰ]
Emma	hãːnig	**maːrax**	hũnig	hən	heː	**nˀimərd**	ʃɔ	mwĩ	**tɑgiʃ**
Rory	hãːn	maːriç	hũn	hən	----	[nˀimərd]	hɔ	----	[tɑgiʃ]
Elsie	hãːn	**maːrax**	**hũnig**	hən	ʃeː	**nˀimərd**	ʃɔ	----	tɑgiʃ
Lorna	**hãːn**	**maːrax**	hũn	ʃən	ʃeː	ˀimərd	ʃɔ	**mwiç**	tɑʃkʰ

Boldface, 100 percent use; double underline, 99–90 percent use; broken underline, 89–70 percent use; no special marking, 69 percent or less use. Square brackets, only one or two instances available; two entries in a single cell, equal use.

did not use at all, as Rory did in the case of ('in') and both Ada and Rory in the case of ('would go').

This same table makes it possible to gauge the extent to which each family member agreed and differed from the others on variant preferences. As well as agreeing with all of her children on a variant preference for ('along with'), Ada agreed with all of three of her daughters on a variant preference for ('tomorrow') and with her two daughters Emma and Elsie in the cases of ('when') and ('saw'). What little material is available from Ada suggests that she and Emma and Elsie might also have agreed in the case of ('needing'). Emma agreed with Elsie on variant preferences for ten variables overall (eleven, if each of Elsie's equally favored variants of ('would go') is allowed validity) and with Lorna on variant preferences for seven. She agreed with neither of her younger sisters on variant preferences for ('family'), ('came'), and affirming ('is/are'). Elsie and Lorna agreed with each other in seven cases (eight, if both of Lorna's equally favored variants of ('would go') are again acknowledged). Rory's variant preferences coincided with those of Elsie (seven instances) more often than with those of his other two sisters (four instances in Emma's case, four in Lorna's).

Disagreements on variant preferences are slightly more numerous than agreements among this set of siblings. Emma and Elsie showed the highest level of agreement on variant preferences, ten of sixteen, or 62.5 percent. Rory and Elsie also agreed at a level well above 50 percent (eight of thirteen, or 61.5 percent). But Emma agreed with Lorna at only a 38.9 percent level (seven of eighteen) and with Rory at a similar 38.5 percent level (five of thirteen). The lowest level of agreement was that of Rory and Lorna, at 30.5 percent (four of thirteen).

5.4.1 Full-Family Comparison in the Lexical-Retention Study

The fact that eight family members completed the 1974/1976 lexical-retention study allows an unusually complete picture of family usage to emerge, albeit for a small number of variables and via a single elicited response in each case. Table 6.6 presents the results of the lexical-retention study based on the lexicostatistical core vocabulary word list of more than 200 items.

With Angus, Euphemia, and Colin added to the sibling set, Rory's singularity with regard to the variable ('in') is eliminated; Euphemia also produced the variant /sčax/. Angus and Colin agreed with Emma, Elsie, and Lorna in giving /sčɛ/. The four siblings who agreed on a variant preference for ('along with') in their materials overall remained in agreement in the lexical-retention elicitations, but Angus, Euphemia, and Colin all gave /kʰɔ̃rna ri/ in response to the item 'with' on the lexicostatistical word list. Where 'this' and 'that' are concerned, the single-lexical-item environment of the lexicostatistical word list is of course not that of the verbless lead-in demonstrative tracked in the corpus generally, and one would expect to find less variation here, as indeed was the case. For ('that'), every family member gave /ʃə̃n/, even though Emma, Rory, and Elsie proved to favor /hə̃n/ in their corpora overall; for ('this'), Rory gave /hɔ/, while all other family members gave /ʃɔ/. Elsie's

TABLE 6.6. Responses to variable items in the lexicostatistical core-vocabulary word list from members of kin group 4

variable	'in'	'with [him]'	'that'	'this'	'wet'	'near'
Ada	stɛ	kʰɔ̃nariʃ	ʃə̃n	ʃɔ	fyux	faʃkʰ
Emma	sčɛ	kʰɔ̃nariʃ	ʃə̃n	ʃɔ	fyuxkʰ	fagiʃ
Angus	sčɛ	kʰɔ̃rnariʃ	ʃə̃n	ʃɔ	fl′uxkʰ	fagiʃ
Euphemia	sčax	kʰɔ̃rnariʃ	ʃə̃n	ʃɔ	fyux	fagiʃ
Rory	sčax	kʰɔ̃nriʃ	ʃə̃n	hɔ	fyuxkʰ	fagiʃ
Elsie	sčɛ	kʰɔ̃nariʃ	ʃə̃n	ʃɔ	fyux	faʃkʰ
Lorna	sčɛ	kʰɔ̃nriʃ	ʃə̃n	ʃɔ	fl′ux	faʃkʰ
Colin	sčɛ	kʰɔ̃rnariʃ	ʃə̃n	ʃɔ	fyuxkʰ	----

Responses date from 1974 and 1976 except for those of Emma, who produced this set of lexical items in 2004. No shading = older fluent speaker, light gray shading = younger fluent speakers, darker gray shading = semi-speakers and (near-)passive bilingual.

lone instance of /faʃkʰ/ for ('near') appeared in this lexical-retention elicitation; otherwise she proved regularly to produce /fagiʃ/ instead. In the case of a variable not presented in this study because of one speaker's exceptional idiosyncrasy, responses were thoroughly various.[5] For ('wet'), Ada, Euphemia, and Elsie gave /fyux/; Lorna gave /flˊux/; Emma, Rory, and Colin gave /fyuxkʰ/; and Angus gave /flˊuxkʰ/. This wide variety of forms is not out of line for Embo, since all of these variants were in use among other Embo speakers as well. Among the children, Elsie's responses come closest to Ada's, with five identical forms. The three sons, Angus, Rory, and Colin, produced only two responses apiece that agreed with their mother's, though in Colin's case one possibility for agreement was eliminated by his inability to recall the word for 'near'.

5.4.2 Across-the-Family Variant-Preference Differences

The obvious question in confronting the usages of a relatively large family like this one is how the four well-represented siblings came by their particular variant patterns.

How is it that Rory alone used /sčax/ exclusively, and Lorna reversed the dominant family pattern by preferring /tə/ to /tənə/? How did it come to be that Rory's and Emma's patterns for ('wasn't/weren't) are very nearly diametric opposites, he using /xa rɔ/ exclusively and she using /xa t rɔ/ almost as regularly, although both are younger fluent speakers by age-and-proficiency grouping? Equally striking are the facts that only Rory used /rɛu/ exclusively for ('would go') and Lorna alone used /ˈimərd/ almost as exclusively for ('needing'). In each of these cases we have some idea of the mother's patterns, but not the father's. Assuming that his variant-selection patterns were to some extent different from the mother's (a solid assumption for Embo, certainly), they would still not as such account for the varying strengths at which the same or different variants were used by individual children, any more than the mother's did. The troublesome question of how variant choices might establish themselves so differently within a single sibling set will be revisited in chapter 8.

At this stage it is useful to recall that Embo child-rearing practices allowed for the possibility that some children would spend considerable time in early childhood with older relatives who might influence their variant choices. In this case the possibility also arises that Emma's variant preferences might influence Euphemia, a same-sex sibling enough younger than she (seven years) to have fallen to the care of an oldest daughter, but not so much younger as to have been still only an infant (or not yet even born) when Emma left the household to take up wage work, as was true of Lorna and Colin. But the cases of ('in') ('along with'), and ('wet') in table 6.6 indicate that Emma's variant-preference patterns did not completely carry the day with Euphemia, any more than Ada's variant-preferences produced identical patterns in any of her children.

It is not realistic, in view of Embo's social patterns, to suppose that each child in the family had a distinct peer group that colored her or his individual variant choices. For one thing, a number of pairs or sets of children in this family were close enough in age to have fallen into what constituted a single peer group in Embo terms: Angus was only two years younger than Emma, and Euphemia, Rory, and Elsie were all within three years of each other's ages. Lorna was four years younger than Elsie, but she and Colin were within two years of each other in age. The chief argument against any strongly norm-setting peer-group influence, however, consists of the identifiable variant-selection patterns of a group of individuals who did in fact constitute part of an Embo peer group.

6 VARIANT-PREFERENCE PATTERNS
AMONG MEMBERS OF A SELF-IDENTIFIED
PEER GROUP

In a recorded 1974 conversation between E30 (Derrick) and E27 (Murdo), with E34 (Lexie) and me also present, the two men discussed the whereabouts of their childhood age cohort by way of reviewing who among the group was still available to them as a Gaelic-speaking conversation partner. On the basis of that conversation, it is possible to say definitively that Derrick considered Murdo and E30* (Emma) peers of his; he did not name E26* (Sheila) as one of the group, but if it is true, as Embo natives claimed, that all children near in age played together in childhood, then Sheila, identical in age to Murdo, was presumably a member as well, and there is independent evidence for this from the testimony of Emma.[6] Some members of the cohort that Derrick named had emigrated or moved away from the Highlands, one was dead, and one or two apparently as adults did not interact in Gaelic (or in one case at all) with Murdo and Derrick. As is true with several of the kin groups discussed here, then, there are missing individuals whose usage is not determinable. But Sheila, Murdo, and Emma are all core members of one or another of the kin groups whose variant-use patterns are presented in this chapter, and a modest amount of evidence is available for Derrick's speech patterns as well. This allows us to consider variant-preference patterns for four members of one acknowledged Embo peer group and arrive at some assessment of their degree of uniformity and of the norming power of peers versus siblings. Table 6.7 presents the variant-preference patterns for four members of Derrick's age cohort, including him.

Agreement is not exceptionally high among these speakers. Each of them had some variant preferences unique to him- or herself (with Murdo showing three distinctive preferences, Sheila four, Derrick five, and Emma six), and there are only two cases in which the full group agreed on a variant preference, ('tomorrow)' and—apart from Derrick's missing data—('out'). Disagreement was highest on ('family'), for which each of the three speakers with established variant preferences favored a different variant. Only in the cases of ('in') and ('near') does the group divide along male versus female lines, and only in the cases of ('when') and affirming ('is/are') into older versus younger; the division with regard to (when')

TABLE 6.7. Variant preferences of available members of one self-identified Embo peer group, younger fluent speakers aged 54 (E26*, E27), 50 (E29*), and 49 (E30) in 1970

variable	'in'	'when'	'along with"	'would go'	'family'	'from, off'	pret. part.	'potato'	'wasn't/ weren't'
E26* Sheila	sčɛ	nu(ə)rə	kʰōna ri	č⁽ʰ⁾eːǰu	tʰəːrtiç	yɛ	tə y	matʰaːtʰ	xa rɔ
E27 Murdo	sčax	nu(ə)rə	kʰōrna ri	raxu	čʰəːrtax	yɛ	č	matʰaːtʰ	xa rɔ
E29* Emma	sčɛ	tənə	kʰōna ri	č⁽ʰ⁾eːǰu	čʰəːrtiç	čɛ	t	mədaːtʰ	xa t rɔ
E30 Derrick	sčax	tə	kʰōna ri	[č⁽ʰ⁾ɛu]	----	[tə, yɛ]	[č]	[matʰaːtʰ]	xa rɔ

variable	'came'	'tomor-row'	'saw'	'that'	affirming 'is/are'	'needing'	'this'	'out'	('near')
E26* Sheila	hãːnig	maːrax	hūnig	hən	ʃeː	ĩmərd	hɔ	---	---
E27 Murdo	hãːnig	maːrax	hūnig	ʃən	ʃeː	nⁿĩmərd	ʃɔ	mwĩ	faʃkʰ
E29* Emma	hãːnig	maːrax	hūnig	hən	h eː	nⁿĩmərd	ʃɔ	mwĩ	fagiʃ
E30 Derrick	hãːn	maːrax	[hūn]	hən	h eː	[nⁿĩmərd]	ʃɔ	mwĩ	faʃkʰ

Variants of variables for which only one or two instances are available appear in square brackets.

is in terms of initial consonant, the older pair preferring variants in initial /n-/ and the younger pair variants in initial /t-/. The fact that both women were formerly fluent speakers probably contributed to their shared preference for the analogically formed variant /č⁽ʰ⁾eːǰu/ for ('would go'); they did not agree on a next most favored variant, Sheila preferring /raxu/ and Emma /rɛu/. At least in this one case of what remained of a Gaelic-speaking childhood peer group, agreement on preferred variants was not notably higher than it was within the kin groups of three of them.

If we look again at family-group aberrance in the light of available peer-group usage, we find that Murdo's preference for /mwĩ/, as opposed to his sister Elspeth's preference for /mwĩç/, is in line with the variant preferences of his peer group according to table 6.7, and he agreed with three of his four peer-group members in favoring /hãːnig/ as opposed to Elspeth's preference for /hãːn/. There is no majority peer-group support, however, for his preferences for /sčax/ or /nu(ə)rə/ and /nə/ as opposed to Elspeth's preferred /stɛ/ or /tə/ and /tənə/, and he was just as much out of line with his peer group on ('family') as he was with Elspeth. The same is true for Emma's preferences for /čʰəːrtiç/ and /xa t rɔ/; they are no more consonant with peer-group preferences than with those of most of her family. There is little in these data, therefore, to encourage us to look to peer-group influence as a way to explain individual variant-preference differences within family groups.

7 SUMMARY

Family usage is very far from uniform when it comes to variant-selection patterns among groups of siblings. The available sibling sets do not make it possible to compare same-sex versus opposite-sex sibling pairs at various age levels, but at the same time no strong pattern of variant preferences linked to same-age or same-sex groupings has turned up within the Embo data as a whole. Consequently there is no reason to expect that we would find uniform patterns even if same-sex sibling pairs and opposite-sex sibling pairs actually were available at various age levels. The one peer group for which some members' variant preferences are known offers no reason to expect uniformity in that quarter either.

The apparent persistence of distinct individual variant-preference patterns within the family and the peer group raises again the issue of the failure of focusing to take place in the linguistic sphere in Embo when focusing in the social sphere was so pronounced there. Why did the anticipated "reduction of variants that accompanies focusing" (Trudgill 1999:297) not suppress some of the more exuberant variation in variables with as many as four or five variants, or eliminate some of the variables altogether by doing away with the less widely used variant of some of the two-variant variables? Another way of posing this question is to ask what role accommodation played in the community. This question is taken up in the next chapter.

Speech Norms, Accommodation, and Speaking Well in Gaelic Embo

1 INTRODUCTION

The idiosyncratic inter-speaker and intra-speaker variation characteristic of Embo Gaelic was evident across the full age-and-proficiency continuum and does not appear to have been eliminated either by childhood upbringing in the same family or by membership in the same childhood peer group. Consciousness of within-the-community variation—age-related as well as personal-pattern variation—was low, which surely encouraged the persistence of such variation, but this only raises the still more fundamental question of why awareness of within-the-community variation should have been as low as it was. This is an all the more interesting question because inattentiveness to Gaelic speech behaviors was selective rather than global. Remarks quoted verbatim in chapter 3 demonstrated that resorting to English loanwords or phrases when the Gaelic equivalents were well known gave rise to very negative reactions, including self-reproach on the part of speakers who displayed the behavior. Community members also had strong feelings about language choice, finding it extremely offensive when individuals known to have been raised in Gaelic-speaking households used English for within-the-community interactions. In addition, local Gaelic speakers identified strongly with their own village variety, showing keen sensitivity to geographically based variation. Bilingual speakers were conscious, furthermore, of differences between their own Gaelic and varieties of Gaelic spoken by outsiders, and certain adjustments in their Gaelic were likely to appear in interactions with speakers of other dialects. For some individuals, though much less so for others, translation tasks could likewise introduce a certain self-consciousness and heighten the likelihood that less common local forms, and even non-local forms, would turn up in their responses.

This chapter looks at all these phenomena again and also at the one disfavored variable of which awareness was relatively strong—analogical gerund-formation with the high-frequency suffixes /-u/ and /-al/. A more general question is also raised: if neither personal-pattern variation nor age-related variation is much attended to, on what basis besides avoiding a few disfavored speech behaviors (such as use of unnecessary English loanwords and analogical gerund formation) does a community like Embo, with its unwritten minority-language vernacular, recognize the ability to speak that vernacular well?

2 SOCIAL RESPONSES TO LINGUISTIC DIVERGENCE

Social responses to Gaelic linguistic divergence differed within the fishing communities according to where the divergence lay. The weakest response (no response at all, more often than not) appeared in connection with divergent *variant* choices, where both personally patterned variation and age-related variation were concerned. Social response to divergent *language* choice (English as opposed to Gaelic) was, by contrast, extremely pronounced. Social response to geographically based linguistic divergence fell between the two. Village-based differences were very well known, and each set of village-based variants was considered appropriate for the natives of the village in question but decidedly *not* appropriate for natives of the others. Cross-village use of an other-village variant could be disruptive in its unexpectedness, acceptable only as a joke or as a personal idiosyncrasy, the result perhaps of a mixed-village kinship network.

2.1 Social Responses to Divergent Variant Choices

Accommodation theory, pioneered in the 1970s by Giles and various associates, predicts that people will attempt to converge linguistically toward the speech patterns of conversation partners if doing so might decrease social distance between them without incurring obvious social penalties (Giles and Powesland 1975). Convergence is thought to increase the prospects of two sorts of rewards. One is social approval, on the theory that "the more similar we are to our interlocutor, the more he or she will like or respect us" (Sachdev and Giles 2004:356). The other is increased communicative effectiveness "associated with increased predictability of the other and hence a lowering of uncertainty and interpersonal anxiety, and gains in mutual understanding" (Sachdev and Giles 2004:357).

With respect to the variables considered in chapter 5, conditions were not conducive to socially sensitive norming. There were no Joneses to keep up with among the local Gaelic-speaking population, and only rarely were there teachers at the Embo primary school who taught a little book Gaelic, holding up for emulation exotic forms that they promoted as superior to the local forms. Without socioeconomic subgroupings within the village population, and essentially free of the pressures toward a normalized Gaelic that serious schooling in Gaelic and an active literacy might have produced, community members did not attend to the variant-selection patterns of fellow villagers, even to those of their nearest and dearest.

The contrast between people's inattention to personally patterned variation and the close attention they paid to the other speech behaviors already mentioned could be striking. A recorded telephone conversation with E29* (Emma) can illustrate the very different responses evoked by two sorts of language behaviors, in one of which—personally patterned variation—accommodation was not at issue and in the other of which—language choice—the presence or absence of accommodation was very much an issue. During a phone conversation early in 2004, I called Emma's attention to the fact that her sister Lorna (E40) regularly used /k ĩmərd/ (citing for her benefit the full contextual form for a vowel-initial gerund, complete with the obligatory, phonologically prefixed, prepositional element /k/ 'at'), while she and her sister Elsie (E38) equally regularly used /nˊĩmərd/. Emma first looked for a semantic difference between the two forms: "/nˊĩmərd/ is 'needing'. /kĩmərd/ is—. Yes! It's the—it can be the same thing, can't it?" Finding no semantic distinction, she next tried to explain the difference by reminding me that Lorna had spent time in the Outer Hebrides when she was working in the herring industry, the implication being that she had acquired an outlandish form from speakers of a different dialect. But I pointed out that Elsie, who used /nˊĩmərd/ as regularly as Emma herself did, had been *with* Lorna in the Outer Hebrides, doing the same work. At that point in the conversation, Emma abruptly changed the subject to a difference between Elsie's linguistic behavior and Lorna's that she herself had noticed independently: she brought up Elsie's current reluctance to speak Gaelic, compared with Lorna's willingness.

The change of subject was telling. Emma was clearly unaware, at least at any conscious level, that Lorna and a good many other people in Embo routinely used the form /ĩmərd/ instead of her own favored form /nˊĩmərd/. But like every member of the community, she was acutely aware that some people responded in English when spoken to in Gaelic, as Elsie had increasingly been doing of late. In a village where shared fisherfolk ethnicity was the very ground from which continuing use of the local Gaelic sprang, differences in the forms that local variables took was not a matter for accommodation. All of the variants were part and parcel of Embo Gaelic, rarely noticed unless they showed a phonological or morphological deviation that had come to be associated with imperfect mastery of the language. But in a village where social stigma had always attached to being a local Gaelic speaker, failure to reply in the local Gaelic when addressed in that language was a failure of accommodation indeed: it was a divergent behavior commonly interpreted as expressing "the desire to emphasize distinctiveness from one's interlocutor" (Sachdev and Giles 2004:357), in effect to disassociate oneself from the stigmatized identity.

In socioeconomically stratified communities, community members' social aspirations can be as significant as their actual social background, as Fasold et al. (1975) found when they tracked stigmatized features in the speech of two working-class and two middle-class African American teenagers. The stigmatized features turned up in proportion to the class orientations of the young men rather than in proportion to their actual origins. The highest frequencies occurred in the speech of the two young men who were working-class—oriented, even though only one of them was actually from the working class, and lower frequencies occurred in the speech of the two who were middle-class—oriented, even though only one of them was actually from the middle class. The authors concluded: "Clearly, we need to know where a person's head is with respect to social class as well as where he is, if we are to understand the influences on linguistic variation" (1975:11). The parallel in Embo is the actual use of Gaelic as opposed to knowledge of Gaelic. The children from an early twentieth-century Gaelic-speaking household did not all necessarily remain life-long Gaelic speakers. In search of economic well-being, some left the community and ceased to use a language that lacked utility in their new environments; a few who stayed at home also ceased to use Gaelic, alienating fellow community members by declining to speak the language they had spoken at home during their childhoods.

2.2 Social Responses to Divergent Language Choice

As Emma's concern about Elsie's language behavior indicates, language choice was a matter of real social import and was seriously attended to. In each of the three bilingual fishing communities, courtesy dictated that one should reply in the language one was addressed in. A few individuals had a habit of code switching, and by this local courtesy rule they imposed code-switching behavior on their conversation partners, too, willy-nilly. A fluent Brora bilingual complained in 1972: "There's a woman down there at the end of the street, she starts off with the Gaelic. I answer her back; but in the middle of it, then she starts the English, so English then I've got to answer back."

This may have been an annoying behavior, but it was not offensive. Failure to reply in Gaelic when spoken to in Gaelic was a very different matter. A Golspie bilingual who got replies in English after speaking in Gaelic to two members of the Golspie fisherfolk community, one a slightly younger woman of her own generation and one a woman of the next generation down, responded with deep indignation: "Why aren't they speaking what I would call the Gaelic: '*the mother tongue*?' Which they were born with. It's the first thing that went into their mouths, and why would they be so proud and not speak it?" (1968, translated from the Gaelic original). "Pride" is the key concept here. By the 1960s, speaking the local Gaelic established a person's identity as a member of the fisherfolk community. Declining to speak that Gaelic was a repudiation of ethnic identity, an attempt to set oneself apart from the stigmatized group. Fellow speakers recognized this clearly, and Gaelic refusers were generally described as "too proud to speak the Gaelic". Social sensitivities on this issue were acute, and members of the community were ever on the lookout for this strongly resented behavior (Dorian 1981:102–104).

One measure of local sensitivity in this matter was the degree to which former community members, away for some time in English-speaking regions or overseas, were evaluated during their visits home according to how well they had retained their Gaelic and how willing they were to use it. Those who came home speaking Gaelic fluently, or even somewhat less than fluently but still eagerly, were warmly approved of and were boasted of by their home-community family members, especially if they had been away for a consider-able time. Those who came home speaking Gaelic poorly and unwillingly, or refusing to speak it at all, were subject to widespread criticism and were a source of some embarrassment to their home-community relatives. E26* (Sheila) in a 2004 phone conversation told of her father's vigilance in this matter early in her life, after she had gone to England to take up a job: "I came home from London. My holiday...Someone came in and I was speaking English. [Quoting her father:] 'Don't be—! Are—are you too proud to—?'...I got a bawling out—for—...for English."

The response from Emma, when I called her attention to a difference in her two younger sisters' variants of ('needing'), was fully in line with local language sensitivities. Even though one sister's usage agreed with Emma's own and the other's did not, she had never noticed the difference; when it was pointed out to her, it surprised her but had no deeper social resonance for her. But the other difference between Elsie's and Lorna's language behaviors had clearly caught Emma's attention without my making any mention of it, and it had troubled her: Lorna would usually answer in Gaelic when spoken to in Gaelic, but Elsie was more and more inclined to answer in English.

2.3 Social Responses to Geographically Divergent Forms

Language choice was a sphere in which convergent behavior was expected of local speakers across all three villages, with all *maraichean* held to the same expectation of reciprocity in language choice whenever they might meet, provided the conversation was among themselves. Geographically distinctive usage called by contrast for convergent speech behavior within each village but for divergent speech behavior across villages. Even though the fisherfolk in each village asserted that they felt closer to the *maraichean* of the other villages than to the *tuathanaich* in their own immediate vicinity, they nevertheless identified strongly with their respective local communities and insisted on the proper linguistic expression of local community identity.

Local dialect identities remained strong throughout the twentieth century in those areas of the Highlands and Islands that retained a native-born Gaelic-speaking population. This was the case in Brora, Golspie, and Embo, despite the fact that East Sutherland's fishing communities had come into being only at the beginning of the nineteenth century. I have already noted the prominence of a small set of geographically based stereotypes, brought up repeatedly by local speakers, and also the frequency with which people in one or another of the fishing communities spontaneously commented to me on the forms used in another village when they supplied their own village forms. Even though local differences were no barrier at all to communication and speakers from all three of the fishing communities understood one another perfectly well, residents of each village tended to characterize their own local forms as "plainer" than those of the other villages. Especially between Embo and the other two villages, a strong sense of linguistic difference prevailed; being among relatives of one's own in a village on the other side of the linguistic divide did not necessarily lessen that sense of difference. As a middle-aged woman living in London in 1978, E21L told a poignant story of being sent to stay for a time with an aunt in Golspie.

> *E21L*:   [I was] about seven. And I couldn't understand their Gaelic, be gosh! And I was—och, I was so homesick. I wanted to come home....
>
> *NCD*:   And was it a big difference, between their Gaelic and yours?
>
> *E21L*:   To me, it was, then. It was, to me, as a kid. I can always remember that. To my dying day. I was—I didn't like their Gaelic. "/kʰur ə gɔr er ə ʃɔ̃n/!" What else? Oh, I don't—I can't remember, really, but—we didn't speak Gaelic like that.

The phrase E21L objects to as disturbingly alien to her, /kʰur ə gɔr er ə ʃɔ̃n/ 'Put the kettle on the fire', is in fact identical to the same phrase in Embo Gaelic except for the final word, 'fire,' which in Embo would have been /ʃĩn/ in this phrase instead of /ʃɔ̃n/. This high-frequency word, with its village-related difference of a single vowel, is one of the stereotypes of Brora/Golspie versus Embo dialect difference, and it evidently resonated down the years for E21L in her memories of a painful exile in a linguistic world not her own. The fact that she was among relatives did nothing to ease the alienness of that world for a seven-year-old child.

Just as local Gaelic speakers were on permanent alert for signs of a "pride" that might keep fellow community members from acknowledging their fisherfolk identity by using Gaelic, they were also vigilant about local dialect norms to which they expected adherence. This expectation emerged, for example, in 1970 when I asked a few Golspie and Embo speakers, among them the Golspie sisters

G1 and G2, to produce the phrase 'my good teapot' in translation tasks. The younger and more assertive of the two sisters rapidly produced four versions of the sentence 'my good teapot got broken' as she explored the ways two different words for 'good' (one that obligatorily preceded the noun and one that obligatorily followed it) might appear in a possessive construction. All four of her versions rendered 'teapot' as /pʰačʰ tʰeː/, with a distinctively Brora/Golspie vowel in the word 'pot': /pʰačʰ/, as opposed to the equally distinctive Embo /pʰɔčʰ/. In the phrase 'teapot', however, Embo speakers usually also assimilated the final consonant of /pʰɔčʰ/ to the initial consonant of /tʰeː/, to give a compound noun with long medial consonant: [pʰɔtːʰeː].

The older of the two Golspie sisters, when she came to give her rendition of the translation task sentence, supplied a form with impeccably Golspie vowel quality, but at the same time she produced an Embo-like consonant assimilation: [pʰatːʰeː]. The reaction of her younger sister was swift and scathing: "/a vi u mər nəh ẽːrəbəłiç/" 'Don't you be like the Embo ones!' Possibly somewhat older Brora and Golspie speakers had once made use of the consonant-assimilated form that G1 gave; but it was at any rate true that no one else among my Brora and Golspie sources rendered 'teapot' with an assimilated medial consonant in the 1960s or 1970s, and the younger sister was reacting to an apparent violation of current Golspie norms. It was illegitimate in her eyes for a Golspie speaker to produce a form that mimicked Embo linguistic patterns, and she promptly took her older sister to task for the lapse.

2.4 Language and Identity

The two spheres in which speech behavior evoked these particularly strong responses had a central issue in common, that of identity. In the first case the identity was ethnic, *maraichean* versus *tuathanaich*, fisherfolk versus nonfisherfolk. By the mid-twentieth century, the fisherfolk community was deeply identified with the use of Gaelic; members responded by assessing ethnic loyalty in terms of willingness to speak Gaelic. In the second case, the identity issue was local. If you "belonged to" Golspie, as the very telling Scottish expression has it, you signaled that geographical connection by speaking Golspie Gaelic. If it was Embo you belonged to, then you spoke Embo Gaelic.

As far as it was possible to tell by the usage of adult speakers in the 1960s and 1970s, it seems that children with only one locally born parent acquired the Gaelic of the community in which they were raised. Kin groups being as large as they typically were, however, and local usage as variable as it was, such children were exposed to the general village-wide variation and showed as adults the same diverse array of variants for local variables as children with two locally born parents. E15L had one Outer Hebridean parent, but though he could sing very authentically in his mother's Hebridean island dialect he spoke conversationally like anyone else in his Embo generation. (This was the judgment of fellow villagers as well as mine.)

3 ABSENCE OF COMMUNITY-INTERNAL ACCOMMODATION TO PERSONAL-PATTERN VARIATION

Whereas ethnic identity was at issue in connection with the use of Gaelic or English in an interaction where both were possible choices, and local identity was at issue in connection with geographically based variant choices in cross-village interactions, no issues of identity other than the purely personal (a speaker's own individual variant-selection patterns) were raised by the choice of one or another variant for the variables introduced in chapter 5. An Embo speaker who declined to use Gaelic stood out sharply as a kind of ethnic renegade, and an Embo speaker who said /pʰačʰ/ instead of /pʰɔčʰ/ would have been an oddity sure to attract negative comment. But an Embo speaker who said /rɛu/ for 'would go' was no less an Embo *maraich'* than one who said /raxu/ or /hɛu/ or even /he:ʝu/. The use of one variant or another for the eighteen variables considered in this study carried no group-wide social loading that evoked either approving or disapproving responses from fellow community members. Awareness (usually created only if I called differences in variant preferences to speakers' conscious attention) that a conversation partner preferred a variant other than the speaker's own favored variant would neither increase the social distance between interlocutors nor decrease the communicative effectiveness of the interaction. Nor would an individual speaker's use of one variant as opposed to another normally prompt emulation or avoidance among her or his auditors. (The one exception, for some speakers, was analogically formed gerunds in /-u/ and /-al/, which will be discussed shortly.)

It may be that a speaker has most to gain from linguistic accommodation in interactions with someone whom she or he knows only slightly or not at all. If a speaker successfully approximates the forms used by an interlocutor who has little or no previous impression of her, the newly engaged interlocutor might conceivably form a more favorable impression of her because she speaks like him. If the same speaker is talking to a neighbor or a relative, or a neighbor who is also a relative (as might often be the case in Embo), the likelihood of changing the interlocutor's impression of her by making a different selection from among strictly local variants is almost nil. In a small-village minority-language setting like Embo, where the Gaelic-speaking residents were linked to one another by multiple kinship ties and multiplex social roles (and where furthermore everyone already knew an extraordinary amount about everyone else), the mere adoption of an interlocutor's linguistic forms could scarcely be expected to affect that interlocutor's opinions, already well established by long familiarity with the speaker and her entire kin group.

3.1 Accommodation and Non-accommodation to the Usage of Gaelic-Speaking Outsiders: Conversational Interactions with Speakers of Other Dialects

The long-standing stigma attached to both fisherfolk identity and fisherfolk Gaelic made interactions with Gaelic speakers from outside the local communities problematic. Fisherfolk speakers were well aware that their Gaelic had very poor standing in the Gaelic-speaking world overall. During my earliest fieldwork periods, fluent local speakers often apologized for their "poor Gaelic" and advised me that I would have to go elsewhere to get "the right Gaelic". When I did plan a short fieldwork stint in the eastern part of a county to the south, four years after beginning work on East Sutherland Gaelic, an Embo friend to whom I wrote of my plans expressed her certainty that the Eastern Inverness-shire speakers would have "a better class of Gaelic than us up Sutherland way" (E34, in a letter dated January 16, 1967).

Confronted with the necessity of speaking to outsiders in Gaelic, fisherfolk speakers with better than average linguistic flexibility might attempt certain accommodations, but the aberrance of the local Gaelic placed limits on the degree to which they could successfully move toward more mainstream Gaelic. It was not always possible for fisherfolk speakers to accommodate by mimicking non-local pronunciations or locutions. Local phonology and local grammar both lack certain distinctions that would be needed to perform successfully in this way over any longer stretch of speech, and as I can attest from my own awkward experiences, East Sutherland Gaelic speakers who launch themselves on a sentence intending to adopt some approximation of a standard construction may find themselves unable to complete the sentence for lack of the structural wherewithal to carry the alien pattern through.

Lexical borrowing represented one relatively simple form of accommodation that was available to speakers of East Sutherland fisherfolk Gaelic, and a good many speakers did resort to it when they conversed with a speaker of a more mainstream Gaelic dialect. When it was a question of a term that the local dialect did not provide at all, speakers who had some acquaintance with book Gaelic or with more mainstream dialects might import a word wholesale from those sources. When it was a question of competition between a form used only locally and one known to be in use in more widely spoken and better respected dialects, speakers might replace the local word with the more widely used equivalent. A fairly frequent instance of the former strategy involved 'boat', for which East Sutherland Gaelic provided no generic term. Local speakers had words for all the varieties of boat that they themselves used (herring fishing boats, the smaller line-fishing boats, and the little boats known as cobles), and they also had terms for the ships that passed by well out in the Dornoch Firth, including battleships. They had no cover term that meant simply 'boat', however. Both written Gaelic and other Gaelic dialects offered the word *bàta* (originally a loanword from Norse), and

East Sutherlanders sometimes adopted this term when talking to non-local speakers, as G5 did in 1977 when he was interviewed by a fieldworker colleague of mine (and as the lone Golspie informant also did in responding to the Linguistic Survey of Scotland's Gaelic questionnaire; see chapter 9, §4.2). An example of the second (substitution) strategy emerged when E17, talking on the phone to a radio interviewer, substituted the more mainstream term *balaich* 'boys' for the local equivalent *brogaich*. This sort of lexical accommodation was fairly common, but so far as I observed the practice evoked no criticism.

3.2 Accommodation and Non-accommodation to the Usage of a Non-local Speaker of the Local Fisherfolk Gaelic

Conversation with me was a curious affair for fisherfolk Gaelic speakers because I was so thoroughly anomalous. Local categorizations recognized four sorts of people: *maraichean* (fisherfolk), *tuathanaich* (nonfisherfolk), incomers (outsiders who had settled locally), and visitors (the usual local term for tourists). Monolingual English-speaking offspring of Gaelic-speaking fisherfolk were usually recognized as quasi-members of the fisherfolk group, but there was no special term for such people. I spoke fisherfolk Gaelic, otherwise always a reliable sign of *maraich'* ethnicity, but I spoke with some mixture of geographical forms (Golspie and Embo), and I also made mistakes that no native-born speaker would have been likely to make. It was very rare that I encountered a local Gaelic speaker who did not know in advance who I was and what I was doing there, since there is very little that is not generally known about everyone's doings in small-village settings and as a resident foreigner I was conspicuous in any case. On an unusual occasion in 1967 when I was introduced simply as /kʰalag ameri-kanax/ 'an American girl' to an Embo Gaelic speaker who knew nothing about me (E21L, home from London on vacation), she assumed from our brief Gaelic conversation that I was the American offspring of an overseas Embo villager and asked E22 (Elspeth), who had introduced us, whom I "belonged to," that is, was related to. The possibility that I might not be of local fisherfolk descent did not occur to her.

Especially in the earlier years of my fieldwork, mistakes in Gaelic on my part sometimes provoked a code switch into English on the part of a conversation partner. Signs of serious incomprehension on my part produced the same result. The more local my speech became, however, the less reason there was for local speakers to pay any more attention to my usage than to that of other local people, which is to say none at all. (See the next section for a telling example from 1974.) In the 1990s, however, as fluent speakers became scarce and the grammar I had acquired from older speakers in the 1960s and 1970s began to seem conservative, the remaining speakers began to expect my Gaelic to show some resemblance to what older people had used to say and to shift occasionally in the direction of my usage. Curiously enough, it was the oldest surviving speaker, E17, who did this most often, but the one feature on which she was inclined to follow my lead was actually quite predictable. On hearing me use a conservative gerund she dropped any analogically formed gerunds in /-u/ or /-al/ that she might have used and reverted to a more conservative form herself when she next used the same gerund (see §5.3). Even though E17 never expressed any disapproval whatever of analogically formed gerunds, her shifts in the direction of my more conservative gerunds suggest that she was nonetheless aware of the disfavor in which they were held.

3.3 Non-accommodation in Variant Selection within Multispeaker Interactions

In the passage quoted here from a 1974 recording, the non-accommodation of Embo speakers to one another is evident, while in the recording session overall their non-accommodation to me as interviewer is equally evident. At this point in the conversation Murdo (E27) was commenting to Derrick (E30) on the oddity of hearing someone speaking Gaelic on the phone at that date, when there were still few private telephones and Gaelic was rarely used for phoning in Embo village. Lexie (E34), who had been directly involved in the phone conversation under discussion, also contributed briefly to the conversation. The variable of immediate interest here is conjunctional ('when').

Murdo:	/o, ai. hə̃n te ha mi ra:, **nurə** fo:nig—**nurə** fo:nig u ɛ skɔl to:rnax ən uər, n e kʰwĩ:n ad er? ʃ e—ʃ e mə xalag a ʃɔ xa: fo:n, ax hurd i, "an el is am te ha n ɛr ʃə̃n ra: "./
Derrick:	/o, h e:, h e, h e./
Murdo:	/va u prĩ:n ə xa:likʰ, vel kʰwĩ:n ad?/
Derrick:	/va:. ha kʰwĩ:n am er ʃə̃n. hə̃n ad **tənə** xə:xilˊ ə mĩnĩʃĕar./
Lexie:	/a ha./
Murdo:	/xur i re:ʃ mĩʃ kəs ə fo:n: "te: va u ra:?"/
Lexie:	/**tə** xə:xilˊ məkʰ ləu:d./

Murdo:	Oh, aye, that's what I'm saying, WHEN [you] phoned—WHEN you phoned from Dornoch School that time, do you remember? It was—it was my lass here [that] went to the phone, but she said, "I don't understand what that fellow's saying."
Derrick:	Oh, yes, yes, yes.
Murdo:	You were speaking Gaelic, do you remember?
Derrick:	Yes. I remember that. That was WHEN the minister died.
Lexie:	A-hah.
Murdo:	She sent me to the phone then: "What were you saying? "
Lexie:	WHEN MacLeod died.

Among them, the three Embo speakers used three different variants of ('when') in this short passage. In the taped session overall, their variant selections were just as diverse. Murdo used /nurə/ or its equivalent /nərə/ twice and /nə/ once. Derrick used /nərə/ once and /nə/ three times, but /tənə/ twice (possibly also a third somewhat indistinct time) and /tə/ eight times. Lexie used /tə/ once, in the interchange just quoted, but otherwise she used /nə/ four times. There was no suggestion—in terms of comments, pauses in the conversation, voice emphasis or other suprasegmental signals—that they noticed the lack of agreement in their variant choices, much less tried to repair it.

Given that local speakers took little or no notice of each other's variant selections in such interactions, it is hardly surprising that they were generally unaffected by mine. I was neither a flawless speaker nor a reliably local speaker in geographical terms. Provided that my variant choices were not glaringly village-inappropriate (Golspie variants not in use in Embo), they were simply irrelevant, at least when local people were speaking to each other. In theory I was conducting the session from which the passage quoted is taken, in that my recorder was running and I asked a fair number of questions; supposedly I was interviewing Derrick, whom Murdo and Lexie had invited to come by for that purpose. However much the session was an interview with me, however, it was also clearly a conversation among the three Embo villagers, and the fact that I used the variant /tərə/ for ('when') with perfect consistency during the full session (twelve instances) had no effect at all on the others. My usages affected another speaker's only once, when Derrick repeated rhetorically a question I had asked him:

NCD: /kʰɔ̃rn ə **hã:nig** us er aʃ ku ẽ:rəbəł, əs čəi fiçəd pliərn?/
Derrick: /wɛl—kʰɔ̃rn ə **hã:nig** mi er aʃ?/

NCD: Why <u>DID</u> you <u>COME</u> back to Embo, after twenty years?
Derrick: Well—why <u>DID</u> I <u>COME</u> back?

Except for this one rhetorical repetition of my question, Derrick used only monosyllabic variants of ('came') throughout the session (eight instances).

4 ACCOMMODATION AND THE EFFECT OF TRANSLATION TASKS

Because translations tasks represent—especially for speakers of a low-status purely oral vernacular—a relatively formal speech activity involving some degree of self-consciousness, accommodation to whatever concepts of "proper" Gaelic a speaker harbors might be expected to emerge in elicitation responses as compared with ordinary speech. Possible elicitation effects on variant selection in the translation tasks that I posed to Embo sources were discussed in chapter 5, §10, while the primacy of what I've called the interlocutor effect was noted as a mitigating factor in chapter 1, §4.2: in passing along to friends and kin whatever conversational nuggets might be of special interest, bilingual villagers often relayed those nuggets in the form of more or less direct quotes (what Tannen calls "constructed dialogue" [1989:99]). In doing so they automatically used whichever language was routine for them in interacting with the interlocutor they happened to be addressing. This meant in effect that people translated constantly, reformulating in English the Gaelic remarks made by older people for young members of the family circle or for monolingual incomer acquaintances, and reformulating in Gaelic the English remarks made by young monolinguals or monolingual incomers for older people and for their Gaelic-speaking agemates (Dorian 1997a).[1] Producing such spontaneous translations was of course a different matter from producing translations on demand in response to requests for particular structures, and the more artificial translation work of elicitation sessions could require a little getting used to. But with surprisingly few exceptions, people took to the task without much difficulty.

For those speakers who had developed some passive Gaelic literacy and were inclined to style shifting, the translation tasks I set to obtain direct grammatical comparisons were a little more likely to produce efforts at accommodation to "good" usage than general conversation, especially in the lexical sphere. Providing translations on demand focused attention fully on language, heightening passively literate speakers' consciousness of the distance between the local Gaelic and written Gaelic. In view of that fact, distortions arising from translation tasks were much less in evidence than might have been expected.

4.1 Elicitation Responses to an Outsider Speaking the Local Gaelic

Most Gaelic speakers from the fishing communities found it hard to credit, at the beginning of my work in East Sutherland, that it was their own everyday local Gaelic I was interested in. Those who had become at least passively literate sometimes offered Bible Gaelic or book Gaelic in place of their usual local lexicon, and in one case an elderly speaker proved permanently unable to suppress his impulse to supply biblical or church-Gaelic terms in place of ordinary Brora words. Fortunately, the rest of his family (wife, Embo son-in-law, and semi-speaker daughter) all quickly came to understand that my focus was strictly local, and they objected whenever he made a substitution of this sort; over time his wife, a reliably local speaker, took over the main language-consultant role in this household. Other speakers with the ability to make substitutions in the direction of book Gaelic or Bible Gaelic (G3 and E13, for example) soon accepted the local focus of my Gaelic work. G3, the most actively literate of all my sources and a formidably intelligent man, made an explicit resolve to ban all extraneous influences from his Gaelic, and for the most part he managed to do this. E13 (Flora), equally intelligent and incomparably generous-spirited and helpful, was still working to suppress the impulse to "improve" her Gaelic when she died, a year after my second field trip to East Sutherland; but she, too, had been making a conscious effort to be local.

Not all local speakers shared the impulse to change their Gaelic in response to elicitation tasks. A good many of the women in particular showed no tendency toward the importation of lexicon or the lifting of constructions from mainstream dialects, church Gaelic, or book Gaelic. In response to my questions and translation tasks, they spoke the same way on my last field trip to East Sutherland that they had on my first, giving their responses in a fully East Sutherland fashion. Unaffected local speakers of this sort were invaluable to me, since their translations provided a template by which speakers more given to importations and style shifts could be evaluated.

Not only did elicitation work prove easy for a good many fisherfolk Gaelic speakers, it proved genuinely congenial for some. Those who were linguistically resilient and were themselves interested in how things could be said in Gaelic (notably G3, E13, and E27) relished considering structural alternatives and making judgments about what could or could not legitimately be said. The challenge of wrestling an English sentence into Gaelic appealed to some individuals; G2 was one such, and at the far extreme of Gaelic proficiency so was E42L. For a substantial number of people, the opportunity to be a source of expert knowledge was gratifying, perhaps especially because formal schooling had often been a far from positive experience; destined to be early school leavers, these minority-community bilinguals quite often experienced neglect and discrimination as children in the local schools (Dorian 1981:65, 81). Apart from all this, many people showed a degree of helpfulness that went beyond any reasonable expectation, an extraordinary generosity that represented the legendary "Highland hospitality" transferred to the linguistic sphere: much as they would have offered a bountifully laden table, they offered almost limitless access to the rich linguistic knowledge they possessed. For some individuals, the wish to be helpful was powerful enough to overcome a natural shyness (E27, E34, and E37) or the absence of any natural interest in the undertaking as such (B6). The most unusual response, because of its incongruity with her verbal skills, was that of E17. She was a conversationalist of verve and skill as well as a fine anecdotalist, but she remained permanently wary of translation tasks. She did them in limited numbers, but never with enthusiasm. Her exact opposite in this respect was E27, to whom casual conversation did not come easily; translation tasks were his forte and he was inclined to abbreviate conversational forays on my part and recall me to what he saw as our proper work together, the exploration of how anything and everything could be expressed in Embo Gaelic.

The facts that I worked with so many different speakers and worked in the same place over many years constituted the main advantages I enjoyed in evaluating the results of elicitation work, especially in Embo. At the same time, however, there were Embo speakers whom I worked with only once or twice or only at rare intervals, and whose variant use I consequently could not evaluate in terms of its relative formality or informality for the speaker in question, and there were a good many speakers for whom I had no freely spoken material to set beside their elicitation responses as a measure of relative unselfconsciousness. For a better assessment of the effects of translation tasks on accommodation impulses and on variant selection in particular, I needed an opportunity to see how speakers whose usage I knew well would respond to someone else, a stranger to them, in translation task work.

4.2 Elicitation Responses to a Speaker of Non-local Gaelic

An excellent opportunity to assess the pressure local speakers might feel to alter their Gaelic in elicitation work came when my colleague Dr. Seòsamh Watson made a field trip to Embo in 1993 and posed on my behalf a good many translation tasks to five of my sources. Seòsamh Watson had done extensive fieldwork among the former fisherfolk of Easter Ross on the Tarbat Ness peninsula just south of Embo years before, roughly at the time I was beginning my work in East Sutherland, and though he was most at home with Irish Gaelic and also knew standard Scottish Gaelic, he understood East Sutherland Gaelic readily and was able to tilt his own Gaelic in that direction. A personable man with an unassuming, easy manner, he was someone I felt confident would be as little intimidating as possible to my Embo friends. He was a stranger to them on this first visit, all the same, and his status as an outsider who spoke Gaelic had some discernible effect on their Gaelic in several cases.

The important question for this study was just where in the translations that people provided him accommodation effects might appear: would they be largely lexical, or would they include adjustments in the variants that speakers used for the personal-pattern variables? With one of the five speakers, E29* (Emma), there was no discernible effect of any kind; she made no adjustments in her Gaelic to accommodate the stranger. With three others, certain substitutions appeared in pronunciation or lexicon. E24 (Una), in my experience not much of a style shifter and normally quite a natural, unaffected speaker, made a pronunciation substitution in the direction of mainstream Gaelic very early in her session, twice pronouncing the word 'house' as /tʰəi/ rather than the strictly local /tʰɛ/; very late in a long session, in a different sentence, she reverted to the local pronunciation. E27 (Murdo) substituted the more formal terms /tʰɔrʃtʰ/ 'thirst' and /tʰɔrʃtax/ 'thirsty' for the usual local /pau/ 'thirst', and for /yo:rnĩʃ/, the invariable fisherfolk version of the place name 'Inverness', he substituted mainstream /ĩnərnĩʃ/. E17, who drew on mainstream /paɫiç/ 'boys' instead of local /prɔgiç/ in conversation with the radio interviewer, did so in elicitation work with my colleague, too, but erratically (just once out of four instances of 'boys' within her translation task sentences).

One other likely accommodation effect appeared in E17's translations, however, a gradual movement from more conservative to less conservative forms of ('family'), as noted in chapter 5, §10.3. Her first two instances of ('family') in response to stimulus sentences took the form most in line with the written-language form; her next two versions took the form favored by a number of older speakers; and her final two versions took the form that was most common among Embo's younger speakers and actually predominated in her own usage overall. E17 seemed to pass through the two more conservative options before, like E24 with her final instance of 'house', she arrived at her normally preferred form late in the session, when she was more comfortable with the questioner. In E17's elicitation session with Watson overall, her variant selections for the rest of the variables at issue here were typical of her usage generally, showing no conspicuous movement toward variants that coincided with book norms and no avoidance of distinctively Embo fisherfolk forms. She also made no attempt to avoid or alter several grammatical forms peculiar to fisherfolk Gaelic that are not treated in this study but would be considered aberrant from the point of view of mainstream Gaelic dialects as well as from that of book Gaelic.

The fifth Embo speaker from whom Watson elicited translations during this visit was E38 (Elsie). She showed several deviations from her ordinary usage during the session, each connected with a variable of interest here, but the presence of her older sister Emma was a major factor in her elicitation results. Emma contributed a number of audible prompts during Elsie's translation efforts and may well have made others that were not so audible on the tape. All three of Elsie's unusual variants coincided with Emma's preferred usage and most likely reflected Emma's direct influence: one instance of /čʰəːrłiç/ 'family' (instead of Elsie's otherwise overwhelmingly preferred /tʰəːrłiç/); one instance of /a t rɔ/ (instead of Elsie's otherwise completely invariant /a rɔ/) as an echo of a very audible prompt from Emma; and one instance of /kə d rɔ/, a dependent form of ('wasn't/ weren't') after the conjunction /kə(n)/ 'that', with the voicing of the preterite particle that conjunction requires (instead of Elsie's otherwise invariant /kə rɔ/, without preterite particle at all). The particular direction of Elsie's deviations suggests that Emma's active role as prompter in Elsie's elicitation session, rather than Seòsamh Watson's role as task-setter, had the determining effect on the younger sister's usages. In ordinary conversational interactions, an older speaker's variant preferences had no perceptible impact on the variant selections of younger speakers. By contrast, in this elicitation session with an outsider, Emma's prompts evidently did affect her younger sister's choices. In effect, an older and more fluent speaker was giving instructions to a younger and less proficient sibling for the proper accomplishment of a quiz-like task. Semi-speakers were more inclined than fully fluent speakers to respond to prompts, in any case, and the unusual circumstances on this occasion lent special weight to Emma's modeling of responses.

With Emma's influence the most likely source of Elsie's deviant variant choices, the only probable case of variant-choice accommodation in connection with the variables treated here is E17's ('family'). Otherwise the relative immunity of variant choices to the pressures for accommodation to a stranger suggests once again that for the most part the variant options of personal-pattern variables escaped social weighting.

5 THE EXCEPTION TO THE RULE: A VARIABLE WITH NEGATIVELY WEIGHTED VARIANTS

Although individual patterns of variant selection did not typically evoke comment among community members, some linguistic behaviors did, as we have seen: replying in English when spoken to in Gaelic, code-switching with too much frequency, and using English borrowings in place of familiar Gaelic equivalents. Semi-speakers were criticized for exhibiting these traits more prominently than other speakers, but they were criticized in addition for two prominent linguistic features of their Gaelic: for substituting an unvelarized lateral for the traditional velar lateral (a phonological failing otherwise associated with English learners of Gaelic), and above all for their habit of extending the two most common gerund-forming suffixes, /-u/ and /-al/, to verbs whose gerunds were traditionally formed by other suffixes or by some process other than simple suffixation. Apart from disapproval of over-liberal resort to English borrowings, the strictly linguistic purism to be met with in Embo seemed to focus almost entirely on this feature. Older fluent speakers tended to associate this usage with younger speakers generally, while younger fluent speakers tended to associate it with semi-speakers; both groups, that is, considered it a fundamentally age-related phenomenon. In point of fact it was a community-wide phenomenon, exhibited by speakers across the entire age-and-proficiency continuum. It differed from the likewise analogical structure /(x)a t rɔ/ only in that the change-over to an analogical structure was complete among the youngest speakers.

5.1 Older Speakers' Practices and Attitudes with Regard to Gerund Formation

Among my sources E13 (Flora) stood out as the severest critic of analogical gerund formation. She strongly disapproved of suffixing /-u/ or /-al/ to verbal roots that did not traditionally form gerunds with those suffixes (see chapter 3, §7.2.5), and she earned a certain right to her severity by herself adhering to conspicuously conservative models in gerund formation. In her freely spoken material, all gerunds were traditionally formed with only a single exception (one instance of /fiaxal/ 'trying, showing' in place of traditional /fiaxən/), and in her elicited material there was likewise only one gerund that was analogically formed, a single instance of /tʰigal/ 'understanding', offered as an alternative to traditional /tʰikʃən/. Flora claimed that it was younger speakers who were producing the objectionable gerunds in /-u/ and /-al/, but this was a claim that she could only make by failing to acknowledge her older brother Duncan's use of analogical gerunds such as /kʰɫĩ:nˈal/ 'hearing' in place of conservative /kʰɫĩ:nčən/, /fwɔ̃ĩ:niçal/ 'asking' in place of conservative /fwɔ̃ĩ:nax/, and /priʃal/

'breaking' in addition to conservative /priʃu/ (all drawn from his freely spoken material). In Duncan's elicited material, furthermore, he used the same non-traditional gerunds occasionally used by Flora herself, namely, /fiaxal/ 'showing' and /tʰigyal/ 'understanding', and as in his freely spoken material he used /priʃal/ in addition to /priʃu/.

Duncan was by no means the only speaker older than Flora to use analogically formed gerunds in /-u/ and /-al/. E4's greater use of /furiçal/ 'waiting, staying, living' than of /furax/ and of /kʰyɔ̃rniçal/ than of /kʰyɔ̃rnax/ was noted in chapter 3, §7.2.5, and in addition his one instance of 'meeting' was /kʰõn´ĩçal/ rather than conservative /kʰõn´əxu/. Like Duncan, E4 also occasionally used an /-al/ suffix where /-u/ was traditional for Embo: one of his two instances of 'telling' was /ĩːʃal/ instead of conservative /ĩːʃu/ and three of his eighteen instances of 'doing, making' were /čẽːnal/ instead of conservative /čẽːnu/. E6, though he provided much less freely spoken material, also showed a few analogically formed gerunds. In his elicited materials, furthermore, E6 produced a version of the gerund 'saying,' /kʰanal/, that was fully as startling a departure from conservative /kʰa(n)tən/ as E38's notorious and much criticized /kʰanu/ (chapter 3, §7.2.5). E7, whose available freely spoken materials consist only of a single personal anecdote, produced a particularly interesting case of analogical gerund formation in that one short anecdote. She used the gerund 'meeting' twice, but neither instance took the conservative form /kʰõn´əxu/. Instead, both of her versions used the verbal root /kʰõnç-/ plus simple suffixation, but one was formed with the suffix /-u/ while the other was formed with the suffix /-al/, giving /kʰõn´ĩçu/ and / kʰõn´ĩçal/.

As with most of the other variables, variation in gerund formation among Embo speakers included both lack of uniformity from speaker to speaker and lack of consistency in each individual speaker's usage. Every speaker who provided more than a handful of gerunds showed repeated inconsistencies in producing the gerund of one and the same verbal root, and indeed, as the case of E7's /kʰon´ĩçu/ ~ /kʰon´ĩçal/ shows, even some of those whose gerund tally consisted of the merest handful of instances showed this sort of variation. And while conservatism in gerund formation was generally greater among older speakers than among younger, elderly speakers could certainly be heard producing some striking instances of analogical suffix extension.

5.2 Younger Speakers' Attitudes and Practices with Regard to Gerund Formation

Although younger speakers all produced a good many analogical gerunds, the degree to which younger speakers were conservative or innovative in gerund formation varied markedly from individual to individual. Among the younger fluent speakers with whom I worked, three were exceptionally given to analogical extension of one or the other of the two overused suffixes. For E22 (Elspeth) and E26* (Sheila), the preferred suffix was /-al/, while for E29* (Emma) it was /-u/.

All three produced analogically regularized suffixes more frequently in elicitation than in freely spoken material, and in fact it must be said that very few speakers seemed to be making an effort to avoid analogical gerund formations in elicitation, despite the presumed greater self-consciousness of that mode and despite the strongly puristic attitudes expressed by some Embo natives about these formations.

Even younger speakers with conservative attitudes were often far from conservative in practice. E27 (Murdo), for example, was highly critical of E38 (Elsie) for her analogical /kʰanu/ 'saying', and yet his wife E34 (Lexie) had occasion to reprove him for his own translation task use of /fa:gu/ 'leaving' in place of /fa:gal/ (chapter 3, §7.2.5). Murdo's purism was more ideological than practical, in actuality. He produced many analogically formed gerunds in freely spoken material and additional examples in elicitation. Lexie, more conservative in gerund formation than her husband despite her younger age, and distinctly puristic in attitude, produced only two analogical gerunds in her somewhat limited freely spoken material but a surprising number of analogical gerund formations in elicitation.

5.3 Individual Differences in Sensitivity to Analogical Gerund Formation

Analogical gerund formation was highly unusual as a variable in that it had become the subject of explicit comment, and quite harsh comment at that, for some Embo Gaelic speakers. But despite the distinctly negative social weighting it had developed, some speakers appeared to be quite unaffected by puristic views about analogically formed gerunds. Elspeth, for example, was untroubled by the purism of her brother and sister-in-law and produced analogical gerunds frequently, especially in elicitation. The fact that *all* speakers continued to produce analogical gerunds not just in conversation but also in elicitation indicates that puristic attitudes had only a limited effect on actual usage—not an unusual outcome where linguistic purism is concerned. Some analogical gerunds were so well established in village usage that they appeared to be well on the way to replacing the traditional gerunds, in fact; this was true of /tʰig(y)al/ 'understanding' and of /fiaxal/ 'showing', the two that even Flora used.

Even speakers who never expressed any disapproval of analogical gerund formation could display behaviors that suggested self-consciousness about them. E17, for example, never made any remarks that reflected a gerund-related purism, but she showed a tendency to remodel her gerunds to match mine during our telephone conversations. Though she had used /ʃi:ʃal/ herself in an immediately preceding sentence, when I used /ʃi:ʃu/ in replying she likewise shifted to /ʃi:ʃu/. Her *only* uses of /tʰikʃən/ 'understanding' and /kʰɫĩ:nčən/ 'hearing' occurred as immediate echoes of my usage (she used /tʰigal/ otherwise and heavily favored the variant /kʰɫĩ:n′al/, though she made single uses of /kʰɫĩ:nčal/ and /kʰɫĩ:nču/ as well).[2] In one surprising case, she actually echoed my use of /fiarax/ 'asking', a gerund form current in Golspie, where I had acquired it, but no longer in use in Embo. The form was known in Embo, even if no longer in active use, and had not taken on an exclusive association with Golspie, but the fact that E17 echoed what would have been an archaic gerund from the point of view of an Embo speaker strengthens the impression of self-consciousness about gerund formation that her other echoes suggested.

E29* (Emma) provided a sharp contrast with E17 in this respect, very rarely reforming her gerunds to conform to mine when she used the same verb in an immediately succeeding sentence. She followed my /tʰikʃən/ with a /tʰigal/ of her own, for example, and my /kʰumal/ 'keeping' with her own preferred /kʰumu/. She mirrored my usage only once, in fact, using /kʰau:ɫ/ 'losing' immediately after I had, in place of her more usual /kʰəi:lʹu/. Only one other adaptation emerged in Emma's freely spoken materials: after I had produced a conservative, Golspie-acquired /faraxkən/ 'feeling', she produced a moderately conservative Embo equivalent, /fanəxu/. This form was unusual both because most Embo speakers were inclined to use /faniçal/, suffixing /-al/ to the verbal root, and because Emma herself normally pressed English *feel* into service, using the loan verb /filigu/.

5.4 Gerund Formation with Verbs Borrowed from English

Where English loanwords were concerned, any disapproval that surfaced was more likely to relate to the act of borrowing than to the manner of gerund formation. English verbs were routinely gaelicized by suffixing a verbal formative /-(i)g(y)- ~ -k(y)-/ to the English root, a practice that had the positive effect of allowing speakers to maintain conversation in Gaelic without regard to topic: any verb not readily supplied by the local Gaelic, such as 'to phone' (plus a good many whose semantic range was imperfectly matched by a Gaelic equivalent, like 'to watch') was simply gaelicized and drafted into use. All such verbs showed gerund formation by suffixation of /-u/ or /-al/; they also showed personal-pattern variation, with individual speakers using one or the other or both. There was a community-wide preference for /-u/ overall (despite a scattering of strong individual preferences for /-al/), but variation was common, especially where the most frequently used loan verbs were concerned. E17 for example used /fo:nigu/ 'phoning' invariably; but E26* used both /-u/ and her more generally favored /-al/ variably for the same verb. E17 also used /waǒku/ 'watching' invariably; but E38, despite heavily favoring /waǒku/ overall, used /waǒkal/ as well. And although she was invariant on /fo:nigu/ and /waǒku/, E17 herself alternated between the two suffixes for /tʰraig-/ 'try', /wərig-/ 'worry', and /fidig-/ 'feed' (this last a loan verb that came up several times in connection with her cat).

5.5 Responses to Variation in Gerund Formation Compared with Responses to Variation in Other Linguistic Forms

No strictly linguistic factors can account for the negative social loading that ana-logical extension of /-u/ and /-al/ in gerund formation had developed for some Embo speakers. Many other analogical regularizations were under way in Embo Gaelic, and none of them had attracted any widespread negative comment. Replacement of the synthetic first-person singular conditional suffix /-ĭn'/ by analytic /-u mi/ represented another analogical simplification, for example, yet it went without comment; and no one remarked on the fact that three of the five semi-speakers in my Embo sample appeared to have gone over to invariant use of the preterite particle in ('wasn't/weren't). Analogically formed /he:ʃu/ for ('would go') likewise attracted no comment. Among the analogical simplifications under way in Embo Gaelic, analogical extension of the most common pluralizing suf-fixes to the roots of nouns that traditionally formed their plurals irregularly was the closest parallel to the case of gerund formation (Dorian 1973). In the formation of the plural, as in that of the gerund, a considerable number of different suffixes served as allomorphs of the same morpheme, and in forming the plural, too, processes other than simple suffixation traditionally appeared, especially with a number of high-frequency lexical items. Substituting the suffixes that had the highest frequency of occurrence for some of the less common plural allomorphs reduced the number of irregularities, and naturally enough some speakers (and all semi-speakers) occasionally did just that. In spite of the close parallel to analog-ical gerund formation, analogically regularized noun plurals drew none of the criticism that analogically regularized gerunds did.

The amount of grammatical change under way in Embo Gaelic was substan-tial, considerably greater than in Brora and Golspie. It is not entirely obvious why this should have been so, but a major contributing factor must have been the per-sistence of Embo Gaelic into a period when young people were growing up in Gaelic-speaking households as the last to do so and in a steadily increasing linguistic isolation. With the dying away of the local fishing industry, contacts between the Embo fisherfolk and their counterparts in Brora and Golspie (smaller populations in any case) decreased. As Embo people took part to a lesser extent in the national herring fishery, they also had fewer interactions with Gaelic speakers from other parts of the Highlands. Embo village became a very small, if lively, pocket of Gaelic speech, enclaved in an ever more English-speaking environment. With transmission falling off and English obviously on the rise even in Embo itself, whatever braking effect a linguistically conservative oldest generation might ordi-narily have had within a small speech community seems to have dwindled. Active literacy, another familiar constraining factor, was also absent, of course.

In any event, the variety of change processes in evidence in Embo during the second half of the twentieth century was notable. Instances of all of the following were to be met with, for example: the replacement of synthetic structures by analytic structures, the merging of alternative syntactic structures into one compromise structure, the extension of one traditional structure into environments previously reserved for another (with loss, or partial loss, of the competing structure), and the disappearance of traditional structures without replacement. Conversations among speakers whose usage represented various stages in all these developments proceeded without any apparent notice taken of the differences, and in this setting neither schoolteachers nor an educated elite was on hand to promote the use of one construction while opposing the use of others. Younger community members occasionally expressed the opinion that their elders had been better Gaelic speakers than they were themselves, but they couched this difference in terms of lexicon: their predecessors had had more "words for things" than they now had.

It is not unusual for grammatical changes in progress to go unnoticed, even in speech communities where literacy is widespread and standardization is strongly promoted by formal education. A change may move at various paces through different segments of a population, the differences in pace obscuring its progress for speakers, while general lack of a metalanguage for identifying and discussing linguistic change may make explicit recognition of its nature difficult. Considerably more mysterious, particularly in the absence of standardization, is the process by which a single analogical regularization process among many comes to be negatively weighted. I noted in §7.2.5 of chapter 3 that the /-u/ endings famously associated with eastern Sutherlandshire Gaelic may have been stereotyped enough to create a certain self-consciousness about them among local speakers. Some of the final /-u/ pronunciations in East Sutherland Gaelic correspond not to suffixes but to word-final -bh or -mh (e.g., Embo balbh /paɫu/ 'deaf', talamh /tʰaɫu/ 'earth, land'), but by far the greatest number represent the gerund-forming suffix -(e)adh. Because verbs that form their gerunds with -(e)adh are extremely common in Gaelic, the frequency of gerunds in final /-u/ is very high. This is all the more true because all varieties of Gaelic make exceptionally heavy use of progressive verb phrases using the finite verb 'to be' and the gerund.

In one important setting for the use of Gaelic in East Sutherland, the contrast between local speakers' high-frequency gerund-marking suffix /-u/ and the equivalent mainstream and book-Gaelic /-əɣ/ was particularly conspicuous, namely in the singing of the metrical psalms during church services. Where Embo natives at the Dornoch Free Church produced their usual /-u/ suffixes in rendering gerunds in -(e)adh, the minister and those resident Gaelic speakers who had moved to Sutherland from the west rendered the same gerunds with /-əɣ/. The difference in the rendering of this high-frequency suffix no doubt seemed more prominent when sung out at high volume and unaccompanied (as was the practice in Free Church psalm singing) than in ordinary conversation. It is at least possible that heightened consciousness of this singular feature of East Sutherland Gaelic arose in this setting, where local Gaelic was unusually audibly in contrast with the church-Gaelic and mainstream-Gaelic norm, and that this gave rise to a rejection of its analogical extension to still more verbs than already used it in traditional gerund formation. A more generalized rejection of analogically formed gerunds might then easily carry over to /-al/ as the only other gerund-forming suffix similarly extended to gerunds not traditionally formed with it.

While this is a possible scenario, it cannot be confirmed or disconfirmed. What is certain is that analogical gerund formation with /-u/ and /-al/ remained unique with respect to its disapproved status within the Embo speech community, and those who rejected the usage rejected it in rather strong terms. Even so, the rejection was not shared by all speakers, and actual avoidance of the usage was much less widespread than was a negative view of it. Despite the negative social loading in the case of analogically extended /-u/ and /-al/, these variants remained very much part of the picture of inter-speaker and intra-speaker variation in Embo Gaelic.

6 LOW AWARENESS OF WITHIN-THE-COMMUNITY VARIATION REVISITED

The question raised at the beginning of this chapter—why awareness of within-the-community variation should have been so low—appears to have two answers. One is that the extreme socioeconomic homogeneity of the fishing village populations, combined with their distinctive ethnic solidarity as fisherfolk living apart from all other social groups in the region, acted to block the development of internal social groupings with which differences in language usage could be associated. Without such social groupings, the linguistic variation that abounded in the community remained a phenomenon of the individual level.

But even exceptional homogeneity and a whole-group identity forged by a socially stigmatized, poverty-level, group-wide occupation would probably not have prevented awareness of variation from developing, and perhaps giving rise to socially significant weighting, if Gaelic had served as the medium of education in the region. This second factor is fully as important as the first. The role of education in establishing and maintaining overarching language norms against which all other usage is measured is unequaled: "Education is the institution wherein all language-related facets of culture are maintained and dispensed in Western civilization, and whether it is restricted to an elite or open to the masses, the presence of this institution is indispensable to the establishment and the maintenance of a standard language" (Joseph 1987:45).

Because education is so central to promoting adherence to language norms, one can expect to find maximum latitude for the emergence and persistence of socially unweighted variation, even in socioeconomically homogeneous communities, only when no form of their language is used in the region as a medium of education. Provided it has no established presence in the schools, the language of a socioeconomically undifferentiated minority-language community can escape the development of a conscious awareness of competing variants, an awareness with consequences described by Joseph as inevitable:

The awareness of variants seems inevitably to be accompanied by value judgment. For any number of possible reasons, wherever variants are in competition, one will always be preferred to the other, creating hierarchies which it is the task of language education to inculcate. The canonical form of such education is "Say *x*, not *y*." (1987:16)

The minimal Gaelic instruction offered at one time or another in the Embo primary school (never in the Brora or Golspie primary schools, where English monolinguals predominated) was sufficient to make Embo children aware of the low standing of their local speech forms but not nearly sufficient to provide them with workable linguistic alternatives to local Gaelic usages. Quite evidently it was not sufficient to create the crucial awareness of variation identified by Joseph as the prerequisite for the emergence of value judgments.

The conditions that permitted the long-term persistence of socially unweighted variation are not unique to Embo, and in the next chapter other communities are introduced in which similar conditions have prevailed, with similar linguistic results.

7 SPEAKING WELL IN A COMMUNITY WITH AN UNWRITTEN VERNACULAR

So far it appears that abundant personal-pattern variation attracted almost no negative attention among Embo Gaelic speakers, and even age-related variation involving such seemingly conspicuous changes as regularization of the first-person singular conditional or loss of the distinctive locational-adverb category evoked no negative comment. Speaking Gaelic well meant avoiding analogical gerund formation with /-u/ and /-al/, certainly, and not resorting to English loanwords when Gaelic equivalents were readily available, and perhaps also avoiding excessive code switching (see §2.2). But on what other basis did community members recognize the "good" speakers among them, and how do their judgments compare to those of linguists?

In a 1927 article deriving from his experience with the Menomini Indians of Wisconsin, Leonard Bloomfield related his surprise on finding that members of this compact community of about 1,700 members, with no written language and no dialect differentiation, readily made distinctions between people who spoke well and those who spoke badly. They were able to identify individuals who used incorrect forms, for example, and people who spoke in preachy fashion or with archaic turns of speech (Bloomfield 1964 [1927]:394). Bloomfield proceeded to offer characterizations of the speech of a number of Menomini individuals as follows: Red-Cloud-Woman spoke "a beautiful and highly idiomatic Menomini"; Storms-At-It used "unapproved—let us say, ungrammatical—forms which are current among bad speakers" or, alternatively, "elevated speech" with "long ritualistic compound words and occasional archaisms"; Stands-Close produced speech that was "well up to standard" but "interlarded with words and constructions that are felt to be archaic"; Bird-Hawk, "as soon as he departed from ordinary conversation", spoke "with bad syntax and meager, often inept vocabulary, yet with occasional archaisms"; and White-Thunder, a younger man, produced a Menomini that, according to Bloomfield, was "atrocious", with "small" vocabulary, "barbarous" inflections, and sentences constructed on "a few threadbare models" (1964:395). Though the precise characterizations offered are Bloomfield's own, his phraseology occasionally suggests that he based them on community judgments: he equates the local expression "the way the old, old people talked" with his own term "archaic", for example (1964:394). Without written language or educational institutions to explain the Menominis' capacity for distinguishing among speakers in this fashion, Bloomfield looked for an explanation in more general terms:

> The nearest approach to an explanation of "good" and "bad" language seems to be this, then, that, by a cumulation of obvious superiorities, both of character and standing, as well as of language, some persons are felt to be better models of conduct and speech than others. Therefore, even in matters where the preference is not obvious, the forms which these same persons use are felt to have the better flavor. This may be a generally human state of affairs, true in every group and applicable to all languages, and the factor of Standard and Literary Language versus dialect may be a superadded secondary one. (1964:396)

Superior character and standing are here taken to make an individual a model to others in terms both of conduct and of speech; the term "model" implies that emulation will (or at least should) follow. In a community with recognizable distinctions of wealth or social standing, this may be a reasonable assumption, but in a community as occupationally uniform and socioeconomically homogeneous as Embo, it may not be.

7.1 The Menomini Indians and the Embo Fisherfolk as Bilingual/Multilingual Communities in Transition

There are a number of features of the Menomini community to keep in mind, in connection with Bloomfield's sketch of some of its speakers. The community still contained some monolinguals: Stands-Close is described as speaking only Menomini. There were also some individuals who were bilingual in two Indian languages but without knowledge of English: Storms-At-It is described in these terms, and Bird-Hawk may have belonged to this category as well, speaking either only Menomini or "possibly a little Ojibwa" in addition (Bloomfield 1964:395). There was apparently still an elevated register in use by shamans such as Storms-At-It, yet at the same time there were younger speakers like White-Thunder, bilingual in Menomini and English, whom Bloomfield describes as speaking "no language tolerably" (1964:395). Where levels of proficiency and style are concerned, this is a diverse picture. By the time Bloomfield worked with the Menomini, the community was evidently in transition; the language in today's terms would have been described as potentially endangered, its speakers characterized by an age-and-proficiency continuum.

Embo no longer had any Gaelic monolinguals by the mid-1960s, though the memory of near-monolinguals lingered in comic anecdotes about such people's struggles with English. There were still some elderly people who were more comfortable in Gaelic than in English and more proficient in Gaelic as well, and a number of men, especially in the older half of the speech community, had some capacity to use an elevated style of Gaelic marked by biblical lexicon and phrases characteristic of religious usage. Older males produced this sort of speech in prayer and in such relatively formal speech events as taking leave of someone not likely to be seen again for a long time. Certainly community members recognized good speakers and singled out their gifts for praise; they also recognized a low-proficiency group of speakers, those whom I have called semi-speakers, who did not say things "correctly" by local standards. But comparing my experience of the Embo speech community at a somewhat more advanced transitional stage with Bloomfield's experience of the Menomini speech community, it seems possible to me that Bloomfield conflated two of at least three potentially separate issues when he assessed the "good" and "bad" speech of the Menomini speakers within his acquaintance.

7.2 Components of Being a "Good" Speaker in a Community without Mother-Tongue Literacy

Comments met with in Embo suggested to me that the foremost element in producing speech admired by community members was sheer verbal (rather than strictly linguistic) skill. Verbal skill encompasses such things as the ability to draw on a rich lexicon effectively, to tell stories with a point, to recount or allude to a local repertory of well-known anecdote, to compliment or insult with subtlety or verve, to converse with liveliness, to prevent or fill awkward conversational gaps, and generally to maintain and make use of the verbal tradition of the community (including material such as proverbs, local rhymes, songs, by-names, prognostications, and the like). The more of these abilities a speaker had, the more admired her or his speech was likely to be. Someone who had one of these skills in marked degree but lacked some of the others equally markedly (e.g., Duncan, with his extraordinary repertory of proverbs but his lack of easy conversation) was assessed realistically—admired for the notable skill, even while the notable lack might be acknowledged. Conformity to conservative grammatical norms was not a requirement for success in these facets of speaking well.

A second component of speaking well comes closer to what linguists and other highly literate judges might deem "good" speech: speech performance that conforms to traditional models of grammar. Approval of this more specifically linguistic skill was inferable in Embo in the criticism of semi-speaker lapses, but was seldom to be heard in any positive form. A rare exception was an admiring reference from Murdo to an older member of the community, deceased by then, who had teased Murdo's generation about their use of a local adverb not in use in written or mainstream Gaelic.[3] While speakers did not in my experience make spontaneous judgments of grammatical preferability between constructions that represented approximate conservative and innovative parallels, some were willing and able to do so when I asked them to make such a distinction, demonstrating that judgments on the basis of grammatical conservatism could be evoked in this community.[4]

7.3 The Committed Speaker as a "Good" Speaker

A third apparent component of good standing as a speaker came as more of a surprise to me: degree of commitment to the minority language. This factor emerged only gradually, as I confronted linguistic skills that seemed to be seriously out of line with speaker status. From the results of the large-scale elicitation batteries of 1974 and 1976, in which I presented the same set of 270 stimulus sentences to eight fully fluent speakers and seven semi-speakers, it became clear that brother and sister E37 and E38, Rory and Elsie, both produced an Embo Gaelic that departed sharply from conservative grammatical norms. Since the community judged them to be speakers of different proficiency (Rory a fluent speaker and Elsie a semi-speaker), I took a closer look at their respective responses to the elicitation batteries to see whether there was any difference in linguistic skills that could reasonably account for the difference in speaker status.

I found one difference that seemed potentially significant. Rory consistently preserved most of the traditional irregularities in four different structures (first-person singular conditional, noun plural, irregular verb stems, and the first-person singular future of regular verbs), whereas Elsie leveled them out to a very conspicuous degree (Dorian 1977). The difference between their responses in this respect was quite extreme. Rory was just one year older than Elsie, and yet the forms he supplied resembled those of his mother, twenty-nine years his senior, much more closely than they resembled Elsie's. In view of the fact that the only seriously disfavored personal-pattern variants in Embo Gaelic were analogical regularizations (extension of gerund-forming /-u/ and /-al/ to additional verbs), it seemed possible that analogical regularization might generally have the effect of lowering the speaker's linguistic standing, even though explicit comment emerged only in the one case of gerund formation.

But while on the one hand Rory preserved irregularities remarkably well, on the other hand he preserved certain other aspects of traditional grammar remarkably poorly. In the test batteries his mother, E9 (Ada), marked personal names and other nouns for the vocative case 100 percent of the time (eight out eight opportunities), but Rory marked the vocative only once out of seven opportunities; Elsie outperformed him in this respect, in fact, marking the vocative in four out of seven opportunities. Ada marked the passive correctly for person (by means of appropriate initial mutations for third-person singular and plural) in five out of seven opportunities, but Rory and Elsie marked *no* such passives correctly in the seven instances each of them provided. Ada used a feminine pronoun replacement for four of seven feminine nouns tested, but Rory and Elsie replaced feminine nouns with masculine pronouns in all seven cases. Ada used a conservative negative-imperative particle once, correctly (without initial consonant mutation of the verbal root), with the verb 'to be', and in her other three negative-imperative instances she used the more ordinary negative particle equally correctly (with initial consonant mutation of the verbal root). Both Rory and Elsie joined many other young speakers in using the dummy verb 'go' in all four of the negative-imperative forms they provided (i.e., 'don't go___ing'), a periphrasis that appeared in their usage even with the verb 'to be'). Their mother retained the imperative plural inflection, but neither Rory nor Elsie did so.

With Rory's grammar departing in so many respects from the grammar of more conservative speakers, it seemed curious to me that he was universally regarded as a "good" Gaelic speaker and unlikely that the retention of irregularities—one of only a few conservative features in his Gaelic—could counterbalance the decay or absence of so many other grammatical features well enough to account for his being firmly assigned to the fluent-speaker category. And indeed, more extensive experience with Rory and Elsie over the longer term did reveal a difference in their speech behavior that now strikes me as more significant in accounting for their community-assigned speaker statuses.

Rory's preferred language was well known to be Gaelic. Whereas Elsie had no conversation partners with whom she regularly and by preference spoke Gaelic, Rory used Gaelic routinely with *all* of his most frequent bilingual conversation partners and by preference with anyone who would reciprocate. Rory spoke with normal fluency in both Gaelic and English, but he was more at home in Gaelic; his self-presentation was considerably more confident in Gaelic than it was in English. Elsie interacted easily and comfortably with people who spoke Gaelic regularly, and her translation test results indicated a reasonably wide-ranging active knowledge of Gaelic structure, even if not of the more conservative constructions. She tended to make active use of Gaelic in short bursts rather than in extended conversations, however, and she was not in any case a woman who talked a great deal in either of her languages. Rory, like his agemate E36, had been a member of the last class at the Embo school among whom Gaelic was said to be used regularly on the playground; both remained regular Gaelic speakers all their lives. According to the recollections of several sources, Elsie's class at school was the first that did not revert automatically to Gaelic on being released from the schoolroom to the play-ground, and her agemates did not go on to make the routine life-long conversa-tional use of Gaelic that Rory's agemates did. Community recognition of Rory as a fully fluent speaker rested, I've come to believe, above all on his commitment to Gaelic as his preferred medium of communication, with grammatical intactness a negligible consideration by comparison.

7.4 "Good" Menomini Speakers Compared with "Good" Fisherfolk Gaelic Speakers

There seems to be some mixing of the first two elements—verbal skill versus con-formity to traditional grammatical models—in Bloomfield's depiction of the Menomini speakers whose usage he describes. He mentions "elevated speech" with "ritualistic compound words" and "occasional archaisms" on the part of Storms-At-It, archaic words and constructions on the part of Stands-Close, and departures from ordinary conversation in connection with the "meager...inept vocabulary" but "occasional archaisms" of Bird-Hawk, references that suggest the persistence of special verbal registers among the Menomini. There is no sure way of telling from his sketches how the community (as distinct from Bloomfield) responded to such speakers' ability to produce archaic words and constructions. It is well within the realm of possibility, however, that Menomini speakers appreciated the ability of a man like Storms-At-It to use elevated speech that retained ritualistic compound words and archaisms, regardless of whatever "forms...current among bad speakers" (1964:395) he may also have used; these two facets of his speech may have been considered two entirely separate matters. Or, equally possibly, community members may have considered his use of forms typical of "bad speakers" painfully inappropriate for a man with the ability to use elevated speech, as Bloomfield seems to have done. Bloomfield's description of the "well up to standard" speech of Stands-Close as "*interlarded* with words and phrases that are *felt to be* archaic" (1964:395, emphasis added) creates the impres-sion that archaisms were not appreciated by fellow community members; yet if the father of Stands-Close was "known as an oracle of old traditions" (1964:395) and Stands-Close himself was a well-spoken man, it is not clear why anyone should have found the son's use of archaic turns of speech at all out of place.

Commitment to the heritage language of the community does not come into Bloomfield's considerations in any direct fashion. Nonetheless his description of White-Thunder as a man with "atrocious" Menomini and one who spoke "no lan-guage tolerably" certainly suggests that White-Thunder's linguistic identity was weak by comparison with that of the other tribal members described; quite evi-dently his commitment to the language was not strong enough to keep him in the fluent-speaker fold. This was despite the fact that his exposure to English does not seem to have been sufficient to give him English skills even to the "atrocious" level of his Menomini skills.

7.5 Speaking Well Reconsidered

Bloomfield's association of "character" and "standing" with forms considered to have a "better flavor" (1964:396) sounds reasonable enough for a small community, provided that there are genuinely discernible differences in standing within the community. Though there were no doubt individuals of particularly good character in Embo, differences in standing (except insofar as character itself creates a variety of moral standing) were too small to create an elite that inspired linguistic emulation. The pace of linguistic change was also very great in Embo; a large number of grammatical features were in flux, with consensus on linguistic form correspondingly weak. It cannot be said of Embo that speakers simply took an "anything goes" attitude, since they recognized and criticized certain deficiencies in semi-speaker performance. But at the same time, the fact that they voiced no criticisms at all of the performance of a younger fluent Gaelic speaker who deviated broadly and sharply from conservative grammatical norms, as Rory did, indicates that the latitude for deviation was very large by comparison to the latitude for deviation in a community whose mother tongue is written and the medium of education.

No doubt there is some level of deviation that cannot be compensated for by even the most pronounced language loyalty. The structural gaps in the Gaelic of the exceptionally language-loyal E42L would surely have aroused comment and criticism even if she had resolved to use Gaelic regularly with every speaker she encountered, instead of only fitfully and within a small kin circle as she actually did.[5] High-proficiency semi-speakers such as Elsie and Lorna might conceivably have changed their speaker status in spite of all, however, if they had become more regular speakers. Indeed Lorna, highly verbal and with a fluency beyond the expectations of most who knew her abilities only from previously quite limited conversations, moved somewhat in that direction in the late 1990s and after, even while Elsie moved the other way. Lorna surprised and pleased the finest speaker remaining in 1998, the verbally gifted E17, winning praise (expressed to me in a subsequent phone conversation) for her unanticipated fluency as she used only Gaelic in the making of the Embo videotape that she brought along when she visited me in the United States that year.

8 ASSESSING SPEAKER SKILLS

Speaker skills are in actuality very difficult to assess. A speaker's willingness and motivation are so crucial to outcomes that neither the speaker nor the assessor can take it for granted that a performance represents the speaker's true capacities. Self-consciousness and inhibitions created by fear of making a bad showing can prevent an imperfect speaker from using the language as effectively as she or he is capable of doing. In addition, personality differences are often reflected in the ease or lack of ease with which an individual carries on a conversation. On one hand, a natural taciturnity can prevent the display of a speaker's reasonably good structural knowledge, as was true in Elsie's case; her translation test results indicated a better control of Gaelic structure than her very limited conversation could display. On the other hand, a pronounced language loyalty can divert attention from the limited extent of a speaker's structural conformity, as seemed to be true in Rory's case. Unusual circumstances can call forth correspondingly unusual efforts from people whose capacities have not previously been revealed. The making of the videotape gave Lorna a reason to speak much more Gaelic than she usually did, with a larger number of people. She rose handsomely to the occasion, and E17 was not the only person in Embo to express surprise at how extensively and readily Lorna could speak Gaelic when she wanted to. (For a similarly striking example of unexpectedly strong language skills, evoked in this case by a child's desire to use a novel technology, see Kulick 1992:220–22.)

In speech communities where the ancestral language is passing out of use, the obstacles to achieving a realistic assessment of speaker skills strike me as enormous, in particular in the case of the final speakers to use the receding language. Surprises are common, if the researcher's experience of the community continues for a substantial number of years. Hard-and-fast speaker typologies for obsolescent-language communities can only be misleading in view of the disparate skills that an imperfect speaker may show—grammatically skilled enough to be good at conditional verbs, say, but bad at the passive; verbally skilled enough to engage in ordinary conversation, but not skilled enough to tell an amusing story that reaches a properly pointed conclusion. Our assignment of particular individuals to particular categories (including the ones I have used here) will inevitably be oversimplified and misleading. In the Embo case, differences in personality between Elsie and Lorna, and the resultant differences in their verbal performances, would not have permitted Elsie's better grasp of grammatical structures to emerge without extensive translation task testing; yet translation task testing will only rarely be possible or productive in similar settings.

Even willingness to undertake translation tasks on the part of a speaker will not make it easy to assess language skills if the speaker's personal history or individual personality traits have produced special inhibitions, as was true in the case of the three Brora semi-speakers who participated in some or all of the large battery of 1974 and 1976 tests. One of the three women had very painful memories of discrimination suffered because of her fisherfolk ethnic identity and her local fisherfolk Gaelic; this appeared to prevent her from accessing her Gaelic as well as she might otherwise have done. The other two semi-speakers tested in Brora were uncertain of their grasp of the language and were made more anxious than most by translation task testing; but the mere prospect of speaking Gaelic in any extended fashion raised anxieties for them as well, whether with me or with others. There may simply have been no deliberate assessment measures that could have determined how well they were still capable of speaking Gaelic, so that only a lucky chance would have allowed a glimpse of their full abilities. Such lucky chances do occur, but the linguist may not be on hand to witness them. One of the Brora semi-speakers told me of a visit she had made to a hospital, during which she happened across a lonely Hebridean patient with limited English. She attempted to cheer the islander up by conversing in Gaelic, and though the attempt failed because of her difficulty in understanding the Hebridean's Gaelic dialect, the effort was heartfelt and very likely produced a better flow of Gaelic than I had ever succeeded in drawing forth from her.

The three main speaker types recognized here and in my previous writings about Embo Gaelic do not represent any supposedly universal speaker typology, consequently, but rather what I take to be a rough but useful categorization of proficiency levels for describing this particular speech community: a highly fluent older group whose usage was by and large relatively conservative; a younger group, also fully fluent, still speaking Gaelic by preference with regular conversation partners but less conservative with regard to a number of grammatical structures that were undergoing change; and a final group who still made some active use of Gaelic but whose Gaelic was said by their more fluent elders to contain errors and who had no conversation partners with whom they regularly used Gaelic. In addition I recognize formerly fluent speakers whose childhoods in thoroughly Gaelic-speaking homes guarantee that they were fully fluent at one time but whose skills were diminished by lack of regular use; in my Embo sample all such individuals fell into the YFS age range and are therefore discussed as atypical members of that group.

All of these are group designations, however, and like all such groupings they disguise pronounced individual differences. Individual speakers at each proficiency level differed considerably in the degree of conservatism they displayed in particular structures. Older fluent speaker E17, for example, marked the vocative case 100 percent of the time, but she reserved the traditional first-person singular conditional suffix almost exclusively for negated sentences, using analytic /-u mi/ elsewhere (except in traditional rhymes). Rory (E37), twenty-three years her junior, produced vocative markings in only three of twelve environments where it would traditionally have been required in his materials overall, but he was far more conservative than she in his use of the traditional first-person singular conditional suffix. Such deviations as these from the age-related norm serve as reminders of the inevitable crudity of group-based speaker categories and proficiency labels; they should make us cautious about creating the categories and deploying the labels.

8.1 Disparate Skills at the Low End of the Proficiency Continuum

Among the Embo semi-speaker group itself, there were pronounced differences in speaking ability, both in terms of grammatical control and in terms of conversational ease. In Embo, as Gaelic was passing out of use, speakers at all three proficiency levels showed certain imbalances among the components of "good" speech, with only a rare individual such as E13 (Flora) ranking equally high on all three (verbal skill, adherence to traditional models of grammar, and loyalty to the minority language). Imbalances tended to be most pronounced among the semi-speakers, however. E42L was far and away the most committed of the Embo semi-speakers, insisting on continuing some use of Gaelic with the last speakers among her kin group and going so far as to develop a writing system of her own to use Gaelic in correspondence with a physically removed "conversation" partner. But E42L's control of Gaelic grammar was particularly weak, limiting what she could do in terms of verbal skills; her ability to tell stories, for example, or to engage in repartee, was reduced by her inability to produce grammatically intact sentences with ordinary conversational ease. E38 (Elsie) proved by translation task testing to have a better control of traditional grammatical structures than might have been anticipated, but neither her verbal skills nor her level of commitment to Gaelic matched her grammatical control. E40 (Lorna) was testably just a little weaker than her sister Elsie in grammatical control, but stronger both in verbal skills and in commitment. E41 was weakest overall; she controlled traditional grammatical structures very slightly better than her cousin E42L in translation task testing, but by her own account used Gaelic chiefly when she did not want her son to understand what she was saying.

As this sketch of four of the five Embo semi-speakers shows,[6] speakers at the low end of the proficiency continuum may, like their seniors, be relatively strong in one or two components of speaking well but weak in another; they differ from their seniors above all in that the weak aspects are usually very weak indeed. It is more accurate, and possibly more useful, to tease these facets of their speech behaviors apart and recognize them as separate elements than to try to characterize imperfect but still active speakers more globally.

The Embo community members whom I've termed near-passive bilinguals were even harder to evaluate. Like the semi-speakers, they had outstanding receptive skills. They followed fluent speakers' verbal interactions with apparent ease, even in noisy conditions, and they demonstrated their full social integration in such interactions by the appropriateness of their social and verbal responses. When they interposed remarks of their own during Gaelic interactions among more fluent speakers, it was usually in English, but occasionally they used Gaelic words or phrases. A very good-natured individual who was willing to participate in some translation task testing proved to have modest lexical resources but a very limited ability to construct grammatical phrases and sentences with them. Another resisted testing but spontaneously contributed two very short but complete and grammatically intact sentences when I was conducting an interview in Gaelic with someone else. She also demonstrated her outstanding passive skills by undertaking an extensive interview in which I posed all my questions in Gaelic and she answered them in English. Furthermore, this same near-passive bilingual and her low-proficiency semi-speaker cousin (E42L) were able to listen to a short and rather indistinct section of OFS Embo speech that had been unintelligible to me on a recording and provide the translation.

8.2 Assessing Speaker Skills: Conclusion

The mix of speaker skills to be encountered when a community is moving from bilingualism to monolingualism is dauntingly complex.[7] Certainly in the case of Embo, the inclination linguists typically show to assess speaker skills primarily, or even solely, in terms of grammatical control would be unduly one-sided and would fail to capture the Embo speech community's own perspective on what being a good speaker entails. Linguists' preoccupation with structural conservatism needs to be recognized as a view with a distinct professional skewing, akin to that other professional preference for "a *general* linguistic description for the entire speech community" (Collins 1998:267; see chapter 1, §7.4). Each of these approaches takes a single criterion as central (one that values above all a kind of grammatical orderliness), and is therefore relatively easy to pursue, but since neither represents fully or adequately what linguists actually encounter in the field, they should not stand entirely without a challenge to their dominance in linguistic description and in the evaluation of proficiency or verbal skills. An approach that takes the speech community's views into account as well does more justice to the untidiness and complexity often encountered in the local setting.

Socially Neutral Linguistic Variation: Where, Why, What For, and How?

1 INTRODUCTION: DISCOUNTING VARIATION

Possibly the hardest preconceived notions to shed, when setting out to engage with a previously un- or underdescribed language, are the ones that arise from extensive, often exclusive experience with standardized languages. Knowing mainly or only such languages, we expect to find a consensus of choice, even if not of practice, among speakers who share birthright community membership, the same geographical location, socioeconomic status, and a speech variety. That is, we expect them to agree at least that there are "correct" or "better" forms, even if they do not regularly use them. Consciously or unconsciously, we are in search of a consensus description for the language overall. Inter-speaker differences according to distinct locations, by sex, by contrasting socioeconomic position, or by social network patterns are expected and accepted, but if these factors are ruled out and sources still disagree on a good many linguistic forms, a likely first impulse is to look for reasons to disqualify some of the competing forms.[1] It may seem reasonable to discount a younger speaker's forms if they differ from the forms offered by an older speaker,[2] or the forms supplied by individuals who have lived elsewhere if they differ from the forms supplied by a speaker who has always lived in the core location.[3] Forms that clearly derive from some other language spoken in the region can be classed as borrowings and disqualified on that basis.[4] Forms supplied by a less thoughtful or less careful speaker may be dismissed if they differ from those of a notably thoughtful and careful speaker, and a marginalized individual's forms may be deemed marginal themselves and disregarded for that reason. Forms that are analogical or are less internally consistent in terms of the typological structure of the language may be left out of account on those grounds. Forms that depart from the canonical pattern expected for a language belonging to a particular language family may be set aside for their aberrance.

These are all more or less rationalized approaches to reducing lack of consensus in field data; to convince oneself that rationalizations of these sorts can be very appealing to field linguists, one has only to try to imagine Bloomfield placing the "bad syntax and meager, often inept vocabulary" of the very elderly and quite possibly monolingual Bird-Hawk on a descriptive par with the "beautiful and highly idiomatic" Menomini of Red-Cloud-Woman. Yet Bird-Hawk was as much a Menomini speaker as Red-Cloud-Woman. If an elderly and possibly monolingual Menomini speaker used "bad syntax," then that syntax was part of Menomini usage and would merit description as part of community speech patterns, even if it did not merit commendation from a linguist looking for maximally rich, conservative, and internally consistent structures.

A particularly seductive rationalization for selectively choosing elderly speakers' most conservative forms when framing the description of a language is that the grammar or phonology so constituted offers the maximum number of distinctive categories, even if some of those categories appear only vanishingly rarely in the elderly speakers' actual usage and not at all in the usage of others. This practice is justifiable in the view of some analysts, since it captures the most "intact" linguistic pattern available to the linguist and presumably preserves the echo of patterns that were previously more widespread. If other grammatical or phonological patterns are currently in regular use among the great majority of speech community members, however, they also merit scrupulous description. For one thing, the differences between the most conservative forms still in sporadic use and less conservative forms in widespread use illuminate change processes and direction of change. For another, genuinely descriptive practice requires that the speech variety be presented as it is, rather than as it was or may have been; to do otherwise is to inject a prescriptivism of the linguist's own into the description. (See in this connection the comments of Klein-Andreu, Mougeon and Beniak, and Mitchell quoted in chapter 1, §7.2.)

The process of standardization acts to create an idealized uniformity of structure, as a model if not as an actuality. In the standardized-language model, a single set of societally ratified forms is taken to constitute the standard language and all others are delegitimized. The non-ratified forms are then characterized as inferior (ungrammatical, dialectal, careless, vulgar, etc.), their use disapproved of and discouraged. Those whose linguistic socialization takes place in societies where a standardized language is powerfully promoted as the written language of formal education absorb what James Milroy terms an "institutionalized ideology" in which "uniformity or invariance is valued above all things" (Milroy 1999:27). Striking and unexpected findings are required to dislodge the expectation that an underlying consensus form of a community's language can be discovered by diligent analytic and interpretive work on the part of the field researcher. A finding of just that sort has surfaced in this volume: persistent and apparently socially neutral disagreement on variants among siblings and other close kin and/ or among agemates who share deeply similar backgrounds.

2 INTER-SPEAKER VARIATION AMONG CLOSE KIN AND AGEMATES

Trudgill's surprise on finding that close kin (affines who had grown up together and still lived in friendly proximity in adulthood) differed considerably on phonological realizations in Arrowtown, New Zealand, was reported in chapter 6, as was Duran's even greater surprise on discovering that an elderly brother and sister in the Aran Islands displayed a large amount of variation despite sharing a single household all their lives. The differences displayed in these cases reflected no social distinctions and appeared to be socially neutral themselves. Oftedal, though he followed a conservative descriptive tradition in treating only Roddy Martin's speech fully, was sufficiently struck by the differences between Ishbel Martin's Leurbost Gaelic and that of her husband and childhood next-door neighbor to acknowledge some of them in a note, if not to give them equal descriptive status. In another instance of the same surprising sort of finding, Bruce Connell reports as follows on sound-system variation in Cambap, a receding Benue-Congo language in Cameroon (2002:182): "Its few remaining speakers obviously all know each other intimately and have known each other for their entire lives;...many of them are closely related to each other, a fact that makes the variation all the more remarkable."

Tracing the complex effects of centuries-long language contact between northwest Russian dialects and Karelian in the northwest region of the former Soviet Union, Anneli Sarhimaa likewise reports surprising variation among individuals of seemingly identical background (1999:93):

> The analysis of the Russian-modeled necessitative infinitive construction in Karelian...that I carried out in 1992 did not suggest any correlations between the construction and any typical sociolinguistic variable such as the informant's age, gender, or the level of education....On the contrary, the results showed notable differences in the linguistic behaviour even between people who were born in the same year in the same village, had simultaneously attended the same school, and then had started their own families in maximally similar conditions, that is they got married to another Karelian and stayed in their native village.

Sarhimaa does not indicate whether any of the individuals concerned were affines or blood kin, but the situation as depicted certainly leaves that possibility open.

Ruth King, working with recessive Acadian French in four Newfoundland communities, encountered great variation and was struck by the erratic-seeming appearance of one conspicuous variable feature across two generations of a particular family. The brother in a brother-sister pair exhibited a feature known as <j>-*saintongeais* (after Saintonge province, France, where the feature originated): written <j> and <ge> are realized as voiceless or voiced velar fricatives or as [h]. The sister in the sibling pair did not herself show <j>-*saintongeais*, nor did her husband, but despite the absence of the feature in the parents' speech, their daughters did (King 1983).

Trudgill's is the odd case among these reports, in that his New Zealanders were speaking a highly standardized language. Since they had all been born in New Zealand, albeit to parents from different parts of the English-speaking world, they might have been expected to show the sort of leveling reported by Kerswill and Williams in the newly created towns of late twentieth-century England (Kerswill and Williams 2000, 2002). Trudgill fully expected that the children of this first native-born generation would subsequently show such leveling and was surprised only by the one-generation delay in its appearance.

3 FACTORS IN THE PERSISTENCE OF SOCIALLY NEUTRAL VARIATION

In the reports of field linguists who acknowledge their surprise at encountering variation in the speech of closely related people or of neighbors with identical backgrounds, certain factors are typically discussed as possible contributors to the variation. These are reviewed here.

3.1 Absence of Linguistic Codification and Home-Language Literacy in Small, Isolated Minority-Group Communities

By their very nature as the speech varieties of small and isolated minority-group populations, languages of the sort already mentioned (Arrowtown English obviously excepted) are generally not written by their speakers, even when they are isolated forms of languages that exist in standardized form elsewhere. Of the French-speaking population in Newfoundland, King reports (1989:141): "Most French Newfoundlanders have received little or no education in their mother tongue: only a very few French speakers are literate in French; many over the age of 60 cannot read or write either English or French."

Duran does not discuss Irish literacy among the Aran Islanders, but it is likely that schooling in Irish has been offered in local schools from the 1930s at least, if not before then. As in the sporadic teaching of Gaelic in the Embo school, however, the local dialect would most likely have been excluded from formal classroom use and a book-Irish of one sort or another introduced instead.

Among Karelians, literacy has nearly always meant literacy in Finnish or (more recently) in Russian. Official-language policies for Karelia in the turbulent twentieth century were marked by inconsistency and radical reversals, as Soviet policies toward minority languages swung wildly over the decades. Despite a very brief period in the late 1930s when Soviet ideology favored the standardization of local languages, these policies did not have the result of introducing a standard Karelian into regular written use (Sarhimaa 1999:34–41).

Connell is silent on the subject of literacy, but given the social and occupational circumstances he reports, it seems extremely unlikely that Cambap was available to its speakers as a written language.

In several villages in northern Norway, a minority population known as Kvens speak a language derived from Finnish dialects brought to that part of the country by settlers arriving from far northern Finland mostly in the eighteenth and nineteenth centuries (with lesser strands of Finnish settlement both before that period and since). Anna-Riitta Lindgren, working with Kven speakers, reports very high variation in lexicon, phonology, and morphology (Lindgren 1999:141, 143). According to Lindgren, standard Finnish is little known to Kven speakers in Norway, either in written or in spoken form, and Kven has passed from generation to generation as an unwritten vernacular (1999:146).

Whatever codification has existed in the communities where these languages are spoken has applied either to other languages altogether or to different forms of the same language. In most communities where considerable socially neutral inter-speaker and intra-speaker variation has been reported, Arrowtown excepted, the small size of the population in question, its isolation within an allophone region, community-wide modest or low socioeconomic standing, and a minority-language position in the nation or region as a whole have kept local speech forms out of schools and books and have at the same time kept any written forms of the local language out of the home-language sphere. That is, *community-external* norms have little or no presence in the local community.

3.2 Socioeconomic Homogeneity, Together with Weakness of Other Potential Social and Linguistic Correlations

In most of the cases instanced so far, a single common socioeconomic standing characterizes the minority-language group as a whole. The undifferentiated socioeconomic structure of the East Sutherland fisherfolk communities was set forth in chapter 2. Duran twice refers to the small communities of the Aran Islands as "egalitarian" (1992:13, 16); the co-resident brother and sister in Corrúch obviously shared the same standard of living and presumably the same socioeconomic standing overall. Connell describes the Camba as subsistence farmers who "to some extent are able to supplement their livelihood through cultivation of coffee and maize as cash crops", and states that "the society is essentially undifferentiated" (2002:170). Sarhimaa gives almost no details about the life patterns followed by villagers in the sites where she worked, but she does speak to the general inapplicability of Western notions of social class in Soviet Karelia (1999:84):

> It would be very difficult to define what "social mobility" actually means in the Karelian-Russian framework. Considering that my recordings were mainly made in the late Soviet period, and that even today Russian society still bears the impact of the state ideology which aimed at abolishing the whole concept of social class, including the supposed prestige differences between, say, academic professionals and working people with vocational training, my data would not permit direct application of the traditional social class divisions (income, occupation) used in sociolinguistics [*sic*] studies of Western societies. A fundamental reworking of sociolinguistic theory and methodology would be required.

A few researchers who have encountered inter-speaker variation in the speech patterns of small, minority-language populations have made a point of considering the possible effects of socioeconomic status in particular, in addition to those of age, sex, and proficiency. Jane and Kenneth Hill investigated different manifestations of the element -āška 'possession' in the Mexicano (Nahuatl) of two neighboring towns on the southern flanks of the Malinche Volcano in central Mexico, finding that the differences

> do not appear to be associated consistently with age, sex, dominant source of income (such as whether a speaker is a factory worker or a farmer...), or whether a speaker was Mexicano- or Spanish-dominant (all respondents are bilingual).... Speakers like S93, S96, and S53, all of whom exhibit irregular paradigms, are Mexicano-dominant bilinguals. Therefore, the position of a community on the language-shift continuum may not be an important factor in the -āška variability. We conclude that developments of -āška may be quite idiosyncratic. (1986:410)

The 'possession' suffix is the sole case of variation that Hill and Hill report on, but King, in her study of Newfoundland French, looked at a number of variable features in phonology and grammar. The area of western Newfoundland where the four French-speaking villages are located was economically depressed, dependent on a fishing industry in decline; there was a conspicuous absence of socioeconomic differentiation in terms of such factors as occupation, income, or type of housing among the villagers of the receding francophone population. Despite some difficulties created by the limited number of older speakers in one village and an absence of young speakers in another, King was able to construct a reasonably balanced sample differentiated by age and sex within each village. She made a close study of clitic pronoun usage, reporting that while age proved to be a significant factor, other social factors were undetectable in the statistical analysis. Younger speakers cliticized object pronouns less than older speakers (e.g., showed more tendency toward constructions such as *A donne le livre à lui* 'she gives the book to him' rather than *Elle lui donne le livre* 'she gives him the book'), suggesting that a linguistic change was in progress, but the speaker's sex and even geographical location were non-contributory (King 1989:144–45). King looked at variation in agreement marking as well as in clitic pronoun usage, and in contrast to Flikeid's (1985) findings for agreement marking in healthier Nova Scotian Acadian French, it appeared that factors of geographical location, sex, and education were also not significant for variation in agreement marking (King 1989:146).

Working in a very different language environment in Australia, but also with a receding language, Bavin reported similar findings. A number of changes had been introduced into the complex pronominal system of Warlpiri in the imperfect version spoken by young people from this Aboriginal group, but though the changes were clearly age-graded, the variation in question was otherwise without social correlates (Bavin 1989:283–84).

Just as absence of the local language from schooling and literacy blocks the introduction of community-external norms in the cases discussed here, absence of socioeconomic stratification limits the development of community-internal norms based on social group in a number of these cases. Perhaps more surprisingly, the speaker's sex also seems to play little or no role, even when women and men have clearly defined work roles, as in the East Sutherland fishing communities.

3.3 Population Mixture and Language Contact

For some languages that show high levels of inter-speaker and intra-speaker variation, a history of population mixture is detectable. Such mixture may contribute to the emergence of multiple variants that persist over the course of a good many generations, without the variants developing social weighting in communities with an egalitarian social structure. A long history of contact with one or more other distinct languages is nearly always involved as well and may also play a role in increased language variation.

3.3.1 The Process of Dialect Leveling

Trudgill, reviewing the process of dialect leveling, posits a three-stage chronological process of new-dialect formation for colonial situations, for newly founded towns, and for settings of rapid urbanization. In the first, adult speakers of different regional and social varieties come into contact, with some accommodation and "rudimentary" dialect leveling. In the second, children with diverse parental linguistic models as targets show a good deal of inter-speaker and intra-speaker variation, and in the absence of a single peer-dialect model, the influence of the parental generation remains stronger than is otherwise typical. In the third stage, the new dialect finally emerges in stable leveled form (Trudgill 1999:197–98). He takes the varying phonologies of the Arrowtown New Zealand speakers (see chapter 1, §7.6) to represent the second of these stages, one that reflects the diverse overseas origins of their parents. It must be taken into consideration, however, that Trudgill is concerned with various settings for English, with a powerful history of standardization going back several centuries. It seems on the evidence of East Sutherland fisherfolk Gaelic that the process of dialect leveling can be significantly delayed, or even largely avoided, in homogeneous communities where the speech variety is not subject to the pressures for conformity that are exerted by comparison of the spoken vernacular with a codified written form of the same language.

3.3.2 Population Mixture with Limited or Absent Leveling

Among the Embo fisherfolk a significant group of in-marrying wives from neighboring Ross-shire was evident in the census of 1851, and Embo Gaelic indeed shared some dialect features with the Ross-shire dialects to its south that Brora Gaelic and Golspie Gaelic did not show. Each of the fisherfolk villages also provided evidence, among its very small selection of family names, that males from outside the local area were at some point important elements in the Gaelic-speaking population. The alien names (in terms of clan territories) MacRae and MacDonald in Brora and Golspie and Cumming, Fraser, Grant, and Ross in Embo were sure signs of the in-marriage of men from outside Sutherland (see chapter 2, §4.2.1). The occasional large family using a certain number of distinctive forms could conceivably produce a proliferation of non-local forms, perpetuating some of them within their own subsequent families. It is likely, however, that fisherfolk Gaelic showed some degree of variation from the first, arising from admixture of geographically distinctive features, even without the contributions of outsiders. Groups of Clearance evictees from a few different though nearby inland glens would probably have been sufficient, at the beginning of the nineteenth century, to produce a certain number of variant forms in the newly emerging fishing settlements, augmented perhaps by additional variants after a few people from outside the area joined the community. This is in effect the Arrowtown model *without* the subsequent standardization that leveled New Zealand English in the next generation.

Duran found Inis Mór linguistically divided into an eastern half and a western half, in spite of the absence of any geographical features dividing the halves and in spite of the fact that the Irish of both halves was closely linked to a single dialect area on the nearby Connemara mainland. He suggests that in earlier times, when the population of each half was considerably larger (the eight-mile-long island had over 1,800 residents at the time of the first population census in 1821), marriage tended to be endogamous within each of the two halves of the island, giving rise to a certain degree of linguistic differentiation, especially in the more populous eastern half. Where his brother-sister pair was concerned, he speculated that some of the phonological differences between them might have reflected male versus female speech differentiation, and he considered it possible that some morphological differences might be "possible chance products of elicitation"

(Duran 1992:7); but he also noted that the father in this family came from the western side of the island's isogloss bundle and married into Corrúch, on the eastern side. On Inis Mór, it was more typically the woman who moved to the husband's location on marrying, and the tradition of in-marrying women suggested to Duran that a careful study of marriage patterns within Aran Island populations (and, because of continuing connections with kin on the mainland, within adjacent mainland communities as well) might shed light on individual as well as geographical variation (Duran 1992:8).

The French speakers in the Newfoundland villages studied by King did not have a long settlement history in that area, but they represented two different origins. One group of settlers were Acadians with a nearly 300-year history in North America; they came to Newfoundland from Nova Scotia from the middle of the nineteenth century to the early twentieth century. Another group of French-speaking settlers arrived during the same period directly from France (King 1989:140). Despite these two strands of settlement, King did not find population mixture to have a major effect on Newfoundland French; it accounted for "only a small amount of phonological variation...and for perhaps half-a-dozen lexical alternations" (1989:142). While dialect differentiation in terms of Acadian versus more recent French regional forms does not appear to have played much role in the Newfoundland French variation, there was some indication that family groupings did play a role, that is, that social-group boundary marking had developed within that particular community.

Lindgren's analysis is closer to Trudgill's, in that she views the mix of original Finnish dialect forms as fundamental to present-day variation in Kven. She reports that the Kven settlers in Norway originally came from different dialect areas of Finland, and because of that history she considers that "variation is to be anticipated" (Lindgren 1999:146).

The situation Sarhimaa looked at in Soviet Karelia was one of intense, centuries-long language contact not between various Karelian dialects but between Karelian and northwest Russian dialects. The result has been remarkable convergence, in spite of the fact that the languages in question belong to different language families (Sarhimaa 1999:194):

> The Karelian and the (northwest) Russian phonological systems have converged to such an extent that in numerous cases it is impossible to show that a given lexical entry has assimilated to Karelian phonologically. Similarly, it is often impossible to show morphological and/or syntactic integration into Karelian, because the structures of the languages in contact match each other. Furthermore, in contrast with contact situations involving languages that are very different typologically and have only come into contact with each other only relatively recently (such as English and Finnish), the Karelian-Russian setting is characterized by longstanding intensive contacts between two language systems which were not so typologically different from each other even originally; for instance, both Karelian and Russian have rich case systems and relatively free word order; in the course of time, under conditions of adstratum convergence these languages have gradually grown even more similar in many respects; the necessitative

construction systems discussed...[earlier] are one example of this....On some occasions, Karelian-origin and Russian-origin lexical and grammatical items may amalgamate to such an extent that the distinction between the two languages or codes grows completely dim, giving rise to syntactic constructions that are "mixed" in the sense of "impossible to derive from one source language only".

Sarhimaa's study looks closely at a single syntactic construction, the "duty and obligation" construction (DOC) in Karelian, one of many Karelian necessitative constructions with striking syntactic parallels in northwest Russian (though not in all cases with standard Russian). Karelian and northwest Russian, spoken in the same region for 1,000 years, have developed extraordinarily convergent systems of necessitative constructions, among others, and Sarhimaa convincingly identifies four linguistic systems showing distinct degrees of independence or merger with Russian (Karelian, neo-Karelian, Russian-Karelian, and Karussian, in her terminology).

In others of the settings looked at here, cross-language (as opposed to cross-dialect) contact is less in evidence. None of the personal-pattern variation in East Sutherland Gaelic arises from the direct influence of English, and Connell had to abandon cross-language contact as an adequate explanation for individual variation after examining the phonological systems of Cambap's neighboring languages. He concludes (2002:179):

> A comparison of the consonant and vowel systems of Cambap with those of the replacing language, Kwanja, and the majority language of the area, Ba-Mambila, does not account for the range of phenomena associated with the contraction of Cambap. Only some of this variation may be directly attributed to the influence of Kwanja, and none to Ba-Mambila.

The abundant variation Duran encountered in the forms of irregular verbs in Inis Mór Irish was unrelated to English structure. The Newfoundland French of the speakers studied by King showed influence from English in some of the syntactic variation they displayed, but, as with Cambap, language contact did not account for the full extent of the variation.

Sarhimaa's and Trudgill's findings of persistent and apparently socially neutral inter-speaker variation are included here, despite the fact that they represent different sorts of linguistic settings from most of the other cases, because they indicate that inter-speaker variation akin to the some of the personal-pattern variation of East Sutherland Gaelic can appear under several sorts of conditions: not only from the mingling of different dialects of a single language but also from cross-language mixture in an intense contact situation between nonstandard forms of two languages (Karelian and Russian); not only in isolated minority-language settings but also, transitionally, in a mixed-origin majority-language population despite the presence of a standardized form of the same language (Arrowtown English). Sarhimaa notes that the extremes of variation in the Karelian of northwest Russia have previously gone unreported because of researcher biases some of which are by now quite familiar: a preference among researchers for concentrating on the most traditional "unspoiled" forms of Karelian (1999:73); "correction" by editors of dialect texts collected for Karelian (1999:63);[5] exaggeration of the difference between Karelian and Russian as a result of comparing Karelian with standard Russian rather than with local dialects of Russian (1999:66).

4 ABSENCE OF SOCIAL WEIGHTING OF VARIANTS IN INTER-SPEAKER AND INTRA-SPEAKER VARIATION

Social evaluation of a variable's variants goes underdiscussed or even undiscussed in most of the studies introduced here, but absence of social weighting follows logically from the factors discussed in 3.1 and 3.2. Duran mentions that the people with whom he worked on Inis Mór "struggled to grasp what [he] was talking about" when he asked about a particular variant and "denied in all honesty that they use[d]" it, but then "clearly and spontaneously produced the variant in a later taped interview" (1992:15). In the case of gerund formation in particular, he notes that he encountered "a good deal of variation" but that "little apparent use is made of variant [gerund] forms as social or regional markers" (1992:11).[6] From these remarks it appears that awareness of variation was low and that normative evaluation was applied to variants little if at all. He identifies one exception, the monophthongization of two diphthongs; but this feature is geographical rather than social, with people on the western side of Inis Mór viewing the monophthongization as a shibboleth that characterizes the speech of people from the eastern side of the island (1992:15).

Lindgren refers repeatedly in her study of Kven to what she calls "low normativity", that is, a very high tolerance for variation (Lindgren 1998). Implicit in her term is an absence of social judgment applied to the rampant variation (phonological, morphological, and lexical) characteristic of Kven speech. In view of the slight or nonexistent knowledge of written and spoken Finnish that she reports (1998:146), it seems that the local Finnish-origin minority language escapes comparison with standard Finnish and therefore also escapes the social evaluations usually evoked by dialectal deviation from standard-language norms.

King's careful treatment of Acadian French in western Newfoundland provides explicit comment about speaker response to variation in clitic pronoun usage (1989:144):

> Speakers of Newfoundland French themselves pay no attention to variation in clitic pronoun usage, with the exception of a few geographically scattered older speakers who volunteered that indicative constructions with postverbal *en* [e.g., *Ma mère me fait en manger* versus *manger-z-en*] was the bad French of a limited group of young people, and at that of young people from another community [illustrative example inserted].

In the case of East Sutherland fisherfolk Gaelic, chapter 3 offered evidence of six kinds for absence of social weighting in connection with the personally patterned variables discussed in this book: contrasting variant selections of which the speakers seemed to be unaware, even though they were closely connected and highly interactive (next-door-neighbor siblings and co-resident husband and wife); variant substitutions that went unnoticed when one of a pair of speakers repeated part of what another speaker had said; rapid-succession variant alternations on the part of a single speaker without any change of topic, audience, affect, or syntactic environment; equally unmotivated variant alternation in what is usually regarded as "fixed form" traditional material, such as proverbs and children's rhymes; and in striking contrast to all these cases, sharp awareness and strong disapproval on the part of some community members of the analogical extension of one pair of high-frequency suffixes in gerund formation and equally strong disapproval of use of English loanwords when well-known Gaelic equivalents were available. The strength of the disapproval in these last two cases served to highlight the lack of response to variant-selection differences other than analogically extended /-u/ and /-al/ in gerund formation.

5 SOCIALLY NEUTRAL INDIVIDUAL VARIATION AND OBSOLESCENCE

One particular constellation of features that frequently appears in conjunction with a high level of socially neutral individual variation (small population, absence of socioeconomic differentiation, a minority language used as the traditional language of the home but excluded from written use) immediately suggests another common feature: the speech varieties in question are recessive, facing either the possibility or the certainty of passing out of use. Minority languages are typically under considerable pressure from at least one language of wider communication, and when they are not written (and are therefore excluded from educational use), as is very often the case, their position is particularly weak. Absence of socioeconomic stratification, furthermore, is not a feature of prosperous communities; it appears rather in subsistence-level communities where economic circumstances do not allow significant differences in income level to emerge. Again, many such communities are in decline, with their languages as well as other aspects of their traditional lifeways under threat.

If most speech varieties that display socially unweighted inter-speaker and intra-speaker variation are recessive, spoken by small populations that are in the process of becoming still smaller, the question naturally arises of whether the process of obsolescence is the underlying cause of the variation displayed. Dressler, in a review of language death and its literature, identifies the presence of notable variation as one of several features distinguishing dying languages from pidgins (1988:189): "Dying languages, much more so than pidgins, are characterized by great variation, as represented by massive occurrences of free allophones.... This variation is due to increasing lack of performance in the recessive language and the accompanying relaxation of sociolinguistic norms in general."

Connell, whose study deals exclusively with phonological variation, takes up Dressler's thesis and assesses its applicability in the case of Cambap. At the time of his research, only about thirty speakers of Cambap remained, all middle-aged or older. They lived dispersed among six villages (now Kwanja villages, although Connell notes that at least two of the six were originally Camba villages) and used Kwanja at home with younger members of their own ethnic group and with fellow villagers. Most Cambap speakers were of mixed Camba-Kwanja parentage and had both languages as joint "first" languages. In spite of these circumstances, Connell does not find Dressler's explanation for high variability applicable to Cambap phonological variation. He points out that those who still spoke Cambap did so on a daily basis and continued to use it by preference with one another, remaining fully fluent speakers of the language. In this the final Cambap speakers paralleled those fluent Embo Gaelic speakers of the 1960s who were middle-aged or older: despite their ability to speak a language of wider communication (one they spoke regularly in interactions with their own children and other monolingual fellow villagers), the fluent Embo Gaelic speakers continued to use Embo Gaelic as the normal language of interaction among themselves, their Gaelic language skills remaining impressively high. In both cases, lack of performance did not emerge as a feature of daily life and proficiency was notable despite the fact that transmission had ceased.

Where sociolinguistic norms are concerned, Connell (2002:180) takes a position distinct from Dressler's: "Rather than 'relaxation' of norms it is probably true to say that in situations such as that of Cambap, there never have been strict or standardized norms; and therefore less rigid standards regarding phonetic and phonological aspects of language need not be seen as part of the contraction process at all." Connell points to accounts of phonological variation in other languages, including some which have very large numbers of speakers such as Kanuri (Cyffer 1998:26), Afar (Hayward, personal communication to Connell), and Khoekhoegowab (Haacke 1986; Haacke et al. 1997). But he notes that in the cases of large-language phonological variation, the variation is typically reported for dialects spoken by small and isolated groups of people within the overall population of speakers, leading him to bring a different perspective to the question of a "relaxation of sociolinguistic norms" (2002:181–82):

> In most of these cases the dialects in question are said to enjoy normal vitality; they are used for the full range of daily functions and undergo normal intergenerational transmission.... What they have in common, and what sets them apart from other languages usually treated in scholarly studies is their relative isolation and small populations. In such situations, speakers would come to know everyone in the community intimately, just as is likely the case for a contracting language, and it is this familiarity that may well lead to the relatively relaxed sociolinguistic norms that permit the kind of variation seen also in Cambap. In short, the phonetic and phonological variation reported in previous studies on dying languages...may be a phenomenon inherent not to the lan-

guage contraction process, but rather to a more general one, one associated with the familiarity found among members of small relatively cohesive groups of people.

Connell had already noted the absence of socioeconomic differentiation in the Cambap setting earlier in his publication, and though he does not reiterate that factor here, it is most likely an important additional condition for an absence (rather than a "relaxation") of strict phonological norms, since it eliminates the social stratification in connection with which one set of linguistic features easily takes on higher social value than another.

The combination of features that gives rise to what Connell calls "familiarity" can be restated in more conventional sociological and sociolinguistic terms, along the lines of the Embo sketch provided earlier in this study: absence of socioeconomic differentiation, a face-to-face community structure characterized by shared background knowledge and multiplex social roles, and, as a result of the first two features, an absence of linguistic accommodation. In more multilingual settings like that of the Kven-speaking villages of northern Norway, duration and degree of multilingualism may also play a role in the degree of variation. Lindgren found that the smallest of the three Kven-speaking villages showed the greatest phonological and morphological variation (the lowest normativity, in her terminology). In Connell's terms, this would also be the setting offering the greatest familiarity; but Lindgren points out in addition that Raisi, the smallest village, was already trilingual in the nineteenth century with both Sami and Norwegian residents using Kven as a second language, and that norwegianization began earlier in Raisi than in the other two Kven villages (Lindgren 1998:163). The somewhat lesser degree of variability in the other two villages may also reflect the facts that the number of Kven speakers is larger in one of the two, and that Norwegian came into use considerably later there; and that in the other of the two, the most easterly, fewer other co-resident ethnic groups speak Kven, while immigration from Finland was also later than in the more westerly villages. Use of the high-variation language by speakers of allophone ethnicity has not been a factor in the other cases looked at in this chapter, since, by comparison with thriving languages, receding languages are relatively seldom used by other ethnic groups. But Lindgren's work indicates that use of a small, isolated language as a second or third language by co-resident allophone groups may join dialect diversity arising from early population mixture (as in Arrowtown and Embo) as a factor in producing inter-speaker and intra-speaker variation.

In present-day conditions, nearly all small languages are at least potentially endangered, and "large" languages spoken in isolated settlements by small, high-interactivity subpopulations (e.g., the Kanuri and Afar cases identified by Connell) may also be threatened by a variety of modernization pressures. It may therefore not be possible to rule out processes of linguistic recession or obsolescence as a factor in high idiosyncratic variation, or at least as a co-factor along with social and geographic isolation, and indeed the difference between Flikeid's findings in Nova Scotian Acadian French and King's in Newfoundland Acadian French suggest such a possibility: Flikeid found that age, sex, and level of education were linked to certain variables in the more vigorous Acadian French environment, while King found only age to be a factor in the contracting Newfoundland environment for Acadian French (see §3.2). At the same time, however, Trudgill's finding that individual variation could emerge in a first native-born generation with dialect-differentiated parentage, even in the context of a highly standardized language and close personal relationships, suggests that individual variation may be more robust than previously supposed.

Striking evidence for the robust nature of idiolectal variation has emerged as well from extensive studies carried out in Hyde County, North Carolina, an isolated rural setting with a remarkable degree of historical, social, and linguistic continuity (Wolfram and Beckett 2000; Wolfram and Thomas 2002; see §7.2.1). In Hyde County, the researchers encountered "considerable variation among different individuals" despite "common demographic profiles (e.g., level of education, socioeconomic status, etc.)" (Wolfram and Thomas 2003:24). And in the Embo setting, the fact that it was not just younger speakers who showed idiosyncratic variation but also the oldest speakers, born in the late nineteenth century and more comfortable in Gaelic than in English, indicates that inter-speaker and intra-speaker variation was more than just the product of Gaelic decline in the village.

In the current state of our knowledge it would be premature to rule out any of the proposed causal factors decisively, but we are more likely to make headway toward determining which factors have significant effects if we resist any temptation to achieve tidier descriptions by discounting unexpected and unexplained variation. Keren Rice, in her fieldwork experience with the Athapaskan language Slave, gained the insight that the members of a speech community can tolerate a large amount of variation of which they are not necessarily consciously aware. On the basis of her own experience, she gives advice akin to Foley's advice about not "papering over" variation (Rice 2001:235):

> It is important that the linguist not try to make judgments of what is right and what is wrong, but take all of the language, and figure out what it is, including all of its internal diversity and variability. Diversity can be as systematic and rule-governed as uniformity, and such diversity is not to be dismissed as mistakes, poor speech, and the like, something that is often tempting to do in the presence of overwhelming amounts of material to sort through. It is rather to be embraced, and an understanding of diversity in addition to uniformity leads to a deeper understanding of both the language in question and language in general.

6 CONTRIBUTORY FACTORS IN SOCIALLY NEUTRAL INDIVIDUAL VARIATION: SUMMARY

The studies cited here treat a wide variety of linguistic features. Some, like Trudgill's and Connell's, share with the majority of variationist studies a focus on phonological variation. Some, like Lindgren's, King's, and Wolfram and Thomas's, include both phonological and syntactic variation. Most report an age-related element in the variation that suggests change in progress, but some appear to be describing stable individual variation, for example, Duran, Sarhimaa, and Hill and Hill. There are thus similarities both to age-related variation and to personally patterned variation in fisherfolk Gaelic, each of which appeared to be socially neutral in the fishing communities of East Sutherland.

Researchers typically find several of the elements that contribute to high inter-speaker and intra-speaker variation co-occurring in a given case. A representative example of multiple contributory factors appears in Silvia Dal Negro's study of the German speech form in use in the village of Formazza in alpine Italy. In reporting that the Walser German spoken by her oldest sources was not uniform in spite of the elderly speakers' similarity in fluency, linguistic loyalty, age, social class, and education, Dal Negro points to lack of a written tradition and to the absence of a standard-language model as contributing factors in "a degree of variation that is accepted and probably overlooked by fluent and traditional speakers" (2004:118); but she also stresses centuries-long isolation from other varieties of German and an equally long history of contact with Italian (2004:117). She takes the cumulative effect of this constellation of factors to have given rise to the absence of linguistic consensus.

A review of the factors discussed so far as likely contributors to the emergence and especially the persistence of idiosyncratic linguistic variation produces the following list, of which several usually appear in concert, as in the case of the Walser German of Formazza:

- dialect mixture via population mixing;
- geographical isolation and/or enclavement within a larger allophone population;
- minority status for the language in question, with either no relationship or distant relationship to the dominant language of the country or region;
- absence of community-external language norms and exclusion of the minority language from written use among its speakers;
- absence of social stratification related to socioeconomic differentiation;
- absence of social evaluation of variants vis-à-vis one another;
- a homogeneous small-community social structure characterized by dense face-to-face interaction and multiplex social roles;
- absence of linguistic accommodation;
- obsolescence (with declining use as an exacerbating, if not originating, factor).

Some of these features are causally related to one another: absence of social evaluation of variants relates to the three features that precede it and absence of linguistic accommodation to the community structure specified in the preceding feature.

If we consider the features of the settings in which the great majority of linguists and linguistic anthropologists (as the likeliest describers of the languages in question and the communities in which they are spoken) are socialized, the list consists of precisely the opposite characteristics: social stratification is a prominent feature of our urbanized societies, and the various expressions of linguistic variables are strongly correlated with class and/ or ethnic group membership, for which reason they also evoke strong social evaluations; our own first languages are, more often than not, the dominant and official languages of a nation (or at least a major region) and are taught in the schools and routinely used in writing; interactions among community members are multiplex only in the relatively infrequent instances where a co-worker is also a relative, a relative is also a neighbor, or the like, while most community members have no personal acquaintance with one another at all; linguistic accommodation is an effective and therefore widely used practice; our primary languages are spoken by large populations and are not threatened with recession to the point of likely or certain disappearance. As researchers whose linguistic expectations and practices are formed in environments as different as this from those of the usually rural dwellers whose idiosyncratically and socially neutral high-variation speech we are encountering, we have major adjustments to make in the assumptions we bring to language description before we can expect to make useful appraisals of what we are encountering.

Of central importance, ultimately, is the recognition that socially unweighted idiosyncratic variation, which might have seemed in the East Sutherland fisherfolk context merely a bizarre phenomenon of an obsolescent speech form, is in actuality a reasonable outcome of a particular set of social, historical, and linguistic features. That this constellation of features should exist, producing this sort of variation in a minority-language population enclaved in a distinctly first-world British setting, should make us alert to the possibility of social and linguistic conditions with consequences we have not fully appreciated previously.

7 IDEOLOGICAL FACTORS BEARING ON SOCIALLY NEUTRAL LINGUISTIC VARIATION AND ITS RECOGNITION

Least well documented (because they are the least easy to recognize) in connection with high-frequency, socially unweighted, idiosyncratic variation are ideological factors that may contribute either to the phenomenon itself or to lack of recognition of it. Two sets of ideologies come into question: those of the community under study, and those of the researchers undertaking the study.

7.1 Recognizing Alternative Ideologies

Linguists socialized in standard-language environments bring their own ideologies to their descriptive work, importantly including what James Milroy calls "the belief that a 'language' must exist in some authoritative, invariant form" (1999:17). Only when confronted by manifestations of a very different sort of orientation are they likely to recognize the existence and effect of divergent language ideologies. Milroy (1999:34) offers two examples from scholars of Pacific languages, both cited in Mühlhäusler (1996). From Grace (1991:15): "One of the things I found most puzzling was that in some areas the people seem to have no conception of what their language is and no sense of belonging to a linguistic community." And from Heryanto (1990:41): language "is not a universal category...though it may sound odd, not all people have a language in the sense in which this term is currently used in English".

Collins's experience with Tolowa speakers who had no expectation of uniformity of usage and did not acknowledge the appropriateness of a general structural description was noted in chapter 1; their conception of "a language" differed, startlingly for Collins, from the dominant Western conception. Of another Californian tribe, the Western Mono, Paul Kroskrity reports that they espouse a position he terms "honoring variation" (2002:174):

> Speakers of Western Mono recognize many regional dialects, formerly identified with various bands but today identified with the neighboring town....Local ideologies of linguistic differentiation for the Western Mono rarely elevate one regional dialect over another. But regional differences are not the only ones recognized among Mono people. Monos recognize the shaping role of families in creating speech differences in the community. They also recognize and even celebrate individual variation and do not expect all members of the group to conform to a single way of speaking. Just as all members of the community once had their own traditional Mono names and personal songs that they would sing when approaching others, so each person is expected to have his or her own distinctive verbal style.

This orientation is radically different from that cultivated by standardization, and it creates a potentially very different environment in terms of latitude for linguistic idiosyncrasy.

7.2 Recognizing One's Own Ideology

It is difficult for most of us as life-long users of standardized languages to recognize the likely contribution of unfamiliar ideologies to the persistence of socially unweighted inter-speaker and intra-speaker variation, but it can be just as difficult for us to recognize the ideological factors that constrain our own viewpoints, which tend to be familiar to the point of invisibility. As Irvine and Gal point out, the ideological underpinnings of assumptions are most easily recognized if the assumptions are someone else's, especially if they are those of a previous time and therefore no longer prevail (Irvine and Gal 2000:36, 59).

Entrenched ideological positions can also be surprisingly difficult to modify. Silverstein offers a striking example of persistent ideological intransigence on the part of anthropologists. In the face of abundant evidence to the contrary, he states, anthropologists have ignored the plurilingualism characteristic of Native American life in accounts reflecting five post-contact centuries and have persisted instead in treating Native American communities as if they conformed to the conceptions of European one-nation, one-language ideology (Silverstein 1997:127):

> Even in the face of long-known linguistic documentation to the contrary, most anthropological work has proceeded out of its own ideological condition of Andersonian (Anderson 1991) linguistic-cultural nationalism, in which "stable, language-bounded, one-language cultural units"...have been assumed to be the basic condition of "traditional" Native American discursive life, and plurilingualism the remarkable exception. In North America this has not been the norm for the entire record of written evidence over 500 years, and to use an assumption of unilingual sociocultural units based on such a conception of the relevant type of "community" has long been considered incorrect and known to be unsupportable. Why has it persisted so long?

Anthropologists are not alone in playing down the incidence of multilingualism. The rise of Western ideologies that disfavor bi-and multilingualism has permeated linguistic thinking as well. Irvine and Gal (2000:63) point out that metropolitan Europe took "the ideal political order of one nation, speaking one language, ruled by one state, within one bounded territory" to be the prerequisite for technological progress, economic development, and civilization. Europeans regarded regions lacking in this order as backward as well as disordered. Again, despite much evidence to the contrary, Western social sciences persist in the unwarranted assumption that the communities they study "will normally be linguistically homogeneous," as Irvine and Gal point out (2000:76).

Some of the ideological barriers to recognizing the potential for linguistic heterogeneity in highly homogeneous communities were identified in chapter 1: the assumptions that linguistic differences are bound to correlate with social groups within the community (§1); that "good" speakers will recognize some forms or structures of their language as preferable ("better," "more correct") than others (§7.1); that small, tight-knit communities will show less variation than larger, more complex, and anonymous communities (§7.4); that speakers will be inclined to accommodate to one another linguistically (§7.5). One other researcher assumption has been identified that takes on special importance here, because it operates even among linguists with a special interest in variation, increasing the likelihood that individual variation of the personally patterned type will go unrecognized.

7.2.1 The "Homogeneity Assumption"

After extensive field experience with dialects of the southeastern U.S. seaboard, Wolfram and his co-workers have identified a firmly established viewpoint in linguistic studies which they call "the homogeneity assumption". It prevails in their view in the variation analysis of correlational sociolinguistic work: "Data are presented for a set of speakers as if they were a homogeneous group", carrying the implication that "individual variation is insignificant in the description of linguistic and social covariance" (Wolfram and Beckett 2000:5–6). The homogeneity assumption allows the data from a grouped set of individuals to be treated as undifferentiated; if in-group variance should appear too prominently, division of the group into additional subgroups is taken to be the corrective, a subdivision strategy that allows the homogeneity assumption to be maintained. The existence of anomalous individuals as exceptional cases may be acknowledged (as in the discussion of the atypical Nathan B., in Labov 1979), but the underlying assumption remains (Wolfram and Beckett 2000:6): "Notwithstanding such exceptions [as Nathan B.], the guiding rule of variationist investigation remains the assumption that socially meaningful divisions of groups of speakers will not be linguistically heterogeneous." Their own findings in an isolated, rural, biracial Outer Banks community in North Carolina did not justify such an assumption. They found "patterns of inexplicable individual variation" that led them to consider that individualized life histories and personal identities were significant in patterns of variation and that a "much more complex array of variables... must be considered in the explanation of intragroup diversity" (Wolfram and Becket 2000:27).

Le Page, influenced by years of work in multilingual, multiethnic societies, contends that what really needs explanation is not linguistic variation but the formation of such a concept as the homogeneous language (Le Page 1997:31). Certainly linguistic variation in small and homogeneous groups can be so extensive as to make the very concept of community linguistic homogeneity seem faintly exotic. Recall in this connection Foley's report of working in Papua New Guinean language communities with no more than 200 people and finding their languages to be non-homogeneous (chapter 1, §7, quoting Foley 2003:86). Lack of isomorphism between individual speakers and the group was identified early on as a potential problem for correlational sociolinguistics (Romaine 1982:20), and certainly East Sutherland Gaelic and the other minority languages discussed in this chapter pose a serious challenge to the homogeneity assumption. The stubborn persistence of idiosyncratic and apparently socially neutral variation in such communities has surprised every researcher who has encountered it, and some particularly engaging questions remain. One such question is this: what purpose does it serve?

8 THE "WHAT FOR?" ISSUE IN SOCIALLY NEUTRAL INDIVIDUAL VARIATION

Earlier parts of this chapter looked at the questions of where idiosyncratic variation has turned up, what features the speaker populations who display the phenomenon have in common, and what makes the phenomenon difficult for linguists to discern and acknowledge. We come now to the question of what role such variation plays in the communities where it persists—what it is good for.

Here I think we must turn to Barbara Johnstone's work on "the linguistic individual", the phrase that serves as the title of her 1996 book. Johnstone points out that individuality asserts itself in speech not just when it might be expected to (in telling a story, for example, or in emotion-laden talk) but also in talk that is supposedly anonymous, highly referential, and disengaged (1996:x). As an extreme instance of the latter, she examined a set of telephone interviews that were to be conducted according to rigid scripting under the auspices of a communications firm in Texas. Not surprisingly, interviewees frequently resisted the script (which required them to use the words "agree" or "disagree" and choose by number one of several possible answers). More surprisingly, the twenty-four interviewers who conducted the phone calls also resisted the careful scripting of their own parts in the interviews. In the opening segment of the phone interviews, the callers introduced themselves and the survey. Despite the fact that this part of the interview was entirely scripted, each interviewer deviated in small ways; in addition, when more than one of an interviewer's opening segments was examined, each was found to deviate slightly differently (1996:95–118). The urge to individualize one's voice appears to be irresistible, even when the success of one's work (and the receipt of one's pay) depends on suppressing the individuality of that voice.

Johnstone reminds us that "language is just as crucially self-expressive as it is referential or relationship-affirming, poetic or rhetorical" (1996:186). Lexical and syntactic choices have long been recognized as a matter of not just referential precision but also individual style. When the language in use within a small community offers many variable elements, with multiple variants available for a number of them, variant choice can likewise be a matter of individual voice.

Many of the speakers who served as sources for the study of East Sutherland fisherfolk Gaelic made use of recurrent phraseology or fixed phrases highly characteristic of their own personal styles. Some used relatively unusual endearments, for example, and several had recognizable favorites among the range of exclamations that they drew on. In expressing surprise or wonder at something said by another speaker, for example, G2 favored /hiarn/ 'lord!', E13 (Flora) favored /mə ruar (mĩʃ)/ 'mercy (me)!', and E29* (Emma) favored /pyɔːrniç/ 'bless!' Some used distinctive phrases or made unusually fine distinctions between phrases that others used more indiscriminately. E13 (Flora) was the only speaker in my sample who used a calque of the English phrase "Believe you me!" in Gaelic. E29* (Emma) was the only Embo speaker to signal agreement with another speaker's evaluations by means of frequent repetitions of the phrase / te: el/ 'what else [could one expect]?' E30 (Derrick) regularly followed explanations or philosophical remarks with the phrase /hɔ̃n ad e:/ 'There you have it'. E17 made a distinction between /an əl əs am/ 'I don't know', used as a recurrent discourse marker, and /an ũrn dɔ̃ ra:/ 'I can't say', used to indicate that she genuinely lacked knowledge of something. Certain markers of conversational involvement were used by speakers to conspicuously different degrees according to sex, with women using both their interlocutor's given name and /ʃ e:/ ~ /h e:/ as a token of affirmation to a greater degree than men. But though these last were clearly gender-related features, individual women differed considerably in the degree to which they made use of them: E13 (Flora) used her interlocutor's given name with great frequency, while her near agemate E17 seldom did so.

8.1 Variability, Variant Selection, and Personal Voice

In something of the same fashion, both degree of variation and particular variant choices reflected speakers' individuality. E26*, E29*, and E13 were conspicuously high-variation speakers, as we have seen, while E24 was an exceptionally low-variation speaker. Above all, however, particular variant-use patterns were an individual matter. Elspeth was a /stɛ/ and /hãːn/ speaker by conversational variant preference, her brother Murdo a /sčax/ and /hãːnig/ speaker. Elsie was a /hɔ̃n/ and /nˊĩmərd/ speaker by conversational variant preference, her sister Lorna a /ʃɔ̃n/ and /ĩmərd/ speaker. The recognizability of personal patterns in variant choices is what made it so particularly painful to me to have to discard all of the variants that appeared on field notebook pages in which I failed to distinguish between Lexie and Elspeth, or between Lexie and Elspeth and Murdo, as initial provider of a particular translation-task sentence (see Chapter 7, §4). If the form /stɛ/ appeared for ('in'), it was perfectly clear that Elspeth had been the speaker whose rendition was initially taken down, given what I knew of these three speakers' variant-selection patterns: both Lexie and Murdo favored / sčax/ and rarely (if ever) used /stɛ/. But to avoid logical circularity I could not use my awareness of variant preferences to make the identification; I was, after all, tabulating known speakers' variant selections precisely to show that these selections were an individual matter.

Speaker identities were especially evident in cases where several variants appeared within a sentence or two, or even within a single sentence. Because many of the variables are high-frequency items, it was common for a number of variants to appear in fairly close succession. Almost any modest stretch of speech was rich in relevant variables, a fact that made the transcription of recordings rewarding even in the bottomless challenge of transcribing the phone conversation tapes (which often increased by two or three as I transcribed one). Here for example is a single sentence from a comic story told by E4 in 1968, in which three of the variables discussed in this study appear in succession:

ɔːx, **tə** xuarɫ iʃ ʃɔ, **xa rɔ** nə kʰasən ɛkʰ puəɫtən ə ɫaːr,
tuɫ ə raʃ **stɛx** n ə dɛ.

Och, WHEN she heard this, her feet WEREN'T striking the ground,
going back IN to the house.

The recurrent /ʃɔ̃n/ ~ /hɔ̃n/ alternations in Elspeth's account of childhood games have already been mentioned (chapter 3, §8.2.3), but many other variables appeared in that account as well, as the following three-sentence section of her description of the game Margaidh Dollach demonstrates:

s **raxu** kʰas ɛkʰ s ə dəurl. ʃən ad marəgi dorlax,
s va i '**mwiç**'. s veru ʃĩnˊ ə stɔrl tə nə suːlən ɛkʰ.

And her foot WOULD GO in the hole. THAT'S Margaidh Dollach for you, and she was 'OUT'. And we would take the strip of cloth FROM her eyes.

In chapter 2, §4.2.2, I noted that a dialectologically well-informed eaves-dropper listening to an out-of-sight East Sutherland fisherfolk Gaelic speaker would know within a minute or two whether the speaker was from Brora, Golspie, or Embo, thanks to the high frequency of distinctive (morpho)phonological elements in the speech of each community. It would be equally feasible, if not as swift, to identify one among many possible Embo speakers as the source of an unattributed transcription of a thousand words or so on the basis of the patterns of variant use that appeared over the course of the transcription. No one variant would determine the identification, but as the number of variant selections mounted, more and more potential candidates would be ruled out until eventually the identity of the individual speaker became evident. To take just the brief extract just given for Elspeth, the use of /raxu/ would not eliminate her brother Murdo or her sister-in-law Lexie as possible producers of these three sentences, but Murdo would be ruled out by /mwĩç/. Lexie would be ruled out by the presence of *either* locational form of the adverb 'out', whether /mwĩç/ or / mwĩ/, since she was one of a number of Embo speakers who used only the originally directional form /max/, and in addition she would be made unlikely by the use of the variant /tə/. A more substantial stretch of transcribed text that provided a few more instances of these and other variables would build up bit by bit a distinctive variant-use pro-file that gradually eliminated various other Embo speakers, until with a generous enough speech sample Elspeth emerged as the uniquely likely source. This association between individual speakers and particular patterns of variant use and variant preference makes any invocation of the concept of "free variation" inap-propriate. Though the variant choices are not in most cases influenced by any syntactic constraints (despite a few exceptions such as E27's apparent preference for monosyllabic variants of ('when') when a form of the verb 'to be' followed; see chapter 5, §11.3.1), they are also not random. Instead they are probabilistically related to the usage of individual speakers.

This individual patterning of variant selections in a speaker's use of variable elements in discourse is of course my reason for adopting the terminology *person-ally patterned variation* (*personal-pattern variation*), for this phenomenon. In the small, remarkably homogeneous, deeply interrelated fisherfolk communities, it was the individual speaker who adopted and deployed a distinctive selection of variants in characteristic fashion. The use of Gaelic rather than English distin-guished each fishing community as a collective social body, and the use of a dis-tinctive set of local forms marked out each community as opposed to each of the others; but within each community patterns of variant selection that could easily have developed into a means of distinguishing one family, one kin group, one peer group, or one social network from another did not do so. As chapter 6 demon-strated, some sibling pairs showed variant-use patterns that agreed at a better than 50 percent level whereas other such pairs did not, and one identifiable Embo peer group agreed as a group in only a few of the eighteen cases followed there. Within the village individuals went their own way, each speaker using a unique mix of variants at levels peculiar to her-or himself.

Coupland, writing about the handling of style in sociolinguistics, calls attention to the inappropriateness of attempting to study style via social aggregates. He acknowledges that following individual speech patterns will not suffice when the goal is to reveal social stratification by class, gender, or age, since the patterns of greatest significance operate beyond the scope of the individual case. But he points out that the situation is different in the case of style (Coupland 2001:191–92):

> When it comes to the analysis of style, we see individuals interacting within their own space, time, and relational context. We can of course seek to generalize about "what most people stylistically do", and the results are informative and important. But this exercise is reductionist in that it rules out any possible interpretation of the local intra-and inter-personal processes which are style's domain... The basic problematic of style... is inherently established at a local level which makes aggregation inappropriate.

The personal-pattern variation of East Sutherland fisherfolk Gaelic does not constitute style as it is usually conceived of in linguistic studies, since style in the more usual sense implies speech choices that have a common interpretation for the community of speakers as a whole. Repeated avoidance of contraction on the part of an English speaker would convey a sense of formality in communities where English is spoken natively, for example, as would repeated use of genitive case marking (as opposed to various dative constructions with or without preposition) on the part of a German speaker in communities where German is spoken natively. Personal-pattern variation differs from such cases in that repeated use of a particular variant could not be counted on to convey a stylistic message with a common, community-wide interpretation for Embo Gaelic speakers.

The shifting forms of ('when') in the usage of E10 (Duncan) are a good case in point. Duncan's preference for /nu(ə)rə/ in proverb recitation took on stylistic significance in his usage, since it contrasted with his preference otherwise for /tə/. It cannot be assumed, however, that /nu(ə)rə/ had any fixed stylistic significance for all Embo speakers. Quite a few speakers never used the variant /nu(ə)rə/ at all, and some used it more routinely than E10. Some used it just occasionally, without any obvious change in speech genre, degree of formality, or change of topic or mood as a motivating factor. No one else reproduced E10's variant choices in proverbs. E4, who overwhelmingly favored the variant /tə/ for ('when')—the same variant E10 preferred when not reciting proverbs—shifted not to /nu(ə)rə/ in the one proverb he provided that included ('when') but to /tərə/. E17, who also favored /tə/ conversationally (though less overwhelmingly than E4), made a shift almost as pronounced as Duncan's in reciting proverbs, but in her case it involved not /nu(ə)rə/ but an almost exclusive use of /tənə/. E40, whose ordinary variant for ('when') was also /tə/, made a shift in speaking to a radio broadcaster, but likewise to /tənə/ rather than /nu(ə)rə/. On the basis of shifts such as these in variant selection, one might come to believe that disyllabicity as opposed to monosyllabicity conveys some sense of increased formality; but even that general supposition is weakened by the absence of co-occurrence patterns that oppose paired use of disyllabic variants of ('when') and ('came')/('saw') to paired use of monosyllabic variants of the same variables, by absence of any clear-cut stylistic shift between disyllabic and monosyllabic variants across story-telling styles and in interaction with both familiar and unfamiliar interlocutors on the part of the E17, and by lack of evidence for any formality factor that might motivate the alternation between disyllabic and monosyllabic variants in the usage of E30, for whom ('when') is an especially high-variation variable.

Owens (1999) makes a valiant attempt to fit the linguistic variation characteristic of Embo Gaelic, as described in Dorian (1994b), into a comprehensive characterization of speech communities and the variation found within them. He applies the label "unordered uniform variation" to the personal-pattern variation discussed in that paper and describes this as variation that is "uniform throughout, but unordered relative to social categories" such as age, sex, kin-based social networks, and different linguistic styles (Owens 1999:666). The second part of his description is accurate, but the first is not. Speakers had their own patterns of variant preference, and variant use was predictable in a probabilistic sense though not in an absolute sense. It was imaginable, for example, that E37 (Rory) might use the variant /stɛ/ for ('in') at some point, even though his preferred variant (invariant in the materials available for this study) was /sčax/, but not that he would go over entirely to /stɛ/ within a stretch of speech. It was far from inconceivable that high-variation speaker E27 (Murdo) might produce an instance of /stɛx/ at some point, but it was not conceivable that he would use more /stɛx/ than /sčax/ in an extended stretch of speech. It is unworkable, therefore, to describe Embo's personal-pattern variation as an "unordered uniform variation" in which "[two variants] A and B are equally distributed among all groups", as Owens does (1999:668). All Gaelic-speaking Embo constituted one group in terms of the universal presence of personal-pattern variation as well as in terms of class and ethnicity, but the variants of each variable show distinctly unequal distribution across the members of that group, appearing in greater or lesser numbers (or not appearing at all) on an individual basis.

9 HOW IS PERSONALLY PATTERNED VARIATION TRANSMITTED?

The final very basic question in connection with the socially neutral idiosyncratic variation so prominent in Embo Gaelic is a "how" question: how does a set of siblings develop speech patterns that leave some of them favoring one variant and others a different variant for a variable that all of them frequently use? Early in my investigation of personally patterned variation, I imagined that if I had only been able to investigate the speech patterns of *both* parents fully I might have been able to see how each of the children in a set of siblings came by their particular patterns of variant use. But this was highly unrealistic (not to say wishful) thinking. The variant-use patterns of parents whom I did not have the chance to record or test would undoubtedly have been just as diverse as those of the few parents whose usage I did have the chance to explore, and the process by which children came to adopt one particular variant or set of variants from among the many to which they were exposed would still have remained mysterious.

The most suggestive hint of a solution to this problem comes from the findings of Alison Henry and her collaborators, working with children in Belfast, Northern Ireland (Henry et al. 1998). As in Embo, the input to which the children were exposed was highly variable. The Belfast researchers looked into the acquisition of a local syntactic feature known as "singular concord", which allows optional subject–verb agreement if the subject is a full noun phrase rather than a pronoun, so that both 'the kids is out late' and 'the kids are out late' occur. They found that children in the two-to four-year-old age range were acquiring variable use of singular concord, their own usage reflecting the proportion in which variants occurred in the input that the children received, and that even low-frequency variants were acquired (Henry 2002:277– 80).

Input sources for Embo children went well beyond those of the two most commonly invoked major influences in variationist linguistics, the parents and the peer group. Caregivers for fisherfolk children were necessarily more routinely various than has been typical in industrialized Western societies. With fathers and sometimes also mothers away for extended periods during the herring fishing season, and fathers out fishing and mothers out all day marketing fish during the line-fishing season, younger children were more often than not under the care of an oldest sister (and often two older sisters in succession, as the original oldest went away to work or moved out of the home to marry). Grandmothers and great-aunts were also important stand-in caregivers for children. The peer group, too, was larger and more various than those of contemporary urban societies, comprising all the children, male and female, within several years of one another in age. At no point in a child's life could there have been only two parents or a few same-age friends providing the bulk of the input for language acquisition. Instead, the child must have been exposed from the start to a generous sample of the variation typical of Embo fisherfolk Gaelic. Most likely the particular mix and proportion of variants that each child was exposed to early in life was unique, depending on the child's own emotional ties with and degree of interaction with parents, older siblings, grandparents, great-aunts and -uncles, siblings of the parents, and older cousins. Because the peer group was relatively large and diverse, and because each child came to the peer group with the same sort of varying exposure to a variety of kin-group caretakers, the peer group was without question a less potent linguistic influence in Embo than it has been in urban and suburban settings where peer-group members are typically of the same sex and are also more often than not confined to the age range of a single school class. Under these circumstances it might have been more surprising to find that Embo children did *not* acquire a wide range of variants, occurring in proportions peculiar to each child, than to find that they did. In the absence of accommodation, community-external norms, and hence also dialect leveling, the persistence of personal-pattern variation in Embo Gaelic was perfectly in line with local social realities.

Conclusion

1 INTRODUCTION

Each time researchers have engaged with a distinctive type of social setting, new findings with respect to variation in speech have emerged. Labov's trail-blazing work in New York City identified one type of social setting quite widespread in the contemporary world, a socioeconomically stratified society oriented to a standard-language norm, as demonstrated by the consistent direction of style-shifting and subjective-evaluation responses (Labov 1966). The Milroys' work in Belfast, Northern Ireland, identified a working-class community in which dense, multiplex social network structures operated powerfully to maintain distinctively local, non-standard speech forms, despite the seemingly irresistible pressures exerted by the standard language (Milroy and Milroy 1978; Milroy 1987a). Le Page and Tabouret-Keller (1985), working in a Caribbean setting, faced such multiethnic complexity that they recognized not speech communities with boundaries aligned with one or more prestige norms, but innumerable individual "acts of identity" representing a multiplicity of overlapping social orientations with highly fluid boundaries.

Embo represents yet another kind of social setting, distinct from any of these. Instead of the socioeconomic complexities of New York City or Belfast, there was at the start of the twentieth century great socioeconomic homogeneity: essentially a single occupation, a single income level, and a single educational level. The community lacked an effective external norm in terms of which local speakers might orient or evaluate their own speech, since the only higher-prestige forms of

Gaelic available as potential models were too alien to serve as reference points for speakers of the local dialect. Instead of the complex ethnic identities of the Caribbean, with their corresponding linguistic complexity, Gaelic-speaking Embo consisted of a single sharply bounded ethnic group, the Embo *maraichean*, all of whom spoke a single dialect, Embo fisherfolk Gaelic. Not surprisingly, then, the profile of linguistic variation in Embo when the present study began in the latter half of the twentieth century was also distinctive as compared with the profiles of variation in these other already well-studied settings. Variation correlated with class and ethnic groupings was absent, since class and ethnic differences themselves were absent, but variation deriving from early dialect mixture throve on the individual level, manifested in many co-existing and socially neutral variants. With Gaelic no longer transmitted and its use receding, an age- and proficiency-related variation reflecting gradual obsolescence had become apparent among the remaining speakers. Obsolescence was not a major factor in the personal-pattern variation treated here, however, its limited influence appearing chiefly in the rising incidence of a few analogical variants; nor did bilingualism in English produce any of the variants that appeared in personal-pattern variation.

2 CONTRARY TO EXPECTATIONS: PERSONALLY PATTERNED VARIATION IN EMBO GAELIC

A number of aspects of the personal-pattern variation so prevalent in Embo Gaelic run counter to general expectations expressed in the sociolinguistic literature. The most striking of them are reviewed here.

2.1 Rampant Inter-Speaker and Intra-Speaker Variation in a Small, Densely Interactive, and Socially Homogeneous Community

Possibly most striking among contrary-seeming findings in connection with Embo personal-pattern variation was simply the fact that there was so much of it in a very small, very homogeneous, face-to-face community. The expectation seems generally to have been that the level of variation would be lower in such communities, as the comments of researchers across three decades indicate (see Haas 1982:20 in addition to the quotations from Sankoff 1974 and Milroy 1992 cited in chapter 1, §§7.4 and 7.5). This notion was reinforced by the Milroys' findings in Belfast, where regularity in the patterning of variable elements proved to be greater in the relatively focused community of Ballymacarrett than in less focused Belfast communities (see Milroy 1987a, in addition to Milroy 1992:90).

The expectation of lesser variation with greater social focusing was not fulfilled in Embo, however. In social terms it would be hard to imagine a much more focused community than Embo, yet Embo Gaelic showed remarkable linguistic diffusion. Common occupation, comparable socioeconomic status, multiplex social roles, dense kinship ties, and enclavement did not eliminate inter-speaker or intra-speaker variation, which were instead conspicuously prevalent. It would seem that there is more, not less, latitude for variation when a single ethnic group at a single socioeconomic level makes up the speech community.

2.2 Ongoing Maintenance of High Variation Levels

By apparent-time evidence, the personally patterned variation characteristic of Embo Gaelic was not showing the "reduction of variants accompanying focusing" anticipated in Trudgill's model (Trudgill 1999:197; see chapter 8, §3.3.1) and documented for one of Britain's new towns by Kerswill and Williams (2000). This reflects not only the absence of an effective and accessible community-external model for Embo Gaelic speakers but also the fact that linguistic accommodation in Embo and the other fisherfolk communities involved not inter-speaker and intra-speaker variation, whether age-related or personally patterned, but language choice (Gaelic or English) and village-appropriate choices where geographically distinctive forms were concerned. The truly vast body of social knowledge shared by birthright community members worked against any role for accommodation in terms of strictly local forms, just as did the absence of any linkage between local variants and social stratification.

2.3 Non-participation of Personal-Pattern Variables in Marking Group Membership

The very prevalence of personally patterned variation makes its absence in social boundary marking another instance of an unexpected finding. According to Chambers (2002:349), "The essential function of linguistic variables is to mark group membership." But in Embo village Gaelic-speaking households did not reliably share variant preferences, nor did Gaelic-speaking sibling sets, nor (at least in the one case available) did peer-group networks. Sources also denied any possibility that residence in one street as opposed to another produced shared variant preferences (Dorian 1994b:681).

Personal-pattern variation was an extremely conspicuous phenomenon in Embo Gaelic, and in the light of variationist studies the sheer presence of so much variability raises an expectation of some correlation between all that variation and locally identifiable social groups. But lack of a social boundary-marking function for personally patterned variation confounds such expectations: as far as the available materials can demonstrate, this sort of variation does not have any regular correlation with social groups internal to the community.

2.4 The Social Neutrality of Variants

The last-mentioned feature of personal-pattern variation underlies this one. On the evidence of Gaelic dialect geography and surnames, the variants of most Embo personal-pattern variables arose from early dialect mixture. The fact that they did not acquire social weighting over time arises from the classless, single-occupation social environment of Gaelic-speaking Embo and the absence of groups who differed by their position in a social hierarchy. In a context where variants are not systematically related to the social positions of their users, social significance need not attach to their use.

2.5 Low Awareness of Acoustically Salient Variation

Perhaps also related to the absence of any correlation between social position and use of particular variants is the apparent weakness of phonological salience as a factor in awareness of within-the-community variation. Trudgill (1986:11) suggested that degree of phonetic difference and the presence of change in progress might contribute to speakers' awareness of some variables as opposed to others, but there was very little indication of this in Embo. Compared to the rather small differences in vowel quality that have often been found to carry socially significant weighting in English, phonological differences between the variants of personally patterned Embo variables seem large and obvious. Yet the more substantial phonetic differences between variants of ('family') (initial aspirated stop versus aspirated affricate, final back vowel and voiceless velar fricative versus final front vowel and voiceless palatal fricative) did not seem to make speakers any more aware of variation than the smaller phonetic difference between the variants of ('out') did (presence or absence of final voiceless palatal fricative). Only in the case of a variable with variants formed on entirely different roots, ('would go'), was there any indication of speaker awareness of variation, and at that it was slight: two individuals volunteered the information, on one occasion in each case, that some speakers used a variant other than the one they had just used; but each mentioned only one additional variant out of the three others actually in use (chapter 5, §7.1.2).

Any awareness of flux that might have arisen from use of the local vernacular in writing was of course ruled out by the purely oral use of Embo Gaelic. This was as true of age-related change in progress as of more stable personal-pattern variation: even an age-related change as dramatic and rapid as the change-over from a synthetic first-person singular conditional suffix /-ĩn'/ to an analytic construction using suffix /-u/ + free-standing pronoun /mi/, apparently complete within less than thirty years (see table 3.1), went entirely unmentioned by Embo speakers and produced no apparent self-consciousness among them.

3 REMAINING QUESTIONS

Embo's personal-pattern variation raises a number of provocative questions about generally accepted notions and practices: about the realism of uniform descriptive accounts of languages, for example; about the greater regularity of the speech of the community as opposed to that of the individual; about structured heterogeneity; about the place of the individual in linguistic analysis; about field techniques. While it would be premature to try to resolve such questions on the basis of the highly suggestive but incomplete data from Embo Gaelic, it is not premature to initiate discussion about them.

3.1 Are Largely Uniform Descriptive Accounts Justified?

A number of linguists have suggested that our views of language are constrained by our own life experience and our preference for homogeneous language descriptions. Le Page, for example, observes (1994:115): "Linguistic systems are in the mind of the beholder—both as speaker-listener and as descriptive and as theoretical linguists. Strenuous efforts are made by each to assert the integrity and the homogeneity of systems in terms of conventional grammars." James Milroy agrees that linguists are overly inclined to expect homogeneity and invariance, attributing this inclination to the effect of a standard-language background on linguists' conceptions of language, in particular their belief that a standard form exists "in some abstract dimension" (1999:17). Woolard (1998:26) sees covert influence from prescriptivism as a determinant of what late twentieth-century linguistics chose to focus on. Gal, reviewing Collins's lack of success in persuading elderly Tolowa speakers to confirm his judgment that certain textbook Tolowa forms were incorrect, comments (1998:327): "While Athabaskanist linguists argue about who speaks 'real Tolowa', Tolowa speakers themselves resist this implicitly standardizing position, conceiving of Tolowa as the resource of extended kinship groupings. They question the effort to have a general linguistic description for the entire valley, let alone all possible speakers."

People may differ significantly, it seems, in the degree to which they have, or recognize, any canonical form or status for their language. Elderly Tolowa speakers rejected anything more than a kin-based and local model of Tolowa usage, and apparently speakers in a given community may not so much as recognize that they speak any language in particular (see the quotes from Grace and Heryanto in chapter 8, §7.1). Accordingly, James Milroy suggests that "different methods and different underlying assumptions about the concept of 'a language'" may be needed for the study of variation in language communities that are without standardization of the native language (1999:36).

I have noted previously (chapter 1, §7.3) that prevailing descriptive-linguistic frameworks accommodate the differences between Golspie Gaelic and Embo

Gaelic more comfortably than they accommodate differences within Embo Gaelic, even though a few of the latter are just as great as (and quite similar to) some of the former. That is, general acceptance of geographically based distinctiveness allows for ready recognition of differences between the Gaelic of two different villages, but the convention of presenting a uniform description of a single community's language variety renders it uncomfortable to find oneself obliged to present variant forms for a Brora conjunction or an Embo conjugational paradigm, as I did in my 1978 description of East Sutherland fisherfolk Gaelic. Ó Dochartaigh's assumption, in reviewing that study, that obsolescence must account for the lack of a single Brora conjunctional form and a uniform Embo prepositional paradigm indicates that it is equally uncomfortable for readers to accept a non-uniform description, at least for fully fluent speakers.

Although the force of standardizing tradition in grammar-writing and dictionary-making is strong, what might be dubbed "the Tolowa position" has begun to receive some consideration from lexicographers. Dealing with small languages characterized by a good deal of individual variation, some lexicographers are acknowledging the validity of co-existing forms. In preparing a dictionary of North Slavey, an Athabaskan language of Canada, linguist Keren Rice and the North Slavey standardization committee did not doubt the need for a phonemically based, one symbol–one sound alphabet, but in view of the level of individual variation found in North Slavey, they did depart from the Western dictionary model that demanded a single standard spelling for every word (Rice and Saxon 2002:150–51). Comparing the resultant, more multivocal outcome with traditional Euro-American dictionaries, they offer the following comment (Rice and Saxon 2002:153):

> Variations in spelling are a reflection of variations in language, a fact of any language whatsoever. Rather than see dictionaries of First Nations languages as deficient in being unable to reach standardization in spelling, we might view many Western dictionaries as deficient in not recognizing the full range of pronunciations that a word can have but hiding them with a common spelling.

In a similar spirit I cannot envisage a conscientiously compiled dictionary of Embo Gaelic that did not include co-valid entries of, say, /maːrax/ and /maːriç/ for 'tomorrow', of /nʼĩmərd/ and /ĩmərd/ for 'needing', and of all five variants of adverbial 'in'.

3.2 Is the Linguistic System of the Community More Regular than That of the Individual?

One of the most striking facets of Labov's Lower East Side study in New York City was the uncovering of an underlying order in what had appeared to be linguistic disorder. Looking at phonological features in relation to the class membership of the speaker and in relation to style shifting and subjective evaluations of phonological variables, he was able to show that the speech community was much more unitary than it had appeared: "In this particular community, New York City, the system of the individual speaker appears to be less coherent than that of the speech community as a whole" (1966:v). Community members may have produced different realizations of certain speech sounds, but they shared a common sense of what those speech sounds represented, as they demonstrated by the common direction of their style shifting and by their general agreement in subjective-reaction-test responses on the social value of certain phonological realizations as opposed to others. One of the recurrent themes of the study, according to Labov, was "that the speech community as a whole is unified by a common set of norms" that are "best exemplified by speakers with middle class orientation" (1966:412).

Since there was surprisingly little phonological variation apparent in Embo Gaelic, and what did appear was entirely age-related, the abundant phonological variation in well-studied urban centers such as New York, Montreal, and Norwich and the equally abundant variation appearing in the phonological shape of morphemes in Embo Gaelic make a less than perfect comparison. Within the East Sutherland setting, however, we can still ask whether the community as a whole presents a linguistic system offering greater coherence than that of the individual speaker.

In the East Sutherland setting the most profound social division was the binary division between *maraichean* and *tuathanaich*, reflected linguistically in continuing use of Gaelic as opposed to exclusive use of English. Within Embo village itself, near-uniform social and economic conditions offered little scope for social distinctions in the late nineteenth and early twentieth centuries, when most of the Gaelic speakers who served as sources for this study were children or young adults. There were no better-off or better-educated groups whose usage might have attracted emulation, and as we have seen, the large age range encompassed by siblings sets, together with diffuse responsibility for child-rearing and the relatively generous social scope of peer groups, did not encourage the development of variant-use patterns associated with social groups. Whereas changes in progress showed the usual correlation with age (and in this receding speech form also with proficiency), personally patterned variation did not do so at all routinely, nor did it correlate reliably with the sex of the speaker. It was possible, accordingly, for female semi-speakers like E39 and E40 to share a variant preference with E4, a male more than forty years their senior, as the former did in the case of ('in') and the latter did in the case of ('when').

The usages reviewed in §11 of chapter 5 indicated that where variables had longer and fuller forms as well as shorter and less full forms, the former might show some association with relative formality and the latter with greater casualness or ease—but not for all speakers, not for all such variant pairs (or sets), and not for all potentially relevant genres. Patterns that might indicate style shifting in one speaker's variant usage did not hold for the speaker sample as a whole, or even for recurrent subgroups within the sample. Patterns that might indicate an effect of the speaker's sex are likewise incomplete rather than general, and even sharing both the same age and the same proficiency level did not ensure that speakers would share variant-use patterns. Precisely for the reason that it does not yield convincing whole-group patterns, the idiosyncratic inter-speaker and intra-speaker variation so prevalent in Embo Gaelic merits the appellation *personally patterned variation*.

3.3 What of "Structured Heterogeneity" and Implications for Language Change?

In chapters 1 and 3, a distinction was made between age-related variation and personal-pattern variation. Age-related variation embodies change in progress, evident in differences between the forms and structures used by the oldest speakers and the forms and structures used by their juniors. The variants of a personally patterned variable may also show some degree of change according to age, as in the cases of ('family') and ('wasn't/weren't'), but the change patterns are neither as rapid nor as convincingly unidirectional as those of age-related variation (see tables 3.2, 3.3, and 3.4).

While heterogeneity is the hallmark of personally patterned variation, that heterogeneity is clearly less structured, and less directly related to change processes, than the class-, style-, and ethnicity-related phonological variation that has been intensively studied by variationists. This does not necessarily mean, however, that it provides no basis for language change. The presence of any coexisting variants at all offers the potential for change, since the number of people using a particular variant can always increase to the point where consolidation of one variant and elimination of another takes place. Some variants of certain personally patterned variables did show apparent tendencies toward change (as with increasing /čɛ/ and declining /yɛ/ for ('from, off, of'), for example, and the analogically regularized variants increasingly used by younger speakers), indicating that this kind of variation is not entirely immune to change processes under conditions of language shift.

Developments in the London-Embo group suggest that some change processes not directly related to language shift may have begun within the exile group living in London and vicinity. Chapter 5, §14.1.3, noted that the level of agreement on variant preferences was unusually high among members of this group (apart from the poorly represented E21L), though the number of variables for which evidence was available was small. All members of the London-Embo group were fully fluent, except for semi-speaker E42L, and all maintained an extremely strong connection to Embo. Most returned to the village at least annually for their summer vacations, while their most significant social interaction from week to week was with one another. They remained oriented to home-village people and events to an extraordinary degree. Contacts with English-monolingual workmates and neighbors were weak and superficial by comparison with their involvement with one another, which was profound. They were connected by kinship ties of varying degrees, as were many groups of people within the home community, but in the London environment both kinship and social-interaction ties were intensified by the emigrants' common origin and shared exile.

In Embo itself the level of agreement on variant preferences among household members and sibling sets was various, relatively strong for certain pairs of speakers but not for others, and it was strong across the complete household or sibling set for only a modest number of variants. Agreement levels among the London-Embo group, so far as they could be discerned, were unusually high by comparison with Embo-village agreement levels; this suggests that fragmentation of the Embo population along residential or social lines had the potential to follow this apparent line of development in the home village, too, creating incipient subgroups with variant preferences shared among themselves. Such a development could eventually lead to distinctive group-wide variant-use patterns and to the emergence of variant use as a marker of social groups after all. The fact that the speech form has meantime all but passed out of existence makes this possibility moot, of course, and apart from E42L there was also no descendant generation of Embo-born Londoners whose usage could be monitored for further signs of a distinctively London-Embo variant consensus.

3.4 Is There a Place for the Individual in Linguistic Analysis?

Some linguists take a strong position on the exclusion of individual grammatical and phonological patterns from consideration in linguistic analysis, as in the following (Labov 2001:34):

> Linguistic analysis cannot recognize individual grammars or phonologies. Individual rules or constraints would have no interpretation and contribute nothing to acts of communication. In this sense, the individual does not exist as a linguistic object. However, each individual shows a personal profile of the comparative use of resources made available by the speech community.... All sociolinguists agree that the productions and interpretations of the individual speaker are the primary site for linguistic investigation. The position of this study is that these individuals are not the final units of linguistic analysis, but the components that are used to construct models of our primary object of interest, the speech community.

This position has increasingly been challenged, however, with a number of researchers reconsidering the importance of the individual as cogently urged by Hymes (1979:36). Wong Fillmore, in the same volume in which Hymes made his case for consideration of the individual (Wong Fillmore 1979:205), pointed out that researchers in pursuit of universal features of language acquisition processes never raised or discussed the question of individual variation in childhood second language acquisition, even though children in the process of acquiring a second language could readily be seen to show considerable variation as to the rate and ease of acquisition and ability to use the second language. Johnstone (1996, 2000), like Le Page and Tabouret-Keller (1985), recognizes individual and therefore idiosyncratic features of language use; she considers language "fundamentally the property of the individual", asserting bluntly that "people have different grammars" (2000:410, 411). Schilling-Estes (1998), like Fasold et al. (1975), considers that individual notions of identity and community membership can produce individually distinct language use; and Wolfram and Beckett's research in a long-established co-resident population of European Americans and African Americans, historically and geographically isolated among the swampy wetlands of coastal North Carolina, establishes that "some variation is a function more of personal history, interactional relations, and attitudes and values than of conventional social divisions or even constructed social identities" (2000:27).

Based on their own research and a review of the literature on variation, Wolfram and Beckett take a strong position that can serve as a counterpoise to Labov's position quoted above (Wolfram and Beckett 2000:28):

> Descriptions that ignore the individual—theoretically, descriptively, and methodologically—cannot provide an adequate explanation of synchronic and diachronic sociolinguistic variation. The recognition of individual variation does not . . . negate the extensive patterning of linguistic variation in terms of group affiliations and social boundaries—in small rural insular as well as in large urban settings. Obviously, a range of social factors, including social boundaries of various types and varied interactional relationships, correlate with some of the linguistic variation. However, even when the group is broken down into smaller subgroupings based on different permutations of demographic, sociocultural, and sociopsychological factors, individual dimensions of variation remain. Speakers are both individuals with idiosyncratic life histories and affiliated members of a complex array of social groups.

Focus on the group (notwithstanding increasing attention to particular group members who act as leaders in linguistic change in recent variationist work [Labov 2001:323–411]) is anchored in the Saussurean distinction between *langue* and *parole*. The former is, as Johnstone points out (1996:11), "by definition superindividual and self-replicating . . . the property of the community, not the individual". The latter has been viewed as too disorganized or too ephemeral to constitute the object of linguistic study—or more particularly of linguistic "science." Science, after all, abstracts from the individual case to the general case; the individual case is taken to be of interest chiefly as a signpost to a larger significance that may lie in repeated (and repeatable) cases. Disciplines seeking the intellectual respectability of science have an understandable but perhaps undue inclination to eliminate consideration of the individual (who may after all prove to be a deviant or otherwise atypical case) and concentrate on the group. Making a distinction between "user-centered" versus "language-centered" linguistic theories, Simone notes that user-centered theories have been considered too informal and too much focused on individual variation, while language-centered theories have been favored for their use of formalisms, a presumed marker of rigor, and for a recognition of inter-individual regularities: "The main inconvenience with the user is that he intrudes a typical factor of disturbance, from which theoretical linguistics has always striven to stay off—variation" (1995:234).

But as Wolfram and Beckett demonstrate in their study, the individual cannot be ignored in language data without distorting the result. The contemporary disregard of the individual in linguistics, whether by discounting discrepant data or by routinely subsuming the individual within the group, risks a distortion akin to that produced by the editors who discounted the variation in Middle English texts by declaring it to be the product of Anglo-Norman scribes. Invariance is certainly far less common than theorists might wish, and as Johnstone notes, fieldworkers confronted with the idiosyncratic data produced by their native-speaker sources can be led to "wonder in what sense an individual speaker can embody a language or represent its other speakers" (2000:410). Just as syntacticians acknowledge in private conversations, if less often in print, that their sources do not reliably agree on grammaticality judgments, so, too, some fieldworkers acknowledge when questioned directly that their sources do not reliably provide identical grammatical patterns, even if they are seldom as open as Foley (chapter 1, §7) and Rice (chapter 8, §5) have been about the prevalence of variation.

Simone's "factor of disturbance" was high in Embo fisherfolk Gaelic. Even speakers at the same general age-and-proficiency level did not necessarily produce uniform paradigms for some of the conjugating prepositions, for example, as the paradigms for 'through' and '(away) from' provided in Dorian (1978) demonstrate. As chapter 5 indicated, the individuals who produced historically oblique forms as citation forms of ('family') did not necessarily do so for ('tomorrow') or ('old lady'), and speakers who favored the lenited variant of ('that') might or might not also favor the lenited variants of ('this') and affirming ('is/ are'). Chapter 3 offered evidence that speakers might shift from one variant to another in rapid succession without a change in setting, interlocutor, topic, or affect, as E22 (Elspeth) did in her use of ('that') when summing up her account of each childhood game and as E30 (Derrick) did in his use of ('when') in conversation with E27 (Murdo) and E34 (Lexie). Failing to acknowledge this lack of consensus and uniformity in Embo Gaelic would also be to fail to understand the social structure of the Embo speech community and its implications for language use, a considerably more serious shortcoming than simply not recording the full range of variant forms.

4 METHODOLOGICAL IMPLICATIONS OF EMBO PERSONAL-PATTERN VARIATION

Once it is clear from a consideration of the Embo personal-pattern data just how prevalent idiosyncratic inter-speaker and intra-speaker variation can be in a community that offers the requisite extra-linguistic conditions, it seems equally clear that field practices need to be modified or adapted to allow for this possibility. Some examples follow.

4.1 Beginning with the Variants or Beginning with the Group That Uses Them

Winter (1999:69) points out with regard to methodological approaches to variation that it is theoretically possible for linguists to take either of two routes in studying living languages. They may either begin with linguistic variants and determine what group uses them, or they may identify a group defined by nonlinguistic criteria and look for the linguistic usages of that group. The Embo findings demonstrate that there are communities in which only the latter approach would be productive, since in such settings groupings by common use of variants would be very large in number and more or less unique in each case, as demonstrated for Embo by tables 5.7 and 5.15. In the stratified New York City setting with its overarching standard-language reference point, natives of the Lower East Side showed similar patterns of phonological variation, by social class and by style, for the variants (th) and (dh) (Labov 1966:244–53). In Embo, where the native Gaelic-speaking population constitutes what amounts to one undifferentiated social class, individuals who produced monosyllabic variants of ('came') could not be counted on to produce monosyllabic variants of ('saw'), nor, as noted in §3.4, could individuals who favored the lenited variant /hə̃n/ for ('that') be counted on to favor the lenited variant /hɔ/ for ('this'), even though these two instances of variation involve quasi-phonological distinctions. Still less could one predict that someone who favored /raxu/ for ('would go') would also favor /ĩmərd/ for ('needing'), and so forth.

4.2 Implications for Dialect Geography

The East Sutherland findings also demonstrate that a large-scale dialect survey such as the Linguistic Survey of Scotland can fall short of its goals if the existence of high-variation communities like Brora, Golspie, and Embo is not recognized and taken into consideration in carrying out the basic questionnairing. The Gaelic Division of the Linguistic Survey of Scotland had extremely limited objectives, by general descriptive standards. Its questionnaire was oriented above all to determining "the synchronic reflexes of the Common Gaelic phonological system" (Ó Dochartaigh 1997, vol. 1:54), but with only a single speaker each to represent Golspie and Embo, and insufficient avoidance of at least passive literacy on the part of male informants, the results of the Survey's work in the Gaelic-speaking fisherfolk villages of East Sutherland were sometimes compromised.

Kenneth Jackson, director of the Gaelic Survey, was concerned above all to secure purely local speakers as survey sources; if at all possible, speakers with a parent from some other location or with a non-local spouse were avoided (Jackson 1958:232, quoted in Ó Dochartaigh 1997, vol.1:80). Jackson's criticisms of an earlier Breton dialect survey indicate that he was well aware of the dangers of drawing responses from a single source by means of a single question (Jackson 1967, quoted in Ó Dochartaigh 1997, vol. 1:52), but in the face of the enormous

task the Gaelic dialect survey represented, he gave highest priority to the requirement of strictly local provenience. In Brora and Golspie the result was, in two
cases, a genuinely local man who sometimes offered non-local forms, as each
fieldworker duly noted. In the Brora case it was only one brother in a multisibling
household who offered non-local forms, with the other siblings acting as a corrective, and in addition the survey consulted a second Brora source; but non-
local forms did occasionally make their way into the record, as the case of one
Brora entry for *oirre* 'on her' demonstrates. In the Golspie case, Oftedal as a
Survey fieldworker noted that the literate male informant's wife "often reminded
him of a local word or local expression when he gave literary words" (Oftedal
field notation quoted in Ó Dochartaigh 1997, vol. 1:91), but he made no entries
for her usages, despite the fact that she was clearly an important corrective for
her husband.

In the Golspie Survey work, Oftedal thus followed his Leurbost working
principles, since in Leurbost, too, he noted that Roddy Martin's wife's Gaelic
differed from Roddy's in a number of respects but refrained from entering her
forms into the official record. This policy may have made his record of Leurbost
Gaelic incomplete, but since Roddy Martin was an excellent source and Oftedal
an excellent linguist, the resulting treatment remains outstanding, even though
for a linguist interested in the latitude for individual variation the data that got
away will always be tantalizing. The consequences are more unfortunate in connection with the survey entries for Golspie. The fact that the literate Golspie
source was inclined to give non-local responses resulted in numerous distortions in what is likely to be the most frequently consulted lexico-phonological
record of Golspie Gaelic, a problem made worse by Oftedal's tendency to
prompt his sources heavily.[1] In addition, because of reliance on a single source
in Golspie and Embo, there is simply no way of knowing from the Survey volumes that certain items might take more than one form in the fisherfolk villages,
although this would presumably have been particularly important and interesting information in terms of diachronic phonological development.[2] In view of
what Oftedal reported from Leurbost—a wife whose Gaelic differed from her
husband's despite her having been his childhood next-door neighbor, a village
with dialect differentiation across its two-mile length—it seems probable that
the variation characteristic of Embo, Golspie, and Brora was not unique in
Highland Scotland, in type at any rate, if not in extent. Recognizing the existence of communities of the Embo sort (face-to-face, socioeconomically highly
homogeneous, with the local form of the minority language excluded from written use and with weak or absent extra-community norms), and taking steps to
acknowledge the latitude for individual variation that such communities allow,
would improve the likelihood that a dialect geographical survey would capture
the actualities of local speech forms. Essential precautions would include drawing on more than one source, drawing on female sources in rural communities
where males have greater experience with outsiders and are more likely to be
somewhat literate, and reducing or avoiding prompts with literate or passively
literate sources.

4.3 Selection of Sources and Inclusion or Exclusion of Data

Paradoxically, it seems that variant use may be less predictable rather than more so when neither the constraints of ethnic and social class distinctions nor the constraints of literacy and schooling are present within a small, face-to-face community. This is all the more true if child-rearing is not the exclusive province of the parents and peer groups are relatively inclusive in terms of children's age and sex. It might easily be supposed that in the absence of differences in ethnicity, occupation, income, and educational level, the researcher in Gaelic-speaking Embo could make do with a smaller speaker sample than the urban variationist, but exactly the opposite is the case. Since it is impossible to predict the degree to which diverse usage will appear in a minority-language community where standardization and literacy are absent (though a prediction that a good deal of diversity will appear seems safe enough), it behooves us to draw on a number of sources, even when one particular source is outstandingly gifted at the language consultant's work, and to aim at relatively multifaceted and well-contextualized documentation, as is increasingly advocated currently (see the papers in Austin 2003) rather than settling for more limited grammatical description.

A major question raised by linguistic research in the Gaelic-speaking East Sutherland communities is whether any field data at all should be discounted—set aside as too unimportant or aberrant to merit further inquiry or entry into the record. I offer three encounters with East Sutherland fisherfolk Gaelic, the outcomes of which suggest that it is wisest to set little or nothing aside. The first demonstrates the value of imperfect speakers, the second the importance of illiterate or otherwise naïve sources, and the third the value of divergent sources.

1. During my first year of fieldwork in East Sutherland I was directed to the speaker coded in this study as B10, who was well recognized as a member of the residual fisherfolk community in that village and as having an interest in Gaelic. When her responses to translation tasks showed her to be an imperfect speaker, the established conventions of dialect geography required that I rule her out as a source and look for older and more fluent speakers instead. Yet B10 and her fellow semi-speakers were invaluable ultimately to establishing how East Sutherland Gaelic was changing in the process of obsolescence (e.g., which features of the language were remaining relatively intact and which were showing evidence of regularization, increasingly sporadic retention, or loss).

2. Oftedal, pursuing dialect geographical ends in Golspie five years before my arrival there, apparently asked no questions directly of his source's considerably younger wife (she was sixty, he seventy-five at the time), despite the fact that she took an active role in reminding her husband of local words and expressions. Women in the fishing communities were very seldom literate in Gaelic, and lack of Gaelic literacy would have made her a more reliably local source than her husband. Oftedal explicitly acknowledged her usefulness in checking her husband's tendency to supply non-local forms, but he allotted her no Golspie entries in the Linguistic Survey.

The number of non-local forms in the Golspie survey entries makes it quite evident that she did not succeed in recalling her husband to strictly local forms in every relevant case, and Oftedal's preferential treatment of the older husband's lexicon leaves Golspie village inaccurately represented, precisely in dialect-geographical terms, at a good many points in the Survey's official publication.

3. Providing a full and accurate record of East Sutherland Gaelic certainly proved more difficult than I could have anticipated at the time when I undertook to prepare a descriptive monograph on the fisherfolk dialect, since neither I nor in all likelihood anyone else could in the late 1970s have explained or interpreted the degree of individual variation that appeared in intra-village and intra-speaker usage. But faithfully recording that variation and including it in the monograph in question was the key to my eventual return to the perplexing issue of individual variation, since it was the inclusion of so much inter-speaker variation that prompted Ó Dochartaigh's reasonable yet incorrect assumption, when he reviewed the volume, that obsolescence accounted for the level of variation recorded.

In view of these outcomes in connection with one small dialect area it would seem wise, as a general principle, to make the linguistic scrapheap—the discard pile where we leave the findings that seem to have no clear-cut place in our analyses—as small as we can and to acknowledge untidy and unexplained findings when we encounter them. Other researchers may see significance where we do not, or at some later point we may see new significance ourselves.

5 SOCIAL STRUCTURE AND LINGUISTIC VARIATION

Labov's warning against extrapolating from contemporary societies with familiar social organization to societies with an entirely different social organization, quoted on the opening page of this study, is important, but it must be applied laterally, to contemporary populations, and not only, as in his suggestion, "backward in time" (Labov 1994:23). There was nothing to suggest, in the appearance of Embo or its inhabitants in 1963, that the village might present a distinctive social structure— one without the class stratification tacitly treated as a universal social feature by Labov, despite his recognition that stratification *systems* might be differently organized (2001:437)—and that its residents might be manifesting a kind of idiosyncratic linguistic variation that had not yet been adequately recognized or described. But despite the appearance of ordinariness, this was in fact the case: one form of variation characteristic of Embo Gaelic did not fall into generally recognized categories or patterns of linguistic variation. The importance of the Embo case lies not just in the fact that the village proved to have a lot of a form of variation generally absent from the sociolinguistic literature but also in the fact that it did *not* have the form of variation that generally *did* feature in the sociolinguistic literature—variation directly correlated with class, ethnicity, speaker's sex, and so forth. The absence of the one is as striking as the presence of the other.

I emphasize the apparent ordinariness of Embo village to make the point that what might be deemed "exotic" findings can appear in settings that do not appear the least bit exotic. If unexpected linguistic findings can emerge from a village in present-day Scotland, squarely within the industrialized Western world, it seems reasonable to suppose that there are other settings, some of them perhaps equally ordinary-seeming and some more obviously different from the settings most linguists are personally familiar with, that harbor equally unanticipated sociolinguistic phenomena. In chapter 8 I pointed to other language settings for which individual variation akin to that of Embo Gaelic had been described, offering a list of features that these settings seemed to have in common. Some of the social, social-historical, and sociolinguistic features characteristic of the relevant communities differ from those found in Embo, however, and the extent to which such features have an effect on the degree of variation and its character deserve further investigation: the multilingualism of the Cambap and Kven settings, the second-language use of Kven by other ethnic groups, the structural convergence deriving from centuries of intensive contact between two unstandardized language varieties in Karelia, the apparent family factor in Newfoundland Acadian French.

Still unexplored, so far as I am aware, is the scope for linguistic variation in societies with much more dramatically different social structures than any of these: the so-called family-level societies of the Siriono in the Bolivian rainforest and the Matsigenka in the Peruvian Andes, for example, or the almost family-less society (in Western terms) of the Kapsiki of Cameroon, among whom marriage is a short-term arrangement:

> The frequency with which [Kapsiki] women contract new marriages forces many fathers-in-law to refund the brideprice to a former son-in-law, thus increasing the tensions concerning mobile women. It should be readily apparent that marriage does not cement long-lasting relationships between clans. Kapsiki society is kept divided by the touring women. On the other hand, the sheer number of unions—especially the resulting children—unite the autonomous social units in some way. Of course this situation is not conducive to an intimate relationship between husband and wife. Friction, even antagonism, between the marriage partners is a standard feature of social life. (van Beek 1987:82)

The author of this study of the Kapsiki does not treat language at all, let alone linguistic variation, but the family is a highly unstable institution in Kapsiki society, with frequently changing adult female figures. The children remain behind when a mother passes on to another husband, and there are ultimately more half-siblings than full siblings. The father is a potentially stable source of linguistic socialization, but we have no information about whether the "touring women", most of whom remain only a year or two in the household, might serve as the introduction point for competing linguistic forms. The scope for linguistic variation in such societies remains to be investigated.

In family-level social organization the individual household is the basic social unit. Such peoples engage in no supra-family activities and typically live as dispersed households much of the year, aggregating on occasion around the harvest of a seasonally available food resource. Once doubted as a normal type of human social organization, the family-level social scale is now recognized on the basis of archaeological findings as well as ethnographic descriptions (Johnson 2003:2–3). Once again we know nothing of the scope for linguistic variation among such peoples. Johnson, who describes one such people minutely (2003), does not deal with language use. Still awaiting detailed investigation, too, is single-language variability in the smaller languages of profoundly multilingual areas where regular transmission of all the local languages continues uninterrupted, as reported by Blench (1998) for parts of Plateau State, Nigeria.

The fact that one sort of social organization is exceptionally well entrenched and widely distributed in regions of the world that are more likely than others to produce linguists cannot be taken to mean that that particular social organization and its linguistic effects are universal or that its historical depth is great. It seems clear that family-level social organization is older, and since examples survive in Africa (Lee 1979), North America (Steward 1955), and South America (Holmberg 1969; Johnson 2003), it seems equally clear that it was at one time very widely distributed.

Without a doubt there is still more to be learned about language use, including variation, in complex societies characterized by pronounced class and ethnic distinctions, but societies of this sort are still expanding and will be with us for the foreseeable future. For those interested in language use and language variation in societies with a different social organization, the horizon is narrower. There is limited time remaining within which researchers can expect to find traditionally organized societies showing relatively little disturbance from the increasingly urbanized outside world, societies still using an ancestral language in ways that bear some resemblance to the ancestral fashion. There are still too many linguists providing language descriptions without giving adequate information about societal structure or socially contextualized language use, and too many anthropologists describing societies without giving any information about language structure and language use. A more useful model arises from the studies of linguistic anthropologists who merge the approaches of both fields. Representatives of this blended field are among the researchers who have provided some particularly rich insights for this study, for example, Collins, Kroskrity, Gal, and Irvine.

Many years ago, in a brief review of my oral history of the East Sutherland fisherfolk (Dorian 1985), Dell Hymes took critical note of the total absence of references to my linguistic work in that ethnographic and folkloric work, commenting that the volume perpetuated the "long-standing distance between...linguistic description and description of ways of life" (Hymes 1988:622). The point was well taken, and of course Hymes was right: in the end it has proven impossible to treat language use in an East Sutherland fishing community without close attention to fisherfolk ways of life.

Notes

Chapter 1

1. In 1963 public transport scheduling did not allow for a return trip between Golspie and Embo in a single day. To make my multiple-village assignment possible, the Gaelic Division of the Linguistic Survey of Scotland made one of their vans available to me during my original year of fieldwork. I am grateful to the late Professor Kenneth Jackson for this enabling generosity.

2. Given the rapidity with which children can lose as well as achieve fluency, the former acquisition history did not necessarily confer any advantage in adult proficiency. The least proficient semi-speaker in my Brora sample, in terms of translation-test results and apparent conversational skill, was the one Brora semi-speaker whose full fluency as a child at school-entering age was completely certain (see Dorian 1981:81).

3. One young speaker appeared on the basis of material recorded for me in 1992 to be somewhat more fluent than most of her semi-speaker agemates. I had worked with her mother and older brother during the 1960s and 1970s, but up to 2004 she contributed to my recorded materials only via that one recording. From 2004 on she became a fuller participant via both recording and telephone, but it was impossible at that stage to repeat the very extensive proficiency testing that all other Embo speakers close to her in age had participated in. Since she did not move in the circle of the fluent speakers who had identified other semi-speakers for me by their linguistic failings, I also have no community-based evaluation of her proficiency. In some respects (conversational ease and some grammatical features) she is probably the most proficient of the five youngest Embo speakers in this study, but at the same time her Gaelic shows many characteristic semi-speaker features (including the apparent absence altogether of at least one grammatical category, the passive voice). In addition, she has stated that she did not have interlocutors with whom Gaelic was her

unmarked conversational language when she was growing up. She can be clearly grouped with the Embo semi-speakers, therefore, but the parameters of her language proficiency are less well established than those of the other four members of that group.

4. Deciding on a citation form for the variables discussed in this study presents a number of problems. Choosing any one of the phonemic variant representations for the variable would suggest a "main" or "preferred" variant. Using the orthographic representation of the equivalent term in standard Gaelic would similarly suggest primacy for the forms of the written language. See §6.4 in chapter 4 for a fuller discussion of this issue.

5. One instance of thoroughly anomalous /ɔir/ was collected in Brora, from a household in which the eldest sibling was reported to have offered suspect (non-local) forms. This man was no longer alive when I reached East Sutherland, and the Brora form in apparently universal use (by a surviving sister of his as well as by all others) was /ɛr/. The second of the Brora households sampled by a Survey fieldworker also offered /ɛr/.

6. So many high-frequency words and constructions show personal-pattern variation in fisherfolk Gaelic that any two- or three-sentence sequence usually offers at least one personal-pattern variable. For a rough measure of frequency of occurrence I counted the personal-pattern variants appearing in 1,000-word recorded stretches from E4 and E27. The older man produced personal-pattern variants at a rate of 1 per 18.2 words (55 instances in 1,000 words, proper nouns excluded) and the younger man produced them at a rate of 1 per 22.7 words (44 instances in 1,000 words, with the same exclusion). See also chapter 8, §8.1.

7. See in this connection Bloomfield 1964 [1927], discussed in Chapter 7 below.

8. Labov however demonstrates that sound changes resulting in splits and mergers, that is, in changes in phonemic inventory, escape this evaluative process (1994:344).

9. It is possible at least in theory that this pair were the only Golspie speakers who made use of the variant /kɛruax/, since Golspie speakers otherwise produced /kɛrəvax/. More probably, my small Golspie sample simply did not happen to include others users of that variant. The word for 'sand' belongs to a small set of words in which /v/ or /u/ or zero correspond to one another, either across villages or among the speakers of a single village. For 'wild', for example, another word from this same lexical set, various speakers in Brora and Golspie used either /fiəuiç/ or /fiəviç/ (most speakers using only one of the two variants); all Embo speakers, by contrast, used /fiəuiç/ invariably. Because all three villages share the variant /fiəuiç/, 'wild' has escaped becoming a stereotype of inter-village variation. In the case of 'sand', with Brora and Golspie sharing the variant /kɛruax/, the additional Golspie variant /kɛrəvax/ seems to go similarly unnoticed, but Embo's unshared and highly distinctive /kãnax/ becomes the very embodiment of inter-village dialect stereotyping.

10. Working boats were, of course, present in great numbers, but women were not taken on board; see chapter 2, §5.3.

Chapter 2

1. The differences include for example the following: the absence in Brora Gaelic of one morphophoneme prominent in Golspie Gaelic (but absent in Embo, too, curiously enough); a unique initial allophone of one initial phoneme in Brora fisherfolk Gaelic; different gender assignments in Brora and Golspie Gaelic for two high-frequency nouns; invariant Brora forms for several nouns in common use that have variant forms in Golspie Gaelic (as in the case of the word for "sand" instanced in chapter 1).

2. In a sample of thirty-two fully fluent East Sutherland Gaelic speakers born before 1910 whose nuclear-family histories I compiled, eighteen married fellow Gaelic speakers from the same village and eight did not marry at all, while only one person married a local individual not of fisherfolk background. Five women married men who were not fishermen but were also not local.

3. Nonsensical or mocking elements of the by-names of parents and grandparents are frequently incorporated into the genealogical by-names of current community members, so that a great many by-names are in fact offensive to their bearers. For this reason, by-names are universally used in reference but only very selectively used in address; in this respect they differ very clearly from nicknames.

4. The well-established residence of a few English monolinguals serving the Embo village population had no bearing on the personal-pattern variation that is of special interest here. In personal-pattern variation all variants were peculiar to Gaelic and were also of Gaelic origin, with the exception of the well-established early borrowing of the word for 'potato'; none of the variants showed English influence.

5. The census is taken by parish, and the parishes extend in each case beyond the single village at its center. The estimates given here for all village populations, as opposed to parish populations, were supplied through the courtesy of the Registrar-General's Office in Edinburgh, but they remain estimates rather than actual village population counts.

6. For a fuller account of this and all other matters treated in this section see Dorian 1985.

7. I was told that the women who occasionally acted as precentors stayed in their regular seats and declined to take the precentor's seat at the front of the room.

Chapter 3

1. No instances of conjunctional 'when' happened to appear in the jokes I recorded from E10, but given his strong tendency to shift into a performance style, the same change-over might have been expected to turn up there, too, with a larger collection of jokes.

2. In her freely spoken material, the youngest of the older fluent speakers, E17, showed idiosyncratic conditioning in the use of /-ĭn'/ versus /-u mi/. Except in traditional material, such as a children's rhyme, where her usage was as traditional as the material itself (three instances), she made almost exclusive use of the analytic form in positive clauses (thirty-four out of thirty-five instances), whereas after the negative particle she strongly favored the synthetic form (seven out of eight instances). No conditioning pattern of this sort appeared for other speakers.

3. Because I was selecting more items to track according to village-by-village and speaker-by-speaker incidence, I did make some new discoveries of this sort. I chose 'money' as another instance of geographically based variation to follow, and in the process of sorting every Brora and Golspie instance of the word by individual speaker, I realized belatedly that variation between pronunciations /ɛrigəd/ and /ərigəd/ was not haphazard within the villages, but rather speaker-based: some individual Brora and Golspie speakers quite consistently used the one pronunciation while others quite consistently used the other, making this another case of inter-speaker (but not intra-speaker) variation for Brora and Golspie. Where the phonological difference is small and the word is common, it is surprisingly easy to fail to recognize the *speaker-specific* nature of an already-documented variation. Variations I had simply not consciously attended to also emerged as I resurveyed earlier materials. For example, reviewing the lexicostatistical word list I had elicited from

ten Embo speakers in 1976 reminded me that two variants of the adverb ('near') coexisted in Embo (and in Brora and Golspie, for that matter), and I began belatedly to track this variable as well (Embo /fagiʃ ~ faʃkʰ/). There were also contracted and non-contracted variants of the phrases 'ought to' (/pə xɔːr/ ~ /pɔːr/) and 'used to' (/p aːviʃ(čʰ)/ ~ /p aːʃ(čʰ)/), which likewise became late additions to my expanding list of variables with idiosyncratic variant distribution.

4. Other visits were paid me in the United States by monolingual English-speaking kinfolk of my sources. Such visits did not of course provide Gaelic data, but it is no exaggeration to say that they never failed to deepen my understanding of East Sutherland fisherfolk lifeways, especially of the intricacies and social ramifications of fisherfolk kin relationships.

5. Additional material turns up occasionally in notebooks originally used for other purposes or in old recordings that prove to contain untranscribed elicited material. In spite of repeated passes through field notebooks and phone conversation transcriptions, overlooked instances of variables still emerge with some frequency, and many of the entries in the tables in this volume have changed as the writing progressed, either because of late notebook finds or because of ongoing transcription. Late-emerging data have rarely produced changes of more than a percentage point or two in the tables, however.

6. This was particularly true with regard to vowels, curiously enough, though vowels have been the most common locus of change in variationist studies. Only one example of change in progress appeared in Embo Gaelic vowels. The oldest Embo speakers used the vowels /a/ and /aː/ for written a before -r and -ll, representing historically "dark" forms of those consonants, and before one or two other consonants in a few words, whereas younger Embo speakers used /ɔ/ and /ɔː/ in the same environments. There were, however, no gradual changes in vowel quality across the population of speakers. Rather, a certain number of intermediate-age speakers among the OFS group showed some alternation between /a/ (short and long) and /ɔ/ (short and long), while everyone older than they used short and long /a/ and everyone younger used short and long /ɔ/.

7. Scottish Gaelic has two initial consonant mutations, one known as lenition and the other as nasalization. Realizations of the mutations differ somewhat from dialect to dialect; the description here applies to East Sutherland fisherfolk Gaelic in particular. In lenition, initial stops become fricatives, by and large, and fricatives become other fricatives or zero. In nasalization, the contrast between initial aspirated and unaspirated voiceless stops is neutralized, with both becoming voiced stops; fricatives tend to become voiced stops or voiced affricates, though initial /f-/ either becomes zero or shows no change. Some initial mutations are grammatically significant (lenition marks the past tense of verbs, for example, and the vocative of nouns, triggered in each case by a preceding particle that often does not appear in the surface structure); but others are simply obligatory after certain function words (such as the adverb /kleː/ 'very' and the numeral /taː/ 'two') or seemingly entirely optional (one of the few adjectives that precede the noun, an adjective meaning 'good', can take either the form /prad/ or the form /vrad/).

8. E34 provided two freely spoken instances of ('from, off, of') plus a person's name, both using /čɛ/; her husband's five freely spoken instances of the same construction used /tə/ in four instances and a third variant, /yɛ/, in the fifth. E38 provided five freely spoken instances of demonstrative ('that') plus a noun, four of them with /hɔ̃n/ and one with /ʃɔ̃n/; her younger sister, E40, provided twenty-six freely spoken instances of the same construction, all of them with /ʃɔ̃n/. The preceding shibilant-final /nĩʃ/ in the instance given here for E40 had no assimilative effect; a junctural pause followed it, and in any case none of her other instances of demonstrative ('that') plus noun, all /ʃɔ̃n/, was preceded by /nĩʃ/.

9. Although /hūnə/ occurred seldom by comparison with /hūnig/, it was nonetheless used occasionally by a good many speakers.

10. In addition to the two initial consonant mutations Scottish Gaelic also has one set of final consonant mutations, much less frequent in appearance than the initial mutations.

11. Duncan had worked in construction crews in which most of the other Gaelic speakers were not East Sutherlanders, and he was inclined to introduce Gaelic terms from other dialects into elicited material and quote proverbs that almost certainly originated in other dialect areas. Una acted as a check on these tendencies, volunteering in many such cases that she didn't know the word or hadn't heard the proverb locally. But after Duncan's death she herself produced one striking non-local, more nearly mainstream pronunciation in translation task work with a colleague of mine whom she was meeting for the first time. See chapter 7, §4.3.

Chapter 4

1. The phone conversations were of course of varying length (though most ran over half an hour and a good many well over an hour), and the amount of Gaelic produced during any given conversation also varied considerably by speaker. The difference in personality and speech style between the two sisters E29* and E38 was such, for example, that a smaller number of sessions with E29* yielded far more material than a larger number with E38. At a point when nineteen conversations had been transcribed for formerly fluent speaker E29*, plus nine additional elicitation-only sessions, the yield in tokens for seventeen variables was 1,230. At that same point in time, when thirty-two sessions had been transcribed for semi-speaker E38, a good many of them chiefly or solely elicitation sessions, the yield was only 700 tokens for the same seventeen variables. Gaelic conversational materials are abundant for four of the seven phone conversation partners, including a semi-speaker and a formerly fluent speaker, each of whom had originally doubted her Gaelic conversational abilities. The phone recordings have in fact long since outrun my ability to keep up with them in transcription. Untranscribed tapes remain for all my phone conversation partners except the single older fluent speaker among them, E17; she died in early 1999, and all thirty-two of our conversations are transcribed, filling five notebooks and spilling over into a sixth. Two speakers whose freely spoken phone materials are relatively limited, E27 and E38, provided less material simply because they were not the easy conversationalists, in either of their languages, that the others were; fortunately, other freely spoken material is available for each of them. Somewhat limited material is available for semi-speaker E39 only because she was late in joining the speaker sample.

2. Any notion of a conservative norm is here necessarily grounded in terms of apparent time differences. There are no earlier texts available for fisherfolk Gaelic, and the isolated words recorded in the 1950s by fieldworkers for the Gaelic Division of the Linguistic Survey of Scotland do not always offer a solid basis even for establishing a slightly earlier phonological form of individual lexemes: especially in Golspie, the forms offered by an at least passively literate source were not all reliably local (see chapter 9, §4.2). At the same time I would not, in the case of the fisherfolk communities, take the position Dal Negro adopts in her study of remnant Walser German in alpine Italy, that "the speech community as a whole is...restructuring language domains, functions, attitudes and values" to such an extent that "this crisis becomes linguistically apparent in the language spoken by all its members", for which reason she declined to recognize a group of fully competent speakers (2004:104). Though similar restructuring was taking place among

the former East Sutherland fisherfolk populations, older fluent speakers' habitual use of Gaelic with kinfolk and agemates maintained their skills in their own local form of Gaelic remarkably well. (For examples of a very few structures which older fluent speakers did *not* continue to maintain well, see Dorian 1986.) Most such speakers displayed not just fluency but impressive verbal skills.

3. Local social norms dictated the use of English in the presence of monolinguals, a requirement that substantially reduced the amount of Gaelic spoken in these communities as the Gaelic-speaking populations in the three villages shrank via emigration and natural mortality. From at least the mid-twentieth century, Embo in particular has had a thriving tourist industry connected with a small hotel and pub made famous by a sentimental song, and a great many trailers were rented out on a beachfront site all summer. Relatively few tourists came into the village proper, since the trailer site had its own access road, toilets, and shop, but the pub was patronized both by villagers and by outsiders and at least in summertime much more English was spoken there than Gaelic.

4. The Embo man coded as E15L had one parent from the Outer Hebrides. See chapter 7, §2.4, for a note on the representativeness of his Gaelic.

5. In a few cases, additional information became available belatedly and has resulted in a numerical reordering compared to that of Dorian 1994b; the inclusion of one entirely new source, E32*, has also resulted in renumbering.

6. Constantinidou's suggestion (Constantinidou 1994) that women led in the abandonment of Gaelic in East Sutherland fails to recognize this feature of the local language scene (and for that matter the presence of men who had deliberately stopped using Gaelic, like B2 and E32*, the latter the formerly fluent brother of E26* and E34). And while she notes that the two youngest daughters in the Embo family she knew best were imperfect speakers, she does not mention the fact that the same family's only member who did not speak Gaelic at all was male, the last child and youngest son, a (near-)passive bilingual. Jaffe (1999:108) speaks of a "discourse of culpability" according to which women are scapegoated in language shift and suggests several lucid reasons for its emergence.

7. The term *semi-speaker* has been widely adopted since I first used it in connection with East Sutherland fisherfolk Gaelic (Dorian 1973:417; 1977), but it should be noted that I am defining it here in a way that is not necessarily directly transferable to other obsolescent language communities.

8. The latter variant, /hã:n/, can actually appear in either of two phonetic alternatives: [hã:n] and [hãn:]. The former is the underlying phonological form, but before unstressed elements that belong to the same phrase or clause, notably personal pronouns consisting of a single vowel, the syllable's length can be transferred to the final consonant instead of residing in the vowel. The same is true of a few other stressed monosyllabic words in final /-n/, for example, /pu:rn/ 'water, rain'.

Chapter 5

1. In that case, however, it was being used in a different function, namely, to make an existential statement (with /ʃ e:/, the copula, and /ãũ:n/, a conjugated third-person singular masculine form of the preposition 'in', used in formulating existential utterances).

2. In mainstream Gaelic dialects the directional form of adverbial 'in' shows a final consonant that would be congruent with Brora and Golspie /sčɛx/ and Embo /sčɛx, stɛx, sčax/, while the locational form of adverbial 'in' has no final consonant and would be congruent with Brora and Golspie /stɛ/and Embo /stɛ, sčɛ/.

3. Many of the conjunctions that require dependent verb forms also produce the initial consonant mutation known as nasalization, which voices initial voiceless stops and affricates. Since both /čʰ-/ and /č-/ are voiced to /ǰ-/ by this mutation, no difference in the aspiration of an underlying form's initial consonant is discernible in nasalization; /...kə ǰɛu a/ '...that he would go' might equally well derive from /čʰɛu/ or /čɛu/.

4. Since telephone work with E38 continued while this book was in preparation, I thought I might settle, at least temporarily, the issue of which ('would go') variant she used more frequently by including one more transcription beyond the point at which I had necessarily stopped tallying variant instances in order to arrive at figures for tables. But when I looked for E38's next instance of ('would go'), I found that she had offered two translation task versions one right after the other, one with each of her usual variants. Confronted by this additional evidence of her persistently variable usage, I concluded that it was after all quite realistic to present her figures for ('would go') just as they were, at 50 percent for each of her variants.

5. See chapter 3, §6.1, on the emergence of originally oblique forms as citation forms in East Sutherland fisherfolk Gaelic. Many such forms are in use locally, most of them common to all three villages but a few established in one or two villages and not the other(s). The historical nominative/accusative form in /-ax/ has usually dropped out of use altogether, but in a few cases it remains in competition with the oblique form, as with ('family') and also the variable ('tomorrow'); see especially §9.3.3.

6. This applies also to verbs with initial /f-/ which lose that /f-/ when they appear as complements and so become vowel-initial.

7. In its written-language form *buntata* 'potato', there is an apparent folk etymology that makes the word appear bimorphemic by identifying the first syllable with *bun* 'root' (MacBain 1982:59); this would suggest compounding, making second-syllable stress less anomalous. An intrusive /-n-/ appeared very occasionally before the stressed consonant in Embo Gaelic (3 instances out of more than 150 renditions of the word), but 1 of those 3 was in an /m-/-initial form that would preclude the first syllable's being identified with /pun/ 'root' and the other 2 had medial /tʰ/ rather than /d/. Perhaps the voiced medial consonant of the variant /mǝda:tʰ/ arises by incorporating voicing from a preceding /n/, but if so, the nasal itself is eliminated from the surface form in the process.

8. The formerly fluent speaker E29* produced one such analogical variant conversationally not long after her first return to Embo, but never again. One Golspie speaker used such an analogical past tense form routinely. He was by all odds the most literate individual in my entire three-village sample and was undoubtedly aware of the deviance of his past-tense form, but he showed no self-consciousness about it. Possibly other high-proficiency Golspie speakers had at one time shared his comfortable use of the analogical form, but no others in my small Golspie sample did so in the 1960s and 1970s; just one other senior Golspie speaker produced an analogical form on a single occasion but never did so again.

9. Given that the two irregular verbs ('came') and ('saw') show this pattern in East Sutherland fisherfolk Gaelic, it might be expected that a similar irregular past-tense form, *ràinig* 'reached', would show parallel disyllabic and monosyllabic variants. But the verb *ruig* 'reach' is regular rather than irregular in this dialect and *ràinig* is non-occurrent in any form.

10. Several speakers also occasionally produced lenited /hɔn/ in the truncated relative clause used when the demonstrative modifies a noun, for example, /ə burn:ax a ʃɔn/ 'that woman', derived from /ə burn:ax ə ha ʃɔn/, literally 'the woman who is that', but only E37 used forms like /ə burn:ax a hɔn/ with any great frequency.

11. Affirmatives could readily be elicited by asking questions using the copula, which would then also require affirmative responses with the copula, but variation would be unlikely to appear in such directly cued question-and-answer pairs; most or all responses would be /ʃ eː/.

12. Because I had tracked ('near') as a geographical variable for all my phone-conversation partners, I already had a record of their instances of the variable. I reviewed perhaps two-thirds of the relevant field notebooks, omitting exclusively Brora and Golspie notebooks since only Embo instances were to be tabulated here.

13. Consistency would call either for including the 40 percent level of disagreement or excluding the 60 percent level of agreement in tables 5.28 and 5.29. Because there were so few speaker pairs with a relatively high level of variant-preference agreement and so many with a relatively low level of variant-preference agreement, however, I included the 60 percent level of agreement and excluded the 40 percent level of disagreement.

14. This finding contravenes, as far as communities with the distinctive social-setting features found in Embo and the communities treated in chapter 8, §6 are concerned, the assumption that "near relatives" will have particularly similar grammars (Davies 2003:42). Such variables as ('wasn't/weren't') and ('preterite particle') clearly involve grammatical differences, and they are among the variables on which Embo siblings disagreed.

Chapter 6

1. E29*, the oldest daughter in her family, reported that this situation was accepted as an inevitability even by the school authorities. The school inspector would come to the house to assess the progress she had been able to make by spotty school attendance and her own efforts at home; he was understanding and kind, according to her account. E13, likewise an oldest daughter, loved school and badly wanted to go but was seldom able to. She told of rocking the current baby in its wooden cradle with her foot while reading a school book and calling out a false report to her mother (/ha ə lʹanu nə xɔrdərl eː/ 'The baby's already asleep') in hopes of being allowed to attend school. E26*, again an oldest daughter, reported that she and her next oldest sister went to school by turns; each would go two days one week and three the next.

2. I have considerable freely spoken materials for E4 precisely because of the primacy of Gaelic for him. It was more congenial for him to speak in Gaelic, even with a less than perfectly fluent conversation partner, so that recording with him was uniquely easy.

3. I had no prior personal acquaintance with the brother identified here as Angus. Because of his tenuous health situation I would certainly not have pressed him to undertake linguistic work. It was his siblings who did so, as also happened later with Emma, the oldest daughter, who returned to live in Embo late in life. Unlikely though it may seem, this is not a unique response where a large family is concerned. I found in working with a twelve-sibling family of Pennsylvania German speakers in Berks County, Pennsylvania, that the mother and the more central siblings exerted pressure on the more far-flung siblings to take part; they also insisted that I appear and carry on working at a social event, which struck me as a highly inappropriate setting for fieldwork. It seems that a large family can come to have an investment of their own in such work, looking on it as a sort of family project.

4. Duncan produced only a single variant of ('along with'), namely, /kʰɔi/. But /kʰɔi/ cannot be used in conjugated form with a pronominal object, and Duncan would have been obliged to use one of the other variants if he had given any ('along with') forms with pronominal object. This would have made ('along with') at least a two-variant variable for

him, and he would therefore have had seven one-variant variables and nine multivariant variables overall.

5. Material from Lorna in later years showed her usage to be exuberantly variable in this case. It was the fact that she produced three variants unique to herself that dissuaded me from including the variable ('wet') in the present study, since Lorna's exceptional variability would have made the statistics of variant usage for ('wet') too unlike those for other variables: the variable ('wet') would have had a unique seven variants, placing it in a class of its own.

6. Further evidence for her inclusion comes from the warm memories E29* had of E26* from their childhood years. Sheila helped the younger Emma learn to be a caddy at the Dornoch golf course, for example, where Sheila was already working when Emma first began there.

Chapter 7

1. These cross-language "quotes" were so routine that it was impossible to be sure without asking whether the person being quoted was a Gaelic speaker or a monolingual. In one instance the appearance of repeated Gaelic quotations from a woman whom I had believed to be an English monolingual in a narrative told by a Golspie Gaelic speaker led me to become uncertain about the quoted woman's ethnic identity. Inquiry confirmed that she was indeed a monolingual, but since the lengthy story in which the quotes were embedded was being told in Gaelic to an interlocutor who expected Gaelic, the woman's remarks were, with just one brief exception, produced in Gaelic exactly as if the woman in question had made them that way herself.

2. The verb 'hear' in fisherfolk Gaelic was usually formed on a root /kʰɫiː.n-/, but an alternative root /kʰɫiː.nčʰ-/ also existed, evidenced for example in an imperative form /kʰɫiː.nčʰ/ 'hear!' (i.e., 'listen [to that/him/her]'!). This latter form is then susceptible to analogical gerund formation by the suffixes /-al/ or /-u/, as in E17's forms /kʰɫiː.nčal/ and /kʰɫiː.nču/.

3. Murdo implied that the man in question had criticized other younger-generation speech habits as well, but when asked by his wife what other sorts of lapses had met with disapproval, he offered no further examples.

4. Not all speakers were prepared to make such judgments. Some could not grasp the issue of grammatical acceptability, assuming that any question raised about a possible construction must relate to a potential difference in meaning, and others became uncertain when the issue was raised, seeming to lose touch with their own sense of structural acceptability.

5. This was not in actuality a realistic possibility in the East Sutherland setting. After the death of the last family member with whom she occasionally used Gaelic, E42L urged that she and I use more Gaelic together since I was her only remaining Gaelic interlocutor. I suggested that she speak Gaelic with the scattering of fluent Gaelic speakers who still remained in Embo whenever she visited the village, but she replied that she had already tried that tactic without success. The problem was her generational inappropriateness as a Gaelic interlocutor: older people regarded her as too young to be a Gaelic speaker and automatically responded to her in English even when she spoke to them in Gaelic.

6. E39's translation task participation became more extensive only from 2004 onward, too late to provide a measure of her capacities comparable to the measure provided by participation in the 1974/1976 translation task batteries. See chapter 1, note 3.

7. Grinevald 2001 presents a particularly complete and sensitive account of the difficulties fieldworkers are likely to face in communities where seriously endangered languages are spoken, offering a challenging sample of the many potential obstacles to gathering speech material that represents the community's verbal life and also represents the verbal skills of individual speakers at all adequately or fully.

Chapter 8

1. Just such a tidying-up approach was taken in the nineteenth century by the first French scholar to write a grammar of the Sereer language in Senegal; see the examples in Irvine and Gal 2000:55–59.

2. The community may well share this and others of the viewpoints noted here. Dal Negro reports, for example, that "the speech community was rather skeptical about my resolution to contact and record less competent dialect speakers who were substantially different from the stereotyped ideal informant, who could generally be defined as old, rustic, and 'genuine'" (2004:104). See also Woodbury 2003:44.

3. Angus McIntosh, who assumed directorship of the Linguistic Survey of Scotland in 1949, advised fieldworkers to seek out "resistant" individuals whose speech was relatively unaffected by "recent influences from outside" (McIntosh 1961 [1952]:85). (See also Jackson 1958:232, discussed in chapter 9, §4.2.)

4. According to Irvine and Gal (2000:58), nineteenth-century European linguists dealing with Senegalese languages saw their differentiation as a reflection of supposed "differences in mentality, history, and social organization" on the part of the speakers of each language; features that did not conform to the differentiating profile of a given language were regarded as "borrowings, forms that could be omitted from a grammar or dictionary".

5. Cf. J. Milroy's discussion, quoted in chapter 1, §7.1.1, of the variation-eliminating editing of Middle English texts (Milroy 2000:21).

6. In this respect, Inis Mór Irish differs from its distant relative East Sutherland Gaelic. The negative evaluation attached to two variants used analogically in gerund formation make gerund formation the sole variable in connection with which social weighting actually does appear in fisherfolk Gaelic.

Chapter 9

1. In a questionnaire with 893 lexical items, Oftedal recorded that he prompted his literate Golspie source in 107 instances (Ó Dochartaigh 1997, vol. 1:99), and it would appear that some of the prompts were all too readily accepted. This was certainly a very high figure for prompts, the second highest recorded in any location, in fact. (The figures on prompts from each fieldworker appear in Ó Dochartaigh 1997, vol. 1:95–100.) The Brora sources questionnaired by fieldworker Fred MacAulay in 1953 were not prompted at all, nor were any of MacAulay's sources in other locations; in this procedural matter MacAulay matched Survey director Kenneth Jackson, who also never prompted a source. Three of the other fieldworkers limited themselves to a handful of prompts in the case of any given source. While one other fieldworker prompted with some frequency, his highest number of prompts to a single source was 38, as against Oftedal's highest total of 129 prompts to a female source in Shandwick, Easter Ross. The Embo source, also interviewed

by Oftedal in 1958, was prompted 73 times, itself a very high figure; but the risks to the local character of the record were a good deal lower with a non-literate female source, and as a result the Embo Survey record is much more locally authentic than the Golspie record. The literacy-based distortions include—to give examples from just one of the Survey's four volumes of entries—acceptance of a word not in local use (*bàta* 'boat'); inauthentic vowel quality in the entries for *allt*, *Beurla*, *banais*, and *cainnte*; inauthentic consonants in *ainm* and *balbh*; and the representation of a word-final unstressed vowel that normally goes unpronounced in East Sutherland, *bliadhna*. Examples of written-language variants misleadingly entered for items discussed in this study include a Brora entry for 'on her' influenced by written *oirre*, a Golspie entry for 'taking' influenced by written *gabhail*, and a Golspie entry for 'old lady' influenced by written *cailleach*.

2. Examples of extant but unrepresented variants of items included in the Survey volumes, for variables either discussed or mentioned in passing in this study, are the following: Golspie variants /ɔi, ɔir, ɔiç/ 'on her', Golspie variant /fiəuiç/ 'wild', Golspie variant /kɛruax/ 'sand', Embo variant /mwĩ/ 'out', Embo variants /kʰɫ̃ĩ:nčən, kʰɫɔ:sčən/ 'hearing', Embo variants /fyux, fl'ux, fl'uxkʰ/ 'wet', Embo variant /hã:n/ 'came', Embo variant /hũ(r)n/ 'saw', Embo variants /čər:ɫax, tʰə:rɫax, tʰə:rɫiç/ 'family'.

References

Adam, R. J., ed. 1972. *Papers on Sutherland Estate management, 1802–1816*, Vols. 1–2. Edinburgh: T. and A. Constable, for the Scottish History Society.

Anderson, Benedict. 1991. *Imagined communities: Reflections on the origin and spread of nationalism*, 2nd ed. London: Verso.

Austin, Peter K., ed. 2003. *Language documentation and description*, Vol. 1. London: Hans Rausing Endangered Languages Project.

Bavin, Edith L. 1989. Some lexical and morphological changes in Warlpiri. In *Investigating obsolescence: Studies in language contraction and death*, ed. Nancy C. Dorian, 267–86. Cambridge: Cambridge University Press.

Bell, Allan. 1984. Language style as audience design. *Language in Society* 13: 145–204.

———. 2001. Back in style: Reworking audience design. In *Style and sociolinguistic variation*, ed. Penelope Eckert and John R. Rickford, 139–69. Cambridge: Cambridge University Press.

Blench, Roger. 1998. Recent fieldwork in Nigeria: Report on Horom and Tapshin. *Ogmios: Newsletter of the Foundation for Endangered Languages* No. 9, Autumn: 11–12.

Bloomfield, Leonard. 1964 [1927]. Literate and illiterate speech. In *Language in culture and society: A reader in linguistics and anthropology*, ed. Dell Hymes, 391–96. New York: Harper and Row. [Reprinted from *American Speech* 2:432–39.]

Chambers, J. K. 1995. *Sociolinguistic theory*. Oxford: Blackwell.

———. 2002. Patterns of variation including change. In *The handbook of language variation and change*, ed. J. K. Chambers, Peter Trudgill, and Natalie Schilling-Estes, 349–72. Oxford: Blackwell.

Cheshire, Jenny. 1999. Spoken Standard English. In *Standard English: The widening debate*, ed. Tony Bex and Richard J. Watts, 129–39. London: Routledge.

Christy, Craig. 1983. *Uniformitarianism in linguistics*. Amsterdam: John Benjamins.

Collins, James. 1998. Our ideologies and theirs. In *Language ideologies: Practice and theory*, ed. Bambi B. Schieffelin, Kathryn A. Woolard, and Paul V. Kroskrity, 256–70. New York: Oxford University Press.

Connell, Bruce. 2002. Phonetic/phonological variation and language contraction. *International Journal of the Sociology of Language* 157: 167–85.

Constantinidou, Evi. 1994. The "death" of East Sutherland Gaelic: Death by women? In *Bilingual women: Anthropological approaches to second-language use*, ed. Pauline Burton, Ketaki Kushari Dyson, and Shirley Ardener, 111–27. Oxford: Berg.

Coupland, Nikolas. 2001. Language, situation, and the relational self: Theorizing dialect-style in sociolinguistics. In *Style and sociolinguistic variation*, ed. Penelope Eckert and John R. Rickford, 185–210. Cambridge: Cambridge University Press.

Crystal, David. 1980. Neglected grammatical factors in conversational English. In *Studies in English linguistics for Randolph Quirk*, ed. S. Greenbaum, G. Leech, and J. Svartik, 153–66. London: Longman.

Cyffer, Norbert. 1998. *A sketch of Kanuri*. Cologne: Rüdiger Köppe.

Dal Negro, Silvia. 2004. *The decay of a language: The case of a German dialect in the Italian Alps*. Bern: Peter Lang.

Davies, Alan. 2003. *The native speaker: Myth and reality*. Clevedon: Multilingual Matters.

Dorian, Nancy C. 1973. Grammatical change in a dying language. *Language* 49: 413–38.

———. 1977. The problem of the semi-speaker in language death. *International Journal of the Sociology of Language* 12: 23–32.

———. 1978. *East Sutherland Gaelic: The dialect of the Brora, Golspie, and Embo fishing communities*. Dublin: Dublin Institute for Advanced Studies.

———. 1980a. Linguistic lag as an ethnic marker. *Language in Society* 9: 33–41.

———. 1980b. Language shift in community and individual: The phenomenon of the laggard semi-speaker. *International Journal of the Sociology of Language* 25: 85–94.

———. 1981. *Language death: The life cycle of a Scottish Gaelic dialect*. Philadelphia: University of Pennsylvania Press.

———. 1985. *The tyranny of tide: An oral history of the East Sutherland fisherfolk*. Ann Arbor: Karoma.

———. 1986. Making do with less: Some surprises along the language death proficiency continuum. *Applied Psycholinguistics* 7: 257–75.

———. 1994a. Stylistic variation in a language restricted to private-sphere use. In *Sociolinguistic perspectives on register*, ed. Douglas Biber and Edward Finegan, 217–32. Oxford: Oxford University Press.

———. 1994b. Varieties of variation in a very small place: Social homogeneity, prestige norms, and linguistic variation. *Language* 70: 631–96.

———. 1997a. Telling the monolinguals from the bilinguals: Unrealistic code choices in direct quotation within Scottish Gaelic narratives. *International Journal of Bilingualism* 1: 41–54.

———. 1997b. Males and merger: Dative third-person pronouns among secular Berks County Pennsylvania German speakers. In *Languages and lives: Essays in honor of Werner Enninger*, ed. James R. Dow and Michèle Wolff, 39–52. New York: Peter Lang.

———. 2006. Negative borrowing in an indigenous-language shift to the dominant national language. *Journal of Bilingual Education and Bilingualism* 9: 557–77.

Dressler, Wolfgang U. 1988. Language death. In *Language: The socio-cultural context*, ed. Frederick J. Newmeyer, 184–92. Linguistics: The Cambridge Survey, Vol. 4. Cambridge: Cambridge University Press.

Duran, James J. 1992. Branching trees, waves, and rising tides: Some reflections on the notions of "speech community" and "diffusion of linguistic traits." Paper presented at the Fourteenth Annual University of California Celtic Studies Conference, Los Angeles, 1992.

Duranti, Alessandro, ed. 2001. *Linguistic anthropology: A reader*. Malden, MA: Blackwell.

Fasold, Ralph, Carolyn Bins, Lucienne Skopek, Barbara Tully, and Conan Louis. 1975. *Influences on social lect level: Where you are and where your head is*. Bloomington: Indiana University Linguistics Club.

Flikeid, K. 1985. L'accord dans les propositions relatives: Le cas d'un parler acadien. Paper presented at the annual meeting of the Canadian Linguistics Association, Université de Montréal.

Foley, William A. 2003. Genre, register and language documentation in literate and preliterate communities. In *Language documentation and description*, Vol. 1, ed. Peter K. Austin, 85–98. London: Hans Rausing Endangered Languages Project.

Friedrich, Paul. 1971. Dialectal variation in Tarascan phonology. *International Journal of American Linguistics* 37: 164–87.

Gal, Susan. 1998. Multiplicity and contention among ideologies. In *Language ideologies: Practice and theory*, ed. Bambi B. Schieffelin, Kathryn A. Woolard, and Paul V. Kroskrity, 317–29. Oxford: Oxford University Press.

Giles, Howard, and Peter F. Powesland. 1975. *Speech style and social evaluation*. London: European Association of Experimental Social Psychology and Academic Press.

Grace, George. 1991. How do languages change? More on "aberrant" languages. Paper presented at the Sixth International Conference on Austronesian Linguistics, Honolulu, Hawaii.

Grinevald, Colette. 2001. Encounters at the brink: Linguistic fieldwork among speakers of endangered languages. In *Lectures on endangered languages: 2*, ed. Osamu Sakiyama and Fabito Endo, 285–314. Kyoto: Endangered Languages of the Pacific Rim.

Haacke, Wilfrid. 1986. Preliminary observations on a dialect of the Sesfontein Damara. In *Contemporary studies on Khoisan: In honour of Oswin Köhler*, Vol. 1, ed. R. Vossen and K. Keuthmann, 376–96. Hamburg: Helmut Buske.

Haacke, Wilfrid, E. Eiseb, and L. Namaseb. 1997. Internal and external relations of Khoekhoe dialects: A preliminary survey. In *Namibian languages: Reports and papers*, ed. W. Haacke and E. D. Elderkin, 125–209. Namibian African Studies 4. Cologne: Rüdiger Köppe.

Haas, W. 1982. Introduction. In *Standard languages: Spoken and written*, ed. W. Haas, 1–36. Manchester: Manchester University Press.

Haddican, Bill. 2007. Suburbanization and language change in Basque. *Language in Society* 36: 677–706.

Henry, Alison. 2002. Variation and syntactic theory. In *The handbook of language variation and change*, ed. J. K. Chambers, Peter Trudgill, and Natalie Schilling-Estes, 267–82. Oxford: Blackwell.

Henry, Alison, J. Wilson, C. Finlay, and S. Harrington. 1998. Language acquisition in conditions of variable input. Report to Economic and Social Research Council.

Heryanto, A. 1990. The making of language: Developmentalism in Indonesia. *Prism* 50: 40–53.

Hill, Jane H., and Kenneth Hill. 1986. Variable developments of -äška 'possession' in Modern Mexicano (Nahuatl). *International Journal of American Linguistics* 52: 404–10.

Hinskens, Frans. 1996. *Dialect levelling in Limburg: Structural and sociolinguistic aspects.* Linguistische Arbeiten 356. Tübingen: Max Niemeyer Verlag.

Holmberg, Allan R. 1969. *Nomads of the long bow: The Siriono of eastern Bolivia.* Garden City, NY: Natural History Press.

Holmquist, Jonathan Carl. 1988. *Language loyalty and linguistic variation: A study in Spanish Cantabria.* Topics in Sociolinguistics 3. Dordrecht: Foris.

Honey, John. 1997. Sociophonology. In *The handbook of sociolinguistics*, ed. Florian Coulmas, 92–106. Oxford: Blackwell.

Hymes, Dell. 1979. Sapir, competence, voices. In *Individual differences in language ability and language behavior*, ed. Charles J. Fillmore, Daniel Kempler, and William S-Y. Wang, 33–45. New York: Academic Press.

———. 1988. Brief notice on Dorian 1985. *Language in Society* 17: 622.

Irvine, Judith T., and Susan Gal. 2000. Language ideology and linguistic differentiation. In *Regimes of language: Ideologies, polities, and identities*, ed. Paul V. Kroskrity, 35–83. Santa Fe, NM: School of American Research Press.

Jackson, Kenneth H. 1958. The situation of the Scottish Gaelic language, and the work of the Linguistic Survey of Scotland. *Lochlann* 1: 229–34.

———. 1967. *A historical phonology of Breton.* Dublin: Dublin Institute for Advanced Studies.

Jaffe, Alexandra. 1999. *Ideologies in action: Language politics on Corsica.* Berlin: Mouton de Gruyter.

Johnson, Allen. 2003. *Families of the forest: The Matsigenka Indians of the Peruvian Amazon.* Berkeley: University of California Press.

Johnstone, Barbara. 1996. *The linguistic individual: Self-expression in language and linguistics.* New York: Oxford University Press.

———. 2000. The individual voice in language. *Annual Review of Anthropology* 29: 405–24.

Joseph, John Earl. 1987. *Eloquence and power: The rise of language standards and standard languages.* New York: Basil Blackwell.

Kerswill, Paul, and Ann Williams. 2000. Creating a new town koine: Children and language change in Milton Keynes. *Language in Society* 29: 65–115.

———. 2002. "Salience" as a factor in language change: Evidence from dialect leveling in urban England. In *Language change: The interplay of internal, external, and extralinguistic factors*, ed. Mari C. Jones and Edith Esch, 81–110. Berlin: Mouton de Gruyter.

King, Ruth Elizabeth. 1983. Variation and change in Newfoundland French: A sociolinguistic study of clitic pronouns. Ph.D. diss., Memorial University of Newfoundland.

———. 1989. On the social meaning of linguistic variability in language death situations: Variation in Newfoundland French. In *Investigating obsolescence: Studies in language contraction and death*, ed. Nancy C. Dorian, 139–48. Cambridge: Cambridge University Press.

Kroskrity, Paul V. 2002. Language renewal and the technologies of literacy and postliteracy: Reflections from Western Mono. In *Making dictionaries: Preserving indigenous languages of the Americas*, ed. William Frawley, Kenneth C. Hill, and Pamela Munro, 171–92. Berkeley: University of California Press.

Kulick, Don. 1992. *Language shift and cultural reproduction: Socialization, self, and syncretism in a Papua New Guinean village.* Cambridge: Cambridge University Press.

Labov, William. 1966. *The social stratification of English in New York City.* Washington, DC: Center for Applied Linguistics.

————. 1972. *Sociolinguistic patterns*. Philadelphia: University of Pennsylvania Press.

————. 1979. Locating the frontier between social and psychological factors in linguistic variation. In *Individual differences in language ability and language behavior*, ed. Charles J. Fillmore, Daniel Kempler, and William S-Y. Wang, 327–40. New York: Academic Press.

————. 1994. *Principles of linguistic change: Internal factors*. Oxford: Blackwell.

————. 2001. *Principles of linguistic change: Social factors*. Oxford: Blackwell.

Lee, R. 1979. *The !Kung San*. Cambridge: Cambridge University Press.

Le Page, R. B. 1994. The notion of "linguistic system" revisited. *International Journal of the Sociology of Language* 109: 109–20.

————. 1997. The evolution of a sociolinguistic theory of language. In *The handbook of sociolinguistics*, ed. Florian Coulmas, 15–32. Oxford: Blackwell.

Le Page, Robert, and Andrée Tabouret-Keller. 1985. *Acts of identity: Creole-based approaches to language and ethnicity*. Cambridge: Cambridge University Press.

Lindgren, Anna-Riitta. 1999. Linguistic variation and the historical sociology of multilingualism in Kven communities. In *Language change: Advances in historical sociolinguistics*, ed. Ernst Håkon Jahr, 141–66. Berlin: Mouton de Gruyter.

Loch, James. 1820. *An account of the improvements on the estates of the Marquess of Stafford, in the counties of Stafford and Salop, and on the Estate of Sutherland*. London: Longman, Hurst, Rees, Orme, and Brown.

MacBain, Alexander. 1982 [1911]. *An etymological dictionary of the Gaelic language*. Glasgow: Gairm.

McIntosh, Angus. 1961 [1952]. *An introduction to a survey of Scottish dialects*. Edinburgh: Thomas Nelson and Sons.

Miller, J. E., and R. Weinert. 1998. *Spontaneous spoken language*. Oxford: Oxford University Press.

Milroy, James. 1992. *Linguistic variation and change: On the historical sociolinguistics of English*. Oxford: Blackwell.

————. 1999. The consequences of standardization in descriptive linguistics. In *Standard English: The widening debate*, ed. Tony Bex and Richard J. Watts, 16–35. London: Routledge.

————. 2000. Historical description and the ideology of the standard language. In *The development of Standard English, 1300–1800*, ed. Laura Wright, 11–28. Cambridge: Cambridge University Press.

Milroy, James, and Lesley Milroy. 1978. Belfast: Change and variation in an urban vernacular. In *Sociolinguistic patterns in British English*, ed. Peter Trudgill, 19–36. London: Arnold.

————. 1999. *Authority in language: Investigating Standard English*, 3rd ed. London: Routledge.

Milroy, Lesley. 1987. *Language and social networks*, 2nd ed. Oxford: Basil Blackwell.

————. 2002. Social networks. In *The handbook of language variation and change*, ed. J. K. Chambers, Peter Trudgill, and Natalie Schilling-Estes, 549–72. Oxford: Blackwell.

Mitchell, T. F. 1982. More than a matter of "writing with the learned, pronouncing with the vulgar": Some preliminary observations on the Arabic koine. In *Standard languages: Spoken and written*, ed. W. Haas, 123–55. Manchester: Manchester University Press.

Mougeon, Raymond, and Édouard Beniak. 1991. *Linguistic consequences of language contact and restriction: The case of French in Ontario, Canada*. Oxford: Clarendon Press.

Mühlhäusler, Peter. 1996. *Linguistic ecology: Language change and linguistic imperialism in the Pacific region.* London: Routledge.

Newman, Paul, and Martha Ratliff. 2001. Introduction. In *Linguistic fieldwork*, ed. Paul Newman and Martha Ratliff, 1–14. Cambridge: Cambridge University Press.

Ochs, Elinor. 1979. Planned and unplanned discourse. In *Syntax and semantics, Vol. 12: Discourse and syntax*, ed. T. Givón, 51–80. New York: Academic Press.

Ó Dochartaigh, Cathair. 1983. Review of Dorian 1978. *Scottish Gaelic Studies* 14: 120–28.

Ó Dochartaigh, Cathair, ed. 1997. *Survey of the Gaelic dialects of Scotland: Questionnaire materials collected for the Linguistic Survey of Scotland*, Vols. 1–5. Dublin: Dublin Institute for Advanced Studies, School of Celtic Studies.

Oftedal, Magne. 1956. *The Gaelic of Leurbost, Isle of Lewis.* A linguistic survey of the Gaelic dialects of Scotland, 3: Norsk Tidsskrift for Sprogvidenskap, supplementary vol. 4. Oslo: Aschehoug.

Owens, Jonathan. 1999. Uniformity and discontinuity: Toward a characterization of speech communities. *Linguistics* 37: 663–98.

Newman, Paul. 1998. We has seen the enemy and it is us: The endangered languages issue as a hopeless cause. *Studies in the Linguistic Sciences* 28: 11–20.

Rice, Keren. 2001. Learning as one goes. In *Linguistic fieldwork*, ed. Paul Newman and Martha Ratliff, 230–49. Cambridge: Cambridge University Press.

Rice, Keren, and Leslie Saxon. 2002. Issues of standardization and community in aboriginal language lexicography. In *Making dictionaries: Preserving indigenous languages of the Americas*, ed. William Frawley, Kenneth C. Hill, and Pamela Munro, 125–54. Berkeley: University of California Press.

Romaine, Suzanne. 1982. What is a speech community? In *Sociolinguistic variation in speech communities*, ed. Suzanne Romaine, 13–24. London: Edward Arnold.

Ross, John Robert. 1979. Where's English? In *Individual differences in language ability and language behavior*, ed. Charles J. Fillmore, Daniel Kempler, and William S-Y. Wang, 127–63. New York: Academic Press.

Sachdev, Itesh, and Howard Giles. 2004. Bilingual accommodation. In *The handbook of bilingualism*, ed. Tej K. Bhatia and William C. Ritchie, 353–78. Oxford: Blackwell.

Sankoff, David, and Gillian Sankoff. 1973. Sample survey methods and computer-assisted analysis in the study of grammatical variation. In *Canadian languages in their social context*, ed. Regna Darnell, 7–64. Edmonton, Alberta: Linguistic Research.

Sankoff, Gillian. 1974. A quantitative paradigm for the study of communicative competence. In *Explorations in the ethnography of speaking*, ed. Richard Bauman and Joel Sherzer, 18–49. Cambridge: Cambridge University Press.

Sapir, Edward. 1992. Southern Paiute, a Shoshonean language. In *Southern Paiute and Ute linguistics and ethnography*, ed. William Bright. Collected Works of Edward Sapir, Vol. 10. Berlin: Mouton de Gruyter.

Sarhimaa, Anneli. 1999. *Syntactic transfer, contact-induced change, and the evolution of bilingual mixed codes: Focus on Karelian-Russian language alternation.* Studia Fennica Linguistica 9. Helsinki: Finnish Literature Society.

Sasse, Hans-Jürgen. 1992. Language decay and contact-induced change: Similarities and differences. In *Language death: Factual and theoretical explorations with special reference to East Africa*, ed. Matthias Brenzinger, 59–80. Berlin: Mouton de Gruyter.

Schilling-Estes, Natalie. 1998. Investigating "self-conscious" speech: The performance register in Okracoke English. *Language in Society* 27: 53–83.

Schmidt, Annette. 1985. *Young people's Dyirbal: An example of language death from Australia*. Cambridge: Cambridge University Press.

Silva-Corvalán, Carmen. 1994. *Language contact and change: Spanish in Los Angeles*. Oxford: Clarendon Press.

Silverstein, Michael. 1981. The limits of awareness. Sociolinguistic Working Paper No. 84. Austin: Southwest Educational Development Laboratory. [Reprinted in Duranti 2001.]

————. 1997. Encountering language and languages of encounter in North American ethnohistory. *Journal of Linguistic Anthropology* 6: 126–44.

Simone, Raffaele. 1995. The language user in Saussure (and after). In *Historical roots of linguistic theories*, ed. Lia Formigari and Daniele Cambarara, 231–49. Amsterdam: John Benjamins.

Southerland, Ronald H., and Frank Anshen. 1989. Language in social contexts. In *Contemporary linguistics: An introduction*, ed. William O'Grady, Michael Dobrovolsky, and Mark Aronoff, 326–57. New York: St. Martin's Press.

Steward, J. 1955. *Theory of culture change*. Urbana: University of Illinois Press.

Tannen, Deborah. 1989. *Talking voices: Repetition, dialogue, and imagery in conversational discourse*. Cambridge: Cambridge University Press.

Thomason, Sarah G. 2001. *Language contact: An introduction*. Washington, DC: Georgetown University Press.

Trudgill, Peter. 1974. *The social differentiation of English in Norwich*. Cambridge: Cambridge University Press.

————. 1986. *Dialects in contact*. Oxford: Basil Blackwell.

————. 1999. The chaos before the order: New Zealand English and the second stage of new dialect formation. In *Language change: Advances in historical sociolinguistics*, ed. Ernst Håkon Jahr, 197–207. Berlin: Mouton de Gruyter.

Van Beek, Walter E. A. 1987. *The Kapsiki of the Mandara Hills*. Prospect Heights, IL: Waveland Press.

Voegelin, C. F., and F. M. Voegelin. 1977. Is Tübatulabal de-acquisition relevant to theories of language acquisition? *International Journal of American Linguistics* 43: 333–38.

Watson, Seòsamh, ed. 2007. *Saoghal bana-mharaiche: Cunntas beul-aithris mu bheatha muinntir an iasgaich ann am Machair Rois*. Ceann Drochaid, Perth-shire: Clann Tuirc.

Winter, Werner. 1999. Sociolinguistics and dead languages. In *Language change: Advances in historical sociolinguistics*, ed. Ernst Håkon Jahr, 67–84. Berlin: Mouton de Gruyter.

Wolfram, Walt, and Dan Beckett. 2000. The role of the individual and group in earlier African American English. *American Speech* 75: 3–33.

Wolfram, Walt, and Erik R. Thomas. 2002. *The development of African American English*. Oxford: Blackwell.

Wong Fillmore, Lily. 1979. Individual differences in second language acquisition. In *Individual differences in language ability and language behavior*, ed. Charles J. Fillmore, Daniel Kempler, and William S-Y. Wang, 203–28. New York: Academic Press.

Woodbury, Tony. 2003. Defining documentary linguistics. In *Language documentation and description*, Vol. 1, ed. Peter K. Austin, 35–51. London: Hans Rausing Endangered Languages Project.

Woolard, Kathryn A. 1998. Introduction: Language ideology as a field of inquiry. In *Language ideologies: Practice and theory*, ed. Bambi B. Schieffelin, Kathryn A. Woolard, and Paul V. Kroskrity, 3–47. Oxford: Oxford University Press.

Index

Boldface entries represent chapter sections or subsections that include the subject of the entry in their heading.

Aberdeenshire, 7, 45
aberrance, **200**
accommodation, 5, 29, **30–31**, 194, 213,
    236, 239, **244–52**, 277, 284, 286–87,
    296, 299, 337
  accommodation theory, 238
acquisition, 211, 296, 305, 315
  imperfect, incomplete, 18, 141
admixture, 25, 50, 278
Afar, 283, 284
affect, 75, 93, 189, **190**, 191, 244, 252,
    282, 307
affine, 31, 55, 273
  affinal kin, 212
  affinal ties, 53, 217
African American Vernacular English, 28
age, **13–16**, 22, 25, 59, **69–73**, 74, **78–83**,
    84–85, 96, 104, **105**, 107–8, 110–12,
    122–23, **131, 134, 137, 147, 150, 153,
    156, 158, 164**, 165, 167, **169, 172–73,
    175–76, 178, 180, 182–83, 185**, 199,
    207–9, 210, 211–12, 221–24, 233,
    236, 273, 276, 284, 286, 294–95, 303,
    307, 310, 315. *See also* change;
    difference; variation
age cohort, 38, 234
age-and-proficiency continuum, **15–16**,
    70, 73, 80, 124, 126, 147, 150, 176,
    237, 253, 262
agemates, 11, 249, 264–65, **273–74**,
    291, 315, 320
agreement, 29, 31, 231, 303
  lack of, 21, 23, 248
  level of, 38, 218, 232, 322
  on variant preferences/preferred variant,
    123, 158, 162, **201–8**, 235,
    304–5
allomorph. *See* morphology
alternate
  grammatical, 4
  phonological, 116
  alternative forms, 9, 22, **90–91**
analogy. *See also* change; regularization;
    structure; variant

analogy (*continued*)
  analogical extension, 95, 99, 254,
    257–58, 282
  analogical factor, **164**
  analogical form, 82, 147, 321
  analogical gerund/gerund formation, 96,
    238, 253–54, **255–56**, 257, 259–60, 323
  analogical leveling, 76, 83
  analogical preterite particle, 167, 169
analysis
  analytic structure, 79–80, 258
Anderson, B., 289
anecdote, 34, 102, 254, 262
anthropologist, 288–89. *See also* linguists
apparent time, 125, 173, 299, 319
Aran Islands, 210, 273, 275
Argyllshire, 8
Arrowtown, 209–10, 273–75, 277–78,
    280, 284
assumption, 31, 210, 322
  homogeneity, 28, **289–90**
  underlying, working, 26, 210
  of uniformity, 27
Assynt, 18
attitude, 98, 255, 266. *See also* purism,
    purists
audience, 19, 73, 75, 93, 190, 194, 282
Austin, P. K., 310
Australia, 10, 30, 97, 109, 190, 214, 277
awareness, 33, 60, 62, 66, 86, 90, 125, 204,
    237–38, **259–60**, 281–82, 292, **300**

Ba-Mambila, 280
Banffshire, 45
Barra, 46
Basque, 10, 331
Bavin, E. L., 277
Beckett, D., 28, 285, 290, 306–7
Belfast, 10, 31, 296–98
Bell, A., 194
Beniak, É., 25, 272
bias, 6, 63, 119
  methodological, 16
  researcher, 280
bilingualism, 65, 72, 83, 270, 298
  Gaelic-English, 14, 17, 52, 82
Blench, R., 313
blending, blended structures, 70, 76
Bloomfield, L., 260–62, 265–66, 272, 316
Bolivia, 331

borrowing, 72, 74, 98, 245, 256, 317, 329
  negative, 72, 76–77, 83
boundary, 56, 297
  boundary marker/marking, 32, 56, 279,
    299
  community, 112
  social, 28, 36, 306
  village, **32–38**
Breton, 308
broadcaster, broadcasting, 20, 30, 110,
    188, 194–96, 294. *See also* Gaelic
Brora, 5, 10, 12, 14–15, 18, 21–22, 29, 31,
    33, 35–37, 39, 42, 47–52, 56–58,
    62–64, 67–68, 70, 72, 76, 78, 80,
    86–87, 91, 100–101, 103–5, 107–8,
    112, 115, 118–19, 127, 129, 132, 135,
    144, 148, 151, 153, 155–56, 158, 162,
    165, 167, 169, 171, 175–76, 179,
    181–82, 184, 204, 216, 240, 242–43,
    249, 257, 260, 267, 278, 293, 302,
    308–9, 315–17, 322, 324–25
by-names. *See* genealogy; name

Caithness, 18
California, 27, 329, 332–33
Cambap, 273, 275, 280, 283–84, 312
Cameroon, 273, 312
Cantabria, 32, 332
casualness, 303
  casual speech, 75, 176
  casual style, 20, 191, 193
census, 49–50, 58, 278, 317
Chambers, J. K., 4, 28, 210, 299
change
  age-related, 27, 66, 79, 82–83, 300
  analogical, 66
  apparent-time, 173
  direction of, 76, 79, 83, 103, 272
  grammatical, 106–8, 113, 144, 216,
    257–58
  language/linguistic, **144, 304–5**
  patterns of, 72, 304
  processes, 27, 66, 76, 100, 108, 127,
    147, 257, 272, 304
  in progress, 6, 70, 72, 79, 108, 111, 127,
    173, 286, 300, 304, 318
  stylistic, 75
Cheshire, J., 24, 28
child-care, 45, 61–62
  care of younger siblings, 44

caregivers, 296
childhood, 6, 10, 34, 53, 93, 104, 110,
    189–90, 214, 233–35, 237, 273, 292,
    305, 307, 309, 323
    games, 190, 292
Christy, C., 3
church, church services, 8–9, 10, 37, **51–52**,
    60, 62, 73, 112, 187, 249–50, 258
citation form, 77–78, 169, 316
class. *See* school class; social class
Clearance period, Clearances, **41–43**, 49,
    53, 64
clergy, 49, 51
code switching, 74, 240, 260
codification, **274–75**. *See also* Gaelic
Collins, J., 27–28, 270, 288, 301, 313
community. *See also* exile; speech
    community
    bilingual, bilingual/multilingual, 5, 194,
        261–62
    face-to-face, 21, **55–63**, 284, 298, 310
    fishing, fisherfolk, 16, 34, 37, 51, 63,
        240–41, 243, 310
    homogeneous, **298–99**
    as opposed to individual, **302–4**
    interactive, **29–30**, **298–99**
    membership, 10, **62–63**, 271, 306
    minority-group, **274–75**
    minority-language, 259, 310
    norm, **59–61**
    stigmatized, 63
conditioning (linguistic), 6, 66, 117
Connell, B., 273, 275, 280, 283–85
Connemara, 278
consensus, 26–27, 32, 53, 59, 107, 137,
    141–42, 162, 227, 266, 271–72, 286,
    305, 307. *See also* description
conservatism, 15–16, 25, 73–74, 103, 107,
    254, 263, 270. *See also* grammar;
    variant
    conservative norm, 70, 73, 80, 262–63,
        266, 319
    conservative models, 70, 253
consonant
    buffer/buffering consonant, 91, 121, 155
    consonant mutation, 90, 94, 111, 124,
        264, 318–19, 321
Constantinidou, E., 320
constraint, 305, 310
    interactional, 297

syntactic, 293
contact (language), 7, 14, 25, 48, 90, 120,
    209, 273, 277, 279–80, 286, 312
continuum
    age, age-and-proficiency, **15–16**, 70, 73,
        80, 124, 147, 150, 176, 237,
        253, 262
    proficiency, **268–69**
control
    grammatical, of Gaelic/Gaelic
        grammar, 14–15, 105, 268–70
convergence, 69, 137, 144, 279, 312
conversation. *See also* data; interaction;
    skill; style; telephone; use
    conversational contexts, 149
    conversational material, **91–93**, 94,
        121, 155, 319
    conversational turn, 176–78
    partners, 15–16, 34, 88, 103, 194, 217,
        238, 240, 264, 268, 319, 322
correction, 91, 281
    self-correction, 6, 189
    "correct" form, 23, 271
Corrúch, 210, 275, 279
Coupland, N., 293
courtesy, 25, 317
    rule, 240
covariance, 28, 290
Cyffer, N., 283

Dal Negro, S., 286, 319, 324
data, 32. *See also* elicitation
    control, **25–26**
    conversational, 88
    cross-village, 77
    database, 23, 86, **87–88**, 100–102,
        125
    exclusion, **310–11**
    freely spoken, 101, 125, 176
daughter, oldest, 161, 192, 210–11, 233,
    322
Davies, A., 322
De Moravia, 41, 57
decay (language), 22, 264, 328, 338
description (linguistic), 12, 23, 26–28,
    270, 272, 287–89, 301–2
    consensus, 271
    descriptive accounts/work, 272, **301–2**
    descriptive practices, 32
    descriptive tradition, 11, 27, 273

description (*continued*)
  descriptivists, 25
  structural, 28, 288
deviation, **6–11**, 15, 73, 80, 108, 119, 252, 266, 268, 281
dialect. *See also* difference; differentiation
  area, 18, 22, 67, 70, 76, 78, 279, 311, 319
  cross-dialect exposure, 74
  distinctiveness, **49–51**
  fisherfolk, 311
  forms, 7–**8**, 9, 119, 279
  Gaelic, 8, 17–18, 21, 26, 65, 70, 75, 77–78, 95, 118, 245, 252, 268, 300, 309, 320
  geography/geographer, 16, **18–19**, 21, 25, 76, **308–9**, 310
  leveling, **277–81**, 296, 333
  mainstream, 8–9, 18, 74–75, 78, 192, 245, 250
  mixing/mixture, 18, 30, 76, 118, 127, 209–10, 286, 298, 300
  norms, 242
  peripheral, 8
  regional, 28, 78, 288
  survey, 307–8
dialectologist, dialectology, 4, 24, 32, 51
difference
  age, 65, 70
  age-and-proficiency, 29
  age-related, 27
  cross-village, 33, 69, 156
  dialect/dialectal, 26, 242
  grammatical, 15, 94, 322
  individual, 26, 112, 268
  inter-speaker, **17–18**, 271
  intra-speaker, **17–18**, 271
  lexical, 15, 34, 68
  linguistic, 13, 32, 242, 289
  morphophonological, 15, 51
  personality, 215, 266
  phonological, 15, 51, 278, 300, 317
  stylistic, 19, 76
differentiation
  dialect, 49, 260, 279, 309
  social, 4, **31–32**, 339
  socioeconomic, 7, 31, 276, 282, 284, 286
directionality, 22, 28, 66, 73, 79, 83

disagreement, 23, 38, 120, 123, 201, 207–8, 273, 322
discourse
  extended, **191**
  function, 38, 128
  marker, 97, 291
  purpose, 65
  spontaneous, 176
  unplanned, 24, 336
discrimination, 250, 267
disyllabicity. *See also* variant
  disyllabic form, 84, 94, 115, 165, 167, 171
  disyllabic structure, 114
ditty (genre), 94, 99, 102, 116, 189
divergence, 29, 123, 141, 156
  linguistic, **238–44**
diversity, 65, 284–85, 290, 310
  occupational, 89
documentation, 69, 94, 289, 310, 326, 330, 340
Dorian, N. C., 9, 12–13, 15, 21–22, 36, 41, 43, 51–52, 66, 68, 72, 75, 110, 147, 241, 249–50, 257, 263, 295, 299, 307, 313, 315, 317, 320
Dornoch, 36, 52, 57–58, 60, 245, 247, 258, 323
Dressler, W. U., 282–83
Dunrobin, 36, 41, 57
Duran, J. J., 210, 273–75, 278, 280–81, 286
Dyirbal, 10

Easter Ross, 18–19, 22, 70, 78, 88, 251, 324
Edinburgh, 41, 317
education, 10, 24, 85, 112, 258–59, 266, 272–74, 277, 284–86
  educational level, 21, 297, 310
  educational use, 210, 282
egalitarianism, **59–61**
  egalitarian social structure, 5, 277
elicitation, **186–89**. *See also* variant
  elicited data/material, 86, 88, **101–2**, 115, 121, 124, 128, 167, 181, 213, 216–17, 253–54, 318–19
  material, 88
  responses, 125, 146, 181, 248–49, 251
  results, 252

sessions, 13, 33, 215, 249, 319
tasks, 87, 250
techniques, 13, 69
emigration, 42, 52–53, 63, 85, 104, 320
emulation, 239, 244, 261, 266, 303
enclavement, 10, 286, 299
endogamy, 21, **52–53**, 55, 61–63. *See also*
    marriage
English
    British, 7, 335
    Highland, 7–8
    influence of, 72, 78, 106, 280, 317
    Middle, 24, 307, 324
environment. *See also* syntax
    English-speaking, 106, 109, 257
    linguistic, 23, 66, 195
    semantic, 17
    social, 13, 65, 89, 112, 204, 300
    standard-language, 30, 287
    structural, 170
estate managers/planners, 43, 45, 47
ethnicity, 32, 239, 246, 284, 295, 304,
    310–11. *See also* identity;
    membership
    ethnic group, 6, 85, 283–84, 287,
    298–99, 312
    ethnic loyalty/solidarity, 243, 259
Europe, 289
evaluation. *See* social evaluation
evictions/evictees, 7, 42–43, 47–49, 64,
    67, 118, 278
exile. *See also* London-Embo exiles/group
    community/group, 88, 98, 304
expectations
    established, 32
    unconscious, 23

family, **210–12**. *See also* name; usage
    nuclear, 66
    ties, 213
farm, farmer, farming, 39, 40, 42, 44,
    47–49, 275–76
Fasold, R., 240, 306
field methods/practices, 13, 16, 307
fieldwork, 12–13, 15, 23, 28, 34, 49, 83,
    86, 88, 105–6, 215–17, 245–46, 251,
    285, 310, 315, 322
    fieldworker, 16, 20, 23, 26, 67, 75, 125,
    246, 309, 316, 324

Finland, Finnish, 274–75, 279, 281, 284
fisherfolk, 5, 7–8, 10, 12, 16, 18, 20–23,
    27, 34, 38, 50, 54, 68–70, 72, 74, 78,
    85–87, 89, 107, 119, 122, 152, 169,
    182, 196, 210, 245, 275, 278, 282,
    287, 291, 293–94, 302, 310, 313, 318,
    320–21. *See also* dialect; Gaelic;
    identity
    descendants/descent, 50, 55–56, 63–65,
    246
    population, 6, 12, **36–38**, 50, 64, 87
    residential areas, 40, 48, 56
fluency, 6, 22, 106, 109, 197, 217, 264,
    266, 286, 315, 320
    loss of, 110
focusing, **29–30**, 31, 210, 236, 298–99
Foley, W. A., 23, 285, 290, 307
formality, 20, 74, 97, 194–95, 250, 294,
    303. *See also* Gaelic; style
    formal speech, 116, 192, 248, 262
formula
    closing/concluding, 93, 175
    discourse, 175
France, 274, 279
freely spoken data/material, 74, 87–88,
    101, **102–3**, 110, 115, 125, 128–29,
    164, 167, 175–76, 183, 186–89,
    196, 213, 215–17, 250, 253–55,
    317, 319
French
    Acadian, 273, 277, 281, 284–85, 312
    Newfoundland, 276, 279–80,
    281, 333
frequency, frequency of occurrence, 8, 17,
    22, 24, 33, 35, 38, 41, 51, 68–69, 70,
    73–74, 78, 95–98, 101, 110, 114–15,
    120, 147, 153, 162, 165, 175, 186, 196,
    218, 238, 242, 253, 257–58, 282, 287,
    291–93, 296, 312, 316, 318, 321, 324
Friedrich, P., 26, 32

Gaelic. *See also* dialect; vernacular
    Bible, 8–9, 187, 249
    book, 9, 239, 245, 249–50, 252
    broadcast, 9
    Brora, 51, 67, 72, 103–4, 108, 127,
    155–56, 316
    codified, 9
    decline of, 27, 285

Gaelic (*continued*)
    fisherfolk, 8, 10, 13–14, 17, 22, 27, 29,
       31–33, 36, 43, 65, 67, 75, **76–87**, 96,
       100–101, 108, 180, 245, **246–47**, 250,
       252, **265**, 267, 278, 286, 296, 298,
       307, 316, 319, 323–24
    formal, **8–10**
    geographically based differences in, **51**
    Golspie, 19, 51, 67, 72, 103–4, 108,
       118, 127, 155–56, 243, 278, 301, 309,
       316, 323
    Hebridean, 9
    Leurbost, 273, 309
    Lewis, 9
    local, 8, 10, 16, 31, 35–36, 38, 48, 63,
       65–66, 69–70, 72, 74, 78, 82, 106,
       108, 194, 215, 237, 239, 241–42,
       245–46, **249–51**, 256, 258, 260
    locally distinctive, 62
    mainstream, 8, 10, 20, 65, 95, 118, 186,
       245, 251–52, 263, 320
    maintenance of, 52
    non-local, **251–52**
    normalized, 239
    "the right" Gaelic, 10, 245
    spoken, 10, 49, 127
    Stornoway, 9
    use of, 6, 21, 31, 63, 74, 84, 103,
       105–6, 240, 243–44, 258, 264,
       268–69, 293, 303, 320
    written, 10, 119, 186, 245, 249

Gal, S., 288–89, 301, 313, 324
games, 74, 93, 211
gender, 5, 12, 14, **19**, 38, 54, **61**, 69, 72,
    87, 94, 124, 137–39, 150, 174, 208,
    273, 291, 294, 316
genealogy
    genealogical by-names, 54, 317
    genealogical knowledge, 53
    genealogical lines, 55
generation, 30, 53, 73, 107, 110, 112, 203,
    209, 210–13, 240, 244, 257, 263,
    274–75, 277–78, 285, 305, 323
    cross-generational ties, 55
genre, 73, 75, 127, 294
German, 286, 294
    Pennsylvania, 147, 322
    Walser, 286, 319

Giles, H., 238, 240
Golspie, 5, 10, 12, 14, 17–18, 21–22, 25,
    27, 31, 33–37, 39, 41–42, 47–52,
    56–58, 63–64, 66–68, 70, 72, 75–76,
    78, 80, 86–88, 90–91, 101–4, 107–9,
    112, 115, 117–19, 127, 129, 132,
    135, 144, 146, 148, 151, 153,
    155–56, 158, 162, 165, 167, 169,
    171, 175–76, 179, 181–82, 184, 204,
    216, 240, 242–43, 246, 248, 256–57,
    260, 278, 293, 301, 308–10, 315–17,
    319, 321–25
Gordon (family), 42, 43, 50
Grace, G., 288, 301
grammar, 8, 14–16, 22, 25–26, 51, 88, 90,
    103, 107, 111, 155, 216, 245–46,
    263–64, 269, 272, 276, 306, 322, 324.
    See also analysis; change; difference;
    norms
    conventional, 301
    descriptive, 16, 24
    grammatical conservatism, 107, 263
    grammatical construction, 14, 32, 106–7
    grammatical control, control of, 14,
       268–70
    grammatical feature, 15, 49, 90, 103,
       264, 266, 315
    grammatical form, 8, 33, 66, 85, 107, 252
    grammatical intactness, 107–8, 265
    grammaticality judgments, 24, 307
    grammatical structure, 14, 16, 67, 72,
       91, 107, 267–69
    grammatical usage, 107–8
    individual, 305
    traditional (models of), 263–64, 269
    transformational, 24
grandmother, grandparent, 53–54, 211,
    296, 317
Granville, G., 41
Grinevald, C., 324

H[igh] language, 10
Haacke, W., 283
Haas, W., 298
Hallkirk, 57
Helmsdale, 42, 46, 50
heterogeneity, 304
    linguistic, 5, 289
    structured, 301, **304–5**

hierarchy, 9, 60
  social 4, 48, 62, 300
  hierarchical social structure, 59
Highlands (Scottish), 5, 12, 36, 40–41, 52,
  55, 58, 65, 87, 109, 234, 242, 257
Hill, J. H., 276, 286
Hilton, 22
Hinskens, F., 90, 113
history
  settlement, 67, 279
Holmberg, A. R., 313
Holmquist, J. C., 32
homogeneity, 5, 10, 28, 112, 259, **275–77**,
  289–90, 297, 301
  assumption, 28, **289–90**
Honey, J., 5
House of Sutherland, 36, 41–42, 49
household
  Gaelic-speaking, 237, 257, 299
  household membership, **20**, 212, 217
Hyde County, 28, 285
Hymes, D., 113, 305, 313

identity, 10–11, 30, 241–42, **243–44**, 259,
  293
  acts of, 297
  community, 1, 242
  ethnic, 112, 241, 244, 267, 323
  fisherfolk, 37, 63, 242, 245, 267, 293
  linguistic, 265
  local, 10–11, 37, 242, 244
  social, 28, 306
  stigmatized, 62, 240
ideology, 24, 272, 275–76, **287–89**
idiosyncrasy, 96, 141, 233, 238, 288.
    See also variant; variation
  idiosyncratic variant distribution/
    use, 83, 318
  idiosyncratic variant-use choice/
    pattern, 83, 89
imbalance, 101, 150, 268
"Improvement" era, **40–43**
incomers, 52, 112, 246, 249
individual. *See also* usage; variation
  as opposed to group or
    community, **28–29**, 285, 290–91,
    302–4, 305–7
  speaker/speech pattern, 293–94
inflection, 14, 80, 82–83, 107, 261, 264

informality, 97, 194, 250
informal style, 75
informant, 33, 246, 273, 309, 324
Inis Mór, 273, 278, 280–81, 324
in-migration, 50, 119
innovation, 15, 72, 76, 78. *See also*
    lexicon; structure; variant
  innovative forms, 70, 80, 82
integration, 14, 105, 269, 279
interaction. *See also* constraint
  conversational, 91, 96, 217, **245–46**, 252
  density, 5, 69
  face-to-face, 30–31, 34, 286
  interactional patterns, 112
  language of, 84, 283
  multispeaker, **247–48**
  occupational, 32
  verbal, 16, 101, 269
interference, 25
interlocutor, 13, 31, 65, 75, 93, 188,
    194–95, 238, 240, 244, 291, 295, 307,
    323, 315
  effect, 86, 248
internal vowel change, 95–96
interview, 20, 48, 62, 88, 103, 106, 110,
    194–96, 204, 214, 216, 248, 269, 281, 291
  interviewer, 19, 189, 195, 246–47, 251,
    291
invariance, **142**, 150, 161, 301, 307
Inverness-shire, 18, 51, 245
Ireland, 10, 30, 45–46, 210, 296–97
Irish, 117, 251, 274, 278, 280, 324
irregularity, 79, 145, 257, 263–64
Irvine, J. T., 288–89, 313, 324
Isle of Lewis, 26, 46
isogloss, 35, 279
isolation, 10, 28, 42, 64, 73, 103, 186,
    257, 274–75, 283–84, 286. *See also*
    setting
Italian, 286

Jackson, K. H., 308, 315, 324
Jaffe, A., 320
Johnson, A., 4, 313
Johnstone, B., 24, 112, 290–91, 305–7
joke (genre), 102, 190

Kanuri, 283–84
Kapsiki, 312

Karelian, 273, 275–76, 279–80
Kerswill, P., 274, 299
Kildonan, 49
kin/kinfolk, 5–6, 13–14, 20–21, 31,
    37–38, 42, 46, 52, **53–54**, 55, 58,
    62–63, 69, 85, 104–5, 109–10, 112,
    126, 161–62, 202, 208–9, **212–13**,
    215, 234–35, 238, 244, 248, 266, 269,
    273–74, 279, 293, 295–96, 301, 318,
    320. *See also* affine; network
  kinship, 20, 30, **54–55**, 104, 238, 244,
    299, 301, 304
King, R. E., 273–74, 276, 279–81, 284,
    286
Klein-Andreu, F., 25, 272
Kroskrity, P. V., 288, 313
Kulick, D., 267
Kven (language), Kvens (people), 275,
    279, 281, 284, 312
Kwanja, 280, 283

Labov, W., 3–4, 28, 32–33, 89, 290, 297,
    302–3, 305–6, 308, 311, 316
language. *See also* change; shift
  ancestral, 267, 313
  choice, 237–41, 299
  death, 22, 282
  first, 211–12, 287
  "good," 261
  heritage, 265
  home, 13–14, 36, 62, 274
  of intimacy, 10
  language/linguistic change, **144**, **304–5**
  local, 41, 56, 241, 275, 277, 313, 320
  loyalty, 266–67
  minority/minority-group, 6, 11, 25, 217,
    263, 269, 275, 281–82, 290, 309
  native, 35, 301
  obsolescent, 147, 320
  official, 287
  of power, 10
  private-sphere, 8
  public-sphere, 8
  receding/retreating, 65, 72, 267, 277, 284
  skills, 131, 137, 143, 267, 283
  standard, 6, 24, 27, 30, 119, 259,
    272, 297
  standardized, 4, 7, 23–24, 31–33, 89,
    271–72, 274, 285, 288

  unmarked, 16, 316
  unstandardized, 27, 312
langue, 112, 306
Le Page, R., 29, 290, 297, 301, 305
Lee, R., 313
lenition, 80, 124, 143, 158, 181, 204, 318
leveling, 76, 83, 119, 274, **277–81**, 296.
    See also analogy; dialect
Leveson-Gower, G. G., 41
lexicon, 8, 15, 62, 65, 249–51, 258, 262,
    275, 311. *See also* shifting; variation
  lexical influence, 66
  lexical innovation, 72
  lexical resources, 106, 108, 269
  lexical retention, 216, **232–33**
  lexical substitution, 20, 65
lexicostatistical word list, 232, 317
lifeways, 14, 29, 38, 57, 63, 65, 282, 318
Lindgren, A-R., 275, 279, 281, 284, 286
Linguistic Survey of Scotland,
    Survey, 12–13, 18–19, 21, 49, 78,
    102, 246, 308–11, 315–16, 319,
    324–25
linguistics, 5, 301, 307, 326–28, 332,
    337–38, 340. *See also* sociolinguistics
  descriptive, 16, 335
  variationist, 296
linguists, 3, 5, 11, 23–25, 32, 85, 112, 260,
    263, 270, 272, 274, 286–90, 301, 305,
    308, 312–13, 324
  anthropological, linguistic
    anthropologists, 25, 286, 313
  descriptive, 16, 25
literacy, 9, 33, 65, 204, 239, 249, 257–58,
    262, **274–75**, 277, 308, 310, 325. *See
    also* mother tongue
livelihood, 32, 37, 40, 43, 45, 47, 53, 57,
    60, 62, 64, 275
loanwords, 16, 65–66, **96–98**, 158,
    237–38, 256, 260, 282
Loch, J., 42
Loch Fleet, 36–37, 56, 67
London-Embo exiles/group, 58, 88, 98, 104,
    110, **142–43**, 162, 204, **205**, 304–5
lore, 15
  proverbial, 74, 215
  traditional, 94, 102, 190
loss, 14, 22, 70, 72, 82, 110, 115, 258,
    260, 310

Lower Brora, 56, 63–64
Lower East Side, 89, 302, 308
Lowlands/Lowland Scotland, 53, 213–14, 216
loyalty, 266–67, 269, 286. *See also* ethnicity; language

MacBain, A., 321
maraichean, 36–37, 62, 112, 241, 243, 246, 298, 303
marriage
  cross-village, 37
  endogamous, 53
  in-, 278
  out-, 52, 63
Martin, Ishbel, 273
Martin, Roddy, 26, 273, 309
Matsigenka, 4, 312
McIntosh, A., 324
membership, 10, 21, 62–63, 237, 271, 287, 299, 306. *See also* community
  class, 22, 302
  group/ethnic group, 287, **299**
Menomini, 260, **261–62**, **265**, 272
metalanguage, 90, 258
methodology, 276
  methodological approach, 28, 308
  methodological mistake, 215
Mexicano (Nahuatl), 276
Mexico, 26, 276
Middle English, 24, 307, 324
Miller, J. E., 24
minister, 8, 52, 247, 258
minority language/minority-group language, 6, 217, 263, 269, 275, 281–82, 290, 309
  setting, 244
  vernacular 238
Mitchell, T. F., 25, 272
mixing/mixture, 265
  dialect, 18, 30, 76, 118, 127, 209–10, 286, 298, 300
  population, **277–81**, 284, 286
monolingualism, 14, 52, 63, 73, 270
monosyllabicity. *See also* variant
  monosyllabic form, 84, 167, 173, 191, 193
  monosyllabic verb root, 115
Montreal, 89, 303

Moray, 41
Morayshire, 7, 45
morphology, 275
  allomorph, 95, 257
  morpheme, 4, 113–14, 257, 303
  morphophonology, 12, 67. *See also* difference; variable
  morphophoneme, 67, 316
morphosyntax, 12
mother tongue, 8, 211, 240, 266, 274
  literacy, **262–63**
  speaker, 7, 23, 32, 48
Mougeon, R., 25, 272
Mühlhäusler, P., 288

name
  by-names, 32, 54, 262, 317
  clan, 50
  family, 50
  first/given, 54, 291
  naming practices, **53–54**
  official, 54
  surnames, 41, 50–51, 57, 300
narrative, 11, 75, 102, 106, 127, 190, 323
  style, 75, 190
nasalization, 124, 165, 318, 321
negative borrowing, 72, 76–77, 83
neighbor, 105, 224, 244, 273, 282, 287, 309
neighborhood, 8, 10, 31, 112
network, 10, 100
  kin/kinship, 38, 53, 55, 63, 104–5, 112, 161, 238
  social, 9–10, 13, 62, 66, 86, 97, 102, 104, 122, 271, 293, 295, 297
New York City, 89, 297, 302, 308
New Zealand, 30, 209, 273–74, 277–78
Newfoundland, 273–74, 276, 279–81, 284, 312
Newman, P., 25
Nigeria, 313
non-accommodation, 245, **246–48**
non-fisherfolk, 36, 48, 51–52, 56, 60, 62–63, 243, 246
non-local elements
  forms, 238, 278, 309–11
  speakers, 65, 246
norms, 24, 30–31, 38, 61, 74–75, 78, 89, 243, 252, 259, 283–84, 303, 320

norms (*continued*)
(community-)external, 5, 275, 277, 286, 296–97, 309
conservative, 69–70, 73, 80, 262–63, 266, 319
grammatical, 262–63, 266
phonological, 24, 284
sociolinguistic, 283
standard-language, **6–11**, 281
written-language, 74–75
North Carolina, 28, 285, 290, 306
Northern Ireland, 10, 45–46, 296–97
North Slavey, 302
Norway, 275, 279, 284
Norwich, 89, 303
Nova Scotia, 279

obsolescence, **22–23**, 103, 108, 127, **282–85**, 286, 298, 302, 310–11. *See also* language
occupation, 14, 21, 36, 47, 52, 56, 61–62, 64, 259, 276, 297, 299, 310. *See also* diversity; interaction; stigma
occupational distinctiveness, 48, 52
occupational groups, 36, 47
occupational segregation, 56
stigmatized, 259
Ochs, E., 24, 28
Ó Dochartaigh, C., 21–23, 78, 302, 308–9, 311, 324
Oftedal, M., 26–27, 32, 174, 273, 309–10, 324
Oiartzun, 10
oral history, 34, 102, 313
interviewing/taping, 43, 88, 102
Otago, 30
Outer Banks, 28, 290
Outer Hebrides, 26, 45–46, 239, 320
out-migration, 213
Owens, J., 295

paradigm, 80, 276, 302, 307
paradigmatic consistency, 66
parent-child pairs, 86
parole, 113, 306
peer, 234
circle/group, 11, 126, 208, **210–12**, 233, **234–36**, 237, 293, 296, 299, 303, 310

percentage of use, **125–26**, 127, 141, 150, 187, **217–34**
performance, 94, 195, 224, 263, 266, 283. *See also* style
personality, 203–4, 215, 266–67, 319. *See also* difference
Peru, 4
phone. *See also* telephone
conversation, 108–9, 239, 241, 247, 266
conversation partner, 88, 215, 319
interview, 20, 194–96
phoneme, 89, 113, 316
phonemic contrast, 8
phonemic representation, 117–18
phonology, 4, 8, 14–15, 26, 103, 111, 245, 272, 275–76. *See also* alternate; difference; variable; variation
phonological form, 33, 51, 119, 152, 319–20
phonological realization, 12, 68, 89, 113, 273, 303
phonological structure, 116
Plateau State, 313
playground, 264
plurals, noun, 96, 257, 263
plurilingualism, 288–89
politeness, 97
population. *See also* fisherfolk
crofting, 47
density, 40
distinctive, **47–55**
endogamous, 31
homogeneous, 64, 85
local, 13, 36, 52, 65
minority-language, 101, 276, 287
mixture, **277–81**, 284
single-class, 19
size, 5
urbanized, 3
working-class, 31, 49
poverty, 14, **47–48**, 52, 259
Powesland, P. F., 238
precenting, precentor, 8–9, 60, 204, 317
prejudice, 52, 62
prescriptivism, **23–25**, 272, 301
proficiency, **106–8**
differences, 63
group, 15, 107, 126, 134, 153, 164, 262

high-proficiency semi-speaker, 92, 95, 127, 211, 214, 216, 227, 266
    level, 22, 87, 137, 104, **106–8**, 122–23, 134, 139, 156, 165, 185, 197, 199, **202–3**, **207**, 212, 268, 303, 307
    low-proficiency semi-speaker, 88, 127, 269
prompt (in elicitation), 163–64, 187, 218, 252, 309, 324
pronunciation, 4, 24, 26, 33, 116–17, 245, 251, 258, 302, 317, 319
proverb, 74–75, 94, 99, 102, 116, 189, 190, 195, 197, 262, 282, 294, 319. *See also* lore
pseudonym, 83, 97, 161, 213–14
purism, purists, 25, 95–96, 128, 253, 255
    puristic attitudes/views, 192, 255

quotation (language of), 13, 323

radio, 20, 58, 75, 102, 108, 110, 188, 194–96, 214, 216, 246, 251, 294
Ratliff, M., 25
recorder, 87, 97, 248
    recording, 25, 75, 87, 92, 98, 102, 109, 139, 191–93, 195–96, 215, 216–17, 247, 269, 307, 311, 315, 322
reduction
    articulatory, 18
    of variants/variation, 31, 83, 210, 212, 236, 299
regionalism, 78
register, 62, 74, 261
regularity, 29, 30–31, 66, 298, 301
regularization
    analogical, 70, **79–82**, 144, 164–65, 257–58, 263
religion, 31
    religious life/services, 8, 10, 37, 52, 62
repetition, 8, **91–93**, 99, **120–121**, 176–77, 248
replacement, 72, 257
    pronoun, 72, 264
researcher
    assumption, 289
    biases, 280
    responses to variation, **22–33**

resettlement, 47, 50
residence, 40–41, 48, 53, 62, 109, 193, 214, 299, 317
rhyme (genre), 74, 172, 187, 189, 317
Rice, K., 285, 302, 307
roles
    multiplex, 29, **61–62**, 299
    uniplex, 29
Romaine, S., 28, 290
Ross, J. R., 24
Ross-shire, 50, 119, 278
Russian, 273–74, 276, 279–80

Sachdev, I., 238, 240
Saintonge, 274
salience, 34–35, 90, 113, **146**, 300. *See also* variation
sample
    Embo, 79, 108, 118, 146, 157, 186, 227, 257, 268
    imbalance, 101
    imperfect speaker/semi-speaker, 105, 139
    speaker, 15, 79, 86–87, 100, 105, 108, 126, 139, 157, 162, 169, 186, 213, 303, 310, 319
Sankoff, D., 89
Sankoff, G., 89, 298
Sapir, E., 16, 25, 32
Sarhimaa, A., 273, 275, 279–80, 286
Sasse, H-J., 72
Saussure, 112
Saxon, L., 40, 302
saying (genre), 94, 189
Schilling-Estes, N., 306
Schmidt, A., 11
school, schooling, 6–10, 37, 44–45, 48, 58, 61–63, 73, 85, 192, 209, 211, 239, 250, 260, 264, 273–74, 277, 287, 310, 315, 322. *See also* teacher
school class, 112, 212, 264, 296
    classmate, 210, 212
Seereer, 324
segregation, 40, 52, 56, 61. *See also* occupation
self-consciousness, 11, 65, 96, 98, 125, 189, 191, 195, 238, 248, 255–56, 258, 300, 321
self-correction, 6, 189

semantics, 125, 336. *See also* environment
  semantic distinction, 70, 182, 239
  semantic range, 256
semi-speaker (as speaker category),
    15–16, 106–10
Senegal, 324
separateness, 38, 47, **48–55**, 65
setting. *See also* minority language; social
    setting
  classless, 89
  isolated, 3, 89, 285
  middle-class, 210
  rural, 3, 285
  standardized-language, 89
  suburban, 112, 296
  urban, 3, 112, 210, 296, 306
settlement, 27, 30, 42, 47, 55, 57, 67, 275,
    278–79, 284
  settlement history, **49–51**, 67, 279
sex, sex of speaker, speaker's sex, 19, 66,
    85–86, 100, 104, **105–6**, 111, 122–23,
    126, **131, 134, 137, 142, 147–48, 150,
    153, 156, 158, 161, 164, 167, 169,
    172–73, 175–76, 178–79, 180, 182,
    183, 185, 202–3, 207,** 211–12, 214,
    221, 233, 236, 271, 276–77, 284, 291,
    295–96, 302–3, 310–11
Shetlands, 46
shift, 14, 17, 74–75, 165, 176, 188–91,
    193, 195, 246, 276, 294, 307, 317
  to English, 17
  language, 10, 14, 304, 320
  style/stylistic, 20, 74, 250, 295
shifting
  lexical, 9
  style-, 74, 94, 297, 302
sibling
  half-, 54–55, 312
  missing 85, 214
  older, 98, 112, 296
  pair, **83–85**, 161, 205, 223, 236, 274,
    293
  sets, 55, 85–86, 211, **213–17**, 232–33,
    236, 299, 305
  ties, 161, 208
  younger, 44, 213, 227
Silva-Corvalán, C., 72
Silverstein, M., 90, 288
Simone, R., 306–7

simplification, 70, 145, 257
Siriono, 312
skill. *See also* language
  conversational, 108, 315
  passive/receptive, 216, 269
  speaker, 15, 105, 109, **266–70**
  verbal, 250, 262, 265, 269, 270, 320
Slave, 285
social attitudes, 63
social background, 30, 240
social bonds, 224
social boundary, 28, 32, 36, 299, 306
social class, 22, 240, 276, 286, 302, 308,
    310. *See also* membership; setting
social differentiation, 4, 31
social distinction, 4, 35, 273, 303
social division, 32, 56, 303, 306
social environment, 13, 65, 89, 112, 204,
    300
social evaluation, 31, 33, 89, **98–99**, 128,
    281, 286–87
social groups/groupings, 5, 22, 32, 48,
    259, 289, 299, 303, 305–6
social hierarchy, 4, 48, 62, 300
social identity, 28, 306
social interaction, 21, 31, 37, 48, 102,
    111–12, 161, 212, 304
social judgment, 89, 96, 281
social loading, 17, 244, 257, 259
social network, 9–10, 13, 62, 66, 86, 97,
    102, 104, 122, 271, 293, 295, 297
social neutrality, 6, **300**
social organization, 3, 38, 311–13, 324
social patterns, 31, 40, 67, 233
social response, 106, 238–43
social setting, 27, 38, 85, 297
social significance/value (of variants/
    variation), 4, 55, 89, 117, 196, 284,
    300, 303
social standing/status, 47–48, 112, 261
social stigma, 14, 112, 239
social structure, 5, 59–61, 63, **212–13**,
    286, 307, **311–13**
social weight/weighting, **3–5**, 6–8, 17, 32,
    38, **88–98**, 189, 252, 255, 277,
    281–82, 300, 324
society
  complex, 313
  contemporary, 4, 311

family-level, 312
    multiethnic, 290
    pre-urban, 4
    stratified, 3, 32, 209, 297
    traditionally organized, 313
    urban/urbanized, 209, 287
    Western, 276, 296
socioeconomic class, 21, 111
socioeconomic status, 271, 276,
    285, 299
sociolinguistics, 210. *See also* tradition
    correlational, 290; correlational
        sociolinguistic analysis/studies/
        work, 28, 117, 289
    sociolinguistic literature/studies, 38,
        112–13, 298, 311
    sociolinguistic norms, 283
    sociolinguistic theory, 276
    variationist, 4
sources, **104–8**
    source selection, selection of
        sources, **25–26**, **310–11**
song, 98, 189, 262, 288, 320
Southerland, R. H., 5
Southern Paiute, 16, 25
Soviet Union, 273
speakers, **109–12**. *See also* sample;
        semi-speaker
    formerly fluent (as speaker
        category), 106–7, 109–10,
    fully fluent (as speaker
        category), 107–9
    "good", **262–66**
    high-variation, 152, 221, 292, 295
    imperfect, 108, 110
    low-variation, 292
    native, 25, 328
    near-passive (as speaker
        category), 106–10
    older fluent (as speaker
        category), 106–108
    speaker group, 15, 73, 79, 82–83,
        107–8, **142**, 268
    speaker pool/sample, 15, 79, 86–87,
        100, 108, 126, 139, 157, 162, 169,
        186, 212–13, 303, 310, 319
    speaker status, 63, 263, 266
    younger fluent (as speaker
        category), 106–8

speech behavior, 8, 29, 32, 92, 237–39,
    241, 243, 264, 269
speech community, 23, 27, 89–90, 131,
    194, 257, 259, 262, 270, 299, 303,
    305, 307, 319, 324
speech function, **186**
speech model, 9, 210–11
speech patterns, 93, 113, 210–11, 234,
    238, 272, 276, 294–95
speech performance, 195, 224, 263
speech style, 65–66
spouse, 34, 104, **203–4**, 212, 308
Stafford, Marquis of, 41
standardization, 6, 9, 23, 30–31, 89,
    118–19, 210, 258, 272, 275, 278, 288,
    301–2, 310. *See also* language; setting
stigma, 14, 25, 52, 98, 112, 239, 245. *See
    also* community; identity; occupation;
    variant; vernacular
    stigmatization, 6
    stigmatized group, 241
Stornoway, 9, 46, 178
story, 26, 102, **190–91**, 242, 262, 267,
    269, 291–92, 323
    story-telling/story-telling style, 75, 295
Strathnaver, 49
stratification, 3–4, 6, 277, 282, 284, 286,
    294, 299, 311. *See also* society
structure, 5, 72, 79, 90, 107, 115, 117,
    153, 253, 264, 267, 272, 275, 286,
    313, 318. *See also* analysis;
    conservatism; disyllabicity;
    environment; grammar; phonology;
    syntax
    analogical, 253
    analytic, 79–80, 258
    innovative, 82–83
    synthetic, 79, 257
    traditional, 82, 258
    typological, 272
style, **19–20**, 89, 189–92, 262, 288,
    293–94, 308, 319. *See also* difference;
    story; variation
    casual, 20, 191, 193
    formal, 20, 89, 195
    individual, 291
    informal, 75
    narrative, 75, 190
    performance, 74–75, 116, 197, 317

style (*continued*)
   personal, 175, 291
   relaxed, 191–92
style shift/shifter/shifting, 20, 75, 94, 98,
   192, 195–96, 249–51, 297, 302–3
   style-related patterns of variant
     use, **189–96**
   style-related/stylistic variation, **73–76**,
     86, 89
   stylistic effect, 195–96
   stylistic range, 19, 75
subjective evaluation test, 89
suffix, 80, 95–96, 143, 239, 253–55,
   257–58, 268, 300
   suffixation, 95, 253–54, 256–57
surname, 41, 50, 57
survey. *See* dialect; Linguistic Survey of
   Scotland
Sutherland estate, 37, 42–43, 45, 47,
   50–51, 58, 119
Sutherlandshire
   central Sutherland, 18
   eastern Sutherland, 12, 42–43, 48–50,
     58
syntax, 8, 76, 125, 261, 272. *See also*
   constraint; variation
   spoken English, 24
   syntactic conditions, 114, 178
   syntactic environment, 76, 93, 114, 165,
     174, 282
   syntactic structure, 24, 34, 90, 258
synthesis
   synthetic form, 317
   synthetic grammatical marking, 66
system pressure, 80, 82–83

Tabouret-Keller, A., 29, 297, 305
Tannen, D., 249
tape
   ceilidh tapes, **192–93**, 194–95
   gift tape, **191–92**, 194, 196
teacher, schoolteacher, 8, 57, 220, 258
telephone, 87–88, 102, 109, 113, 139, 169,
   184, 188, 215–17, 239, 247, 315, 319,
   321
   conversation, 88, 108–9, 120, 127, 190,
     194–95, 215, 239, 241, 255, 266, 292,
     319, 322
   interview, 20, 194–96, 291

texts, 19, 60, 102, 281, 307, 319, 324
   connected, 26
   freely spoken, 95, 109, 215
Thomas, E. R., 28, 285–86
Thomason, S. G., 72
Tolowa, 27–28, 288, 301–2
tone, **190**, 191
topic, 33, 35, 55, 74–75, 93, 190, 216,
   256, 282, 294, 307
tourist, 58, 246, 320
tradition. *See also* description; lore; variant
   sociolinguistic, 28
   traditional/non-traditional gerund, 95,
     175, 254–55, 259
   traditional material, **94**, 99, **189**, 190,
     195, 282, 317
   verbal, 262
transcription, 113, 191, 292–93, 318–19,
   321
transfer, 25, 72
translation, translation tasks, 14, 69, 85,
   96, 101, 105–7, 109, 111, 113, 121,
   123, 125, 127, 147, 150, 154, 164,
   173, 187–88, 194, 196, 204, 209,
   215–16, 238, 243, **248–52**, 255, 264,
   267, 269, 292, 310, 315, 319, 321,
   323
   translation-task batteries/sentences/
     testing, 106–7, 188, 216, 251, 267,
     269, 323
   translation-test results, 264, 267, 315
transmission, 14, 21, 69, 103, 211, 257,
   283, 313
Trudgill, P., 30, 89, 209–10, 236, 273–74,
   277, 279–80, 285, 299–300
tuathanaich, 36, 55, 62, 241, 243, 246,
   303
Tübatulabal, 25

unawareness, **90–91**
uniformitarian principle, 3
uniformity, 6, 9, 11, **26–27**, 28, 31, 210,
   234, 236, 254, 272, 285, 288, 307.
   See also assumption
   uniform descriptive accounts, **301–2**
uniplex roles, 29
universal
   sociolinguistic, 4
   universal social feature, 311

urbanization, 277. *See also* setting
    urbanized population/society, 3, 287
usage
    family, 104, 154, 232, 236
    individual, 17
    local, 4, 118, 243
    mainstream, 9
    non-conforming, 35
    non-standard, 7
    standard, 4
use. *See also* variant
    conversational, 36, 217, 265
    formal, 24, 65
    invariant, 142, 150, 152, 181, 257

van Beek, W. E. A., 312
variability, 21, 26–27, 29–30, 65–66, 69,
        86, 92, 114, 123, 127, 150, 156, 181,
        184, **196–97**, 209, 226, 276, 283–85,
        292–95, 299, 313, 323
    inter-speaker, 210
    intra-speaker, 157, 184, 210, 218
    within-the-village, 99, 146
variable
    cross-village, 91
    disfavored, 238
    morphophonological, 114
    multivariant, **128–37**
    personal pattern, **299**
    phonological, 89, 303
    socially weighted, 20
variance
    in-group, 28, 290
variant
    alternation, **93**, 282
    analogical, 66, 80, 83, 95, 145–47,
        186–87, 190, 193, 195–96, 298, 321
    choice, 19, 31, 66, 85, 87–88, 91–92,
        99, 114, 116–17, 125, 141, 146, 172,
        176, 191, 200, 217–18, 223–24,
        233–34, **238–40**, 244, 248, 252,
        291–94
    competing, 21, 76, 170, 259
    conservative, 83, 190
    disfavored, 186
    disyllabic, 74–75, 94, 115–116, 167,
        170, 172–73, 184, **187–88**, 189–91,
        193, 195–96, 221, 294–95, 321
    dominant, 19, 119, 135, 155, 169

elicited, **128**
favored, 89, 92, 94, 134, 147, 149–50,
        154, 161, 164, 167, 182–84, 186, 188,
        202, 223, 227, 231, 235, 244
freely spoken, 19, **128**, 176, 221
geographical, 35
idiosyncratic, 83, 89, 99, 137
innovative, 80, 83, 173
local, 9, 20, 35, 118, 244, 299
monosyllabic, 18, 94, 115, 167,
        169–70, 172–73, 184, **187–88**,
        189–91, 193–94, 196, 218, 221,
        295, 321
negatively weighted, **253–58**
non-analogical, 83, 145–47, 187, 190,
        192–93, 195, 221
non-standard, 188
other-village, 238
preference, 76, 82, 119, 123, 126, 131,
        134, 137, 139, 140–41, 143, 147, 150,
        153, 156–59, 161–62, 169, 172, 175,
        177–78, 180, 182–83, 185, 201–5,
        207–8, 217–18, 221, 224, 227,
        231–36, 244, 252, 292–93, 295, 299,
        303–5
same-village, 31
selection, 19, 21, 66, 75, 80, **88–98**,
        113, 128, 131, 134, 138, 143, 148,
        150, 153, 156, 164–65, 167, 169, 171,
        175, 179, 181–82, 184, 195, **217–34**,
        247–48, 251–53, 282, **292–95**
selection pattern, 122, 147, 156, 162,
        170, 213, 218, 221, 224, 227, 233–34,
        236, 239, 244, 292
socially weighted, **95–96**
standard, 4
stigmatized, 6
structurally parallel, **167–68**
traditional/non-traditional, 79–80, 83
use, 75–76, 79, 82, 93, 95, 123, 125,
        126–28, 131, 134, 137, 139, 141, 143,
        150, 152, 162, 167, 171, 175, 177,
        182, **186–89**, 199, 202, 208, 215, 218,
        250, 293, 295, 305, 310. *See also*
        idiosyncrasy
use pattern, 76, 79, 125–26, 128, 162,
        167, 171, 189–91, 194–95, 212, 215,
        218, 223–24, 234, 292–93, 295,
        303–5